Social Psychology
and
Discretionary Law

Social Psychology
and
Discretionary Law

Edited by

Lawrence Edwin Abt, Ph. D.
and
Irving R. Stuart, Ph. D.

 VAN NOSTRAND REINHOLD COMPANY
NEW YORK   CINCINNATI   ATLANTA   DALLAS   SAN FRANCISCO
LONDON   TORONTO   MELBORNE

Van Nostrand Reinhold Company Regional Offices:
New York Cincinnati Atlanta Dallas San Francisco

Van Nostrand Reinhold Company International Offices:
London Toronto Melbourne

Library of Congress Catalog Card Number: 78-21144
ISBN: 0-442-27907-8

Manufactured in the United States of America

Published by Van Nostrand Reinhold Company
135 West 50th Street, New York, N.Y. 10020

Published simultaneously in Canada by Van Nostrand Reinhold Ltd.

15 14 13 12 11 10 9 8 7 6 5 4 3 2 1

Library of Congress Cataloging in Publication Data

Main entry under title:

Social psychology and discretionary law.

  Includes index.
  1. Sociological jurisprudence. 2. Law—Psychology.
I. Abt, Lawrence Edwin, 1915– II. Stuart, Irving R.
K380.S6   340.1'15   78-21144
ISBN 0-442-27907-8

PREFACE

This book grew from our concern with an attempt to answer two questions: What does the law know about social science, and what does social science have to contribute to the law? It has long been recognized that the two fields have in common an interest in and concern for understanding, predicting, and, to some extent, controlling human behavior. But what are the grounds on which the two fields interact? That is, what is the nature of the interface between the two disciplines?

No single book can aspire to answer such questions fully, and indeed our present knowledge of each field hardly provides the basis for doing so. The present work is, therefore, a more modest effort—that of taking a look in some depth of the principal patterns of interaction, but certainly not at all of them.

From the first, we have sought a single conceptualizing principle—a single thread running through a complex fabric—that would provide a means to begin to lay bare the persistent patterns and the primary intersecting points of the two interacting sets of ideas and practices that constitute the social sciences and the law. We believe we have found the integrating idea in the principle of discretion. For us, discretion is the nexus of two disciplines, binding each yet freeing each to draw on the insights of the other.

We feel that the single thread running through the two disciplines lies in the possibilities of examining behavior, now from one point of view, now in another but significantly similar context, from the point of view of discretion, always thought of as an act performed by a human being that seeks to resolve a problem or to reduce an issue. We see discretion, then, as a human judgment made to settle an issue or to formulate a solution within the confines of a set of principles. In the case of the law, the principles are derived from legal theory and practice, which rest on a body of received knowledge and tradition. Although responsive to contemporary prejudice, the law rarely accepts it fully or maintains itself current with it.

Social science, as a young and growing discipline, with both the bold aspirations and the genuine limits of a new discipline, constantly seeks to stake out new territory and to exploit it. Sometimes the exploitation is extravagent; sometimes it is cautious. But persons conversant with the contemporary American scene can hardly be unaware of the growing contributions, and sometimes the unjustified claims, of the social sciences. We feel that, among other things, social science has a valid claim in its aspirations to contribute to the law—and that the law, with the complexity of its own problems, has a valid reason to seek, but seek cautiously, the aid of the social sciences.

It is to these issues and concerns that this book addresses itself.

LAWRENCE EDWIN ABT
Larchmont, New York

IRVING R. STUART
White Plains, New York

Contents

Part II Discretion in the System of Criminal Justice

Social Psychology
and
Discretionary Law

PART I
THE INTERFACE BETWEEN PSYCHOLOGY AND DISCRETIONARY LAW

Part I examines something of the history of discretion, both as principle and as practice, in early English common law and its translation into current American legal theory and practice. A historian, Joel Samaha, takes us on a long journey back in time to some of the beginnings of a legal system, first under the jurisdiction of the Church and later under the aegis of the state, in which the importance of discretion was early recognized. Many of our current problems and dilemmas were thoroughly familiar to our forebears, and it is likely that our more sophisticated knowledge has not yet provided fully for their resolution.

Wallace D. Loh's contribution on the uses and limits of statistics and social science is an excellent example of the interface between social science knowledge and techniques and legal practice. Loh is cautionary but also optimistic about the value of the knowledge and skills that social science has to offer to legal thinking and practice, and his chapter is a skillful statement of how each interacts with the other to the potential enrichment of both.

Leslie T. Wilkins provides us with a systematic study of the role of information and policy control in relation to the use of discretion in legal thinking and practice. His inquiry is particularly valuable, in the opinion of the editors, because it is informed at every stage by ethical concerns and considerations that are always directed at protecting as fully as possible the human qualities of all who come to the attention of the law. The result of Wilkins' scholarly work is a systematic, comprehensive, and impressive statement of how persons use discretion in legal proceedings, preferably against a background of full information and policy control, and always with an awareness of the essentially human qualities that must be protected.

Michael J. Saks and Meridith Miller give a systems view of discretion in the legal process which springs from their knowledge of current social psychological

1

theory. Theirs is another example of the cutting edge of two sets of disciplines, the social sciences and the law, and of the forms and possibilities of their interactions. In recent years, there has been a widening interest in the use of system analysis in the study of complex social problems and issues, and the Saks and Miller contribution provides another advance in looking at such difficult processes within the context of systems theory.

The final chapter of Part I, written by Milton V. Kline, offers a psychodynamic model for looking at lawyer–jury relationships, stressing as it does the role of suggestibility and its use as a tool in the advancement of the lawyer's presentation of his client. It is clear that Kline looks upon the jury as a psychological entity that has characteristics not unlike those of the individual, and he provides an understanding of the full range of transactions that take place between lawyers and the juries they seek to influence. The chapter is stimulating and should provide impetus for additional research.

Tracing the origin of discretion in the criminal justice system in America, Joel Samaha provides a most informative reference with a discussion of Anglo-Saxon secular and clerical law. Modern attacks against discrimination in the system only replicate ancient problems of providing equality for all, in the face of interpersonal relationships involving status, greed, and individual needs.

The mitigating effects of clerical penitentials upon the mechanical application of secular schedules of punishment in Anglo-Saxon times shifted the emphasis from the crime to the sinner. This system encouraged corrupting influences, however, in the form of the wide powers of discretion that were placed in the hands of priests. Contemporary attacks upon the sentencing powers of judges seem to be only a continuation of the same problem. The clerics eventually left it up to God, in another world, to set the record right. As a historian, the author informs us of what has gone before, and suggests that since perfect solutions to human problems have never been devised, we can only rest with the comfort that some things are beyond human control.

1

Some Reflections on the Anglo-Saxon Heritage of Discretionary Justice

Joel Samaha

Discretion has always been at war with law in Anglo-American history. The fundamental urge to ensure equality before the law—that is, to administer justice consistently and objectively—has been tempered with the basic necessity that the law be sensitive to individual differences, that the punishment fit not only the crime but the criminal. Historically, the essential continuity of this tempering of law with discretion has only been interrupted by a shifting emphasis from one feature to the other. In fact, it may be said that the shift may even have been more in the legal writings of various times than in the actual administration of justice, where the two have played their part no matter what has been written or enjoined by articulate lawyers and enlightened policy-makers.

One could illustrate this proposition by many examples from recent history, and probably would not encounter much surprise from general readers or social scientists. When, however, it is also noted that the discretion/law controversy extends back at least as far as 600 A.D., its ancient lineage seems worthy of some discussion. When it can be asserted that the arguments for and against the one or the other have not really changed and that the solutions that have been proposed have also essentially remained the same, the whole history of discretion becomes an important one to tell. Only a small part of this fascinating story can be told here, but even this treatment will reveal some of the earliest examples and discussions of discretion in English history and of the administration of criminal law in Anglo-Saxon times.

Two sets of sources have survived from the Anglo-Saxons, which shed considerable light on the history of Anglo-American criminal law. The dooms, or so-called laws, of the Anglo-Saxon kings, are a collection of some of the rules that were in force in the several kingdoms now known as Britain. The story they tell is largely one of the working of rules, arbitrarily administered, at least if such rules are to be taken at their face value. This is almost a necessity since so little other evidence concerning the actual administration of justice has survived. The dooms are essentially a list of tariffs for what today would be called crimes. Familiar to most and curious to all is the tremendous detail in which the compensation demanded from an offender to be paid to the victim is spelled out: loss of an ear, 30 shillings; an eye, the tongue, a hand, or a foot, 66 shillings, $3\frac{1}{3}$ pence; the nose, 60 shillings; a front tooth, 8 shillings; a molar, 4 shillings; an eye-tooth, 15 shillings; a thumb, 30 shillings; a thumbnail, 5 shillings; a first finger, 15 shillings; the nail, 3 shillings; a little finger, 9 shillings; its nail, 1 shilling; a big toe, 20 shillings; a little toe, 5 shillings, and so on.[1] Although the dooms most heavily emphasize the rule side of our ancient law, it is not valid to conclude that this is all they were concerned with. Hints appear from time to time which make it clear that the Anglo-Saxon kings reserved some discretionary power to themselves even under a criminal law which had as its primary aim the compensation of the victim for injuries done to him. Thus in the dooms of Alfred, we read that, "If any one fights or draws his weapon in the king's hall and is then caught, at the king's judgment he may be put to death or allowed his life in case the king is willing to forgive him."[2]

Not only was the law, therefore, inconsistently applied, but it had written into it an essential inequality. In the first place, the dooms themselves placed a different value on the injuries done and suffered by persons from different segments of society. Thus was the life or body of a thegn worth more than that of a coerl (the ordinary freeman), that of a cleric more than that of a layman; and the dooms are replete with examples of how these differences were worked out. It should be said in their favor that, at least in theory, the idea behind these provisions was that the higher the rank in society, the heavier the burden for doing wrong, and thus the greater the monetary compensation expected.

Nevertheless, we are entitled to speculate that the appealing quality which Anglo-Saxon compensatory justice has on its face was not so laudatory in practice. The alternative for anyone who could not pay the required amounts was usually slavery or death. We may conclude that a person of ordinary means who was unable to pay 5 shillings for damaging a little toe might find himself sold into a life of slavery, a possibility both very real and one which brings us close to the brutality of a law that allowed a rich man to pay for violence but sent a poor man to eternal suffering for stepping a little out of line. Further than these very general and speculative comments, we cannot really go far in analyzing discretion in the dooms because of the paucity of evidence that has survived to show how they worked in practice.[3]

Much more can be said about the other surviving body of evidence—the penitentials. Christianity had always been an austere religion, setting out and demanding of its membership a very strict standard of personal conduct. From the very earliest days means had to be found to enforce this code, especially in the furthest outposts of the Empire where Christian morality was totally foreign. The Church had, however, committed itself to the "purification" even of its most distant converts. At least in the eyes of the Church, it would have been hard to find more unruly and more challenging candidates for this improvement in morals than the Celtic and the Anglo-Saxon tribes in the cold northern fringes of the Roman Empire. Furthermore, it was difficult to communicate to priests so far from the center of things what penalties ought to be extracted from sinners who had confessed their wrongs. Thus there grew up the practice of enumerating in writing sins and the penances due from them. The result is the fascinating set of books of penitentials containing elaborate schedules of all the transgressions that a Christian could commit and the means by which he or she could rectify them.[4]

The books were not always approved by the power at Rome, especially when they reflected, as well they might, more of local custom and superstition than they did the formal rules and decisions at the center of the highly developed system of what would later become the canon law of the Church. Nevertheless, they were popular with local priests throughout England and Ireland, as well as certain parts of the continent.[5]

The penitentials are not only the earliest, but unlike the dooms they are also the richest, evidence we have concerning the evolution of Anglo-American criminal law. This is so for several reasons. In the first place, and as we shall see intimately related to discretion, the penitentials are one of our earliest sources to reveal the conflict between punishment and rehabilitation as proper aims of the criminal law. During the difficult times of establishing peace in the Anglo-Saxon kingdoms, the secular rulers needed all the help they could get in maintaining order. Thus did King Cnut in the eleventh century mingle secular punishment with penance, thereby effectively turning the penitential system into an arm of the administration of criminal justice.[6]   This contradictory mixture is further revealed in St. Edmund of Canterbury's decree that those who were charged with or convicted of serious crime be summoned three times to confess and undergo penance, and if they refused, that they be required to purge themselves by compurgation in secular courts.[7]

That the Church was called upon to enforce the criminal law led to a total contradiction in the aims of penance, which anyone familiar with modern criminal justice can readily appreciate. So, when one bishop whipped sinners who had committed secular crimes, he told the unwilling receivers that somehow their stripes were not only punishment but that they also contributed to their salvations.[8]

The confusion of punishment with salvation is not the only problem in the penitentials that modern students can recognize and understand. Related to it is the constant reference to the medicinal qualities of penance and the repeated characterization of priests as physicians of the soul. A good example of this occurs when Pope Gregory III, in discussing the administration of penance, writes that, "If physicians of the flesh prescribe different medicines against the infirmities of the body, how much more ought God's priests to repay innumerable comforts of healing against the illicit fruits of the work of the flesh."[9] Sometimes this takes a purely physical turn, as when the school of medicine that taught that "contraries are to be cured by their contraries" was taken up in the penitential prescription that the talkative should be sentenced to silence and the glutton to fasting.[10] At other points it has a more psychiatric quality, as when the aim of penance is said to be directed toward aiding the sinner to recover harmonious relationships with society, the Church, and God.[11] In doing penance, an individual can be restored to society and function again as a normal person. Nothing more need be said here to demonstrate that the so-called medical model in criminal justice is neither a new problem nor a modern discovery by twentieth century criminologists.[12] It need only be mentioned that this model created problems in determining the right doses of the proper medicine similar to those encountered today.

Had punishment been the only aim of penance, and not the cure of sick souls, the penitentials would probably have contributed little to our knowledge about discretion in the administration of justice. As we have already seen, the Anglo-Saxon dooms, in which restitution was the predominant aim of the criminal law, left little room or need for discretion. However, when the question turned to cure for sickness of the soul or bringing the sinner back into the community, penalties could not be mechanistically applied. It is to the sinner and not the sin that the priest must look if he is to save a soul and restore a sinner to the congregation. Here arose the great problems posed by tailoring the penalty to suit the offender.

Two other characteristics of the penitentials must be considered before a proper discussion of the significance of discretion in administering them is taken up. First is the hopeless contradiction and disparity of the sentences prescribed in the various penitential books. One example should make the point. In the penitential attributed to the Venerable Bede, the penance for premeditated murder was four years, while in another English penitential, the one ascribed to Archbishop Theodore, the penalty for the same offense was seven years, or if accompanied by a fast against flesh and wine, three years.[13] What then was an English priest to do, if he had both books at his disposal, if two such lofty authorities prescribed such disparate penalties for the identical offense? The problem, as should readily become apparent, is not a new one to the twentieth century; nor, as we shall see later, are the alternative solutions that were proposed to solve it new to us.

The other pertinent characteristic of the penitentials is the tremendous harshness of the penalties prescribed for breaching the strict code of conduct that the Christians expected of their membership. Consider, for example, the length of penance due for some of the more common sins:[14] 30 days for vomiting while drunk; 10 years for sexual intercourse between men; 40 days for masturbation; attempt to have intercourse, 20–40 days; libidinous imagination, penance until the imagination is overcome. Severity need not be measured by length alone. One church formulary prescribed that penitents were to be imprisoned in the Church and heavily fasted for the whole term of the penance. The imprisonment was described as being "passed in harsh garments, on bread and water, except on Sundays, the penitent daily making a hundred genuflections and reciting a hundred Paternosters every day and as many every night, sleeping on straw, never washing his hands, and speaking to no one before the third hour of the morning nor after complins."[15]

This combination of severity, disparity, and the individualization of sentences all led to the exercise of discretion in the administration of penance.

In the first place, the great contradictions in penances prescribed in the penitentials was a cause of persistent concern in the higher circles of the Church and was reflected in the complaints registered against the penitentials in several councils.[16] Sometimes the criticism was directed at destroying the penitentials on the ground that they were written by unauthorized priests who had no power to determine the proper sentences for various sins. Since the authors, if not granted their power to design penance by Rome, were very popular because they derived their prescriptions from the customs and mood of the particular societies to whom they ministered, this solution was not the best one. Other suggestions were directed toward rationalizing the penitentials so that the penalties they prescribed were more uniform. Thus did Ebo, Archbishop of Rheims, call upon Bishop Halitgar of Cambrai to frame a code that would overcome the difficulties in the existing penitentials.[17] Halitgar's solution is very instructive. Instead of writing a new book of penances by means of codification of existing penances, he rejected the whole idea that tariffs for sins could be scheduled specifically. The only way for a sinner to win God's mercy was by "repentance and amendment and reparation of wrongs and good works ... all of which must vary with the individual and his depth of contrition, and be determined by the discretion of the bishop."[18] So the solution to disparity and contradiction was not a uniform code of penalties that could be mechanistically applied but the exact opposite, a general admonition to base the penalty on the degree of contrition in the sinner, a solution which called for discretion in the extreme, not for rules of precise definition.

The harsh penalties led to the same result. One of the more widely accepted notions among students of the administration of justice is that penalties thought to be excessively harsh will be ameliorated through such discretionary devices as the police in arresting, the prosecutor in charging, the jury in convicting, the judge in sentencing.[19]   The reaction was not markedly different in the Anglo-Saxon penitentials except that in the latter the problem was openly admitted and dealt with frankly, as the following excerpt from the penitential attributed to Bede makes quite clear. After reciting the very severe penances due for the commission of sins which happened also to be secular crimes, he concedes that to expect maximum fulfillment of these penalties was too "hard and difficult" in some cases.

> Therefore [to him] who cannot do these things we give the advice that there should be instead of this, psalms and prayer and alms with some days in penance; that is, psalms for one day when he is due to fast on bread and water. These [requirements] are: Kneeling he shall sing in sequence fifty psalms, and without kneeling, seventy, in a church or in one place. For a week on bread and water he shall sing in sequence three hundred psalms, kneeling in a church or in one place; without kneeling four hundred and twenty. And for one month on bread and water one thousand five hundred psalms, kneeling, and without kneeling, one thousand eight hundred and twenty, and afterward through all the days he shall sup at sext and abstain from flesh and wine; other food, whatever God gives him, he may take after he has sung. And he who does not know the psalms ought to do penance and fast and dispense to the poor every day money of the value of a denarius and fast one day until nones and another until vespers and [then] eat whatever he has.[20]

Harshness in this passage, it is immediately apparent, is judged by the inability of the sinner to perform sentences embodying hard physical endurance, such as long fasts.   For them, psalms, genuflections, prayers, and so on could be substituted.

Physical pain and suffering of the sinner were, however, not the only aims of the sentence. If the amelioration was in the form of commutation to money, especially if paid to the victim, then the purpose of penance was as much to serve the aims of restitution in the secular criminal law as it was to reconcile the sinner to the Church. Commutation in the penitentials for sins that were also secular crimes reinforced the secular laws and was meant to do so. In these cases, discretion took the form of reducing penance in order to induce payment that would satisfy the secular law. Thus was payment of the wergild of a slain man considered sufficient to reduce the penance for homicide by one half, according to one penitential.[21]   And so too it was sufficient penance, according to Bede, to work for an assault victim as a means of compensating for medical treatment of a man whom the sinner had wounded in a fight.[22]   In the same vein were those reductions or substitutions of penance that were made upon the restitution of stolen or damaged property.[23]

Reconciling disparities, mitigating harshness, and reinforcing the secular criminal law were not, however, the only—and indeed not even the most important—reasons for the exercise of discretion prescribed in the Anglo-Saxon penitentials. It was rather a more fundamental aim of penance that was primarily responsible for placing discretionary powers in the hands of the confessor priests. As we have already seen, unlike the Anglo-Saxon dooms in which it was clearly the offense that was the focus in prescribing secular punishments, in the penitentials the sinner was the object of penance. And so with the penitentials we have the first thoroughgoing investigation into the individualization of punishment in Anglo-American history.

When Bishop Halitgar wrote that he could not set down precise penalties for particular sins, he gave as his reason that penalties depended upon the amount of contrition in the sinner, not upon the sin he committed. In this he was eloquently echoed by many other Church fathers who, like Alcuin, stoutly maintained that penance was not to be assessed by the number of years but by the bitterness of the mind. Peter, he said, was quickly forgiven as soon as he denounced the triple denial of Christ because in his denial he had displayed bitterness of heart, and that, not the magnitude of the sin, was the determining element in his reconciliation to God.

In taking up the awesome power of the keys—that is, in assuming to itself the authority of admission to heaven and thereby to everlasting life, or conversely to hell and perpetual suffering—the Church embarked upon an ambitious, a noble, even a Herculean, task. Resting the determination of whether the sinner should spend eternity in heaven or hell upon seeing into his soul may have been a lofty purpose, but it also was little short of madness because it required the impossible task of looking inwardly toward the mysteries of a man's soul instead of outwardly at his more manifest deeds. In that effort, the confessor was forced to contend with the highly speculative question of just what that soul looked like. Yet we read in the penitentials how this can be accomplished boldly and seemingly with little hesitation. Although all of them differ in some details, all follow essentially the same guidelines set out confidently in the penitentials attributed to the Venerable Bede, which bear quoting at length here:

> For not all are to be weighed in one and the same balance, although they be associated in one fault, but there shall be discrimination for each of these, that is: between rich and poor; freeman, slave; little child, boy, youth, young man, old man; stupid, intelligent; layman, cleric, monk; bishop, presbyter, deacon, subdeacon, reader, ordained or unordained; married or unmarried; pilgrim, virgin, canoness, or nuns; the weak, the sick, the well. He shall make a distinction for the character of the sins or of the men: a continent person or one who is incontinent willfully or by accident; [whether the sin is committed] in public or in secret; with what degree of compunction he [the culprit] makes amends by necessity or by intention; the places and times [of offenses].[24]

Thus more than a thousand years ago were the guidelines set for tailoring penances to suit the sinner in ways that are eerily similar to those used to make the punishment fit the criminal in modern-day indeterminate sentencing.[25] Although, to be sure, wealth is not directly a consideration in modern sentencing, it is reflected in the concern for the defendant's income and ability to support himself and his family. More directly akin to today's sentencing criteria are the admonitions to pay heed to the age, occupation, marital status, and education of the sinner.[26] The stress on culpability, that is, whether or not the sin was done willfully, is also familiar to modern readers.[27]

In homicide cases the intention was considered crucial in determining the amount of penance. Soldiers who killed pagans in battle to save Christianity had their penances reduced to 40 days by the Council of Tribur in 895.[28] A woman who negligently and without malice put her baby near a fire where a servant spilled boiling water on it from which the baby died, ought to have light penance because negligence was a lower degree of culpability than malice. To students of the Model Penal Code and its path-breaking attempt to define and grade various levels of culpability, this provision for culpability must surely appear very enlightened.[29] Perhaps the most important feature to note about the guidelines is that, although susceptible to varying interpretations by individual priests, they make quite clear what the criteria are for determining the type and amount of penance.

Correcting disparities, mitigating severities, and curing the soul of the sinner were the aims of penance and the reasons for exercising discretion in the administration of the Church's criminal justice system. From the discussion thus far the parallels between the Anglo-Saxon Church and modern criminal justice have been made obvious. Except perhaps to historians who are accustomed to living at least vicariously in the past, parallels between two such vastly different eras may be surprising to modern readers. It is probably little comfort to learn that the justifications for discretion in administering the law are very old. On the other hand, at least initially, some slight encouragement may be taken from the knowledge that discretion did not go without criticism in those earlier days either. To some of the critics we must now turn.

First were the criticisms directed at outright corruption in the administration of penance. Alms-giving and the commutation of certain forms of penance to money, both of which as we have already seen were fully within the discretionary powers of the priests, were the sources of the complaints. Typical of many others was the critic who accused some priests of selling absolution for a chicken. Another critic, Cardinal Henry of Susa, tells of priests who looked invitingly at penitents' purses and then graded their penalties according to the amount handed over to them. St. Bonaventura warned the Franciscans never to take gifts from penitents.[30] Such complaints are very small potatoes when compared with the many accusations of the aggrandizement of the Church at the willing expense of very wealthy penitents. The churchman Muratori relates:

> When the noble, perhaps stretched on a sick bed, would seek to discharge his conscience of the accumulated crimes of years, after his confession was finished the priest would produce the canons and his ink-horn and proceed to foot up the years of penance incurred. The aggregate would be appalling, and the redemption at the current rate would represent an amount far beyond the means of the penitent to command on the spot, for ready money was scarce in these times. A transaction would be suggested by which an equivalent in lands would be accepted by the church or abbey, perhaps leaving to the owner the urusfruct during his life, and both parties would be satisfied with the bargain.[31]

Second were the attacks on the discriminatory applications of penance, that is, the administration of penance in such a way that the rich and powerful were favored and the poor and weak oppressed. Thus, in the canons of the Council of Cloveshoe held in 747 we find the alleged favored position of the rich denounced in the form of a story about a rich man who, by means of his money and power, was able to accumulate so much expiation that if he had lived for three hundred years, his sins would have been fully satisfied, after which the reporter for the Council wisely queries:

> ... if the divine justice can be appeased ... in this way, why, ye foolish boaster, are rich men—who are able with bribes to purchase limitless fastints ... for their ... offenses—said by the voice of Truth to enter the Kingdom of Heavin with more difficulty than a camel goes through a needle's eye.[32]

Giving considerable credence to the complaints is a canon from the reign of the ninth century Anglo-Saxon King Edgar, in which it was recommended with approval how a rich man with the help of his friends could buy penance:

> After confession let him undertake penance with much sighing, lay aside his weapons and wear woolen or hair cloth garments and so do, that in three days the series of vii years be dispensed with thus; let him proceed with aid; and first let him take with him xii men, and let them fast iii days on bread, and on green herbs, and on water; and get, in addition thereto, in whatever manner he can, seven times cxx men, who shall also fast for him iii days; then will he be fasted as many fasts as there are days in vii years.[33]

If this reflected reality, it is no wonder that critics of discretion which favored the rich were so numerous.

Finally there were the censures of laxity in punishment that discretion engendered. Thus a Council of Chalons in 813 reproached the use of pilgrimages in place of more severe penance because it led people to believe that they could be purged of their sins by taking a simple pilgrimage.[33] Similar was the charge that priests who freely substituted alms-giving for more severe forms of expiation actually encouraged men to sin on purpose in the mistaken belief that they could easily get absolution by the mere payment of money.[34] The commutation of penance into money payments so corrupted the penitential system, according to one critic, that sinners could no longer be made to fast longer than three days in a week, apparently because to do so was considered too severe in the light of discretionary commutations.[35]

To the modern reader perhaps the most striking feature of these criticisms is how much, at least generally, they resemble modern attacks on the criminal justice system. The problem of uncertainty of punishment based on the hope that the rigors of the penitential prescriptions could be avoided through the exercise of the priest's discretionary powers is echoed in most of the literature on the certainty and severity of criminal punishment. Only the most significant of these attacks, but by no means the only one, is the work of the distinguished Norwegian jurist Johannes Andenaes, who has made us aware of the significant role that certainty of punishment plays in deterring criminal behavior.[36] The corrupting influence of the wide powers of discretion held by the Anglo-Saxon priests is mirrored in the wholesale assault on the sentencing powers of modern-day judges, such as that which was recently and so persuasively made by U.S. District Judge Marvin Frankel.[37] And the discriminatory exercise of discretionary power can be documented in the legions of work proving that the poor and the weak in our society are the most likely candidates for arrest, conviction, and long-term imprisonment, while the wealthy, in the few instances where they are arrested and convicted at all, usually receive probation and suspended sentences and only rarely prison terms, in which case they serve only a very short time.[38]

The criticisms of the penitential system were much more detailed in assessing its shortcomings than in spelling out plans to remedy them. A few proposed solutions can be found, but they are tantalizingly brief and are put into the critic's writing almost willy-nilly among other matters. One such proposal was that of Bishop Ebo, whose lament to his learned fellow, Bishop Halitgar, that the books of penitentials were in hopeless contradiction and confusion, leaving priests with no direction as to what to prescribe as proper penance, we have already seen. Let us see his suggested remedy. He pleads with his learned brother to gather up a proper list of penances, which are to be drawn not from local customs but from the exalted Church fathers' writings and the canons of the Church. Having done this, he asks Halitgar to publish them in simple and direct form for the use of uneducated confessors. His solution to the problem was in giving priests proper guidelines to follow so that they would not be left to their own devices in prescribing penance. Specifically, he recommended controlling discretion by rule. We have already seen that Bishop Halitgar rejected this solution because of his belief that contrition had to be determined individually for each sinner. So the solution of making penance more dependent upon rule was rejected in favor of keeping it open to discretion. It was not only the "confusion" in the books that troubled Bishop Ebo; it was also the "slowness" of the priests who administered it. Except for putting a clear set of directions in their hands, we read no more of improving the quality of the priests' exercise of discretion. In part, at least, this was because of confidence in the knowledge that an ultimate and, within the framework of the times, infallible final review of discretion in prescribing penance would take place. Naturally, we are referring here to the judgment day. This is precisely what Peter Lombard had in mind when he wrote confidently that if because of "ignorance or negligence of the priest" insufficient penance was exacted, God would add the required amount. Furthermore, the priest himself might be punished for his error.[39]

The reliance on God to sort out everything in the end and put the improper sentences right was a luxury that no modern judge can fall back upon when he errs in sentencing. Nor is it to God to whom most modern critics of the administration of criminal justice look for solutions to abuse of discretion. Hope today resides in social science and the answers its students can provide. Whether modern social scientists will find a solution that improves upon Bishop Ebo's request for authoritative guidelines administered by good priests with the rest left up to God remains to be seen. A hope seems to be growing that discretion can be eliminated from the administration of justice without sacrificing justice itself.[40] This solution is not only extreme, but also rests upon what appears to be a false hope that all individual cases can be put into general categories that provide the same penalty. The better modern view, better at least in the view of this writer, is much akin to that expressed in the penitentials. It is very well argued by K. C. Davis, who accepts the reality and the necessity of discretion but hopes to stop its abuse by exercising it wisely, that is, by controlling it.[41] How this can be done is, of course, a problem of the utmost importance and complexity but one that can be intelligently addressed by social scientists. Happily, the role of the historian stops in informing them of what has been done in other times and places. The only advice that a historian can give, beyond telling the story of the past as it actually happened, is to remind readers of some things they already know very well—for instance, that perfect solutions to problems have never yet been devised and that even if we cannot take comfort in the hope that God will ultimately put everything right, at least we can be humble enough to admit that some things are simply not within human control.

FOOTNOTES

1. Dooms of Alfred, 871–901 A.D., taken from Carl Stephenson and Frederick George Marcham, *Sources of English Constitutional History*, Vol. I (New York, 1972), p. 12.
2. Ibid.
3. For a very good discussion of the possibilities of taking the evidence to its outer limits, while remaining convincing, see Theodore F. T. Pluknett's brilliant lectures printed in his *Edward I and the Criminal Law* (Cambridge, 1960).
4. The best collection of translations is John T. McNeill and Helena M. Gamer (eds.), *Medieval Handbooks of Penance* (New York, 1938), hereafter cited as McNeill and Gamer. The best discussions of the penitentials, which have been very much neglected, are Henry Charles Lea, *A History of Auricular Confession and Indulgences*, Vol. II (Philadelphia, 1896), hereafter Lea, and Thomas P. Oakley, *English Penitential Discipline and Anglo-Saxon Law in Their Joint Influence* in Columbia University Studies in History Economics and Public Law (New York, 1923), hereafter Oakley.
5. Lea, pp. 102–6.
6. Ibid., p. 112.
7. Ibid., p. 114.
8. Ibid., p. 112.
9. Migne, *Patrilogia Latina* (hereafter Migne), Vol. 89, cols. 587–89. I am grateful to Steven Fanning for the translation of this passage.
10. McNeill and Gamer, pp. 44–46.
11. Ibid., p. 46.
12. For a reasonable discussion of the modern learning, see Nicholas Kittrie, *The Right to Be Different* (Baltimore, 1971).
13. McNeill and Gamer, pp. 224, 187.
14. All taken from the Penitential of Theodore, McNeill and Gamer, 184ff.
15. Lea, pp. 120–21, paraphrasing a church formulary.
16. Ibid., p. 105.
17. Ibid., p. 195.
18. Ibid.
19. For the best scholarship on discretion in these areas, see Frank J. Remington (ed.), *The Report of the American Bar Foundation's Survey of the Administration of Criminal Justice in the United States* (Boston, 1965).
20. McNeill and Gamer, p. 237.
21. Oakley, p. 170.
22. Ibid.
23. Ibid., p. 172, who sees this more as a way to alleviate even heavier penance.
24. McNeill and Gamer, p. 225.
25. Joseph Goldstein, Alan Dershowitz, and Richard Schwartz, *Criminal Law: Its Theory and Practice* (2nd ed., Boston, 1969), pp. 613–56, has a good analysis of modern-day sentencing criteria.
26. Ibid.
27. Ibid.
28. Mansi, *Sacrosancta Concilia*, Vol. 17, MGH, Leges, sec. 2, Vol. 2, pp. 233–35.
29. The American Law Institute, *Model Penal Code*, Reprint, Tentative Draft No. 4 "Commentary," pp. 123–32, (1954).
30. Lea cited, p. 149.
31. Lea, p. 156.

32. McNeill and Gamer, p. 394.
33. Cited in Lea, p. 132.
34. Lea, citing Council of Chalons, p. 137.
35. Ibid., p. 156.
36. See Andenaes, *The Journal of Criminal Law and Criminology 66* (no. 3), (September 1975).
37. See his *Criminal Sentences* (New York, 1972).
38. Leonard Orland and Harold Tyler (eds.), *Justice in Sentencing* (Mineola, New York, 1974) summarizes much of the plethora of materials.
39. Peter Lombard, *Four Books of Sentences*, Migne.
40. See *Justice in Sentencing.*
41. *Discretionary Justice* (Urbana, Ill. 1971).

Sharing his expertise in both statistics and law, Wallace D. Loh discusses the establishment of a reasoned connection between conclusions of law and the supporting substantive evidence. Prudence is suggested in using quantitative methods exclusively in rule-making, as well as in determining the occurrence of an event or the shaping of the perception of an event. He makes an interesting contrast between the differences in legal proof and proof in statistics.

Weighing the evidence in judicial legislation is central to the process of providing justice, and the author cautions against relying upon the presumed objectivity of statistics without considering the subjectivity of the interpretor.

The author concludes with a summary of strategies for applying social science techniques without ignoring the intent of the law.

2

Some Uses and Limits of Statistics and Social Science in the Judicial Process[1]

Wallace D. Loh

A central issue in judicial decision-making is the establishment of a reasoned connection between conclusions of law and the supporting evidence. This chapter will present an analytical overview of some of the uses and limits of extra-legal evidence—that is, facts derived from the application of statistical and social science methods—to support legal conclusions. As early as 1897, Justice Holmes in a classic essay, entitled "The Path of the Law," called for the application of empirical methods to the law. "For the rational study of the law," he wrote, "the black-letter man may be the man of the present, but the man of the future is the man of statistics and the master of economics" (p. 469). In the ensuing two decades, the legal philosophy schools of sociological jurisprudence (Pound, 1912) and realism (Llewellyn, 1930) also urged an empirical orientation to the judicial decision-making process. According to Pound, the main problem is "to enable and to compel law-making, and also the interpretation and application of legal rules, to take more account, and more intelligent account, of the social facts upon which the law must proceed and to which it is to be applied" (p. 512). However, the actual, systematic application of these empirical tools to law, at least by lawyers, is of recent vintage, dating only from the 1950s (Kalven, 1968).

Owing to the breadth of the subject, I have chosen the case method in presenting this overview. I have selected some judicial cases from the 1950s to the present that illustrate different prospects and problems in the application of statistics and social science to law. By analyzing and comparing these cases, I hope to cull some general insights and principles regarding when and how they should be used in the judicial process.

The chapter has three parts. The first is on the use of statistical techniques in judicial adjudication, with special attention to their use in (1) determining quantitative fact issues, (2) testing the reliability of trial procedures, and (3) quantifying judicial standards of proof. It also examines (4) the logic of proof in science and law. The second part is on the use of social science in judicial legislation. It discusses (1) the determination of adjudicative and legislative facts, (2) the sources of legislative facts for the courts, and (3) problems of evaluation of legislative facts. The final part consists of some reflections on strategies of rapprochement between law and social science.

STATISTICS IN JUDICIAL ADJUDICATION

Use of Statistics in Adjudicating Quantitative Fact Issues

The context in which statistics plays perhaps the largest role in litigation is in the inference of numerical characteristics of a population based on sampling operations. Here, the very issues at stake are quantitative. Under the governing substantive law, the content of which is not in dispute, the legal question is one of statistical fact. Sampling statistics have been used, for example, in antitrust cases to estimate the percentage of market control [*U.S. v. United Shoe Machinery Corp.*, 1953; aff'd per curiam, 347 U.S. 521 (1954)] ; in trademark litigation to establish public confusion as to brand names (*U.S. v. 88 Cases More or Less*, 1951); in criminal pretrail motions to show community bias toward the defendant in order to secure a change of venue (Woodward, 1952); and so on (see Zeisel, 1968). These instances of use of statistics seem altogether unexceptionable and pose no special issues of law.[2] Sampling statistics often constitute the best and only evidence available about the quantitative features of a universe of persons or events.

Use of Statistics in Testing the Reliability of Trial Procedures

A different use of inferential statistics is in testing the reliability or fairness of trial procedures. I will illustrate this use by analyzing some cases on racial discrimination in jury selection.

The total exclusion of minority members from grand jury or petit jury venire panels, when such persons are available and eligible for jury service, is "a prima facie case of denial of equal protection" (*Norris v. Alabama*, 1934, p. 587). A more difficult problem arises when there is underrepresentation, not exclusion, of minorities, and consequently discrimination in jury selection is alleged. Three principal cases have come before the Supreme Court.

In *Swain v. Alabama* (1965), black males over the age of 21 constituted 26 percent of all males in the county, but only 10 to 15 percent of the grand and petit jury panels drawn for the preceding eight years had been black. The Court held that this percentage disparity was small and did not constitute evidence of "purposeful discrimination." While not every statistical discrepancy is constitutionally fatal, neither the Court nor counsel offered any criteria for ascertaining where and how to draw the line. There was no reasoned basis for concluding that a 10 to 15 percent disparity is or is not discriminatory.

Relying on statistical decision theory, Finkelstein (1966) has proposed one possible test, using a baseline of chance. There is prima facie evidence of intentional discrimination if the underrepresentation is larger than expected by chance. The procedural effect would be to shift the burden to the prosecution to come forth and account for the disparity. By treating the selection of veniremen as a series of Bernoulli trials, Finkelstein showed that the probability of selecting solely by chance five or fewer blacks in each venire of 30 persons, where potentially eligible black veniremen constituted 25 percent of the population, was .20. But since this result occurred in *Swain* in 30 consecutive cases over eight years, the probability (applying the product rule) was $.20^{30}$. He concluded that veniremen were not selected at random in *Swain*, and, in the absence of any explanation, this was proof of discrimination.

Two years later, in *Whitus v. Georgia* (1967), the Supreme Court appeared to retreated from the statistical test of *Swain*. The selection of an all-white jury, drawn from a venire panel consisting of 7.7 percent blacks, was challenged as discriminatory, since 27.1 percent of the county taxpayers (and potentially eligible jurors) were black. The Court applied Finkelstein's test and found the likelihood of a chance occurrence to be .00006. However, in striking down this jury selection process, the Court held the probability test was "unnecessary to [its] disposition of the instant case" because the process itself was "clearly discriminatory." At that time, Georgia tax return sheets were of different colors for black and white taxpayers, and since juries were selected from these sheets, this procedure was prima facie evidence of discrimination. [See *Jones v. Georgia*, per curiam, 389 U.S. 24 (1967); *Sims v. Georgia*, per curiam, 389 U.S. 404 (1976).]

In the latest Supreme Court case of *Alexander v. Louisiana* (1972), the defendant was indicted by an all-white grand jury. This jury was drawn from a venire panel consisting of 5 percent blacks, which, in turn, was called from a pool of 7 percent blacks, which, again, was culled from a larger pool of 14 percent blacks. The county contained 21 percent male blacks who were presumptively eligible for grand jury service. The Court held that "the progressive decimation of potential Negro grand jurors is indeed striking here, but we do not rest our conclusion that petitioner has demonstrated a prima facie case of invidious racial discrimination on statistical impossibility alone, for the selection procedures themselves were not racially neutral" (p. 626). The Court indicated that it had "never announced mathematical standards for the demonstration of systematic exclusion of blacks but has, rather, emphasized that a factual inquiry is necessary in each case that takes into account all possible factors" (p. 626).

There is, then, an important difference in the use of statistics in these jury discrimination cases and in the cases (mentioned in the preceding section) measuring the numerical characteristics of a population. In population measurement, the issues at stake are numerical. Only the facts are disputed, and statistical evidence from sampling operations can resolve the conflicting factual claims. The rule of law applicable to the facts is not at issue. In the jury discrimination situation, on the other hand, both the facts and the applicable rule are disputed. Statistical evidence is used to determine the extent of minority underrepresentation, and a statistical method is also used to establish a decision-making rule regarding constitutionally significant discrepancies. The analytical question is which is the better rule for finding discrimination: the *Swain* test of "statistics alone" (set without explanation at 10 to 15 percent) or the *Whitus* and *Alexander* test of "statistics plus defective procedure."

I would suggest that *Swain* is not inconsistent with the subsequent two cases but is distinguishable from them. The two elements of a prima facie case—statistical discrepancy and procedural discrepancy—combine to produce four fact situations, as follows:

Statistical discrepancy

		"Large"	"Small"
Procedural discrepancy	"Large"	1	2
	"Small"	3	4

Each of these elements, of course, assumes a baseline for calculating the degree of discrepancy. I will assume, following *Swain*, that a "large" statistical discrepancy is one greater than 10 to 15 percent, and a "small" one is less than that range. The procedural discrepancies are deviations from constitutionally or legislatively (e.g., Federal Jury Selection and Service Act, 1968) established selection methods. Category 4 represents the *Swain* case. There was little or no taint in the selection procedure, and the numerical disparity was under 10 to 15 percent. Category 1 includes *Whitus* and *Alexander*; in both, the procedures were objectionable and the statistical discrepancies large. Under the *Alexander* reasoning, a selection process falling in category 2 would probably be ruled invalid. If a procedure is opprobrious on its face (such as racial identification on jury lists), statistical differences become irrelevant. There is prima facie discrimination based on improper procedure alone. Finally, category 3 represents the difficult fact pattern not yet encountered by the Supreme Court or lower federal courts. Can discrimination be established on statistics alone, when procedural defects are minimal?[2a]

I am unpersuaded that statistical discrepancy alone is sufficient. The difficulty with the Finkelstein test, that significant deviations from a chance baseline are to be equated with unconstitutional discrimination, is that it fails to consider the reason for the deviation. Not all deviations due to design are suspect. Although such discrepancies are usually the result of improper selection criteria (e.g., race), they could also result from neutral or innocent considerations (e.g., hardship excuses, personal predilections not to serve on juries, literacy requirements, and so forth). Indeed, to the extent that the policy is to assure fairness in selection rather than proportional representation in the jury composition, there may be occasions where deliberate reliance on race or other factors, resulting in statistical disparities, may be necessary to avoid discrimination (see *Stephens v. Cox*, 1971). A statistics-alone test seems too inflexible to take into account, on a case-by-case basis, the various factors that may legitimately produce a deviation from chance. The trend in the lower federal courts since *Whitus* also seems to be that statistical discrepancy is not enough, lacking an improper procedure, because of the potential for discrimination or actual discrimination (see, e.g., *Blackwell v. Thomas*, 1973; *Witcher v. Peyton*, 1969).

Use of Statistics in Adjudicating the Likelihood of a Particular Event

Another application of statistics in the trial process is to determine the likelihood of occurrence of certain individual events by chance; that is, to use probabilistic evidence and arguments as an aid to, or even as a substitute for, the application of judicial standards of proof. This use poses difficult problems of law. In the absence of a coherent judicial theory in this area, I will analyze four selected cases—two criminal and two civil—and attempt to derive therefrom some insights and themes regarding this type of use of statistics.

Criminal Liability

In *People v. Collins* (1968), a robbery victim testified that the woman who snatched her purse had a blond ponytail and had fled from the scene in a yellow convertible driven by a black man with a mustache and beard. Lacking positive identification, the prosecution introduced a statistician as expert witness who testified, over defense counsel's objection, to the hypothetical probability of the joint occurrence of the aforementioned characteristics in any given couple, as follows: yellow car, 1/10; man with mustache, 1/4; woman with ponytail; 1/10; blond, 1/3; black with beard, 1/10; interracial couple; 1/1000. Applying the product rule, the expert testified that the likelihood was 1 in 12 million that any couple would possess those characteristics by chance alone. The prosecution told the jurors that the standard of beyond a reasonable doubt was the "most hackneyed, stereotyped, trite, misunderstood concept in criminal law," and that he was presenting a "new math approach to criminal jurisprudence" (p. 41).

The California Supreme Court reversed the convictions and held the statistical testimony inadmissible on three grounds: (1) there was no empirical evidentiary foundation to support the probability estimates; (2) there was no adequate proof of the independence of the characteristics as assumed in the product rule; and (3) apart from the above, the testimony failed to answer the key issue— namely, of the few couples with these characteristics, which one if any committed the alleged crime? "Trial by mathematics," said the court, "so distorted the role of the jury and so disadvantaged counsel for the defense, as to constitute in itself a miscarriage of justice" (p. 41).

The critical question that *Collins* leaves unanswered is whether probabilistic proof would be admissible for establishing the identity of the defendant if the three objections of the Court had been overcome; i.e., there was an evidentiary foundation, the probabilities rules were correctly used, and there was only one couple in the jurisdiction that matched those characteristics. After all, the court saw "no inherent incompatibility" between law and statistics and did not intend any "general disapproval of [statistics] as an auxiliary in the fact finding processes" of the law (p. 33). This position, while reasonable, avoids the problem of defining the proper and improper auxiliary roles. Other courts have also skirted the issue and rejected probabilistic proof on evidentiary grounds. The New Mexico Supreme Court, for instance, held in *State v. Sneed* (1966) that "mathematical odds are not admissible as evidence to identify a defendant in a criminal proceeding so long as the odds are based on estimates, the validity of which have [sic] not been demonstrated" (p. 802).

Put another way, the *Collins*-type situation raises the broader issue of whether probabilistic proof of the identity of an accused criminal is simply another form of expert proof subject to the usual safeguards of cross-examination of the expert, opportunity to rebut, publicly financed assistance of statistical experts for indigent defendants, cautionary jury instructions regarding statistics, and so on; or, whether despite all these safeguards, it is still not admissible because it poses more fundamental issues which run counter to the social value that undergird the legal order. Before addressing this question, I would like to consider another criminal case where probabilistic arguments regarding a specific, unique occasion were ruled proper, and compare it with *Collins* in order to discern the reasoning for the different outcomes.

In *Turner v. U.S.* (1970), the Supreme Court sustained the constitutionality of a federal statutory presumption[3] that permitted, but did not require, a jury to find from the proven fact of heroin possession the presumed fact of knowledge of illegal importation of that heroin, unless the possession was satisfactorily explained to the jury. The prosecution presented evidence that Congress, in establishing the presumption, evaluated statistical evidence showing that 98 percent of all heroin in this country is illegally imported. After proving the defendant's possession of heroin, the prosecution relied on the presumption to take the case to the jury. The Court found the presumption comported with due process because there was a rational connection between the proven fact and the presumed fact, and this connection was established by the 98 percent statistical evidence both beyond a reasonable doubt (the criminal standard) and by a preponderance of the evidence (the civil standard). However, the Court struck down a similar presumption regarding cocaine. It found no reasonable connection, since the evidence showing that less than 50 percent of all cocaine in the country is illegally imported satisfied neither the criminal nor the civil standard.[4]

Thus, in *Turner* the Supreme Court ruled as proper the use of statistics to show that there was a 98 percent likelihood that the defendant knew of the illegal importation of heroin (key elements of the crime charged), but in *Collins* the California Supreme Court ruled as improper the use of statistics to show that there was a 1 in 12 million likelihood that the defendants did not commit the charged offense. Again, assuming the three objections raised by the court in *Collins* had been met, can the different results of these two cases be explained in some reasonable way? To provide a point of comparison, I will turn next to two civil cases, each with different outcomes.

Civil Liability

In *Smith v. Rapid Transit* (1945), the Supreme Judicial Court of Massachusetts sustained a directed verdict for the defendant in an action for personal injuries caused by the negligent operation of a blue bus allegedly belonging to the defendant bus company. The plaintiff showed only that four-fifths of all blue buses were owned and operated by the defendant, who possessed the sole bus franchise in the jurisdiction where the accident occurred. The court noted: "The most that can be said of the evidence in the instant case is that perhaps the mathematical chances somewhat favor the proposition that a bus of the defendant caused the accident. This was not enough" (p. 470).

The court is silent on the main issues—*how* much more or *what* more is "enough" to establish liability for damages? The quoted statement cannot be interpreted to mean that a higher margin of probability is needed. In civil cases, the standard of proof is by a preponderance of the evidence, which is usually understood but seldom expressly articulated as more than a 51 percent chance. In this instance, the probability was 80 percent that the negligent bus belonged to the defendant. Consequently, the statement should be construed to ask what more is enough—what kind of additional, conventional (nonstatistical), particularized proof exists that this specific defendant operated the bus which struck the plaintiff (Tribe, 1971). Here again, as in the jury discrimination cases and in the *Collins* situation, statistics alone is insufficient. Statistics plus individualized proof is needed for liability to attach.

In comparison, consider the following hypothetical case derived from the facts of *Byrne v. Boadle* (1863). A barrel falls from the window of a warehouse onto the head of a passing pedestrian. The issue is whether some negligent act or omission by the defendant warehouse caused the fall. Under the tort doctrine of res ipsa loquitur ("the thing speaks for itself"),[5] if the event was under the control of the defendant, and it is within common knowledge and experience that such barrel fallings do not occur but for negligence, the case can go to the jury for a determination of the defendant's negligence unless the defendant comes forward and rebuts the inference. Suppose that it cannot be said that it is within common knowledge and experience that unexplained barrel fallings are due to negligence. Can the plaintiff introduce statistical evidence to show that four-fifths of all such barrel fallings from warehouse windows are the result of negligent acts or omissions? In *Rapid Transit*, the fact that 80 percent of blue buses belonged to the defendant was not enough to impose liability. In this instance, is reliable proof that 80 percent of barrel fallings result from negligence also not enough to impose liability, or can the two cases be distinguished?

A Proposed Analysis

The foregoing four cases capture some of the issues in probabilistic proof of individual instances. They represent attempts at quantifying the subjective degrees of certainty that the law requires, by verbal formulas or standards, for decisions on adjudicative facts. Hart and McNaughton (1958) note that, in law, "the probabilities are determined in a most subjective and unscientific way . . . the law refuses to honor its own formula when the evidence is coldly statistical" (p. 54). The question is whether there is virtue in the law remaining subjective and unscientific regarding its standards of proof for fact-finders. Is the law not making use of what statistics has to offer, or are there points of basic incompatability between the two disciplines? The response of the courts to statistical proof of individual events has been inconsistent: sometimes they uphold the attempt at such proof; more often they rule it improper (Tribe, 1971). What is needed, then, is a delineation of when and why statistical proof is admissible or not for this purpose. Instead of focusing on case-by-case details and nuances, we need a broader analysis of the proper role of statistics as an auxiliary to fact-finding at trial.

An analysis of the four cases suggests several factors or criteria that the courts appear to rely upon in passing on statistical proof. These are not mutually exclusive but overlapping factors. I do not imply that this is the only way of mapping the field; it is only one way of mapping with criteria which seem intuitively reasonable. I will first state my conclusions regarding the cases. I think that statistical proof was properly excluded in *Collins* (even assuming adequate evidentiary foundation and statistical independence) and in *Rapid Transit*. On the other hand, statistical proof was properly admitted in *Turner* and should also be admitted in the barrel-falling hypothetical case. Next I will turn to the reasons based on the proposed criteria.

The first criterion is the general purpose for which statistical proof is introduced. Is it used as an aid to rule-making to design procedural or evidentiary rules of law by which lawsuits are generally conducted, or is it used as an aid to fact-finding to resolve conflicting claims of a particular lawsuit?

There is less judicial reluctance to the use of statistics in rule-making. Thus, in *Whitus* the Court favorably considered but found unnecessary to adopt a decision rule for jury discrimination based on probability. In *Turner* the court was receptive to statistics for the purpose of sustaining a criminal presumption. The statistics in both instances bear on whether a general proposition of law should be formulated one way or another. The statistics apply not only to the events of the particular case but also to future events of concern to many not party to the immediate litigation. Indeed, perhaps the reason statutory criminal presumptions have survived unscathed for so long from constitutional attack is the policy of the courts of using "legislative facts" (Davis, 1958, §15.03), generated by statistical methods, in the judicial process. On the other hand, probabilistic arguments were used in *Collins* to establish "adjudicative facts" (Davis, 1958, §15.03), facts pertaining to the particular event—who did what to whom? Statistical probability looks to the future and pertains to the realm of prediction. It is more appropriate for use as legislative fact than as particularized evidence.

The second criterion concerns the specific purpose for which statistical proof is introduced. Is it used to determine the occurrence or nonoccurrence of an event and the existence or nonexistence of a state of mind (scienter), or to determine identity?

There is a difference between using statistics to establish what happened (was the heroin illegally imported? was the falling barrel the result of negligence?) and using it to determine who did it (who committed the robbery? whose blue bus ran over the defendant?). Courts seem greatly reluctant to use statistics for proof of identity in an individual case. In *Rapid Transit*, to impose civil liability on an 80 percent chance of correct identification is both unfair and economically unsound. On the other hand, proof that 80 percent of all barrel-falling incidents in warehouses are due to negligence should be allowed to invoke the res ipsa loquitur doctrine and send the case to the jury for its possible inference of negligence; for there may be reasons of social policy to ground liability on a probability of negligence in this type of case. That is, statistics is used to establish a broader basis of liability for all barrel-falling accidents of this type. Particularized, nonstatistical evidence of negligence in this specific case is not needed. There are certain situations—such as warehouse accidents or carrier passenger accidents—where the defendant has a special responsibility toward the plaintiff, and the balance of subjective probability regarding negligence favors the plaintiff. In these situations, as a matter of policy, there is a broader basis of liability, and probabilistic proof is proper to invoke a rule that gives effect to that policy.

Likewise, in a criminal case, it should always be reversible error to allow the use of statistical probability alone to establish the identity of the perpetrator of the crime. Identity is the ultimate fact issue for criminal liability. To establish it beyond a reasonable doubt, particularized evidence is required. In contrast, use of probability evidence to raise an implication regarding an element of the crime—which, furthermore, the jury is not required to find—is less objectionable. The problem in *Turner* was not who possessed heroin but whether the defendant knew of its illegal importation. Probabilistic evidence alone suffices to establish beyond a reasonable doubt the rational connection between the proven and the presumed facts. In furtherance of the policy of controlling the traffic of narcotics, Congress could have sanctioned directly the possession of all heroin (except for certain legitimate purposes) rather than doing so indirectly by a presumption.

The third criterion concerns the source that evaluates the statistical proof. Is it presented to aid the jury or to a rule-making body such as a legislature or an appellate court?

Courts are hesitant about the wisdom of permitting or encouraging lay fact-finders to resolve disputed facts as to unique events with the assistance of statistics and probabilistic arguments. There is a concern that they may be swayed by the overbearing impressiveness of figures such as 1 in 12 million, thereby eclipsing the weight of seemingly less dramatic, conventional evidence. This is not to say that legislators and appellate judges may not also be influenced by numbers, but at least they have independent research capabilities not possessed by trial courts and juries, and they can consider the evidence in a more deliberative setting.

The final criterion concerns the social costs of quantifying the risks of a type I error (false positive). If the costs are high, then courts will likely rule the statistical proof improper regardless of the actual likelihood of a type I error.

Tribe (1971) has argued that a fundamental incompatibility exists between judicial standards of proof in individual cases and their express quantification in probability terms. This precision tends to undermine social values that undergird the law. In criminal cases, proof of every element of the crime must be beyond any reasonable doubt. The Supreme Court in *In re Winship* (1970) interpreted that standard as a "subjective state of certitude" and noted that, if the Government can adjudge guilt without that requisite certainty, the moral force of the criminal law will be diluted (p. 364). Tribe points out that to quantify that margin of doubt, and to state a priori a rate of false positives which we as a society are willing to tolerate, is to undermine the value of respect for the individual person. It would be incompatible with that value to achieve collective security at the cost of convicting a few innocent persons. Although wrongful convictions also occur under the qualitative judicial standard, there is nonetheless a difference between an unintentional false positive and a deliberate acceptance of a given rate of false positives. Individual dignity and liberty are diminished if the state can impose sanctions in the face of a recognized measure of doubt, however statistically unlikely the chance of error.

The *Collins* Court noted that quantification of the standard of proof distorts the role of the jury. The jury is interposed as a cushion between the individual and the state. A jury trial is not only an objective search for truth but a symbolic process of administering justice. The jury can bend the facts—"in effect to find the facts untruthfully" (Hart and McNaughton, 1959, p. 57)—if not satisfied with the humanity and justice of the rules it applies. Deliberately vague, ill-defined formulas of proof permit the jury to inject community values and its sense of justice into the truth-finding process. This is the case in civil trials too, but its greatest impact is in criminal trials.

In sum, I have outlined four factors that should be considered in ruling on the admissibility of statistical proof of individual, unique events. The first two pertain to when it should be admissible or not, the second two to why it should be admissible or not. They illustrate the broader issue that statistical proof of this kind cannot be treated as another sub-category of expert proof, but that it poses special and pervasive problems of its own.

Proof in Science and in Law

As a way of pulling together some of the different strands of the preceding sections of this paper, I will note briefly some of the parallels between the logic of proof in science and in law.

The methods of science and law are different but complementary means of securing and processing information (Loevinger, 1966-67). Propositions of law find their origin in authoritative pronouncements, not in empirical observation, and they are inextricably linked to the political process and to public acceptance. Law seeks to control conduct by prescribing rules of conduct backed by sanctions; science seeks to understand and predict conduct by observing regularities of conduct. Yet, in its functions of control and prescription, law has occasion to use scientific methods. The task is to define the proper occasions.

Figure 1 presents schematically the processes of proof in science and law. In science, the stimulus event is observed systematically, subject to established methodological criteria of reliability and validity. The data so obtained are used to test a research hypothesis of theory concerning the phenomenon under study. This hypothesis is then evaluated in terms of generally accepted standards in the scientific community, such as by statistical standards of significance.

In trial adjudication, there is a parallel logic of inference. Information regarding a historical event is secured by the method of witness testimony. To assure reliability, the testimony is filtered through layers of exclusionary rules of evidence, yielding legal data or evidence. This evidence is used to support or rebut a legal theory, under the applicable substantive law, regarding the event being adjudicated. Finally, the sufficiency of the theory is evaluated by the trier of fact according to judicial standards of proof.

The diagram also indicates the stages at which social science and statistical proof can be applied in the trial process. The first three applications desirable in the diagram are generally unexceptionable. It is only the fourth application— the quantification of judicial standards of proof—that poses problems for law.

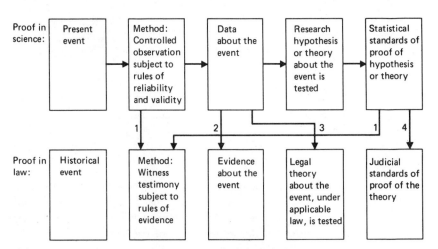

Figure 1. Proof in science and law.

SOCIAL SCIENCE IN JUDICIAL LEGISLATION

Determination of Adjudicative and Legislative Facts

We have considered thus far two types of situation regarding the relationship between law and facts, particularly extra-legal facts. The first involves the application of a rule of law of undisputed content to a disputed state of facts. The
issue is not what the governing rule is, but what the historical events are which
call into application that rule. The extent of market share in an antitrust suit is
an example. In syllogistic form, the rule is a kind of "prescriptive" major premise, the disputed facts (to which statistical and social science methods are
brought to bear) comprise the minor premise, and a legal conclusion follows if
the facts are proved by evidence (Hart and McNaughton, 1959).

The second type of situation is one where both the law and the facts are in
issue. The jury discrimination cases are an example. Not only must a court resolve conflicting fact claims, but it must also choose among alternate rules or
formulate a new rule—when the law in that area is growing and unsettled—to
apply to the proven facts. These two situations can be represented as follows:

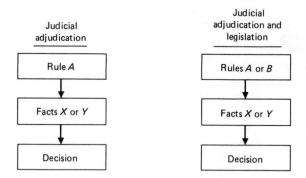

In judicial adjudication, the facts pertain to the particular event at trial. In
judicial legislation, the facts go beyond the particular lawsuit and look toward
the future. They pertain to broad social, economic, and behavioral processes
that are relevant to the formulation of new rules of law (Davis, 1958, §15.03).
Courts are generally reluctant to admit their function of law creation, and when
they do so, it is usually said to be interstitial and elaborative. Yet, as Holmes
(1881) observed, "in substance the growth of the law is legislative" (p. 35). In
the situation where both facts and law are uncertain, social science can play a
role in providing the facts needed to inform and guide judicial lawmaking.

I would like to turn in this part of the chapter to a review of some of the ways
of informing courts of legislative facts derived from the social sciences. I will
focus on counsel's brief on appeal, expert trial testimony, and judicial notice.
Some issues of admissibility and weight of legislative facts will also be discussed.

Appellate Counsel's Brief

One source of information for appellate judges consists of briefs and memoranda of counsel citing research publications, reports of public investigating committees, and the practice of legislatures here and abroad—the so-called Brandeis brief, named for its originator (Doro, 1958). To illustrate how social science is used, or thought to be used, in constitutional litigation, I will again take a leaf from the case method. I will compare this technique as first used by Brandeis as counsel for respondent in *Muller v. Oregon* (1908) and as used by social scientists in appellant's brief in *Brown et al. v. Board of Education of Topeka* (1954).

In *Muller*, the Supreme Court upheld the constitutionality of an Oregon statute forbidding women in manufacturing to be employed for more than 10 hours a day as not an infringement upon an employer's liberty to contract, as guaranteed by the Due Process Clause of the Fourteenth Amendment. In a departure from tradition, the Court cited counsel by name in the text of the opinion because of his unusual brief. It consisted of two pages of legal argument and about 100 pages of social and economic data. The brief combined constitutional analysis and extra-legal data in a novel way. Muller had relied on *Lochner v. New York* (1905), decided three years earlier, in which the Court struck down similar social legislation regulating the work hours of male bakery employees. Brandeis conceded the protected right to contract, but then turned *Lochner* upside down by insisting that this right was not absolute but restricted by the reasonable exercise of the state's police power. To meet the due process test of a state economic regulation that a "real and substantial relation" must exist between the purposes of the legislation (promotion of public health, safety, and welfare) and the legislative classification (shorter working hours for women), he proceeded to present social and economic data in support of the relationship. The data consisted of the physiological differences between men and women, hence the latter's need for legislative protection in industry; the negative effects of long work hours on health and family life; the positive effects of short hours; and the opinions of experts. Although these data do not constitute legal authority, Brandeis cited a case in which the Court said, in dicta, that it would take judicial notice of "common knowledge" (*Holden v. Hardy*, 1898). Thus, he was presenting these facts as common knowledge of which the Court could take cognizance.

Despite the massive array of facts, Brandeis did not argue for their validity. Indeed, he could not do so, since they were not incontestable. Many of the "facts" were in the nature of unsubstantiated hypotheses. Nonetheless, this did not weaken the force of his argument; for the task of judicial review is not to pass on the wisdom of legislation but on its constitutionality, that is, whether it is reasonable or arbitrary. There is a presumption of constitutionality to governmental action. A statute is presumed valid if its supporters can produce evidence showing it is reasonable. As Brandeis later said as justice, "the presumption must prevail in the absence of some factual foundation of record for overthrowing the statute" (*O'Gorman and Young v. Hartford Insurance Co.*, 1931, p. 258). The Brandeis brief serves the purpose of providing the necessary factual support for the presumption. The existence of such facts—not their proven validity—is enough to establish prima facie that the legislature had rational grounds for its action. The burden then shifts to the challenger of the statute to show its unreasonableness. Thus, Rosen (1972) notes that "nascent social science" was all that Brandeis needed to establish his case (p. 84).

In *Brown et al. v. Board of Education* (1954), the Court held that racially separate but physically equal public educational facilities are "inherently unequal" and therefore violate the Equal Protection Clause of the Fourteenth Amendment (p. 487). The Court considered four lines of argument in reaching this decision. It distinguished or overruled (*Plessy v. Ferguson*, 1896) case precedents; it examined the history of the Fourteenth Amendment and found it inconclusive (see Kelly, 1965); it analyzed the importance of public education in modern society; and finally, it cited the social and psychological effects of segregation presented by social science. The Court noted that social science findings of the Kansas trial court and, in the famous footnote 11, referred to the "modern authority" of "psychological knowledge," citing six research publications. The Court also had the benefit of the celebrated "Social Science Statement," akin to a Brandeis brief, on "the effects of segregation and the consequences of desegregation" attached as an Appendix to Appellant's Brief (1953).

I would like to focus on the role of social sicence in constitutional law-making as seen through these two cases. In the wake of *Brown*, some social scientists have taken the position that social science had a direct impact on the Court's decision as evidenced by footnote 11 (e.g., Clark, 1960). On the other hand, some legal commentators have argued that social science did not and should not have any role in the determination of constitutional rights. Cahn (1955) stated: "I will not have fundamental rights of Negroes or of any Americans rest on such flimsy grounds as social science herein presented. . . . (s)ince the behavioral sciences are so very young, imprecise, and changeful, their findings have an uncertain expectancy of life. Today's sanguine asseveration may be cancelled by tomorrow's new revelation—or a new technical fad" (p. 157).

Cahn's position has merit up to a point. If the separate and equal formula is "inherently unequal," then indeed social science evidence is not needed to secure desegregated schools. The language itself indicates the making of a value judgment. Such judgments are beyond factual impeachment. When fundamental social values are involved, "social science cannot play much of a role in law-making at the constitutional level" (Kalven, 1968, p. 65). The merits of constitutional doctrines do not stand or fall solely on scientific facts. Even if the research showed separate but equal schools produced no detrimental effects in minority children, it can still be said as a constitutional matter that it is wrong. As Justice Holmes once warned against tying the Constitution to the wheels of any economic system, so also it should not be made to rest on social science findings.

This is not to say, however, that because constitutional adjudication involves value preferences that social facts are not relevant. Social science can help frame the issue clearly, laying bare the value issues and eliminating mistaken fact assumptions. Better documentation of facts can aid in sharpening the problem. Kalven (1968) has also proposed that the application of social science to judicial legislation is most productive as to facts of "the middle range." That is, social science can best contribute to legal problems which do not involve deeply held values and inaccessible facts or, at the other end, to problems which involve facts too well-known to merit further empirical footnoting. What remains is a critical middle area "where the premises are not that unshakeable and where the facts are not that accessible" (p. 66).

There is another way in which social science of the type presented in Brown can play a role. It can serve to reverse the presumption of constitutionality of the challenged legislation and shift the burden of establishing reasonableness to the state. The brief in Muller and the Appendix to Appellants' Brief in Brown, though similar in social science content,[6] are different in two respects: in Muller, legislative facts were presented by the proponent of the statute; in Brown, they were presented by the opponent. The significance of the distinction lies in the location and nature of the burden of proof. Brandeis only had to establish sufficient social facts to show prima facie a reasonable connection between legislative purpose and classification. The burden was then on the challenger to establish legislative arbitrariness. By the same test, appellants in Brown would have had to negate any factual basis for school segregation legislation in order to press a claim of unconstitutionality.

But there is a second difference between the two situations which illustrates another use of social science. In Brown, the basis of classification is race, and in racial challenges, the test and the burden are different. In upholding the relocation of Japanese-Americans, the Court announced a strict scrutiny test when legal restrictions curtailing constitutional rights are grounded on race (Korematsu v. U.S., 1944). When race is the classification standard, the presumption of constitutionality is reversed (Kohn, 1960; Pollak, 1959). As Brandeis in Muller had only to make a prima facie showing of reasonableness, appellants in Brown needed only to make prima facie showing of arbitrariness to shift the burden of proving otherwise to the state. Consequently, the fact that the social science evidence in Brown (as in Muller) was not incontestable was not critical to its use.

Expert Trial Testimony

The Brandeis-type brief has enjoyed success in supplying factual support for the presumption of constitutionality or, in legislation based on suspect criteria, for the presumption of unconsitutionality. The limited purpose of this method of proof has caused counsel to turn to the trial process for the presentation of legislative facts. The advantage of informing the court of broad social and economic facts by testimony rather than by brief is that it permits cross-examination of the expert. Although a more systematic presentation may be achieved by a brief, the same result can be reached by asking the expert to prepare a trial memorandum detailing his procedures, data, and inference, and subjecting it to cross-examination.

In *Brown*, more than 20 social scientists appeared as expert witnesses for the plaintiffs. The defendant school board relied mostly on cross-examination to rebut the testimony (Tanenhaus, 1968), instead of calling its own experts (Clark, 1953), probably because the defense conceded that most of the testimony regarding the general effects of societal segregation—but not necessarily of school segregation—was essentially correct (Greenberg, 1965).

Most of the expert testimony was directed to the establishment of legislative facts—the general negative effects of segregation. But some of the testimony, particularly by Clark (1953), was of an adjudicative nature—that these particular plaintiff-children were found, after testing, to have suffered negative effects. Of course, this particularized testimony had legislative implications. Overall, though, the distinction between legislative and adjudicative-fact testimony did not seem to have practical importance in the trial process. Although the trial courts reacted differently to the weight of the testimony, none ruled it inadmissible. They tended to view the objections as going to weight and probativeness, not to admissibility (Garfinkel, 1959).

Evaluating Legislative Facts

Admissibility and Weight

The difficult problem posed by the use of social science in judicial legislation— whether by appellate brief or trial testimony—is how to weigh that evidence. The fact-finder or appellate judge, without special training, is in a difficult position to evaluate the data and inferences drawn therefrom. Experts are not only fallible, they have "axes to grind . . . [and] when experts help the courts to make policy, they are not likely to shed their attitudes on the ultimate policy issues" (Karst, 1960, p. 105). In the area of legislative facts, traditional rules of evidence do not apply at all, or apply in distinctive fashion. The development of rules for weighing legislative facts, according to Hart and McNaughton (1959), is "among the most neglected questions of legal scholarship" (p. 63).

In weighing legislative facts presented by social science, there is often a lingering suspicion that the proffered evidence is more "social than scientific," that experts with "axes to grind" go beyond the data in their conclusions (Karst, 1960, p. 105). One safeguard would be to rely on the adversary system. By using counter-experts, one would hope the courts could reach proper decisions when the experts differ. A formalization of this process has been proposed by Rivlin (1973) under the name "forensic social science." I will briefly appraise it and compare it to the forensic or "law office history" (Kelly, 1965) approach used in *Brown*. This example may point out some prospects and limitations of an adversarial approach to evaluating social facts.

Forensic Social Science and Forensic History

The role of social science, as traditionally conceptualized, is not in the formulation of social policy but in the assessment of its results. Rivlin (1973) has proposed that "scholars or teams of scholars take on the task of writing briefs for or against particular policy positions. They state what the position is and bring together all the evidence that supports their side of the argument, leaving to the brief writers of the other side the job of picking apart the case that has been presented and detailing the counter evidence" (p. 25; see Bermant and Brown, 1975).

This approach to resolving the weight of conflicting social science claims is appealing and familiar to lawyers. In fact, it is typical in the resolution of conflicting expert testimony as to adjudicative facts, such as medical evidence in personal injury cases. It works fairly well in that context because the results of that disposition are limited to the specific case at trial. In the adjudication of legislative facts, where the decision usually has a more far-ranging impact, an adversarial approach may be less appropriate. The limits of litigant-sponsored research in constitutional adjudication are illustrated in the effort at forensic history in *Brown*.

After the initial arguments, the Court instructed both sides to re-argue the case in terms of the original intent of Congress in submitting the Fourteenth Amendment. In *Plessy v. Ferguson*, the Court assumed without historical research that the legislative intent was to permit separate but equal public schools. In *Brown*, both sides enlisted noted historians to address this issue. The resulting "law office history" briefs "manipulated history in the best tradition of American advocacy" (Kelly, 1965, p. 144). Yet, the opinion of the Court in *Brown* rejected summarily historical evidence of the briefs as "inconclusive." These briefs exposed a weakness of a forensic approach to scholarly inquiry. In a case where unanimity among the justices was essential to the credibility of the landmark decision, the Court could not rely on a field of knowledge where the leading authorities disagreed among themselves. In contrast, there was very little scientific counter-evidence, by briefs or testimony, to the Social Science Statement. Most of the cited research was conducted to advance basic knowledge and theory prior to the onset of the litigation. In consequence, Kelly (1965) notes, "the Court rejected history in favor of sociology" (p. 144).

There is no ready solution as to how legislative facts produced by social science can best be weighed by the courts. The lesson of *Brown* is that a forensic or adversarial approach has its own hazards. Perhaps ultimately it will be up to each judge to learn enough about the social and economic context of the litigation to fashion his own opinions with the aid, but not the domination, of experts. This leads me to touch upon one other device for taking cognizance of legislative facts, that of judicial notice.

Judicial Notice

Courts rely on judicial notice, explicitly or implicity, to take into account undisputed facts of common knowledge. This suggests another way of looking at how social science is used in judicial lawmaking. Judges are part of a cultural community and, like all other members, internalize its dominant values. Some of these values are derived from science. Major scientific concepts and findings gradually seep into popular consciousness through the mass media and literature. Thus, in the nineteenth century, social science such as then existed was based on a biological conception of behavior—social Darwinism was the predominant social science ideology. This "scientific" perspective, in turn, influenced popular conceptions of the role of instincts in social life and the resiliency of social customs to change. The Court's opinion in *Plessy v. Ferguson* clearly reflects and, indeed, relies on social Darwinist premises (Bernstein, 1963).

Contemporary social science, on the other hand, views social behavior and customs as primarily learned (hence modifiable) rather than biologically determined. Footnote 11 of *Brown* noted that "whatever may have been the extent of psychological knowledge at the time of *Plessy*, this finding regarding detrimental effects of segregation is amply supported by modern authority." Those who claim social science played a decisive role in the decision cite this footnote (e.g., Clark, 1953), and those who argue otherwise treat the footnote merely as a gratuity of the Court to social scientists for their fidelity to the cause (e.g., Cahn, 1955, 1956). In the context of judicial notice, the footnote can be viewed as a shorthand means of calling public attention to the new factual basis of behavior that undermines the social Darwinist foundation of the *Plessy* doctrine which the Court wanted to overrule.

In *Brown*, then, there were two paths for informing the Court of extra-legal facts. One was by direct, litigant-sponsored research relevant to the legal issue, exemplified by the forensic history briefs. The other was by application of an existing fund of knowledge, most of it developed prior to and independent of the litigation, and called to the Court's attention in the appendix of appellant's brief. Kalven (1968) once asked, "For social science learning to have an impact on the living law, will it first have to become popular learning, and thus enter law in the normal political process?" (p. 67) If the social science contribution in *Brown* was possible because an intellectually autonomous body of research had been accumulated, the lesson may be that the production of basic knowledge will, in the long run, have greater impact on important social issues than ad hoc, litigation-oriented research. As the fund of reliable and valid social science learning grows, it will find its way into popular acceptance and then, through judicial notice, into court opinions.

STRATEGIES OF RAPPROCHEMENT BETWEEN LAW AND SOCIAL SCIENCE

I will conclude with some general reflections on strategies of applying social science in law, as disclosed by the case studies considered in this chapter.

One strategy is what Kalven (1968) calls a "collating strategy," whereby one-to-one systematic connections between social science findings and legal problems are attempted. The question asked is, what is available in existing social science knowledge that can be transferred and applied to resolving the disputed facts of this legal issue? The use of social science in *Brown*, or the use of perception and memory research in eyewitness identification, are example of this approach. To diagram this strategy:

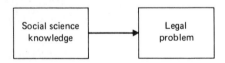

There are limits to collating. Unlike, say, economics, the social sciences have not yet developed any substantial corpus of learning that can be directly applied to a wide range of legal issues. Many of the existing data were gathered in ways and for purposes other than those which are of interest to law. Research geared to theory-construction or to refinement of methodology cannot be easily applied in law to solve or help formulate a particular policy issue (Hazard, 1967-68). Further, even when social science has a direct bearing on a legal issue, that applicability may not always be discerned in advance. Kalven (1968) noted, for example, that although he was familiar with Asch's classic study on conformity (in particular, the greater resistance to group pressure by two persons with similar opinions than one person standing alone), the relevance of these findings to the problem of a hung jury (which is more likely when a deviating juror is not alone) did not become apparent until after he had done research directly on jury decision-making.

A second strategy is what may be called "de novo research." An alternative or complementary approach to reliance on extrapolations of existing social science knowledge is to engage in new research aimed specifically at addressing the factual issues of a legal problem. The question asked here is, what statistical and social science methods can be applied to generate new data to solve the legal issue or, at least, help frame the issue more clearly? Schematically:

In between law and social science is an area of inquiry that neither discipline fully cultivates, namely, problems of law and the legal process that are amenable to joint inquiry by empirical and traditional legal methods.

This strategy too has limitations. New social research can be expensive and time-consuming; and if it is done for purposes of litigation or legislation, decision-makers may not be able to wait for the results. Even if these hurdles are surmounted, it is unlikely that a single study will supply the needed social facts in any definitive manner. As *Brown* illustrated, the kind of social science evidence that commands a high level of confidence by courts tends to rest on the cumulative effect of many duplicative studies.

Finally, there is the basic research strategy I have already discussed in the section on judicial notice. If more attention is given to the accumulation of basic knowledge than to immediate practical applications, that knowledge will eventually filter into popular culture and then into judge-made law via

In the long run, from the perspective of this strategy, law has perhaps more to gain from the perfection of social science as a "basic" science.

FOOTNOTES

1. A preliminary version of this paper was prepared for, and supported by, the National Center for State Courts for presentation at its Conference on Social Research in the Courts, in Denver in January 1977.
2. There are, however, evidentiary problems of proof. Zeisel (1968) notes that "the law has not yet developed a general rule for the treatment of all survey evidence" (p. 323). The principal barrier to the admissibility of opinion surveys is the hearsay rule (Woodward, 1952). The report of the survey researcher in court, as an expert witness, of the opinions of respondents given to interviewers represents hearsay. Courts increasingly have admitted opinion evidence under the state of mind exception to the hearsay rule. Zeisel (1960) has gone further and proposed the creation of a survey exception to hearsay that would admit such evidence in all circumstances subject to certain procedural safeguards and impeachment by adversary or impartial experts.
2a. Since this chapter was written, the Supreme Court has held in *Castaneda v. Partida* (1977) that purposeful discrimination is established by substantial underrepresentation in the venire (79% of the county population was Mexican-American, but only 39% were in venire over a 10-year period) despite a facially neutral selection procedure. Thus, in jury selection, invidious discrimination in violation of Equal Protection can be found by statistical disparity alone. In contrast, in recent employment (*Washington v. Davis*, 1976) and housing discrimination (*Arlington Heights v. Metropolitan Housing Corp.*, 1977) cases, disproportionate impact alone is insufficient, and proof of discriminatory intent (indicated, for example, by tainted procedures) is necessary. Thus, because the values undergirding the jury institution are different from those in other contexts, the consequence of the statistical proof is different: a finding of prima facie discrimination by statistical disparity is tantamount, in effect, to a "conclusive" presumption of discrimination.
3. A presumption is an evidentiary rule established by statute or common law to aid the party with the burden of proof (the plaintiff in a civil case; the prosecution in a criminal case)—that is, the party which loses if after presentation of the evidence the jury remains in equipoise as to the facts—by permitting a jury to infer the existence of an ultimate (presumed) fact "Y" from the proof of some other fact "X." Presumptions thus give the effect of law to normal inferences that most people would draw from a given fact (e.g., heroin possession), in the absence of direct proof of the ultimate fact (e.g., knowledge of illegal importation).

    The procedural consequences of a presumption differ according to whether it is civil or criminal, and according to jurisdiction. Generally, the effect of a civil presumption is to shift the burden of coming forward with evidence to the party who does not bear the burden of proof (i.e., the defendant). If the presumption is not rebutted, the court is authorized to instruct the jury to infer "Y" from "X," or to direct a verdict for the plaintiff (Prosser, 1971, p. 212).

    In criminal presumptions, the effect is not to shift the burden of proof, since the prosecution must always prove beyond a reasonable doubt every element of the statutorily defined crime (which may include a presumption). By proving the basic fact "X" and relying on the presumption, the prosecution satisfies the burden. It is then up to the jury to decide if it has any reasonable doubt regarding any element of the crime, including the inference of presumed fact "Y." The practical effect, then, is that a jury would probably find the defendant guilty unless he came forward to raise a reasonable doubt about the presumed existence of "*Y*." For arguments challenging the constitutionality of statutory criminal presumptions based on denial of the Sixth Amendment right to counsel and the Fifth Amendment immunity from self-incrimination, see Ashford and Risinger (1969), Comment (*UCLA Law Rev.*, 1970), and Holland and Chamberlin (1973).

4. Since *Turner*, several lower federal courts and state courts have required that the reasonable relation test be satisfied beyond a reasonable doubt, not just by a preponderance of the evidence, in order to sustain the constitutionality of a criminal presumption (see, e.g., *U.S. v. Johnson*, 1970; *Wilbur v. Mullaney*, 1973; *State v. Odom*, 1974).

5. This doctrine, as originally announced by Baron Pollock in *Byrne*, was merely a permissible inference from the circumstances of an unusual accident that it probably was the defendant's fault. It developed in the context of cases of passenger injuries at the hands of carriers, such as in railroad derailments. The more common view of the procedural effect of the doctrine is that, as a rule regarding circumstantial evidence, it permits but does not compel a jury inference of the ultimate fact "*Y*" (negligence) from the proven fact "*X*" (accident and injury), unless the defendant produces evidence to explain away the inference. It thus shifts the burden of production to the defendant. As a practical matter, it allows the plaintiff to take the case to the jury, which often, but not always, decides for the plaintiff. The minority view is that unless the defendant comes forward, the court will direct a verdict for the plaintiff. The jury cannot decide what weight to attach to the inference (Prosser, 1971).

6. In both, the conclusions were derived from the general fund of social science knowledge rather than from any specific studies. In both, too, by modern social science criteria, the data were weak. Brandeis' brief, as already noted, contained unsubstantiated propositions of fact that can'only be described as hypotheses. *Karst* (1960) is not incorrect in describing the *Brown* Appendix as "more social than scientific" (p. 107). For a critique of the data presented at the trial level, see Cahn (1955). Finally, both included surveys of opinions of social science experts regarding the effects of the legislation at issue.

REFERENCES

Alexander v. Louisiana, 405 U.S. 625 (1972).

Appendix to Appellants' Brief in *Brown v. Board of Education*, The effects of segregation and the consequences of desegregation: A social science statement. Reprinted in *Minnesota Law Review 37:* 427–39 (1953).

Arlington Heights v. Metropolitan Housing Corp., 429 U.S. 252 (1977).

Ashford, H. A., and D. M. Risinger, Presumptions, assumptions and due process in criminal cases: A theoretical overview. *Yale Law Journal 79:* 165–208 (1969).

Bermant, G., and P. Brown, Evaluating forensic social science. *Approaches to Problem Solving* #5, Battelle Institute (1975).

Bernstein, B. J., Plessy v. Ferguson: Conservative sociological jurisprudence. *Journal of Negro History 48:* 196–205 (1963).

Blackwell v. Thomas, 476 F.2d 443 (4th Cir. 1973).

Brown v. Board of Education, 347 U.S. 483 (1954).

Cahn, E., Jurisprudence. *New York University Law Review 30:* 150–69 (1955).

Cahn, E., Jurisprudence. *New York University Law Review 31:* 182–95 (1956).

Castenada v. Partida, 430, U.S. 482 (1977).

Clark, K., Desegregation cases: Criticism of the social scientist's role. *Villanova Law Review 5:* 224–40 (1960).

Clark, K., The social scientist as an expert witness in civil rights litigation. *Social Problems 1:* 5–23 (1953).

Davis, K. C., *Administrative Law Treatise.* St. Paul, Minnesota: West Publishing Co. (1958).

Doro, M., The Brandeis brief. *Vanderbilt Law Review 11:* 784–99 (1958).

Federal Jury Selection and Service Act, 28 U.S.C. §1816 et seq. (1968).

Garfinkel, H., Social science evidence and the school segregation cases. *Journal of Politics 21:* 37–59 (1959).

Greenberg, J., Social scientists take the stand: A renewed appraisal of their testimony in litigation. *Michigan Law Review 54:* 953–70 (1956).

Hart, H. M., Jr. and J. T. McNaughton, Evidence and inference in law. In D. Lerner (ed.), *Evidence and Inference.* Glencoe, Illinois: The Free Press (1959), pp. 48–57.

Hazard, G., Limitations on the use of behavioral science in law. *Case Western Law Review 19:* 71–77 (1967–68).

Holden v. Hardy, 169 U.S. 366 (1898).

Holmes, O. W., *The Common Law.* Boston: Little, Brown & Co. (1881).

Holmes, O. W., The path of the law. *Harvard Law Review 10:* 457–78 (1897).

Jones v. Georgia, 389 U.S. 24 (1967).

Kalven, H., Jr., The quest for the middle range: Empirical inquiry and legal policy. In G. Hazard (ed.), *Law in a Changing America.* Englewood Cliffs, New Jersey: Prentice-Hall, Inc. (1968), pp. 56–74.

Karst, K., Legislative facts in constitutional adjudication. In P. Kurland (ed.), *The Supreme Court Review.* Chicago: University of Chicago Press (1960), pp. 75–112.

Kelly, A. F., Clio and the Court: An illicit love affair. In P. B. Kurland (ed.), *The Supreme Court Review.* Chicago: University of Chicago Press (1965), pp. 119–45.

Kohn, J., Social psychological data, legislative fact, and constitutional law. *George Washington Law Review 29:* 136–65 (1960).

Korematsu v. U.S., 323 U.S. 214 (1944).

Llewellyn, K. N., A realistic jurisprudence: The next step. *Columbia Law Review 30:* 432–64 (1930).

Lochner v. New York, 178 U.S. 45 (1905).

Loevinger, L., Law and science as rival systems. *U. of Florida Law Review 19:* 530–51 (1966–67).

Muller v. Oregon, 208 U.S. 412 (1908).

Norris v. Alabama, 274 U.S. 587 (1934).

O'Gorman and Young v. Hartford Insurance Co., 282 U.S. 251, 258 (1931).

People v. Collins, 438 P.2d 33 (1968).

Plessy v. Ferguson, 163 U.S. 537 (1896).

Pollak, L., Racial discrimination and judicial integrity. *University of Pennsylvania Law Review 108:* 1–34 (1959).

Prosser, W., *Torts*, 4th ed. St. Paul: West Publishing Co. (1971).

Pound, R., The scope and purpose of sociological jurisprudence: III. *Harvard Law Review 25:* 489–516 (1912).

Rivlin, A., Perspecitives on inequality, *Harvard Educational Review Reprint Series 8:* 22–39 (1973).

Sims v. Georgia, 389 U.S. 404 (1967).

Smith v. Rapid Transit, 317 Mass. 469 (1945).

State v. Odom, 83 Wn.2d 541 (1974).

State v. Sneed, 414 P.2d 858 (1966).

Stephens v. Cox 449 F.2d 657 (4th Cir. 1971).

Swain v. Alabama, 380 U.S. 202 (1965).

Tanenhaus, J., Social science in civil rights litigation. In M. R. Konvitz and C. Rossiter (eds.), *Aspects of Liberty*. Ithaca, New York: Cornell University Press (1958), pp. 91–114.

Tribe, L. H., Trial by mathematics: Precision and ritual in the legal process. *Harvard Law Review 84:* 1329-93 (1971).

Turner v. U.S., 396 U.S. 398 (1970).

U.S. v. 88 Cases More or Less 187 F.2d 967 (3d Cir. 1951).

U.S. v. Johnson, 433 F.2d 1160 (D.C. Cir. 1970).

U.S. v. United Shoe Machinery Corp., 10 F. Supp. 295 (D. Mass. 1953), aff'd per curiam, 347 U.S. 521 (1954).

Washington v. Davis, 426 U.S. 229 (1976).

Whitus v. Georgia, 385 U.S. 545 (1967).

Wilbur v. Mullaney, 473 F.2d 943 (1st Cir. 1973).

Winship, In re 397 U.S. 358 (1970).

Witcher v. Peyton, 425 F.2d 725 (4th Cir. 1969).

Woodward, J. L., A scientific attempt to provide evidence for a decision on change of venue. *American Sociological Review 17:* 447-52 (1952).

Zeisel, H., Statistics as legal evidence. *International Encyclopedia of the Social Sciences 15:* 246-49 (1968).

Zeisel, H., The uniqueness of survey evidence. *Cornell Law Quarterly 45:* 322-46 (1968).

Leslie T. Wilkins, after years of research on many aspects of the criminal justice system, offers a systematic treatment of discretion that makes a distinction between decision rules and procedures. The chapter is informed by ethical concerns and the relationships among policy, ethical considerations, and actual procedures followed.

The model that emerges from Wilkins' treatment of a complex subject is one based on cybernetics that provides both for the development of guidelines for parole decisions and the monitoring of such decisions by means of accountability to various constituencies of the body politic.

"Policy Control, Information, Ethics, and Discretion" is a systematic consideration of the exercise of discretion at many levels of the criminal justice system. Based on information theory and the cybernetic model, the chapter advances ways of looking at the complex relationships between policy and discretion against a background of sound ethical practice.

3
Policy Control, Information, Ethics, and Discretion

Leslie T. Wilkins

INTRODUCTION

The exercise of discretion in judicial decisions is seen as both the strength and the weakness of the system of criminal justice. While discretion may give rise to disparity, it is nonetheless essential if the extreme variability of human behavior is to be accommodated. Without the exercise of discretion, justice cannot be done; justice cannot be automated. Discretion, however, needs to be constrained both by *decision rules* and by *procedures*. In this chapter some information-theoretical concepts are considered, and judicial decisions are analyzed. A cybernetic model is described that provides for the structuring of judicial discretion. This type of model provides for the monitoring of decisions by means of accountability to various constituencies. The analysis that follows provides the theoretical background to the "guidelines" for parole decisions and the related procedures currently in use by the United States Parole Commissioners.[1]*

Some notes on the ethical issues that arise from the use of computer-assisted decision processes are included. The difficulty of reconciling the aims of efficiency and morality in the field of criminal justice is recognized, and a new approach to moral issues is called for.

THE PROBLEM OF DISPARITY IN SENTENCING

It is difficult to find much agreement on the definition of "justice." We are more aware of those things that breach our concept of "just" than we are able to identify the qualities of those that are within the range of our conception of the meaning of the term. This does not mean, however, that "justice" is to be re-

*See Chapter 7, Part II, for a statement of some of the policies and procedures used by this agency.

44

garded as a boundary-setting condition. Law may be boundary-setting, but justice implies more than that. Justice is something that should be both "done" and "seen to be done." It is related to the conception of "equity," and is generally considered to go further and to embrace more; but the additional area to be included is not at all clear. Justice is related to "fairness," but again it is usually seen to have broader claims than that. It is an idea that seems to be learned quite early in life, although the notion may undergo considerable change as we mature. (What parent has not been subject to the objection from the three- or four-year-old, "Mummy, that's not fair!") Uncertain as we are as to exactly what constitutes "justice," there is nothing like "injustice" for stirring emotional, antagonistic attitudes toward the source of that evil.

From time to time the press of all free countries points out decisions by the courts or administrative bodies in the disposition of offenders that are claimed to be unjust, arbitrary, and disparate. In England, in the summer of 1977, a group of women stormed the Court of Appeals that had reduced the sentence on a serving soldier accused of "rape" to one of a "suspended" sentence—which meant that he was able to go free.[2] Demands for the removal of the judges concerned were pressed by several organizations. This case followed quite closely one in which a bank robber was placed in community treatment, and it was noted that he was an "Old Etonian" as well as an ex-officer of the Guards. Most people would agree, however, that there is insufficient information in the nature of the charge to say whether "justice" has or has not been done. (It may not *seem* so, and hence a fault lies in its not having been *seen* to be done.) A finding of guilt for a particular offense is inadequate ground for any assessment of the issue of "disparity." Andrew von Hirsch noted: "Without knowing what the aims are, it becomes difficult even to define precisely what disparity is. If two offenders convicted of the same offense receive different sentences, is that disparity? That depends on what other similarities and differences there are between the offenders and how these relate to the aims of punishment."[3] Thus charges of "disparity" are value-determined and relate to variations in dispositions that the accuser regards as "unjustified." Disparity must involve the consideration of at least three dimensions: the considered seriousness of the criminal act, the considered objectives of the disposition of offenders, and "other things." Only when the "other things" are thought to be sufficiently equal and there is agreement about the aims of the system is it possible to begin to consider "disparity" in regard to the classification of offenses.

Concern for the problem of "disparity" has led some authorities to attack the related concept of "discretion" in judicial decisions. Penalties, it has been argued, should be fixed by statute for each crime so that unwanted variation in sentencing will not be introduced by the judiciary.[4] This, we would assert, is a simplistic approach—when there is something they do not like, they make it illegal! Disparity is bad—therefore deal with it by legislation! The relationship between discretion and disparity is not as straightforward as this approach would suggest.

DISCRETION V. DISPARITY

The elimination of discretion by legislation does not seem to be either possible or desirable. If discretion is eliminated where possible in one sector of the criminal justice system, it will doubtless appear elsewhere in the system. There is an interconnectedness of a crude form between the decisions of criminal justice functionaries at all levels and stages. Squeeze out discretion here, and it will emerge there! (Sometimes this idea is referred to as the "hydraulic theory" of discretion—mainly by those who advocate mandatory sentencing!) There is no need to argue the probable degree of success that could attend any attempt to eliminate discretion; it is both the strength and weakness of the system of judicial decisions. To seek to destroy it is to fail to recognize its value or to think that the weaknesses far outweigh any possible utility.

The claim that it is essential to retain discretionary judgments in the decisions about offenders turns upon concepts deriving from Ashby's Law of Requisite Variety.[5] The human species proliferates variety, legitimate as well as illegitimate. Equity demands that this variety be "matched" by the variety of response in terms of the decisions made about behavior classified as illegal. It is undesirable to seek to eliminate discretion because, in doing so, the "variety of response" of the system will be restricted and the appropriate matching of the gravity of the offense and "other factors" in terms of the determination of sentence will become less likely. It is clearly not possible for any legislature to imagine all the varieties of crimes that could exist. If it is not possible to imagine all varieties of crime, it is not possible to imagine all possible and appropriately matched penalties in advance of the act.

The variety of the *act* demands a high variety-generating mechanism for the decision about the *reaction*. However, where the variety available through the permitted discretion is exercised divergently (as perceived by persons other than the decision-maker), there will be the claim that such discretion has generated "disparity." Discretion is power—power to vary the decisions to achieve more accord with the concept of justice, or, by the same token, power to achieve decisions more in accord with the concept of "injustice." To seek to destroy "discretion" (as in mandatory sentencing proposals) is not to seek to destroy an evil, but to destroy a tool. The tool of discretion is an essential part of the machinery of justice.

The exercise of discretion in decisions reveals an admixture of theory, policy, and probably personal prejudice; but we do not know in what proportions. If discretion is a tool, then, as with other machine tools, we might have some concern for the matter of "quality control." The quality control of policy through the structuring of discretionary justice is the practical outcome of the theory that will be further developed in the next seven subsections of this chapter.

THE CRIMINAL JUSTICE SYSTEM AS A DECISION NETWORK

It is possible to see the system of criminal justice in many ways. Some might deny that it is appropriate to see it as a "system" in the technical meaning of that term. Whether that is so is not at present the issue. What determines the ways in which accused and offenders are treated depends, clearly, upon decisions made by persons having the authority to issue appropriate orders and to see that they are carried out. From the moment the individual becomes a suspect, decisions will be made on the basis of available data which will determine when he is no longer included within the network of decision processes that we call "criminal justice."

Most decisions are not automatic, or, as it were, pre-set in terms of the information. The decision rules that relate information to the determination of an action regarding the offender are often imprecise or even no more than implicit. In addition to implicit (or vague) decision rules, there are procedures. Certain procedures are specified, while others are not laid down in detail. Some of the processes fall within the concept of "due process,"[6] such as the "right to a speedy trial." While the federal courts now have time constraints for their hearings, many exceptions to the time limits are provided. In these and many other matters, the exercise of discretion in the interpretation of requirements of law is essential. The distinction between a "decision rule" and a "procedure" must, however, be kept in mind. There may be rules about "procedures" and procedures to be followed in the application of "decision rules." The significance of this distinction will become more apparent as our discussion proceeds.

It may be useful to visualize a railway marshaling yard. Trucks enter the network and, depending upon the settings of the "points," move into one or another siding. They are removed from the siding and taken into other systems in other parts of the total railway system. There are systems within systems, and there are interconnections between the subsystems. Whether we treat a subsystem as a system in its own right or have to regard it as a mere part of a larger whole, depends upon our purpose at the time. In the criminal justice system, the "points" are "nodes" that are triggered by information. If we have information that a person is of a certain age, we may move him along one track; if he is of another age, this may cause a different track to be entered at the applicable "node." While the information with regard to age may give quite specific indication as to the "setting of the points" (e.g., whether a person may be sent to prison or not), most other "trigger" mechanisms are not as clear or as simple. Seldom does one piece of information determine the decision. The majority of decisions are not directly associated with a specific set of items, but rather with a collection of information. Furthermore, the sum of items of information is usually at the discretion of the decision-maker. When, for example, a judge must decide whether or not he will incarcerate an offender, the items of data that "trigger" this "node" will be selected by the judge in accord with his views as to what is relevant.

It is obvious that the issue of "disparity" may be associated with either the selection of information or the way in which the information is used in various decisions. Is it that decision-makers who reveal bias do so because they are making a biased selection of information, rather than interpreting the information in a particular manner? Clearly different information-search strategies are expected to be employed by different persons. The different strategies may result in the retrieval of different sets of information items. Different sets of information items may be expected to trigger different "points" in the decision network, resulting in different outcomes for the decision processes. The relationship between what we will refer to as *information-search strategies* and decision outcomes is a critical one. If a person says that he has "decided" but continues to seek for more information, we will doubt that he has made a "decision." We may agree that he has made an "interim decision," but this is almost a contradiction in its own terms. A decision *is* an end of the process of information search. (Note that the etymology of the word makes this clear, relating as it does to the concept of "cutting off.")

THE NATURE OF A DECISION

In the field of criminal justice, most decision-makers say that they are making decisions about persons. This is not a precise way of speaking of the activity. Indeed, in almost all of our references to decision-making our language is very imprecise. Decisions are made about information that one may possess about persons, and the persons will be handled according to the decisions made. The *"person"* is not the reference, but the *"information"* is. This is not a trivial point. Of course, decision-makers may point out that their information is not restricted when they are making decisions "about persons," since they can always ask the subject another question and extend their information-set. Even where the particular individual is not available so that the potentially available information is almost without restriction, the information that is available is usually quite considerable in quantity and scope. In technical terms, decisions that determine the treatment of offenders take place in an *information-rich* field. This fact has several important consequences. The main consequence is in regard to the selection of information, whether subjectively by human decision-makers or more objectively by the processes of mathematical modeling. There is a close relationship between the concept of the individual human as a unique person and the richness of the information that may be obtained about him. If we have only limited information, we may find (within that information-set) that there are several persons with the same information-profile. As we add more items to the information-set, the probability that we can describe each person uniquely is increased.

For certain purposes it is necessary to regard each individual as a unique human being. Indeed it may be stated as a moral principle that each individual person should be treated *as though* he is both a unique person and an autonomous individual. But all persons have similarities to other persons, and at times it is also a moral imperative that we emphasize not the distinctions but the similarities. If each person is unique, and if each decision we make about persons is also unique and regarded as such, then it follows that there is nothing that can be learned from the experience of decision-making. No unique or once-for-all event can be any guide to policy while we persist in regarding it as such. When we note the similarities, we can begin to learn through the processes of classification. Classification processes may, of course, be either linguistic or numerical in their basis. This approach means that we are continuously aware of the fact that it is *our* classifications which treat persons as similar, and that we make such classifications for *our* particular purposes. Whether this is legitimate (morally acceptable) depends not upon the process of classification, but upon our purposes in using this method to facilitate our own rational action.

A decision that may be considered to be rational or an efficient selection from among alternatives is not always the decision that should be sought on moral grounds. A rational decision will depend upon the definition of rationality, and there is debate on this. It is simpler to define an "efficient" decision as that decision which, in the light of the information available to the decision-maker, maximizes the probability of the achievement of the purpose sought by the decision-maker in the particular case. A choice of acts is informed by data that are sought in relation to a purpose. If the purpose is not clear, few, if any, sensible statements can be made about the decision or the processes relating to it. In practice, it is observed that decision-makers may change the purpose of their information-search operations in the course of following what appears to them to be a single decision task.

It is interesting that we are not able to introspect very effectively on the procedures we use in information-search and decision-making. It seems almost impossible to step outside ourselves, as it were, while we are engaged in decision tasks and ask ourselves what it is that we are actually doing in the process. This may not be as odd as it might at first seem. In coming to a decision (whatever that process is), we are certainly thinking. If we are asked to describe the process, we are being asked to think about our thinking while we are thinking about something else! This is rather like asking us to become two persons—the actor (de-cider) and the observer, and at one and the same time. Further, however we may think, we cannot think *now* in the same way we thought before we thought as we now think! If we are to understand the process of decision-making, and that may be an inappropriate phrase to use to describe it, we must not rely upon the witness of decision-makers or our own introspection. Only experimental evidence can be satisfactory.

THE LIMITS OF INFORMATION-USE

Research has drawn attention to some important misconceptions regarding information-search and decision. One of concern to us is the widely accepted belief that the more information there is available to the decision-maker, the better are the decisions that can be made. It is, of course, accepted that irrele-vant data should be eliminated, but, almost as by definition, relevant data are seen as useful data. This is not so. Perhaps Hayes (1962) was the first to note this, as he stated;

> It is commonly assumed that the more relevant data one takes into account in making a decision, the better that decision will be. It is clear, however, that as one takes more relevant characteristics into account . . . the opportunities for confusion increase. If confusion were to increase rapidly enough as the num-ber of characteristics increased, it is conceivable that decision-makers would perform better if some of the *relevant* data were eliminated.[7] [Emphasis added.]

The number of items of data that can be processed by humans is much smaller than is commonly imagined. Hayes and others have consistently shown that the number of items is seldom larger than eight. This figure is not in accord with the subjective impressions of most decision-makers, particularly of those who deter-mine the dispositions of offenders in our courts or whose decisions otherwise concern the lives of offenders. Why this impression is so strongly held may be explained by a complex of processes. In the information-search routines adopted by decision-makers, items of information may be glanced at but not, as it were, taken into consciousness—an item may be seen as though it were an irrelevant interruption of the data-search. This can occur in certain kinds of search in filed data. Where the decision-maker can call for the items of information he requires and he receives only those items, the figure of eight stands. Formal decomposi-tion and restructuring of the decision task can permit more data items to be taken into account. In such cases a decision is subdivided, and data are consid-ered in relation to each subdivision. Later the full data can be put together from the parts.

Some restructuring does not seem to be adopted as a conscious process, but rather the decision task changes during the progress of the information-search operations without awareness of the decision-maker. It appears, for example, that the task may begin with the search directed toward the specific task, such as the determination of the appropriate sentence to award to an offender. But after a few items have been examined, the task changes to a search for data to test the quality and meaning of the data that were used in the initial stages. That is to say, the task begins as stated. Information is "used" in this task. Some doubt arises as to the precise value to be given to any item of data. Items of data taken as being most important are tested by examination of items believed to be strongly positively or negatively correlated with them. Certainly there is a tendency for decision-makers to seek correlated items of data, and to expect that under normal circumstances they will be able to predict one item from the other.

Whatever the explanation for the observed strategy of examining correlated items of data, this may account for the strongly entrenched belief that far more than eight items of data are taken into consideration in any decision task. On the other hand, most decision-makers are aware, at least in a vague sort of way, of the problem of information-overload. There is, however, no way for a decision-maker to obtain feedback as to his deteriorating performance under conditions of excess information until his ability to organize his material has broken down completely, and he feels disorganized. It is highly probable that his performance has long since passed its optimal level and that this process takes place gradually after seven or eight items have been examined.[8]

DIVISION OF DECISION TASKS

Interesting as it is to speculate on the mental processes of decision-making, this is not the main objective in this chapter. It has nontheless been considered essential to indicate the complex nature of the processes. Our purpose is not to seek to understand the workings of the human mind, but rather to seek ways of modification of the *external environment* in which the decision-maker functions so as to assist him in his complex operations. It would be simple, but useless, to conclude that in order to get better decisions one should get better decision-makers. If we did get rid of all our judges and obtain a new set drawn, as some would suggest, from different social, racial, or educational strata, we still would have no guarantee that the decisions would be any more acceptable to the critics.

The strategy of action underlying the theory presented here is that it is more rational at this time to seek to modify *procedures* than it is to seek to modify *people*. Decision-making, like other human action, takes place within an environment, and the decision-maker accommodates himself to the environment as best he can. That environment is critical when it determines the ways in which information is made available for use in the decision task. Is it possible to modify the environment so that the decision-maker may extend his limits of data-handling and process more than eight items?

We have noted that the subdivision of a decision task may provide a means for cheating our limits of intelligence. There is some evidence that decision-makers have sometimes happened upon this strategy. This evidence derives from attempts to predict the decisions of judges by the use of various mathematical models.[9] Initially the model was noted as a simple "node":

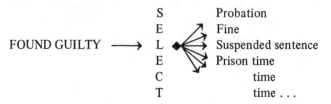

This model did not predict as well as one where it was assumed that the decision task had been subdivided, consiously or unconsciously, by the judicial decision-makers:

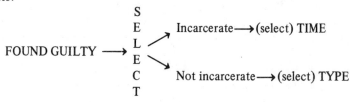

Information which informed the first node (In/Out) was not exactly the same as that which "predicted" (or modeled) time or the type of external sentence to be awarded. Thus, by subdivision of the task, more information could probably be handled than if the first model reflected practice.

If subdivision proves useful in modeling, and, so far as this indicates, in actual practice of human decision-makers, then there seems to be good reason to explore consciously the idea of subdivision of decision tasks. Rather than wait for chance identification of the use of this strategy, we may develop theory to discover useful subdivisions.

THREE MAIN EFFECTS

Research has shown that there are expected penalties for crimes of different levels of perceived seriousness. Most people believe that there should exist some rough calculus relating the seriousness of the offense to the severity of the penalty. This does not mean that there is a conscious or unconscious recognition of a tariff. It is far more vague than that. Nonetheless, the women who stopped the business of the Court of Appeals in London had some idea as to the severity of the penalty that they thought should have been required for the crime of "rape."[2] This rough norm may be regarded as a cultural factor. From the perspective of the social agency or the collective concerned with the decisions, the vague concensus is indistinguishable from a "general policy" which is to provide guidance for all decisions of a particular class. Policy is the collectively determined, loosely stated, set of decision rules.

Judges in a particular court area or circuit, probation officers in a city or state, parole officers in a local office, and all similar decision-makers in similar environments are aware of the views of their colleagues when they make their own decisions about their own cases. No decision is made without the decision-maker's being aware of some audiences who are looking over his shoulder. His perception of these audiences has a modifying effect upon his decisions. The general public, the invisible audience of colleagues, the probable interest of members of the legislature—all these and other factors add up to an element in the individual decision that may be equated with an implicit "policy." Policy in this sense includes the awareness of colleagues' opinions and other collective pressures to have the individual decision-maker conform to the unstated requirements of social expectation.

We may recognize the presence of three elements in a decision made by an individual decision-maker in the setting of a social and culturally constrained environment. It is convenient to use the convention of analysis of variance notation to represent the model proposed. (If any reader is unfamiliar with this technique, the absence of appreciation of the analogy will not matter—read on!) Stating only the "main effects," we may write our explanation of the variance of decisions thus:

$$\text{Decision} = P + C + A \qquad (1)$$

where

P = "Policy" as defined above

C = Unique case elements specific to the particular decision

A = Assessor (decision-maker): the "personal equation" which makes a decision by one decision-maker differ from that of another for the same case.

We will not discuss here the implications for postulating interaction effects. In the simple case, then, if we can identify the "policy" component as it may apply to a particular case, and we know something about the facts of the individual case, we will also need information about the personality of the decision-maker before we can hope to predict the nature of the decision which may be made.

In judicial decisions it is ususally regarded as undesirable that different judges (other things being equal) will make different decisions. Hence, while it may be interesting to seek to predict decisions as a way to try to understand decision-makers' behavior, we are not particularly concerned with doing so for any practical purpose. It will be preferable if we can write the last term of the equation as equal to zero! That is, it would not matter before which judge any case was tried, for the outcome would be the same.

It follows that if we are concerned with establishing a normative system or making recommendations for a revised procedure for decision-making in criminal justice, we are not required to understand *individual* decision-strategies. It would, of course, be necessary to attempt such an understanding if we saw the problem of disparity as being a problem of personalities of judges and wished to devise a training program. If we see the means to change the situation through the modification of procedures rather than through manipulating persons, we can avoid many difficult research questions (not to mention some probably highly embarrassing interpersonal problems also!). The subdivision of decision-tasks that offers a profitable line of exploration is concerned with the processes of decision-making, rather than with the personalities of the decision-makers. We shall concentrate upon the first two terms in the main effects equation, namely (i) the policy (cultural norms, expectations, concensus, etc.), and (ii) the nature of the individual case (specifically whether it is a usual case, and hence a likely fit into the policy, or whether it is sufficiently unusual to demand a departure from the disposition indicated by policy). Clearly we need first to discover something about what we mean by "policy," and to express this in concrete terms of specific decision rules.

According to our theory, it is most important to distinguish, and to keep conceptually separate, the policy element and the individual case element. Moreover, these two elements are dealt with in the recombined decision in quite different ways. In this respect the approach set forth here differs markedly from usual current practice. Usually policy comes from individual case decisions instead of being considered as an issue in its own right. All too often it is the dramatic (unusual) incident that triggers policy change. In our theory the dramatic incident is, by definition, one that does not fit in with policy and is dealt with individually. Clearly, then, the dramatic incident is not, in our terms, any guide to the formulation of policy. Policy is concerned with the usual, normal, uncomplicated decisions that make up the majority of decisions.

If we look to the Courts of Appeal to set policy, this in accord with our theory is quite inappropriate. Appeal cases usually have some characteristics that set them apart from run-of-the-mill cases. Indeed, if this were not so, the Appeals Courts would be flooded with "normal" cases—something for which they are certainly not designed. To suggest that the Court of Appeals is the appropriate body to set standards for sentencing is to suggest that the body which has the least likelihood of obtaining the appropriate data for policy formulation is the body which should be given that task. (Perhaps there is nothing too unusual in this kind of argument!)

If, as we propose, the decision task is divided into two sub-tasks as indicated by the two "main effects," then the policy issues can be addressed specifically as policy issues, and not by means of information obtained willy-nilly from a set of cases that just happen to be taken further up the decision hierarchy.

DESCRIPTION OF THE POLICY ELEMENT

Policy, as we have noted, may be put down as a set of "decision rules." The decision rules underlying any existing policy may be discovered through research techniques. A form of equation, model, or encodification may be found that includes the collective wisdom of all the decision-makers in a particular environment. By environment, in this connection, we mean a court district, circuit or state, probation office, police area, or any other administrative unit where decision-makers are colleagues but act in their decisions as individuals.

Decision-makers are often aware of the presence of a latent policy (or pattern) in their decisions. It is not, however, possible for the items of information to be set forth as exact decision rules with specific weights to each item of data by means of introspection on the part of those concerned. This approach requires the application of research techniques. There are several methods that describe the policy implicitly underlying decisions made by any individual decision-maker who is a member of a group or an administrative unit—a collective of decision-makers. It is not possible to review here the variety of methods that may be considered. It may be sufficient to note that a frequently used and often quite satisfactory method is that of multivariate analysis or discriminant function analysis. Such methods involve the selection of a sample of past *decisions* (without regard to the individual decision-maker concerned) made by members of the decision-collective.[10]   Since we are concerned with *decisions* and not with decision-makers, the sample must relate to *decisions*. All decisions made, say, within the last year by members of the court area, probation office, or other administrative unit of decision-making colleagues provide the sampling frame.

The sample is used to obtain information with regard to individual cases—the criterion variable is taken as the decision actually made about the individual case. We then see how it is possible to predict the decision, without knowing the decision-maker, by means of the best prediction equation we can derive from the data set. Thus a "prediction equation" is derived which best "explains the variance" or predicts the *decisions*. The equation may then be turned around, as it were, and seen as a set of *decision rules*, which if applied to individual cases, will provide an estimate of the probable decision. It should be stressed that this provides a statement of policy in a form considerably different from the usual general vague terms which permit so much variation of interpretation by individual decision-makers. The "equation" or the retrospectively discovered "decision rules" permit no distinction between decision-makers. Decision rules may be seen as representing the decision-making behavior of that fictional individual the average judge of the circuit, or the average decision-maker of the administrative unit that provided the sample. Perhaps a reminder may not be out of place at this point: decision rules should not be confused with procedures. This distinction will become more clear as we proceed with the discussion.

If the initial equations tested do not predict the decisions very well, it is possible to carry out a honing process. Cases that do not fit are discussed with decision-makers to ascertain their reactions to the decision which the average decision-maker might have made (the result of applying the equation). New data can then be fed into a revised model and new tests made. It should also be considered whether a model of a different form, utilizing different sets of assumptions, might not apply. An illustration of the logic of this procedure is given in Figure 1.

A decision made in accord with policy, and *nothing else*, is completely predictable from the descriptive equation. A decision not predictable from the descriptive equation may be one where the decision-maker has departed from policy considerations in order to accommodate factors about the case, or perhaps exercised his own personal opinions. Cases that cannot be "predicted" are cases where a knowledge of the decision which will be made by the average decision-maker in the collective does not indicate how the individual decision-maker will

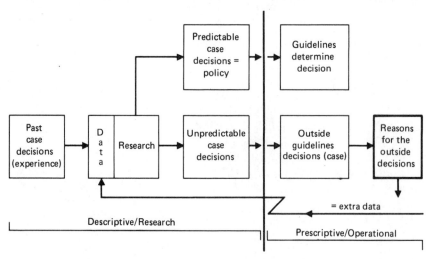

Figure 1. Logic of the decision making system in parole board study.

behave. This is not to say that the departure from policy (or the generalized view of colleagues) in a particular case may not improve the quality of the decision. It is clear, however, that the idiosyncratic element is not covered by the description of "policy" (i.e., the collective wisdom of colleagues as represented in the model).

It has been noted (pp. 44ff.) that mandatory sentences may be legislated in terms which permit variations in interpretation. Where this applies, there would still be scope for the exercise of discretion. Furthermore, the methods which may be employed to structure that discretion may be similar to the methods proposed to structure discretion where the "policy" is discovered by research analysis. In one case the model is one which has been *found to exist* implicitly, whereas in the other case (mandatory sentences) the model is *invented by* the legislature without reference to specific descriptions of current practice.

There may be one major distinction between the structured discretion method that specifically permits and encourages the use of discretion within certain constraints and the mandatory legislative approach. Where members of a decision-making collective unit are both the interpretors of policy and its monitors, changes can be effected quickly to accommodate social pressures and technical change. Legislative prescriptions for decision rules may prove unwieldy and difficult to change, resulting in a system's becoming ossified.

RULES AS DISTINCT FROM PROCEDURES

The decision rules (policy) should, we consider, be only part, but an important part, of any decision system involving the exercise of discretion. The second element accommodates the unusual case and recognizes that the blind application of decision rules (or strict mandatory sentencing) could result in injustice. To deal with the second element in the model (Equation 1), we do not (and this should be emphasized) deal in terms of policy or decision rules, but turn to *procedures*. In the second element we require flexibility. However, it is not the individual decision-maker who is permitted unbridled freedom of action, but the individuality of the case to be decided by him that demands the flexibility. In criminal justice applications it is the high degree of variety generated by individual offenders that is of importance here.

Four classes of *procedures* have been considered to ensure the accommodation of variety while constraining the decision-maker from any capriciousness: (1) Decision-makers may be required to give reasons. (Some legislatures require judges to give reasons for their dispositions.) (2) A panel may substitute for the individual decision-maker. (United States Federal Courts make use of this procedure in some areas.) (3) Review bodies to consider appeals can provide remedies after the event. (In criminal justice determinations, appeals procedures need to have some basis in a code of human rights.) (4) Accountability can be accomplished by the requirement that reports be made to institutions, legislatures, or other public media—the need is for suitable forms of "visibility."

MONITORING POLICY AND MONITORING DECISION-MAKERS

The model proposed makes use of all of the procedures noted, but relies particularly upon accountability to colleagues. However, the admixture of procedures and decision rules must be carefully balanced. It is possible to have too much even of a good thing. Only limited use can be made of panels, appeal systems, and even of the provision of reasons for decisions. If persons are required to give reasons for every decision they make, it is highly probable that the reason-giving procedure will become trivialized. Reasons will become stereotypes and cease to discriminate adequately between decisions. Similarly, if all cases are dealt with by a panel of decision-makers, the panel will find itself dealing with a high proportion of uncomplicated cases and may begin to take shortcuts. The complex case, when it arises, may not be noticed and may fail to be selected for special attention. Where all cases get the "special treatment," none gets special attention! It is, of course, obvious that a system of appeals can deal only with a small proportion of all possible cases. Some process of screening must be applied. The question then arises of whether the screening process is a satisfactory one and in accord with the total system objectives.

Perhaps we may interpolate a further comment on the mandatory penalty legislation which is often seen as an alternative to the structured discretion model. It is not at all clear how mandatory sentencing can deal with these problems, even though it may be decided to permit some discretion in the dispositions. An a priori model, worked out on normative principles, presents somewhat different issues from those that arise from the use (in the form of guidelines) of decision rules derived from a codification of precedent. If it is considered that an a priori model is morally right, then it should be applied without modification as much as possible. If the model is not invented in the belief that it is morally right, then it is a questionable model by its own logic of development. With the descriptive model (precedent) there is no assumption that what has been done in the past is the best that can be done. The decision rules tell us only about the policy implicit in past decisions, not the policy that *should* be followed. The precedent is, of course, a reasonable guide to future decisions unless there are good reasons to depart from it.

In the mandatory sentence case, and with similarly derived a priori decision rules, it is expected that there will be few, if any, departures from the rules. In the "structured discretion" model based upon precedent, the question arises of how often it is reasonable for precedent to be departed from—in other words, how much of the control of decisions is related to "decision rules" (guidelines), and how much to "procedures," hedging the use of individual discretion.

If decision-makers know that the decision rules are based upon particularly efficient equations shown to predict decisions with little uncertainty, they may be reluctant to depart from the decisions indicated by the rules. On the other hand, if the attempt to describe precedent fails to obtain a relatively powerful equation, we may assume that either (a) we have a poor equation, or (b) there has not been much concordance between decisions of decision-makers in the past. In the latter case we have not discovered a latent policy because no latent policy existed, while in the former case we did not discover it because we did not look for it appropriately. The process termed "honing" is designed to sort out this problem. However, it is clear that whatever guidelines are provided, they should neither be too slack nor too tight. We do not wish to limit to too great an extent the definition of the "unusual" case—that is, the case which does not fit the decision rules and "policy" considerations.

It is obvious that the equations may be written in such a form that any level of "fitting" of the indicated decision to the decision actually made can be arranged. If the precision is regarded as too low, the target can be made larger, as it were. If it is too great, we may reduce the size of the target. For purposes of quality control of the decision process, we require around 85 percent of decisions to be within the bounds of the decision rules.

It may be thought that an accuracy of around 85 percent of decisions determined by the description of precedent as a set of decision rules is rather high and unlikely to be achieved. In fact such levels have been obtained without much recourse to "honing." However, this was with groups of fewer than 12 decision-makers in a single urban setting. It must be recognized, however, that the model calls only for precedent to accommodate the first term of the equation (1). Variation between decisions not accounted for by the equation includes both justified discrimination and disparity between decision-makers.

At this point it is not possible to sustain a completely rigorous and scientific argument. It is necessary to move from a level of theoretical sophistication to a pragmatic solution. For the reasons given above and others that will be noted later, we require a level of precision in the prediction equations of between 80 and 90 percent. (Better than 90 percent is also undesirable, and it becomes more difficult, at this point, to fit the procedures to the mandatory, a priori model, even where discretion may be permitted in its design.) Arbitrary as is the selection of 80–90 percent, it is perhaps not totally unreasonable to say that between 10 and 20 percent of cases dealt with by decision-makers are "unusual." The meaning of "unusual" is, of course, subjective. Nonetheless, it is the subjective feeling about the "unusual" that may have a very significant effect upon the performance of the decision-makers. A decision-maker who does not depart from the indicated determinations of the guidelines in, say, 15 percent of cases coming before him may be forcing people to fit policy or failing to recognize the unusual case that needs special attention. Again, by the same token, a decision-maker who departs from the indicated determinations much more frequently than 15% of the time, may be taking too little note of policy and precedent. In other words, he may be arrogating to himself some policy decision element that properly belongs to the collective of decision-makers and not to any one individual. With these considerations in mind, it seemed reasonable to set an "expected value" for unusual cases at 15 percent. The definition of a case as "unusual" (within the 15 percent) triggers the operation of the *procedures;* the other 85 percent of cases are dealt with according to the *rules.* The 15 percent (not more than 20 percent or less than 10 percent) is an *expected* or average value and seems to indicate an appropriate ratio of cases where there is a prima facie case for seeking further information as to atypical decision behavior.

If this reasoning can be accepted, it becomes possible to employ "policy control methods" very similar to "quality control" methods used in industrial production. Decision-makers will be expected to show variation around the expected value, depending upon the number of decisions they make in any review period.

We can now see the nature of the subdivided decision task. Initially, the decision-maker searches for information that enables him to know what decision would be made if it was made solely according to the decision rules. (In the case of mandatory sentencing this would transform into ascertaining the precise terms mandated in the law.) Secondly, in our model, he is required to search for information for any indication that the decision rules *should not* be applied to the case. If he finds that there is no strong indication that policy should be departed from, then he will be expected to follow the rules. If in his view the rules do not apply, then he must follow the procedures, such as seeking the additional views of two colleagues, stating his reasons, or other procedures provided as checks upon discretion. Furthermore, the collected reasons for departure from policy provide another collective of experience that can be taken into account in assessing the operation of policy and procedures.

It is argued that the safeguards should not be seen as onerous. If decision-makers are permitted (or, in our case, specifically encouraged) to exercise discretion, where this leads them to set aside the collective wisdom of their colleagues in the coded precedent of the guideline decision rules, they may be considered to have an additional degree of responsibility. The decision-maker is entitled by the system to exercise discretion, but it seems reasonable that he should be accountable for this. In the models proposed in this chapter, the mechanism of policy setting and control is seen as vested in the local collective of decision-makers themselves. Specifically, the problem of disparity of sentencing is considered to be a matter for the judiciary themselves to deal with. A similar argument may be made in other similar cases. Limiting the "unusual cases" and the concommitant procedures to 15 percent of all decisions seems to facilitate the discharge of the duties involved in appropriate accountability to colleagues and other interested parties.

THE CYBERNETIC MODEL FOR POLICY CONTROL

Situations change so rapidly that no method of decision-making should be designed which does not have built into it a learning system. If the system fails to operate, it should "self-destruct." No system, however good, can remain unchanged and stay sound at the same time. The system of decision control through accountability to colleagues and related procedures may be liable to produce a tendency toward a central philosophical position, which can then become entrenched by means of the same processes of preservation. To achieve a dynamic approach, it is essential to provide for an "open" system element. Some measure of accountability must extend beyond the professions involved, decision-making colleagues, or other administrative unit concerned with monitoring policy. The choice of the external link will depend upon the nature of the decision system. In the case of the United States Parole Commissioners, the final accountability is through the Constitution to the Supreme Court of the United States. Publication in the official record and in journals provides another level of disclosure of information, which affords an aspect of accountability.

The model worked out for the New South Wales, Australia, Bail Commission had two levels of accountability written into the design: a Commission of the Judiciary and the mass media as well as political institutions and public opinion.[11] The logic of this approach is illustrated in Figure 2. The circuit of information feedback should provide for a learning network. There is no actual experience of the operation of this model, and its characteristics are unknown. It is clear, however, that in-house or professional accountability will not suffice either in terms of providing a dynamic system or on ethical grounds.

THE CONSEQUENCES OF POLICY CONTROL FOR THE CONCEPT OF ACCOUNTABILITY

Perhaps the major ethical issue in the exercise of discretion is the difficulty it involves with accountability to the public concerned. Discretion tends to rely upon the qualities of the decision-maker, rather than upon the qualities of the decision, for its justification. The personal characteristics of the individual charged with the responsibility for the decisions, rather than the rules and procedures employed in the decision-task, tend to become the focus for comment.

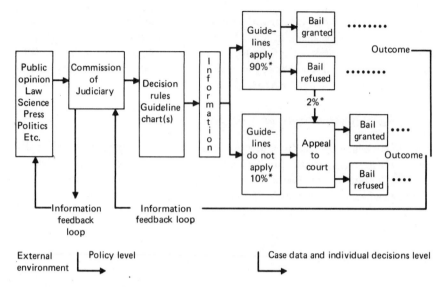

*Indications of possible magnitudes

Figure 2. Chart illustrating the logic of bail guidelines scheme.

The stamp of duly constituted authority does not, in our view, justify the exercise of individual expertise, protected from scrutiny and criticism of the general public. The mere possession of desirable personal qualities and the absence of undesirable traits are perhaps a necessary, but by no means sufficient, basis for a decision-maker's work. This viewpoint is not unusual today, and increasingly a status defense is regarded as unsatisfactory. The idea of "contempt of court" does not now protect the judiciary from criticism. The Church is not regarded as infallible, even by many of the faithful. While crowds or mobs will cheer for or genuflect toward the powerful, the deferential attitudes, even of the uninformed, can quickly swing.

Decisions made in highly technical specialized areas of knowledge or acts that involve complex skills present problems for the concept of public accountability because the public cannot assess them in terms of their content. While the status of the individual has come to be challenged, the public has begun to accept the status of professions as sufficient guarantee. It has been left almost entirely to the medical profession to monitor its own members. In many areas, the police claim the right to investigate for themselves any claims against the police service. These are only examples of a general problem. The problem is one of how to involve the public *appropriately* in the decision process, and not how to avoid such accountability. In this task all levels of technical expertise should be involved. The decision rules approach described in this chapter together with the related procedures makes it possible to disclose material not previously easy to disclose to the public. The professional institutions relating to any decision system also have a role to play in making democracy work—if they believe in it. Some professional bodies lead outsiders to doubt their commitment to the democratic ethic. Problems arise from the marked tendency of some professions to assume for themselves measures of control to which some observers may think they lack ethical title. There is a considerable literature dealing with these matters, which we cannot review here. The matter is raised because it interacts with the procedures advocated in our models.

One example will provide sufficient illustration of the issue. It is, without doubt, a matter of professional expertise to assess whether or not a fingerprint is "properly" lifted from the scene of a crime. Only one who has been trained in the appropriate technique can make a judgment about it. But there are two ways to regard the requirement that the print be "properly lifted"—one is professional and one is not. How well the job is done is a professional matter, but whether the fingerprint *should or should not* have been lifted in the first place is not a matter for professional assessment. It is when professionals arrogate to themselves determinations in the latter category that they are transgressing ethical boundaries of great importance.

Professionals may perhaps be pardoned for some uses of excess power because the public has not been committed to the importance of an open society. It is also clear that professional bodies have not done much to facilitate public comment and have often obscured activities for a variety of reasons. The right to know is being extended, and presents aspects that must be carefully considered by decision-making bodies.

The development of models along the lines proposed makes accountability possible to a far greater degree than previously. The dimensions of defense of and challenge to decision policy and individual discretion are modified and clarified. The public (or some of them) will wish to know exactly what the "decision rules" are, how they were arrived at, and what the procedures are to safeguard the exercise of discretion. There is every reason why they should be told and their comments invited. A form of participant democracy can become much more effective if decisions are defended in terms of their rules, procedures, and content, rather than merely in terms of the authority of the decision-maker or his professional affiliation.

LEVELS OF ACCOUNTABILITY

K. D. Gaver has proposed seven levels of accountability in medical decisions: namely, patients, staff, chief executive, legislative body, public, profession, and oneself.[12]   With a slight change of terminology this classification can apply to almost all decision-making frameworks in modern society. Clearly the kinds of information disseminated to the different constituencies must vary appropriately. The problem is complex and seems to have received little study. As more becomes known about the process we have previously called decision-making, we must develop an appropriate procedure for information dissemination to all levels of accountability.

What we have called decision-making we now know to be information-search, interpretation, and a willingness to terminate the information-search by a selection from a set of available alternatives. What we have previously seen as wisdom, expertise, and authority are not the unitary concepts they were taken to be. Decision tasks can be subdivided and the outcome enhanced by this technique. Input to decision-tasks may be capable of subdivision and result in diversified strategies. Accountability as it will appear in the future cannot be a one-way street. If we "tell the people," we must also have ways whereby we can "hear the people" and let the people know that they are being heard. That justice is "seen to be done" by a small, admiring, silent public gallery in the court is not adequate visibility. The selection of a very small percentage of cases by the press and other mass media for their reporting does not meet the case. The moral philosophy of accountability is a difficult and most important area requiring urgent investigation. Yet such investigations will present dangers. All knowledge may be subject to misuse, but we cannot put the clock back. If we learn more about ways of making participant democracy work—and identify the appropriate ways of informing people—we will, at the same time and by the same research, identify more powerful ways of manipulating the public. We will learn not only how to tell the public that which will enable them to act with more effect, but we shall also learn more of the power of propaganda. In view of the difficulties, some argue for the value of an uninformed public, managed by a benevolent bureaucracy. If that view is taken, then the models set forth here will logically be rejected.

Appropriate accountability, based on ethical standards, will take different forms in relation to different constituencies. The techniques provided by the method of "structured discretion" (subdivision of decision tasks, specification of "policy" by means of open sets of detailed "decision rules," and the safeguarding procedures) can assist by providing a means to focus public, professional, user, and client criticism and comment on the system. For this reason alone, the subdivision of the decision task and the techniques described in this chapter seem to fit the contemporary ethical situation. Indeed, there is an essential element of ethical choice in items of design within the model that must itself be open to challenge and further analysis.

SOME NOTES ON THE ETHICAL ISSUES OF THE MODEL

While the "structured discretion" model has grounding in observation and scientific method, it is, of course, quite capable of being manipulated. Indeed one of the qualities of "modeling" as a scientific method is that the "model" may be manipulated without having any impact upon the system modeled, and by this means the likely results of change can be assessed. It will not have escaped the reader that while the advocated model starts from a base of discovered latent policy (precedent), the decision rules can subsequently be modified at will by the policy-setting body. This fact has two main effects. First, it makes it possible to ask all kinds of "What if . . . ?" questions. For example, we can ask what would happen and to whom if we were to give weight to consideration (x) that we have not done previously. A model can give the answers. In the Parole Commission case, again only as an example of a general point, the seriousness of the instant offense receives more weight than the prior record of the offender.[13] Suppose it is argued that this is "not right" and that the weights to prior crimes and the instant offense *should* be equal. A notional model can be developed to meet this constraint, and cases can be "decided" according to the new set of "decision rules." Of course, there is no reason why these decisions should be acted upon! But they could be. They do provide, in any event, a concrete set of examples of a different philosophy of punishment from that implicit in the current guidelines. It is possible, by such means, to study the probable outcomes of many sets of decision rules as they apply in practice, but without there being any impact upon the cases concerned. However, there can equally well be impact upon the cases if, after study, a set of decision rules, modified in the same way as for simulation exercises, were put into effect by the decision-making body. We will return to this issue after noting the second consequence of the control afforded by models of this kind.

By reason of the procedures, the individual decision-maker is not permitted to employ a different interpretation of policy from that laid down. In the Parole Commission model, for example, the degree of seriousness attaching to crimes is a matter of policy, not a matter of opinion for the individual hearing representative (i.e., the decision-maker) to decide. The level of seriousness is part of the specification of the decision rules, and each crime can be identified by its category. The decision-maker is not permitted to make a more severe or less severe determination merely because he happens to have a particular dislike for tax evaders or for soft drug users (or whatever other views he has about the offenses committed in his cases). If he has views about the seriousness of offenses that do not agree with the decision rules, he must make representations to his *colleagues*, not wrap up his views in the dispositions of his cases. The same situation applies to any item set into decision rules in any similar decision model. This seems to be a rather important consequence of the procedures of "structured discretion" in the establishment of guidelines for decisions. If we have regard to the concept of equity, we may well approve of this outcome. But, it is due to one and the same set of operations that permit the manipulation of policy and the control of decision-makers in ways that may be regarded as unethical. While the method makes the sharing of power by policy-setting bodies possible across a wide range of constituencies, it may also add to the powers of control already possessed by such bodies.

Policy makers, who may be the collective of decision-makers functioning in a different capacity, have in the proposed model a useful tool for investigating many value positions. In a word, the method provides a means for making up models according to different ethical constraints. It is then possible to select the particular model that has the characteristics which the policy-setting body prefers. Moral choices of this kind are often related to assessments of risk, and this method particularly applies where the risk involves some person other than the policy makers. By such means there exists considerable scope for investigating moral choices under different conditions and with different kinds of constraints.

Perhaps another example will clarify this point. Whether a person's arrest record should be available to judges at the time of sentencing or whether the information should be restricted to the conviction record has been hotly debated. Is it necessary that guilt should be established before it should be considered, or is it enough to know that the person has been in difficulties with the police on a few or many occasions? Should both items of data be available? Given models of the kind now available, this issue need no longer remain an abstract philosophical argument. Arrests can be substituted for convictions in the equation forms and a sample of actual cases worked out in the new sets of decision rules. The cases can then be sorted into categories—those who benefit by the rule, including convictions, and those who lose; those who benefit by the rule for arrests, and those who lose; and so on. Examination of individual case information then provides another dimension of information for the assessment of the issues raised previously only in terms of abstractions. In this case, in fact, for federal offenders it is known that there is little or no difference between the decision outcomes informed by models with convictions data and those informed by arrest data.[14] The ethical choice then seems quite clear: since no information is lost with the use of the more tested information, we should use convictions data. This reveals an interesting point. What appeared to be a very important legal and moral question (arrests v. convictions), and which might be expected to have quite significant consequences, is now known to be trivial in its impact upon the actual offenders in a specific system. Perhaps it is easier to make moral decisions when we know that our choice will not influence the consequences.

Be that as it may, the assessment of consequences in this form must be agreed upon as another dimension which can be considered and which may at times assist in value choices.

Obviously one does not need much imagination to visualize a very large number of items that could be substituted in the "decision rules." Items may also be differently weighted, cut, or otherwise modified to provide a changed set of decision rules. These sets of decision rules can reflect different moral choices. The modified rules can then be applied to a sample of actual cases in terms of a simulated decision procedure. The extent of possible combinatory forms leads one to think of the computer as a means to assist in the assessment of values.

Relevance to Computer-Assisted Decision Procedures

The paper file for the recording of information is clearly obsolescent. While there are many problems in the transfer of decision material to a new recording and retrieval medium (such as the loss of serendipitous accessing of items), it is a simple matter to program a variety of sets of decision rules similar to the examples given above. If many models and the related sets of decision rules are computerized, the decision-maker may then search among the outcomes suggested by sets of decision rules. For example, he can begin by saying, as it were, "I prefer not to use information about arrests if I can do as well by making reference only to convictions. However, I do not know exactly what I mean by 'doing as well as,' and therefore I will merely test the size of the difference obtained by the two different approaches. Perhaps this will resolve my problem by showing that it really does not matter!" He may approach the task with a different set of ideas. Perhaps there is a question about the impact of data with regard to "juvenile offenses." A judge may like to ignore the juvenile delinquency record, but may wish to know the consequences of his doing so. Models can be constructed, almost instantaneously, which define "juvenile offenses" as being offenses within any range of ages that seem reasonable to the decision-maker. Clearly this process places considerable emphasis upon the value choices of the decision-makers and leaves much of the technical expertise to the programs and sets of rules. It is possible, at this time with information already at hand, to design computer-interact systems along these lines for parole decisions and for sentencing offenders.

It is necessary to note and contrast decisions based on moral choices and those based on the notion of efficiency. Where decisions relate to outcomes that can be measured and for which preferences can be stated in exact terms, the human intervention need be only in the form of a selection of the desired outcome. For the rest the programs can select the decision which has the highest probability of producing the "most desired" outcome on the basis of information and outcome data recorded in the past. Human intervention is necessary only to inhibit solutions that, although rational and efficient, may be regarded as morally or politically unacceptable. For example, if we require a solution which minimizes the probability of a convicted offender's committing another crime, we may wish to inhibit the solution that suggests the death penalty. However, the death penalty is the only penalty known to reduce recidivism and would doubtless be effective even for car parking offenses!

Efficiency v. Morality

The absurd example of the death penalty for parking offenses indicates that the efficiency of a penalty is not the only dimension upon which it is evaluated. Obviously the dimension of efficiency is moderated in many decisions by the constraints of morality. We do not seem to have a very satisfactory calculus as to the nature, form, and power of the interaction, but it is agreed that such an interaction exists. We may take the view that under no circumstances is corporal punishment acceptable. In other words, even if it is proved beyond all reasonable doubt, that flogging stops certain crimes, we will still not approve its use. On the other hand, we may take the view that we have to select between two undesirable acts—the act of the offender and the act of his treatment. In such a situation, the question turns upon how effective corporal punishment is, how much is required, for whom, and all kinds of other factual (as distinct from moral) questions. A claim at either end of the continuum will have a similar basis. I may make the moral claim that (a) corporal punishment is never justified, or (b) certain crimes not only justify but call for corporal punishment—the offender *should* have a taste of his own medicine! Those inclined to make claim (a) may well be influenced because we have knowledge of some data about the subsequent convictions of persons subjected to flogging in the past. Most moral judgments are in terms of a selection of risk between false positive and false negative predictions.

It follows that moral judgments are "trade-off" choices which often involve the assessment of odds. Such odds may be subjectively assessed or may be actuarially obtained. Probability models are highly amenable to computer-based data sets. If we cannot "train the computer" to make moral judgments, then at least we can program it so that it can assist human intelligence in this choice.

FOOTNOTES

1. Gottfredson, D. M., et al., Making parole policy explicit. In Carter, R., and Wilkins, L. (eds.), *Probation, Parole and Community Corrections*, 2nd ed. New York: John Wiley and Sons (1976).

2. *Times* (London), July 7, 1977, p. 2.
3. von Hirsch, Andrew, *Doing Justice*. New York: Hill and Wang (1976).
4. Kennedy, Edward M., Criminal sentencing: A game of chance. *Judicature 60:* 206–15 (1976).
5. Ashby, W. R., *Introduction to Cybernetics*. London: Chapman and Hall (1961).
6. Cohan, F. The legal challenge to corrections. In Carter, R., and Wilkins, L. (eds.), *Probation, Parole and Community Corrections*, 2nd ed. New York: John Wiley and Sons (1976).
7. Hayes, J. R., *Human Data Processing Limits in Decision-making*. Bedford, Mass.: Operational Applications Lab., Air Force Electronics, Systems Division (July 1962).
8. Wilkins, L. T., Information overload. *Journal of Criminal Law 64:* 190–97 (1973).
9. Wilkins, L. T., and Kress, J. M., *Guidelines for Sentencers*, Research Reports in series 74NI-99-0054. Washington, D.C.: National Institute of Law Enforcement, L.E.A.A. (1977).
10. Any standard statistical textbook. But for early application in criminology, see, Wilkins, L. T., and Mannheim, H., *Prediction Methods in Relation to Borstal Training*. London: H.M.S.O. (1955).
11. Clifford, W., and Wilkins, L. T., *Bail: Issues and Prospects*. Australia: Australian Institute of Criminology, A.C.T. (1976).
12. Gaver, K. D., Accountability. *Journal of Hospital and Community Psychiatry 27:* 635–41 (1976).
13. Wilkins, L. T., and Gottfredson, D. M. (project directors), Reports 1–13 of the Parole Decision-making Project. Davis, California: N.C.C.D. Research Center (1973).
14. Data included in personal communication from Dr. Peter Hoffman, Director of Research, United States Parole Commission, Washington D.C.

Examining the influence of a system upon its component parts, Michael J. Saks and Meridith Miller view the judicial system from the perspective of contemporary social psychological theory and experimental evidence supporting it.

The legal system is considered an interrelated whole, affecting as a system what occurs at numerous "decision nodes." Many choice points exist within the process of legal justice and demand discretionary decisions.

Discretionary decisions, as well as nondiscretionary behavior, in the legal system are shaped and maintained by the same dynamics operating within a social system perspective. The law requires coordinated activity of a number of interdependent components, which influence others by their actions in a given case.

Open systems theory in this context, with discretionary decisions as an operating variable within it, is used to analyze influences upon decisions. The concept of role and its relationship to behavior of any member of the system are related to the shaping behavior of structural relations operating within the social system.

4
A Systems Approach to Discretion in the Legal Process

Michael J. Saks and Meridith Miller

INTRODUCTION

The legal "system" is composed of a number of more or less discrete elements, each having its own structure and functions. Most other chapters in this volume examine the discretionary behavior of members of those individual components, or subsystems, and the social psychological processes that influence such behavior (also see Shaver, Gilbert, and Williams, 1975). The present chapter considers whether the organization of these components into a *system* constitutes a special class of influences that affect what happens at any one decision node (or at all decision nodes). Moreover, it asks what enlightenment social psychological knowledge may offer us concerning such a class of organizational influences, both through facilitating the understanding of individual discretionary behavior and also by way of giving us a lens with which to see these system-level influences (cf. Abelson, 1962).

Consider the following, oversimplified, description of the flow diagram that is the criminal justice system:

A citizen observes what is believed to be a crime and can choose to report it or not. The police can choose to respond or not, investigate or not, arrest or not, ask the prosecuter to prosecute or not. The prosecuter can prosecute, alter the charges, or drop the charges. This decision is likely to be made in negotiation with the defense. A judge can dismiss the case at a preliminary hearing or not. About "one half of those arrested are dismissed by the police, a prosecutor, or a magistrate at an early stage of the case" (President's Commission on Law Enforcement and the Administration of Justice, 1967). The jury can convict or not. If it acquits it can do so regardless of what the evidence shows and the defendant must be freed. If it convicts, the judge can set aside the conviction, choose between a range of penalties, or suspend the penalty imposed. The convicted criminal can appeal to higher courts. Or a governor can issue a pardon. If all of that results in imprisonment, a parole board can exercise its discretion in releasing the person. (Saks and Hastie, 1978)

Even in this brief description (briefer, certainly, than the criminal justice system diagrammed in Figure 1), two points should be evident. One, the system abounds with (explicitly or tacitly approved) opportunities for the exercise of discretion. Many decision nodes exist. Second, it is indeed a system. The several components are interconnected, organized so that most of the output from the system requires the coordinated activity of several components (whether that output be justice, deterrence, resolved disputes, or merely disposed-of cases), so that the operation of any one component depends for its ultimate effectiveness upon the operation of other components. Less immediately evident is the fact that the behavior of actors at any one node may be influenced by the actual or anticipated behavior of actors at other nodes.

Some components influence others by their actions in a given case. Arrests by the police will usually have to be processed by the prosecuter. Actions by the prosecuter will directly affect bargaining options used by the defense.

Some components influence others without ever being called upon to act on the instant case. Prosecution and defense strategies are decided on the basis of anticipated behavior of judges who will never hear the case because it will be disposed of through negotiation. Appellate judges make decisions that are often messages to police or prosecuters about how to handle future cases. Compliance may or may not occur. If it does, it does so partly because the appellate court stated a contingent relationship between behavior and the consequences to be anticipated (fail to prove all the necessary elements in a prosecution, however trivial, and the conviction will be reversed). Many decisions appear to be less concerned with immediate truth in a given case and more interested in impact on the future behavior of the system [e.g., *Watson v. State*, 1957, where the prosecution neglected to offer evidence that a (38-year-old) defendant was over 16, and on this "technicality" the conviction was reversed].

This is not to say, incidentally, that the predictions of legal system actors are correct readings of the behavior of the rest of the system. It has been pointed out that myths develop; lawyers fail to test the predictions of received wisdom, and they fail to act with as much diversity and creativity as the system will in fact allow ("we never file a motion to suppress because we anticipate that the judge will deny the motion, be angry at us for wasting the court's time, and take out his anger on our client") (Bellow, 1977).

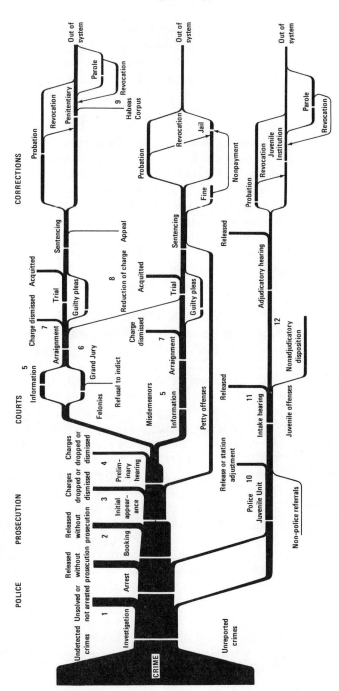

Figure 1. The criminal justice system.

From: *The Challenge of Crime in a Free Society*, A Report by the President's Commission on Law Enforcement and Administration of Justice, U.S., Govt. Printing Office, Washington, D.C., 1967.

In some sense, all behavior is discretionary. Statutes, departmental regulations, codes of conduct, and so on, do not directly compel or limit behavior. Laws do not translate at a stroke into conduct. To paraphase Justice Holmes in a most behavioral moment, the law is the behavior of actors in the legal system. It is the behavior of other actors in the system that regulates the behavior of any given actor, not the written law. The written law is, at best, the statement of a contingent relationship between a behavior and its probable consequence (generally, see Staats, 1975), or a "discriminative stimulus," informing us, for example, that under present norms, if we fail to grant relief to this plaintiff, we are going to be resoundingly overturned on appeal; the behavior of the appeals court will make us look incompetent, a consequence we would prefer to avoid, so we do find for the plaintiff. Other actors "follow the law" because their deviations from it will be looked down upon by colleagues, or they will be fired or prosecuted, or their actions will be neutralized by the actions of other components. We wish to emphasize the largely discretionary nature of all legal behavior not to vitiate the meaningfulness of the concept, but to underscore the role of the system in shaping the behavior of its participants and in regulating the system's output.

If a police officer arrests a person without probable cause, a jury convicts without evidence, an appellate court upholds the conviction, and the defendant is incarcerated, those behaviors are not undone by the fact that they are at variance with the written statutes and case law. Unless a behaver intervenes, these deviant actions will stand. It is because system actors do behave in generally stable and predictable ways that the officer will not make the arrest, or the court will not convict, or the appellate judge will not affirm. But this same "stability" and predictability produce much deviation from written law: laws that are rarely enforced or enforced with systematic selectivity (Packer, 1968), routine violations of law by police (Reiss, 1971; Chevigney, 1969), lawyers who systematically adhere to or deviate from ethical canons as a function of their position in the social structure of legal practice (Carlin, 1966).

Moreover, the distinction normally made between legitimate discretion and illegal deviations probably depends largely upon the concept of role. Behavior that remains within the limits of one's organizational role will be seen as legitimate discretion. Behavior that exceeds the limits of that role (legally and socially defined) will be seen as deviant. We argue that both "nondiscretionary" and "discretionary" legal behavior are shaped and maintained by the same processes, and may be illuminated by a social systems perspective.

In the present chapter we will be examining some social psychological processes which we hope inform us about discretionary behavior within such a social system, and which raise what we think are some interesting questions in need of answering. We will discuss (a) open systems theory, (b) discretion as a variable implicated in such a systems-social psychological perspective, and (c) selected issues in understanding the legal system through this lens.

OPEN SYSTEMS THEORY

The "systems" perspecitve is useful, at a minimum, as an orienting notion. Everyone who refers to the "legal system" or the "criminal justice system" is at least doing that. Each recognizes that police and prosecuters and courts and lawyers are not lone operators, but can accomplish little or nothing without participating as interdependent actors in a coordinated, organized enterprise whose output is achieved only through the joint action of several or all of its components. Beyond this general recognition, few students of the "legal system" do much with the notion, but rather proceed to focus on a component of the system and study that component. One can find many studies of pieces of the legal system, but very few studies of the interdependent action of those pieces. Exceptions are systems engineering studies of case flow, transition probabilities, models, and so on.

In its most developed form, organizational systems theory is a genuine theory, offering hypotheses about the behavior of organizations of people and subsystems. The theory points to such things as the cleavage between individual goals and system functioning (Katz and Kahn, 1966), between latent and manifest functions (Merton, 1968), between espoused and actual functioning (Katz and Kahn, 1966; Argyris, 1975). The theory points to the alterations that occur when individual behavior aggregates into an organization; the organization behaves differently from the sum of its constituent members (see Saks and Hastie, 1978, Chapter 8, for an example using the adversary system).

Open systems theory (Katz and Kahn, 1966) is concerned with problems of relationships, structure, and interdependence among components. The theory is useful in studying such phenomena as the legal system in that it combines the "macro" approach of the sociologist with the "micro" approach of the psychologist. "Open system theory subsumes all of the processes dealt with in experimental social psychology—person perception, social motivation, communication and influence, attitude change, group structure, leadership, group performance, and personality effects" (Lewit, 1975, p. 197). In this chapter we look at social psychological processes that are most likely to operate in an organizational system *and* to affect discretion.

Let us describe what for purposes of this discussion are the relevant parts of the legal system, using selected principles, which we will put to use shortly. An organizational system consists of a set of interconnected components, or subsystems, that work jointly to produce some output. For present purposes, the system we have in mind is that which handles criminal or civil litigation, from the point of entry through exit from the system, and the system's interfacing with its environment. To a large extent, the boundaries of a social system are drawn arbitrarily. The court may be seen as a system unto itself, as may the police, or the "prison system." Or all of these combined may, alternatively, be viewed as but one piece of the "legal system," or the legal system may be viewed as one component of the larger social system which includes religious, economic, educational, and other components that can have as much, or more, to do with people's lives as the legal system, and which shape and are shaped by the legal system (Friedman, 1975). We admit to a certain arbitrariness in focusing on the system of litigation.

A most important decision node is the point where the choice is made to enter the system or not. Of interest here are decisions by citizens and police to report crimes and make arrests, or to handle a matter in other ways, or not to handle it at all. In civil law, the decision of citizens to engage lawyers (Ladinsky, 1976) to bring suit or otherwise resolve disputes (Felstiner, 1974), accessibility to the system, and so on, are of concern. It is interesting to note, in this regard, that the modern world's increase in law, legality, and lawyers has not been accompanied by an increase in litigation rates (Friedman, 1975). Potential clients may lack knowledge about how to find a lawyer, overestimate the cost, suffer genuine economic barriers, or doubt the ability of lawyers or the legal system to help them. A contemporary movement to create pre-judicial community courts to help resolve these unlitigated disputes or to more expeditiously resolve problems that are presently on court calendars (McGillis and Mullen, 1977) may have other, unforeseen, effects (such as increasing accessibility to lawyers and courts and, thus, increasing court caseloads instead of reducing them). Other sociolegal changes may shift the kinds of cases that enter the system. For example, it may be that the rise of medical malpractice litigation ("Medical Malpractice," 1975) can be partially traced to a loss of legal business in other areas (as through no-fault payment for automobile injuries or fast-settling insurance companies). Or the growth of technology may give birth to whole new areas of legal work, as the industrial revolution did for tort law in the nineteenth century (Friedman, 1975). The point in these several examples is that the gateway to the system is an interesting place, and who and what enter the litigation system are determined both by the system's gatekeeping devices and the behavior of people in the world outside the system.

Systems may be relatively closed or open; that is, subject to very limited through very extensive input from the external environment. These inputs may be the material which the system exists to process (laws, cases) or may be input aimed at altering the functioning of the system (political patronage, citizen pressure, publicity, certain other laws and cases aimed at regulating the police, the courts, grand juries, and so on). The litigation system is susceptible to considerable wide-ranging input and is therefore relatively open. However, it believes itself to be a closed, though changeable system (cf. Friedman, 1966), and it adapts sluggishly. It is interesting to consider the role of discretion in a system that is either relatively closed, thinks itself closed, or is slow. Systems which are slow to adapt to changing environments persist in behavior even when that behavior has reduced survival value; such systems become dysfunctional or die (Katz and Kahn, 1966). Relatively open systems have the input and feedback machinery needed to adapt. It is possible that in less adaptable, less open systems, discretion serves the purpose of improving the system's response capability. The formal system cannot track environmental changes quickly enough; so discretionary functions may develop to respond to changes in the environment until the formal structures catch up. They also may add flexibility to the system so that short-term adjustments can be made which ultimately do not warrant formal change. Jury "lawlessness" has been cited as a major example of built-in discretion to take note of societal changes that existing law is not equipped to handle (e.g., Kadish and Kadish, 1971). The preceding has been a speculation on the function of discretion in the legal system, in this case seen as a device that enhances system adaptation. We will offer other speculations later.

The material that flows through the litigation system is most visibly cases. They enter through a citizen complaint or police arrest, or through the filing of a civil action. They may be settled prior to trial and exit from the system, or move to another component of the system, but eventually they always flow through and out of the system. An important concept, then, is that of transition probabilities, which refers to the probability of moving from one to another part of the system, or the probability of moving through one as opposed to other branches at a decision node. Given that a prosecuter has decided to indict, what are the respective probabilities that the case will (a) go to trial, (b) be bargained to a guilty plea, (c) be dropped? And how will changes in other parts of the system alter the transition probabilities at this node? (Bayesian mathematics is useful in handling data within this framework.) But cases are not the only material flowing through the litigation system, and formal legal structures are not the only channels in the system. Information and social influence are two other important flows in the system—and, as we shall see, they may have a good deal to do with discretionary behavior.

Feedback is a familiar aspect of systems, and has been gaining in importance both through traditional behavioral (Skinner, 1938) and cognitive information-processing (Miller, Galanter, and Pribram, 1960; Powers, 1972) conceptions of the determinants of behavior. Feedback has long had a vital place in the study of physical and biological systems (Scientific American Editors, 1955). Perhaps the most familiar physical example of the functioning of feedback is in a home furnace's thermostat. The thermostat's job is to keep a room's temperature above a certain level. The thermostat uses negative feedback to "tell" it when the ambient temperature has fallen below this threshold, and the thermostat then activates the furnace to restore the temperature to some value above threshold. In short, a system's output (its effect on its environment) is fed back to the system, and this "information" is used to maintain or modify the behavior of the system. Obviously, businesses, clients of therapists, revolutionaries, and everyone else uses some form of "feedback" to monitor how they are doing. But the thermostat with its negative feedback loop is much simpler than these other systems. More complex, social systems may have (1) multiple goals, some weighted more heavily than others; (2) multiple channels of feedback, some more accurate and reliable than others; (3) multiple means of altering operations to change the system's outputs; (4) subsystems that provide their own output which serves as feedback about the status of internal operations. (See C. Abt, 1977, for an interesting example of the practical application of feedback in the "social audit" in complex human organizations.)

In addition, intelligent systems are not limited to the "single loop" operation of thermostats, whereby the critical temperature is set by an outside agency and the system merely operates to maintain homeostasis. Intelligent systems are characterized by "double loop" operation: they participate in the setting of their own thermostat, as it were (cf. Argyris, 1975). Police, for example, do not merely read the law as it is set by the legislature. They take that into account as one of several major influences in selecting the kind and level of performance at which they operate. Components of intelligent systems are aware of their own and the system's output. They are able to anticipate changes (sometimes fairly accurately, sometimes not), and can act deliberately to influence the behavior of other components, such as to maintain their own subsystem or to produce a system output they desire. Imagine the inefficiency of living in a home without a thermostat. And imagine the complexity of living in a home where the thermostat has some of its own notions about where its setting should be, and about its own subsystem's well-being.

Another noteworthy feature of human systems is that the appropriate behavior of any member of the system is defined more by *roles*, less by individual actors. Role-appropriate behavior is shaped by the structural relations operating within the social system. Thus, personnel are interchangeable within roles. Different persons may occupy different roles at different times: a prosecuter may become a judge; a generation may pass on and be replaced by entirely new personnel; turnover may be high. Yet the system and its functions will still be distinctly recognizable. That is, the greater proportion of the variance in behavior is due to between-role, not between-individual (or within-individual) factors. [For examples, see Katz and Kahn, 1966, on the failure of psychotherapeutic interventions to change the behavior of organizations; Haney, Banks, and Zimbardo,

1973, concerning prisoner-guard behavior; or Darley and Batson, 1973, concerning the (lack of) altruistic behavior of ministry students; in general, see Mischel, 1969, 1973.]

Broadly speaking, this kind of functioning occurs because the behavior of components is not dependent upon specific personnel so much as it is upon the roles, defined and maintained by sanctions for appropriate in-role performance. Such sanctioning processes are related to the earlier point that all behavior is really discretionary. Behavior that remains within the bounds of a role is not punished or neutralized (as when a judge sentences a convicted defendant to a maximum term). Behavior that exceeds the bounds of the role is unlikely to be tolerated by the rest of the system that maintains the integrity of the roles (a judge gives evidence for the prosecution). Actors closest to the borders of a system are least influenced by the system's norms and sanctions. It may therefore be predicted that judges have the least ability to deviate; police have the most.

One of the more interesting and important features of intelligent (presently, human, social) systems is that they are aware, at least to some degree, of the system nature of the activities of which they are a part, and that their behavior is linked to that of other system components. They can anticipate changes in the system through informational feedback, and change their behavior before it becomes necessary to as a consequence of material feedback. For this reason, human systems may be the most responsive and adaptive, or they may be the most resistant to planned change—because their personnel may adjust so as to sabotage change, or act to influence other components that are trying to change the subsystem of which they are a part. We will give some legal system examples of these points shortly. For now it is important to recognize the intelligent, anticipatory nature of human systems—and to add that subsystem maintenance becomes a most important aspect of the behavior of the people in the system. It is the effective functioning of *our* subsystem that is paramount, not necessarily that of the whole system. Subsystems are often in competition for resources. (Judges need a larger budget, but police have more political clout.)

Consider the following example of a hospital system's (dys)functioning, as observed by a social psychologist who consulted to such organizations (Berkowitz, 1977). The supply department had insufficient resources (sheets, towels, and so forth) to meet the hospital's total demand. Each order from the wards was filled to the extent of, say, only 90 percent of the order. Realizing what was happening, the wards increased their orders to perhaps 111 percent of actual need, anticipating that they would be cut back to the actual need. The supply department, upon discerning the wards' countermove, cut even more sharply its percentage of order filled, say to 82 percent of the order, and the wards countered next time with perhaps a 122 percent of need order, and so on went the moves and countermoves. Note that what was accomplished, despite the increasingly wild oscillations, was a certain homeostasis centering between what the wards actually sought and what the supply department was able to supply. While the actual output will fluctuate above and below the mean, a phenomenon typical .of feedback systems, called "hunting," the average is locked within a fairly stable range. Note also that the several wards, while aware enough of the "system" to maneuver for their individual needs, were willing to compete with each other so as to get more than their share of the scarce resources. Subsystem maintenance (self-interest) dominates. Similar competition goes on within the legal system, and between systems. The judiciary, the police, the public defender, the prosecuter, and the prisons sometimes cooperate and sometimes compete for scarce resources often supplied by the same legislature. They have different abilities to command the degree to which their subsystem's needs will be met.

Also changes in the social and economic environment affect the behavior of the litigation system. Practices of business (Macaulay, 1977) and insurance companies (Ross, 1970), pressure from the news media, elections, and so on, create conditions to which the litigation system must adapt. A dramatic example is that despite internal pressure from their own department, from the courts, and elsewhere in the system, a bottom limit may exist to the amount of heavy-handed tactics the police may be able to drop to. Not only may the day to day contingencies of policing promote a certain amount of brutality (e.g., Reiss, 1971), but there is some historical evidence that when the police fall below a certain level of violence against the "right" groups, vigilantism erupts (Graham and Gurr, 1969), maintaining a certain homeostatic brutality. Thus, police behavior is regulated by a balancing of pressures, internal to the legal system and external, vis-à-vis other social systems. This is not to suggest, incidentally, that a certain level of police violence is somehow woven into the fabric of society. It says instead that a complex of forces conspires to maintain certain balances or to disrupt them, and lack of understanding of the systemic nature of these forces will frustrate planned change. It is not true that we cannot legislate behavior change; it is only that the legislation must change the conditions that maintain the behavior in question (Bem, 1970). This problem of change versus stability will be considered again later.

CAUSES AND CONSEQUENCES OF DISCRETIONARY BEHAVIOR: TOWARD SOCIAL SYSTEMS ANALYSIS

The variable of "discretion" may be measured according to its content (which categorical choices are made) or its amount; and any given discretionary action may be conceptualized as a dependent variable, a mediating variable, or an independent variable.

Considering it as a dependent variable, we may wish to study the determinants of the greater or lesser exercise of discretion or the substance of discretionary decisions (by police, e.g., LaFave, 1965; by judges, e.g., Levin, 1972; by parole officials, e.g., Carroll and Payne, 1976; and so on). Discretion as a dependent variable is the focus of the paper by Shaver et al., 1975.

Discretion may operate as a mediating variable in the system. Where prisons become overcrowded and threaten the welfare of prisoners or the security of the prison, feedback of this information to parole boards, judges, and prosecuters may result in discretionary adjustments in their decisions to ease the overcrowding (Cole, 1975). In this example, prison population is both the cause of altered decision-making patterns and the effect decision-makers try to have; the exercise of discretion is a variable that mediates the changes that need to be brought about to re-stabilize the prison subsystem.

Considering it in still another perspective, the amount of actual or perceived discretion, the unconstrained alternatives available to a decision-maker can vary, and this variation may produce effects. Judges, particularly in continental legal systems, try to appear to have little or no freedom of choice, appearing only to follow the law. It may be supposed that this impression increases the acceptability of their decisions by litigants, other legal system actors, and the public. The exercise of broad discretion by parole boards, making their decisions appear unpredictable and arbitrary, has been found to influence prison operations (Scott, 1974; also see Haney, Banks, and Zimbardo, 1973). (This is not to say, however, that parole decisions are in fact unpredictable; cf. Carroll and Payne, 1976.)

That discretion at a given decision node may be conceptualized as an independent variable, a mediator between causal and resulting components, or a dependent variable influenced by other components, depending upon the matter being analyzed, and may simultaneously operate as all three, is consistent with the systems nature of the organizational behavior that we are examining. Components in a social system often have reciprocal relationships with each other, or mediate the effects of one component on another.

As a Dependent Variable

The question here is, what determines the content of discretionary action, and what determines the frequency with which discretion to depart from routine will be exercised and when it will not be? What determines whether a person initiates litigation, whether police invoke the criminal process or not (Goldstein, 1969), whether a settlement is negotiated or not, what verdict a judge or jury renders? The general answer, from a social systems viewpoint, is that it is determined by the kind and degree of conditions or changes elsewhere in the system. More specific data and speculations will elaborate this point.

At the entry-way to the system, a citizen's decision to litigate will be influenced by personal cost-benefit analyses (intuitive or explicit) concerning the dollars, time, and conflict over pay costs of possible litigation, as against the probability of an improved resulting situation. Changes in the cost of lawyers, the speed of the courts, and the substantive law would be expected to alter litigants' decisions to file or not, or, having filed, to settle or not. Rising population and incidence of conflict, for example, have been offset by increased litigation costs, complexity, and inaccessibility of the courts to hold per capita caseloads constant or, indeed, to reduce them (e.g., Aubert, 1972). The advent of prepaid legal services, legal clinics, and the recent legalization of advertising by lawyers (*Bates v. State Bar of Arizona*, 1977) will likely increase the inflow of cases to the system by making lawyers and litigation less costly and more accessible, unless other, offsetting, changes occur. Similarly, on the criminal side, citizens' reporting of crimes will be affected by their estimates of the likelihood that the police can accomplish anything (or whether the citizen is merely wasting time by reporting) and costs to themselves in time and potential danger (e.g., Latené and Darley, 1970). Changes in police effectiveness and anonymous tip phone-in numbers to police or prosecuters, among other possible system adjustments, will affect citizen discretion.

The advent of pretrial services may represent another response to pressures, such as crowded court dockets, crowded jails, and the unacceptability of keeping presumed innocent defendants in jail awaiting trial (Mullen, et al., 1974). The development of such procedures and programs might be thought of as macro-discretion—it changes the system—and each pretrial release program creates additional decision nodes for the exercise of additional discretion.

There are strong pressures to "cooperate" in plea bargaining, which reduce the likelihood of choosing to defend a case aggressively, such as the expectation of reduced effectiveness in future cases (Blumberg, 1967). Apparently a widely held systems view exists to the effect that plea bargaining has increased in recent decades as a response to increased caseload pressure (e.g., Alschuler, 1968; Yale Law Journal, 1972; *Santobello v. New York*, 1972). Some data, however, reveal that as caseloads have fluctuated, the percentage of cases resolved through negotiated pleas has not changed (Heumann, 1975). Heumann suggests that the defendants' cost-benefit analysis (not his term) is largely responsible for the rate of plea bargaining, rather than the court's changing need to clear its calendar. And defendants now, as a century ago, generally have little expectation of a successful defense in court, and something to gain from making a deal. Here the controlling independent variable is thought not to be caseload pressure, but the operative facts brought into the case. Less effective investigation by the prosecution, and more by the defense, would thus be expected to change these rates—not reduction in cases. If this change occurred, of course, other parts of the system would have to adapt, such as by increasing the number of judges as a means of meeting the increased trial rate, or by increasing the value of prosecutors' offers as a means of holding the rate constant. Another illustration is that of Zeisel (1971), who has argued that as juries are reduced in size, and the standard deviation of jury awards consequently increases, and lawyers consequently can predict with less certainty what the expected trial result will be, more cases will be settled by plea bargaining than under the 12-person jury. (Also, see Saks, 1977.) Again, we see discretionary choices (hypothesized to be) adjusting in response to alterations in other parts of the system.

The legal system is largely a filtering process (Cole, 1975) wherein only a portion of the cases that enter travel very far before being shunted out of the system. Many, many cases leave the system at an early stage (President's Commission, 1967a, b). The further a case travels through the system, the more likely it is that the evidence is adverse to the defendant. The least guilty-appearing defendants are dismissed by the police, a magistrate, or the prosecuter. And even though the most guilty-appearing defendants will enter guilty pleas, the population of cases that reaches each successive decision node may, therefore, in fact be a "guiltier" distribution of defendants than those processed by the preceding decision node. Whether or not the filtering process has this "objective" effect, social psychological processes such as social comparison (Festinger, 1954) and modeling (Bandura, 1965) may successively increase the transition probabilities as cases proceed through the system. The decision nodes are arranged in an invariant order. For a case to reach our decision point, all previous decision-makers had to have judged the defendant as guilty-appearing. A decision-maker's judgment is shaped by the decision behavior of other persons, precisely those persons who satisfy the criteria for social comparison influence or modeling being specified by the principles contained in those theories. These social influence processes will make it monotonically more likely for successive decision-makers to see a defendant as guilty, since all preceding nodes did. And the further along in the system we are, the more such other decision-makers it took to get the case to that point, increasing the number of comparison others we have to contradict in order now to find the defendant not guilty (cf. Asch, 1951). Moreover, since each successive node has a higher threshold (the probable cause of the police, the prima facie standard of the magistrate, the prosecuter's indictment, the grand jury's true bill, and the trial court's beyond-a-reasonable-doubt standard for conviction), the increment required to keep the case moving is never too great; it is easier at each successive node to assimilate the previous decision to our own [in the social judgment theory (Sherif, Sherif, and Nebergall, 1965) sense]. Thus, the transition probabilities increase, perhaps partly for reasons of the objectively more guilty-appearing mix of cases produced by each pass through one of the system's filters, and perhaps also for psychological reasons. We hasten to point out that this is a prediction based on the application of several social psychological principles superimposed on a system, not a demonstrated finding. It would be interesting to test the accuracy of the prediction. Some evidence is provided by citizens and jurors who have endorsed such attitude statements as "our legal system is set up so that people aren't brought to court unless they're guilty" (e.g., Saks, Werner, and Ostrom, 1975). ("If the police arrested him and the prosecuter is prosecuting him and the grand jury indicted him, he must be pretty guilty.") Such social comparison may not be effectively neutralized by the court's admonition that an indictment should not be taken as evidence of guilt. A closely related research controversy, on which contradictory data exist, is whether a court's decision to release a defendant on bail or not affects the probability of conviction at a subsequent trial (see Rankin, 1964; Single, 1972; Landes, 1974).

Our final scenario concerning the effect of system features and social psychological principles on discretionary behavior is a speculation on how the principle of diffusion of responsibility (Latané and Darley, 1970) may lead to a reduced probability of departure from a norm, in spite of the availability of wide discretion to act. Each decision-maker may decline to take the responsibility for a decision because he or she knows that other components are equally capable of taking action:

> The jury convicts a defendant about whose guilt it has some doubts, thinking that if they are wrong, the judge will correct that decision. The judge decides that, although *he* has some doubts, the jury must not have or it would not have made the decision it did and (anyway) if the verdict is wrong, the governor can always pardon the defendant later; the governor decides that if the defendant had not been guilty, the jury would not have convicted him or the judge would have set aside the conviction. By the time the executioners take over, they can rest in the comfort of knowing that the law and penalty were the legislature's, the jury found the defendant guilty, and the judge and governor accepted that decision. Surely if this were not the proper decision, one of these many system components would have said so. (Saks and Hastie, 1978)

The diffusion of responsibility hypothesis makes the unambiguous prediction that the greater the number of other actors (or components), the less the probability that any given one will act. The irony is that while all of these decision nodes exist to ensure due process, the existence of so many may serve to ensure routinization of process and minimization of departure from that routine.

As a Mediating Variable

The conceptualization of discretion as a mediator is perhaps the sine qua non of a systems view. No components or variables are the initial cause or the final effect; all mediate between others. And discretion, we might suggest, is the great mediator. It can facilitate heightened responsiveness of the legal process to social changes, as discussed earlier, or it can be the shock absorber that keeps changes in one part of the system from being felt in other parts, or from affecting the output of the total system. In the following paragraphs we offer some illustrations of discretion as a mediating variable.

One of the more obviously "systemsy" examples of discretion mediating the functioning of the system is the set of responses made to prison overcrowding, discussed earlier. The interesting thing to note is that the various possible adjustive responses require no change in the law; administrative or adjustive discretion is adequate to facilitate the changes.

One of the social products of the legal system is deterrence. Deterrence is information that goes into a person's cost-benefit equation to assess the response cost of a given behavior. The deterrence value may be given by:

$$\text{Deterrence} = \text{Certainty} \times \text{Severity} \times \text{Celerity}$$

with coefficients affecting the relative weights of the terms, and scale values that have both "objective" and "subjective" quantities (a $100 fine is more of a deterrent to a poor person than to a rich one) (Geerken and Gove, 1975). Note that an increase in any term on the right side of the equation may be offset by a reduction in another term. The net result would be that deterrence is kept constant. In an effort to increase deterrence, a legislature may raise the penalties associated with a crime. Other system components can compensate by reducing the certainty or swiftness of the application of the increased penalties. These adjustments which offset the legislative changes can be made rapidly and easily through the exercise of discretion. If the penalty is thought to be too extreme or too certain (mandatory penalties upon conviction), police may slack off in their enforcement, or prosecutors may reduce charges, or juries may convict a smaller proportion of defendants, or some other discretionary adjustment may occur that restores homeostasis to the system, and keeps the left side of the equation constant. Evidently this is not an unusual occurrence. Severity is found to be inversely related to certainty (Bailey and Smith, 1972; Logan, 1972). If jurors think the penalty is too severe, they will refrain from convicting (Kalven and Zeisel, 1966). Police will avoid enforcing laws whose punishment has been made excessive (Campbell and Ross, 1968; Andenaes, 1966). In Massachusetts, the instituting of a mandatory one-year-in-jail for carrying an unregistered firearm was met with dilution through a jump in the acquittal and dismissal rates and, possibly, a reduction in the number of people charged. We should add that this discretionary dilution effect was of a smaller magnitude than one might have expected, but was nevertheless present (Beha, 1977).

Similarly, discretionary behavior by system actors can nullify the impact of Supreme Court decisions (e.g., Wald et al., 1967), police adapt laws to the circumstances they meet (Daudistel and Saunders, 1974), and changes in legal process and resulting impact of the system on society can occur without any formal changes in the law to set them into motion (e.g., Skolnick, 1966).

In these examples, system actors had the discretion to maintain or alter the functioning of the system independent of changes or non-changes in the law, and used that discretion. Clearly, the legal system is open to more input than the promulgated statutes and regulations alone. It should be noted that this is the double-loop feedback "problem." That is, legal process is multiply determined, and the law is only one class of those determinants. While the legislature or the courts set "legal thermostats," system actors may (and apparently do) test their behavior against system output, using something other than statutory or case law standards. Important questions for research and action arise from such an analysis: for example, what those other inputs are and how they work; how one may change the forces that set the norms that are (discretionarily) maintained in spite of the law's norms; and what the conditions are under which discretion is employed to facilitate change, and when, as in most of the examples we have discussed, discretion serves as the insulation in the system that makes change difficult to engineer and makes homeostasis the rule.

Relationships of social exchange have been perhaps the most clearly articulated (Cole, 1975) and severely indicted (Blumberg, 1967) of the social psychological processes that interlock system actors and facilitate the "sausage-factory" stability of the criminal justice system. Prosecutors depend upon defense attorneys to persuade defendants to plead guilty. Defense attorneys depend upon prosecutors to reduce charges, giving the defense counselor a service to sell to the client. The judge depends on both of them to strike a bargain to keep the workload manageable, and both of them depend on the judge to endorse their deal. Et cetera. Each has the discretion to cooperate or not. Each has the discretion to punish others who do not cooperate—from gentle chiding to be more "cooperative" to rendering a role occupant ineffectual. The more integrated into these interdependencies a role is, the more credibility the role occupant has (Careen, 1975). The net result is a degree of mutual shaping that has drawn appalled criticism from advocates of due process (e.g., Blumberg, 1967), but may also be worthy of the awe of students of social behavior. We want to point out that it is discretion that allows these system actors to fine-tune their cooperativeness and responsiveness and mutual conditioning. We want to encourage research on such questions as how young, insufficiently "cooperative" attorneys are socialized, how disturbances in the system or coordinated efforts at reform are "adapted to," what determines when such reform efforts succeed.

As an Independent Variable

Apart from issues of what influences the extent and content of discretionary legal behavior (dependent variable) and what role discretion may play in the adaptability of the system (mediating variable), we may ask what effects discretion may have—that is, as an independent variable. The simplest way of looking at this is to consider the dichotomous conditions of (a) allowing or (b) not allowing discretion, and asking what effects this independent variable might be hypothesized to have.

In an earlier scenario we considered the possible effects of the policy of allowing discretion on the exercise of discretion elsewhere in the system. We hypothesized that too broad an array of interconnected roles and actors, each with certain powers of discretion, will, according to the diffusion of responsibility principle, reduce the exercise of discretion to depart from routine practices. This is the image Jerome Frank (1949) had in mind when he countered the defense of jury lawlessness by speculating that it was sufferance of the jury's discretion to ignore unjust laws that prevented the courts from reforming the law—the judges did not have to change laws they expected juries to "re-legislate" during each deliberation.

To permit or not to permit discretion may have manifold other effects. We have previously mentioned several, which we need only recapitulate here. The fact of and exercise of wide discretion by parole boards may irritate and frustrate prisoners so as to create problems in prison operation (Scott, 1974). Most, and perhaps all, legal systems try to avoid the appearance of such arbitrariness (cf. Weick and Gilfillan, 1971; Jacobs and Campbell, 1961) by either having or appearing to have little discretion ("we only enforce the laws," "we merely interpret the law," "we are a nation of laws, not men") as a (hypothesized) means of gaining greater acceptance of the system's actions or deflecting public dissatisfaction to the legislative branch. On the other hand, legal actors, especially judges, do have broad recognized discretion on many matters; and it is at least in part this ability to act more or less arbitrarily that invests these roles with their power (e.g., LaFave, 1965, p. 29). Much interesting research is possible here, with competing hypotheses about what effects the availability or nonavailability of discretion will have on the behavior of the legal system and its impact on society. Separate policy decisions can be made at each systemic decision node regarding the effects of allowing or trying to limit discretion. And each such policy decision may be expected to ripple its effects through the system, unless of course discretion at other decision nodes absorbs and neutralizes the intended policy effects. These questions are at the heart of the legal system: how do you best control society's most formal system of social control?

CONCLUSION

In this essay we have attempted to apply an open systems orientation to the analysis of discretion in the legal system. We have incorporated into that systems frame a number of social psychological concepts, including modeling, social comparison, diffusion of responsibility, response-cost (individual cost-benefit analysis), norms, exchange, role, feedback, social reinforcement, assimilation-contrast effects in social judgement, and others. We hope that in so doing we have cast new light on the process of discretion and have suggested hypotheses about discretionary behavior in the legal *system*. Perhaps most important, we have tried to make salient a number of issues worthy, we think, of both research attention and practical consideration. Does the structure of the legal system defeat some of its own purposes? Are the "rational goals" of the organization lost or diluted through the struggle of subsystems to maintain themselves? What determines whether the legal system maintains homeostasis or achieves change? What determines when discretion will be used to help the system respond rapidly to environmental changes and when it will be used as the mushiness in the system that facilitates resistance to change?

Some authors view discretion as the basis for uncontrolled, arbitrary behavior in the legal system (cf., Shaver et al., 1975), and have inquired about the usefulness of social psychological knowledge in understanding and perhaps taming legal actors. We have been more concerned with the routinization and assembly-lining of justice and the role of discretion in maintaining that unwanted stability. We prefer to ask how social psychological knowledge may be used to change discretion from a buffer against justice-promoting reforms, and convert it to a device for increasing the responsiveness of the system to society's legitimate needs.

REFERENCES

Abelson, P. H., The need for skepticism. *Science 138:* 75 (1962).

Abt, C. C., *The Social Audit for Management.* New York: American Management Association (1977).

Alschuler, A., The prosecuter's role in plea bargaining. *University of Chicago Law Review 36:* 50–112 (1968).

Andenaes, J., The general preventive effects of punishment. *University of Pennsylvania Law Review 114:* 949–83 (1966).

Argyris, C., Dangers in applying results from experimental social psychology. *American Psychologist 30:* 469–85 (1975).

Asch, S. E., Effects of group pressure upon the modification and distortion of judgements. In H. Guetzkow (ed.), *Groups, Leadership and Men.* Pittsburgh: Carnegie Press (1951).

Aubert, V., The changing role of law and lawyers in nineteenth and twentieth century Norwegian Society. *Juridical Review 17:* 97–112 (1972).

Bailey, W. C., and Smith, R. W., Punishment: Its severity and certainty. *Journal of Criminal Law, Criminology and Police Science 63:* 530–39 (1972).

Bandura, A., Vicarious processes: A case of no-trial learning. In L. Berkowitz (ed.), *Advances in Experimental Social Psychology*, Vol. 2. New York: Academic Press (1965).

Bates v. State Bar of Arizona, 97 S. Ct. 2691 (1977).

Beha, J. A., II, "And nobody can get you out": The impact of a mandatory prison sentence for the illegal carrying of a firearm on the use of firearms and on the administration of criminal justice in Boston—Part I. *Boston University Law Review 57:* 96–146 (1977).
Bellow, G., Turning solutions into problems: The legal aid experience. *NLADA Briefcase 34:* 106–25 (1977).
Bem, D. J., *Beliefs, Attitudes and Human Affairs.* Belmont, Calif: Brooks/Cole (1970).
Berkowitz, N., Personal communications (June 1977).
Blumberg, A., *Criminal Justice.* Chicago: Quadrangle Books (1967).
Campbell, D. T., and Ross, H. L., The Connecticut crackdown on speeding: Time series data in quasi-experimental analysis. *Law and Society Review 3:* 33–76 (1968).
Careen, P., Magistrates' courts: A game theoretic analysis. *Sociological Review 23:* 347–79 (1975).
Carlin, J., *Lawyer's Ethics.* New York: Russell Sage (1966).
Carroll, J. S., and Payne, J. W., The psychology of the parole decision process: A joint application of attribution theory and information processing psychology. In J. S. Carroll and J. W. Payne (eds.), *Cognition and Social Behavior.* Hillside, New Jersey: Erlbaum (1976).
Chevigney, P., *Police Power.* New York: Vintage (1969).
Cole, G. F., *The American System of Criminal Justice.* Belmont, California: Wadsworth Publishing Company (1975).
Darley, J. M., and Batson, C. D., From Jerusalem to Jericho: A study of situational and dispositional variables in helping behavior. *Journal of Personality and Social Psychology 27:* 100–8 (1973).
Daudistel, H. C., and Saunders, W. B., Police discretion in application of the law. *et al. 3:* 26–40 (1974).
Felstiner, W. L. F., Influences of social organization on dispute processing. *Law and Society Review 9:* 63–94 (1974).
Festinger, L., A theory of social comparison processes. *Human Relations 7:* 117–40 (1954).
Frank, J., *Courts on Trial.* Princeton, New Jersey: Princeton University Press (1949).
Friedman, L. M., On legalistic reasoning: A footnote to Weber. *Wisconsin Law Review,* 148–71 (1968).
Friedman, L. M., *The Legal System, a Social Science Perspective.* New York: Russell Sage Foundation (1975).
Geerken, M., and Gove, W., Deterrence: Some theoretical considerations. *Law and Society Review 9:* 497–513 (1975).
Goldstein, J., Police discretion not to invoke the criminal process: Low visibility decisions in the administration of justice. *Yale Law Journal 69:* 543–94 (1969).
Graham, H. D., and Gurr, T. R., *The History of Violence in America.* New York: Bantam Books (1969).
Haney, C., Banks, W. C., and Zimbardo, P. G., Interpersonal dynamics in a simulated prison. *International Journal of Criminology and Penology 1:* 69–97 (1973).
Heumann, M., A note on plea bargaining and case pressure. *Law and Society Review 9:* 515–28 (1975).
Jacobs, R. C., and Campbell, D. T., The perpetuation of an arbitrary tradition through several generations of a laboratory microculture. *Journal of Applied Social Psychology 62:* 649–58.
Kadish, M. R., and Kadish, S. H., The institutionalization of conflict: Jury acquittals. *Journal of Social Issues 27:* 199–217 (1971).
Kalven, H., Jr., and Zeisel, H., *The American Jury.* Boston: Little, Brown and Co. (1966).

Katz, D., and Kahn, R. L., *The Social Psychology of Organizations.* New York: John Wiley and Sons (1966).

Ladinsky, J., The traffic in legal services: Lawyer-seeking behavior and the channeling of clients. *Law and Society Review 11:* 207–23 (1976).

LaFave, W. R., *Arrest: The Decision to Take a Suspect into Custody.* Boston: Little, Brown and Co. (1965).

Landes, W. M., Legality and reality: Some evidence on criminal proceedings. *Journal of Legal Studies 3:* 287–338 (1974).

Latané, B., and Darley, J. M., *The Unresponsive Bystander.* New York: Appleton-Century-Crofts (1970).

Levin, M. A., Urban politics and judicial behavior. *Journal of Legal Studies 7:* 193–221 (1972).

Lewit, D., Social psychology and crime control. *Journal of Social Issues 31:* 193–210 (1975).

Logan, C., General deterrent effects of imprisonment. *Social Forces 51:* 64–73 (1972).

Macaulay, S., Elegant models, empirical pictures, and the complexities of contract. *Law and Society Review 11:* 507–28 (1977).

McGillis, D., and Mullen, J., *Neighborhood Justice Centers: An Analysis of Potential Models* (NILE & CJ Monograph Series). Washington, D.C: U.S. Government Printing Office (1977).

Medical malpractice, *The Center Magazine 8* (4): 25–54 (July/August 1975).

Merton, R. K., *Social Theory and Social Structure.* New York: The Free Press (1968).

Miller, G. A., Galanter, E., and Pribram, K. H., *Plans and the Structure of Behavior.* New York: Holt (1960).

Mischel, W., Continuity and change in personality. *American Psychologist 24:* 1012–18 (1969).

Mischel, W., Toward a cognitive social-learning reconceptualization of personality. *Psychological Review 8:* 252–83 (1973).

Mullen, J., Carlson, K., Earle, R., Blew, C., and Li, L., *Pre-trial Services: An Evaluation of Policy Related Research.* Cambridge, Massachusetts: Abt Associates, Inc. (1974).

Packer, H. L., *The Limits of the Criminal Sanction.* Stanford: Stanford University Press (1968).

Powers, W. T., *Behavior: The Control of Perception.* Chicago: Aldine (1972).

President's Commision on Law Enforcement and Administration of Justice, *Task Force Report: The Courts.* Washington, D.C.: U.S. Government Printing Office (1967a).

President's Commission on Law Enforcement and Administration of Justice, *The Challenge of Crime in a Free Society.* Washington, D.C.: U.S. Government Printing Office (1967b).

Rankin, A., Pretrial detention and ultimate freedom: A statistical study. *New York University Law Review 39:* 641–55 (1964).

Reiss, A. J., *The Police and the Public.* New Haven: Yale University Press (1971).

Ross, H. L., *Settled Out of Court: The Social Process of Insurance Claims Adjustments.* Chicago: Aldine (1970).

Saks, M. J., *Jury Verdicts: The Role of Group Size and Social Decision Rule.* Lexington, Massachusetts: D. C. Heath (1977).

Saks, M. J., and Hastie, R., *Social Psychology in Court.* New York: Van Nostrand Reinhold (1978).

Saks, M. J., Werner, C. M. and Ostrom, T. M., The presumption of innocence and the American juror. *Journal of Contemporary Law 2:* 46–54 (1975).

Santobello v. New York, 404 U.S. 257 (1972).

Scientific American Editors, *Automatic Control.* New York: Simon and Schuster (1955).

Scott, J., The use of discretion in determining the severity of punishment for incarcerated offenders. *Journal of Criminal Law and Criminology 65:* 214–24 (1974).

Shaver, K. G., Gilbert, M. A., and Williams, M. C., Social psychology, criminal justice, and the principle of discretion: A selected review. *Personality and Social Psychology Bulletin 1:* 471–84 (1975).

Sherif, C. W., Sherif, M., and Nebergall, R. E., *Attitude and Attitude Change: The Social Judgment Approach.* Philadelphia: Saunders (1965).

Single, E. W., The unconstitutional administration of bail: Bellamy vs. the judges New York City. *Criminal Law Bulletin 8:* 459–506 (1972).

Skinner, B. F., *Behavior of Organisms: An Experimental Analysis.* New York: Appleton-Century-Crofts (1938).

Skolnick, J. H., *Justice without Trial: Law Enforcement in Democratic Society.* New York: John Wiley (1966).

Staats, A. W., *Social Behaviorism.* Homewood, Illinois: The Dorsey Press (1975).

Wald, M., Ayres, R., Hess, D. W., Scantz, M., and Whitehead, C. H., Jr., Interrogations in New Haven: The impact of Miranda. *Yale Law Journal 76:* 1519–1648 (1967).

Watson v. State, 236 Ind. 329, 140 N.E. 2d 109 (1957).

Weick, K. E., and Gilfillan, D. P., Fate of arbitrary traditions in a laboratory microculture. *Journal of Personality and Social Psychology 17:* 179–91 (1971).

Yale Law Journal, Restructuring the plea bargain. *Yale Law Journal 82:* 286–312 (1972).

Zeisel, H., . . . And then there were none: The diminution of the federal jury. *University of Chicago Law Review 38:* 710–24 (1971).

In the chapter that follows, Dr. Milton V. Kline examines the complex factors operating between lawyers and jury members, giving special attention to the role of suggestibility. As Kline makes clear, it is useful to look upon the jury as a distinct psychological entity in its own right, possessing such qualities as ego functions, memory, and adaptive characteristics not different from those functioning in an individual. To look upon the jury in this manner is to extend considerably our understanding of the play of forces to which its members are subjected.

The psychodynamic model provided offers the reader a new view of the role of influence, manipulation, and suggestion by the lawyer, on the one hand, and the jury's responsiveness and handling and processing of information provided to it by the skillful attorney who seeks to advance the case of his client, on the other hand. We see how the skillful practitioner, moving from the conscious to the unconscious dimensions of jury members, reinforces certain of their attitudes and weakens other developing feelings, in the service of presenting his client in a manner calculated to advance his interests.

Kline's view thus opens up a largely new view of the dynamics of lawyer-jury relationships.

5
The Role of Suggestibility in Lawyer-Jury Relationships

Milton V. Kline

CHARACTERISTICS OF THE JURY

As interest in jury research continues to expand, it is quite natural that many of the variables involved in the interaction between lawyers and juries be examined in increasing depth and detail. Such a focus may be explained by the jury's historical significance, since it is viewed very often as one of the most important aspects of the American criminal justice system. Polier (1968) has pointed out that the jury assumes power more awesome than those of most other groups in our society. It may terminate human existence or it may modify the very quality of such experience. The jury as a psychological entity has distinct ego functions and reacts as an individual might in a bilateral model. At times the jury is an observing ego, taking into account all that it perceives and addresses itself to. As such it is composed of the same system of attention and the subsystems of memory that are characteristic of individual human adaptative experience. Juries also are participating egos and assume the quality of a group ego in that their experiences have a wide range of sensory inputs and reactions. Lawyers traditionally both take advantage of the passive observing part of the jury's ego and tend to count upon influencing the participating ego by shaping the observing ego's inputs.

Whereas jury research may emphasize the fact that the jury is a legal institution designed to render verdicts based upon the evidence presented, it is increasingly clear that other factors, such as personality, demography, and psychodynamic variables, have become significant elements during the course of the trail and thus determine the outcome more often than verdicts based on evidence alone.

Before examining the role that suggestibility plays in the lawyer-jury relationship, it is useful, in the words of Jerome Frank (1930), to take a look at the "basic myth of the jury." The function of the jury is supposed to be fact-finding. According to the official theory, when a case is tried before a judge and jury, there is a rationally composed tribunal; to the judge is left the determination of the rules of the law, while to the jury is left solely the ascertaining of facts. But rarely is anything approximating that concept followed. In most cases, the "general verdict" is used. No one in fact actually understands, and, under our criminal justice system, no one is permitted to investigate a jury to determine how it arrives at its verdict. It may be that its verdict is consistent with the judge's legal instructions, but it is also quite likely that its beliefs, value systems, and response to persuasion and coercion have played the decisive role in the delivered verdict. Whether the jury applied or disregarded the rules of law cannot be, in an objective and certainly in a scientific sense, ascertained. As Frank (1930) has clearly pointed out in assessing an average person serving on a jury, neither is the jury usually able to nor does it attempt to apply the instructions of the court in an objective fashion. It is exceedingly clear that multifaceted variables of a psychosocial nature play a role in shaping the jury's behavior.

While lawyers may view the jurors as individuals, they also address themselves to the collective body, the jury. The organization and presentation of their case are designed not only to be consistent with the legal concepts proposed but also are to be in keeping with what the attorney ascertains to be the feelings of the jury about the judge, the opposing lawyers, the clients, and the witnesses. All these variables constitute a sensory stimulus. They constitute stimuli that are attached to human associations, images, memories, experiences, and fantasies. They constitute the "stuff" of which human cognitive, and affective, behavior, are organized and experienced. Therefore one cannot view the criminal justice system in terms of the lawyer–jury relationship without seeing that the role of the lawyer has to take into account the psychological reactions, the nature and needs of the jury, and try to influence and shape their behavior consistent with reasonable legal expectations.

It has also been stated that aspects of jury-made law, as compared with judge-made law, must be recognized Cahn and Cahn, (1966). Though peculiar in form, such differences do exist. They exist not as a series of precedents, since they are nowhere codified, but each jury makes its own law in each case with little or no knowledge of, or reference to, what has been done before or regard to what will be done thereafter. Yet jury law, although not referred to as law as such, is real law nonetheless and constitutes discretionary behavior influenced at least as much by persuasion as by fact.

The jury is psychologically important in that it provides the necessary humane individualization and flexibility which other parts of the legal system do not directly provide. Society recognizes that the power to determine the guilt or innocence of one accused of a crime should not be relinquished to judges, but must remain with the people. There is a common feeling of confidence in the "common sense judgment" of the jury as opposed to the "legalistic thinking" of lawyers and judges. There may be some question as to the inherent danger that lies in this flexibility, but it is this clear-cut conviction, this basic confidence that society has in its jury system, and for which it maintains a strong affinity, that creates the lawyer's need to understand the dynamics of jury behavior and the individuals who make up the corporate jury body.

For the moment, before carefully evaluating the nature and dimensions of suggestibility as it operates in the psychosocial context of the courtroom and lawyer-jury interaction, we must accept the fact that the lawyer seeks as an outcome his control of the corporate jury body. In this sense there are three major objectives that the lawyer may use as targets for his persuasive tactics and strategies: (1) to influence the jury in its primary observation, assessment, and evaluation of the facts; (2) to influence the thinking, interpretation, and emotional reactions to these facts as they relate to the rules of law laid down by the judge; and (3) to suggest and connect with conviction, rationalization, and emotional input, a general verdict that will be consistent with the previously determined responses.

Thus the lawyer is involved in a complex learning experience, and the lawyer-jury interface is one that in many respects has counterparts in the social structures of modern society involving authority constructs: persuasive images, facilitating images, supportive images, guilt-producing images, and rewarding images.

Any sophisticated theory of jury behavior and jury interaction has to take into account the fact that the manner in which the lawyer deals with the elements described above will determine the degree to which the jury is responsive, cooperative, resistant, adultlike, childlike, logical, or irrational in the organization of its behavioral responses.

Since it is generally agreed that there is no way of enforcing a jury's so-called duty to obey the court, and no way of correcting the so-called abuse of its power to decide the law for itself, we must agree with the refreshingly direct views of Judge Sharswood (Frank, 1930) that "this distinction between power and right— is very shadowy." In 1697 Lord Holt (Frank, 1930) denied that the jury had an "absolute despotic power to disregard the judge's instructions." And judges and legal writers today still impotently repeat that denial. They continue naively to predict dire consequences, were the jury to possess the power to ignore the judge's legal pronouncements. Yet in reality it frequently is the emotional response, the indoctrination and coerciveness, the suggestibility of the material to which the jury has been exposed, that shapes and influences not only its general verdict but the determination of that general verdict which may be at considerable distance from the judge's instructions, from the legal issues involved, and from the "legal" intent of the law. The lawyer, in his address to the jury, does not confine himself to clear and concise legal arguments based on the objective summary of the evidence. He does quite the opposite. He uses every manipulation of oratory and acting to appeal to the atavistic emotions of the jury. He knows only too well that they will not objectively weigh the testimony or discriminatingly consider what the judge has told them of the law. The trial lawyer is a realist, a manipulator, a Machiavellian teacher, an organizer of behavior seeking a result. He seeks out every weakness of the jury that may determine the fate of his client. The influence of the personality of the lawyer in the courtroom is profound, and while we may speak of jury-made law, we may also speak, indirectly, of lawyer-made law. For the lawyer frequently, in effect, determines the behavior of the jury by his strategies and tactics.

In summary, we see that the "defined" jury is in many respects a myth and that intricate technical ritual may often be practically useless, but that the power and the function of the jury are, in effect, a profound determining element in the criminal justice system. The jury is, however, more influenced by psychological mechanisms of ego behavior than by legal pronouncements and judicial procedure.

The lawyer's utilization of suggestion in the manipulation of the jury's behavior must be reexamined within the context in which it takes place. Suggestion can be simply defined, if one wishes, as an attempt to influence or persuade another to accept cognitive values or bahavioral concomitants in keeping with the ideas presented. In a more sophisticated sense, suggestion can be viewed as a process of communication that can lead to atavistic or regressive states typical of induced hypnosis or to more conscious adaptational states involving transferential phenomena which lead to ready identification, acceptance, and commitment. The communication complex in the lawyer–jury relationship leads to mechanisms that, on the one hand, open the doors to persuasion, and on the other, are designed to create resistance to alternate (adversary) persuasion. Thus, the jury is subject to two lawyers' interactions with it, each of which is designed to create persuasive behavior.

It is as if the jury, like a child, is caught between two powerful, seductive, and adversary parents. As such the same dynamics of anxiety, anger, confusion, and mixed identification that develop in such a familial context emerge in the courtroom.

The resolution of this conflict is more frequently influenced by the more powerful "lawyer-parent" and the effectiveness of his suggestions, than by the insightful "working through" of this problem. The dynamics of suggestion appear to play a greater role in the elucidation of jury behavior and verdicts than evidence, logic, and legal pronouncements.

DISCRETIONARY LAW

The concept of discretionary law assumes the right of the jury to exercise volitional discretion, judgment, and choice in relation to its thoughts and actions.

This assumes an idealistic conception that, given certain information, facts, and the ability to logically review these issues impartially and objectively, members of a jury are capable of exercising volitional discretion in the exercise of their responsibilities and power. This assumption becomes increasingly questionable from a psychodynamic point of view as one views the demand characteristics of the jury system to begin with. The fact is that the jury system is embedded within an adversary system, and the interplay of forces in the courtroom is designed to influence, persuade, and coerce, and ultimately modify and shape, the discretionary actions of the jury.

Demand characteristics affecting jurors not only relate to the variations in the adversary role of the lawyers but to the nature of the judiciary and the environment in which the court setting takes place. The manner in which contextual predeterminants of emotions in the courtroom may lead to varying types of decisions is perhaps most dramatically illustrated in connection with the trial and conviction of Jack Ruby for the murder of Lee Harvey Oswald. In the cross-examination of one distinguished expert witness, a clinical psychologist who had administered the Rorschach test as well as other tests to Jack Ruby, the district attorney described the expert witness as someone who "orchestrated a symphony of whines, shouts and supercilious snarls" (Kaplan and Walz, 1965). Unfortunately, such conduct by the district attorney struck responsive chords in the jury, which in turn was reflective of attitudes widely held in the community. This process led in no small way to conviction rather than the use of volitional discretion in the face of factual evidence.

In sharp contrast there is reported the case of an Iowa man who stabbed his 68-year old stepfather to death for cursing the recently assassinated President Kennedy on Sunday, November 24, 1963 (Kaplan and Walz, 1965). On a plea of guilty, the presiding judge referred to the assassination and stated "that the entire nation was under stress and strain from the tragedy." He then added: "But that is not a reason for a citizen of a nation to release his emotions to the extent of causing another tragedy." The defendant was sentenced to eight years in prison and fined $1000.00. The judge then immediately suspended the sentence and ended the hearing by wishing the defendant a Merry Christmas and a Happy New Year.

In considering the role of suggestion and suggestibility in the lawyer–jury relationship, it is essential that one view the suggestibility syndrome on a continuum running from relatively minimal influence on opinion, attitude, and interpretation, to marked alterations in perception, judgment, logical analysis, and the shaping of behavior. Thus suggestibility becomes part of what in a more sophisticated framework may be viewed as the hypnotic syndrome, the nature of interpersonal influence, and the alteration or manipulation of human behavior (Christie and Geis, 1970).

Lawyers have long been aware of the importance of personality factors in the selection of the jury; but only in recent years has greater emphasis been placed on the dynamic structure of personality in a juror which may make that juror more amenable to coercion, persuasion, identification, and the type of behavioral manipulation which is congruent with the goals of lawyer–jury confrontation.

The demand characteristics of the courtroom tend to create in the minds of jurors varied expectations consistent with the priority that the local situation culturally and legally may emphasize. Thus, in some situations, attorneys may work to establish an identification between being a juror and being identified with the enforcement of law and order. As part of an adversary approach, the opposition may attempt to persuade members of the jury that prosecution and judiciary aspects of law enforcement may conspire against the rights and freedoms of individuals brought before the court, and as such move to direct an identification between the jury and the exercise of critical judgment regarding law enforcement practices and procedures.

To a considerable extent, the manner in which individuals accept conformity and resistance appears to identify those who may be more susceptible to pressures regarding social opinions, ideological attitudes, and abstractions that, while not rigidly concrete experiences, nevertheless deal with factual materials from a personal reference point.

As has been pointed out by Blake and Mouton (1961), tendencies toward conformity and conversion are heightened when an individual is with at least three other persons, and when their reactions represent only small departures from the position believed by the individual to represent his own convictions. Resistance is minimized by gradually leading the individual away from his own position in small steps. Those authors have also pointed out that if other individuals present are personally acquainted with the nature of the issues and are persons whom the individual respects, additional conformity pressures are created. It is in this context that the use of expert witnesses plays an important role in determining the nature of jury perception and eventual discretionary behavior.

Thus, regardless of the language which may be used to describe the situation, it appears that attorneys in selecting jurors are motivated strongly to create conditions which will lead to the composition of groups designed to ensure friendliness and conformity among the members of the group, as well as a lack of predisposition to identify with the adversary position, regardless of what it may be.

While it appears that the best single antidote against conformity pressures is intimate data processing and understanding of the issues involved, the courts through the use of adversary practices tend to confront the jury with information, factual data, and expert witnesses that tend not to be in agreement and may actually be oppositional. This situation leads to confusion, lack of respect for the expert opinions reflected, and a tendency to back away from the use of logical analysis in discretionary behavior, and thus to rely more upon empathy, emotional identification, and the extent to which the persuasive and suggestible influences of the court are perceived.

In this context, it is interesting to view the action of the recently formed group of lawyers and social scientists operating as part of what is termed "Team Defense." This group is designed to use relatively new trial techniques in an effort to avoid executions even in supposedly hopeless cases. An Atlanta-based group headed by an attorney organized this group shortly after the United States Supreme Court ruled that death penalty laws in Georgia, Florida, and Texas were constitutional. The techniques employed by the group include the following: (1) appealing to logic rather than compassion in arguments against the death penalty, (2) prolonging trials to allow jurors to become well acquainted with the defendants, (3) using a proliferation of motions to "capture the atmosphere of the trial" for appeal, if necessary, and (4) using social scientists to assist in challenging the composition of jury pools and evaluating the character of prospective jurors. Thus even when a defendant admits his role in a crime, according to this group he can become more of a person to the jury over a longer period of time; and, based on this identification, it may be possible to save his life. This team also desires long trials so that prosecutors will be more cautious. The theory is that if a prosecutor is faced with a defense that plans to fight the case tenaciously, filing motions at every turn, he will be less apt to oppose a plea bargain. This group likewise will not make use of additional impassioned speeches against the death penalty but will argue instead through a panel of experts brought in for each trial that the death penalty is not a deterrent. The success of such an approach must in its final analysis be based upon the careful selection of jurors who will be responsive to suggestions given within a logical framework. Viewed in terms of the hypnotic syndrome, this approach is likely to lead to compliance through identification and understanding rather than through appeal to the exercise of power, authority, and the need to punish the guilty.

The switch from impassioned appeals to punish the guilty and to have the punishment fit the crime has now led to a much more subtle process not unlike that used in the interrogational system. The goal is to have the jury as a group identify with the lawyer and with the lawyer's position and to become amenable to suggestions to bring about articulated changes in attitude, opinion, and interpretation of facts, and a reorganization of thinking based upon this type of "appeal."

This approach may stimulate the interaction that takes place within the therapeutic context in which the therapist carefully articulates the determinants of the problem, focuses upon related and associated issues, has the patient become involved in the transactional process, and then, through carefully placed interpretations which serve as powerful forces of suggestion, brings the patient to a reevaluation of his previous opinion, attitude, and feelings, leading to a change in some aspect of his behavior and his symptoms.

When transposed outside the therapeutic interaction, the use of interpretation becomes the sine qua non of suggestive procedures in what still remains essentially an authoritative relationship. It does so by mobilizing experts and expert testimony, the affirmation of the need to inform the jury of facts, issues, and legal implications with the attorney working toward suggesting variations and alterations in opinion, attitude, and basically identification. Carefully and well placed interpretations can effectively alter the feelings and reactions of a few selected jurors, and, as part of the group process, spread to other members of the jury so that ultimately one can see suggestion and interpretation working as major mechanisms in the shaping or coercion of jury response.

If one views the deliberation and action of the jury as a facet of discretionary behavior in the legal process, it is a discretionary process subject to unusually strong influences and manipulative procedures, making appeal through logic to actually nonlogical aspects of behavior formation through the use of cognitive techniques of interpretation and suggestion. The appeal is made through primary process activity in thinking rather than secondary processes; so while a jury may be led to believe that it is acting in compliance with its own wishes, just like individuals caught in a matrix of the hypnotic process, it may be responding to newly perceived stimuli coming from transactionally imposed suggestions, leading to conclusions that are less than rational, but fully acceptable to the individual and perceived as his own responsiveness. It is important within this conceptual framework to examine what basic factors play a role in shaping lawyer–jury transference within which suggestibility can become such a powerful tool of the behavioral process and thus serve to alter discretionary behavior.

In considering suggestibility in the social context of interpersonal events, we obviously cannot separate it from the hypnotic syndrome, whether one views it as a neodissociative process, as Hilgard (1977) does, or in terms of the social/psychological model evolved by Sarbin (1972). It must still be viewed as a means of altering not only certain aspects of volitional behavior, but also the motivational basis for behavior which permits the linking of both cognition and affect in a manner to bring about the organization of behavior through communicated directions (Kline, 1966). While one may look upon this direction in the therapeutic framework as adaptational, therapeutic, or educational, it still constitutes the manipulation of human behavior even though it may be in the service of the self and society.

Of related interest in terms of the basic psychological mechanisms involved is the work of Brock (1969), who, in reviewing experiments conducted independently in several laboratories, has shown that an individual can be induced to damage another person. In studying the subjects, he found that subjects were willing to comply to a simple request. Interpretation of this transgression compliance effect in terms of possible guilt has been discussed by Brock (1969).

An alternate explanation was imposed, in which it was assumed that an individual who has affected the fate of another will do so again if it is situationally appropriate, in order to maintain social consistency with the self. There seems to be a link between such exercise of power and some of the feelings evoked by being a member of a jury in the criminal justice system. For this reason, the laboratory evidence, apart from the narrow limits of antisocial behavior, has rather convincingly demonstrated that under certain conditions, transgressive behavior can be produced, and that transgression tends to produce compliance with continuing manipulative pressures. It may therefore follow that when transgression is not antisocial but is viewed in the context of identification with social process and specifically with the criminal justice process, it can even more easily lead to suggestibility and compliance. Perhaps this is most clearly evidenced in the behavior and dynamic structures underlying some of the actions of law enforcement officers. At times, those who enforce the law transgress the law more frequently than so-called perpertrators who are transgressors. The use of hypnosis and of suggestion in bringing about what appears to be socially desirable constructive alterations of behavior based on altered attitudes, opinion, and restraints on volitional acts sharply challenges the role of a pure discretionary mechanisms in the deliberation and behavioral process of a jury. The need to punish becomes a powerful element in the suggestion-transgression process in jury behavior.

Christie and Geiss (1970) in their early studies develop some rather interesting experimental observations on the personality constructs that may play a role in the ability of one individual to manipulate another in accordance with the design wishes of the manipulator. This concept is applicable to the model involved in the lawyer–jury relationship. Lawyers, like hypnotists, have traditionally been viewed in the social role of director or operator, a role analogous to, and sharing the characteristics of, being a manipulator. It is therefore possible to think of the successful direction of jury behavior as resulting from the most effective manipulator-lawyer.

In reassessing some of the Machiavellian characteristics evolved by Christie (1970) and redefining them within the lawyer–jury interrelationship, one may observe the following characteristics as being linked to effective manipulation by the lawyer: (1) an increasing lack of personal emotional display in appealing to jury behavior with emphasis upon cold, hard logic and cognition; (2) a lack of concern with conventional aspects of interpreting the determinants of behavior with emphasis upon conformity in perceiving criminal behavior; (3) a projected sense of objectivity, normality, and lack of neurotic characteristics; and (4) the appearance of limited ideological commitment. This may lead to the designation "High Mach." We know from experimental evidence that High Machs are in themselves individuals of lesser suggestibility. High Machs enjoy and are effective in manipulating their interpersonal subjects more than Low Machs. High Machs tend to depersonalize the social interaction and develop instead a cognitive-logical orientation. High Machs manipulate easily and well, and tend to be win-oriented, are not easily persuaded by others, and tend to get great gratification from the ability to persuade others. They are thick-skinned, can withstand enticements and criticism, and like to initiate and control the social structure of groups. In this respect, they tend to be aggressive and act in accordance with predesigned positions of their own. They believe in the effectiveness of their ability to manipulate and alter the behavior of others. Thus the manipulator, by his own personality, is more skillful in and capable of effecting a role in a re-lationship in which he is very little affected by the emotional responses or needs of others. He thus acts primarily in keeping with his own self-detached, cogni-tively directed attitudes and position.

The lawyer who is effective in manipulation on both conscious and uncon-scious levels initiates the selection of jury members who he feels will be more responsive to his suggestions. He may tend to look upon them as being of lesser value than himself, and may in reality have little empathy with them. With this degree of detachment, the lawyer is free to use his manipulative ability against jurors and treat them as objects rather than as persons. He may thus impose upon suggestible individuals the power-image that rapidly develops in authoritarian relationships and leads to compliance and conformity behavior via suggestibility.

The practical aspects of human communication can be subdivided into the three areas of syntactics, semantics, and pragmatics. The first area may be said to cover the process and difficulties of transmitting information and is, therefore, the primary domain of information. This approach to communication lies in the development of coding procedures that channel capacity, noise, redundancy, and the statistical properties of language. The problems encountered are primarily syntactical and semantic. Meaning is the main concern of semantics. While it is perfectly possible to transmit groups of symbols with syntactical accuracy, they would remain meaningless unless sender and receiver had agreed beforehand on their significance. In this sense, all shared information presupposes semantic convention. Very often this presupposition is, in fact, a form of suggestion and yields a state of expectancy by the receiver. Finally, communication af-fects behavior, and this is its pragmatic aspect. While a clear conceptual separa-tion is possible in the three areas, they are nevertheless interdependent. One view is that syntax is a mathematical logic, and thus semantics becomes a philos-ophy of expression, and pragmatics the psychodynamic dimension. It is clear that the lawyer–jury relationship is one of highly intensified and complex communication.

The lawyer is the communicator. The jury is the receiver. The lawyer codes, channels, and delivers the message as information, emphasizing the information content while reinforcing on a subtle, sometimes unconscious, level the meaningfulness of the message by the semantics employed.

The pragmatic influencing and persuading element becomes that of emphasizing the nature of identification with the issues of the bond between jury and defendant, the link between jury, defendant, and lawyer, and the development of positive suggestions that are designed to prevent intrusion of adversary suggestions and to reinforce one's own position against the other's. In sum, the goal is to alter the balance of power and to suggest an appropriate resolution of the dilemma that has been deliberately created.

In effect, all courtroom situations are dilemmas. There is no agreement on the outcome, the issues presented are in conflict, the area is problematical, and it is to be resolved by appropriate information, understanding, insight, and resolution.

The lawyer-manipulator channels this information within an individual group relationship in which he serves as the conductor and orchestrator of group response. His role is clearly designed to lead up to discretionary behavior on the part of the jury. The crux of the issue is the degree to which that discretionary behavior is volitional. To the extent that a hypnotic syndrome develops, the resulting discretionary action on the part of the jury becomes increasingly more atavistic and less volitional.

Dynamic interpersonal interaction creates demand situations that give rise to regressive elements in human behavior and may result in a hypnotic syndrome. The lawyer–jury confrontation is a clear reflection of this process and warrants continuing research into its psychodynamic structure and operations.

REFERENCES

Blake, Robert R., and Mouton, Jane S., The experimental investigation of interpersonal influence. Chapter 6 in Biderman, A. D., and Zimmer, H. (eds.), *The Manipulation of Human Behavior*. New York: John Wiley and Sons (1961).

Brock, T. C., On interpreting the effects of transgression upon compliance. *Psychological Bulletin 72:* 138–45 (1969).

Cahn, E. S., and Cahn, J. C., What price justice: The civilian perspective revisted. *Notre Dame University Lawyer XLI* (No. 6): 927–60 (1966).

Christie, R., and Geis, F. L. (eds.), *Studies in Machiavellianism.* New York: Academic Press (1970).

Frank, Jerome, *Law and the Modern Mind.* New York: Coward-McCann (1930).

Hilgard, Ernest, *Divided Consicousness. Multiple Controls in Thoughts and Action.* New York: John Wiley and Sons (1977).

Kaplan, John, and Walz, Jane, *The Trial of Jack Ruby.* New York: MacMillan (1965).

Kline, Milton V., *Freud and Hypnosis.* New York: Julian Press (1966) (Reprint, Agora Printing).

Polier, Justine Wise, *The Role of Law and the Role of Psychiatry.* Baltimore: The Johns Hopkins Press (1968).

Sarbin, Theodore R., *Hypnosis: A Social Psychological Analysis of Influence Communications.* New York: Holt, Rinehart and Winston (1972).

PART II
DISCRETION IN THE SYSTEM
OF CRIMINAL JUSTICE

Part II examines various levels of the criminal justice system in accordance with the principle of discretion. We think of discretion in the organization of the material that follows as the power of free decision or latitude of choice within the bounds provided by both legal theory and practice. In thus conceptualizing the American criminal justice system, we are able to examine it as an interconnected and interwoven system of individual choices and judgments made by all those involved in the administration of justice.

Such acts of discretion—for every instance of discretion is an act made, a decision arrived at, or a judgment reached—literally initiate the criminal judicial process and either advance it to the next step or terminate it so that it can proceed no further. Legal discretionary judgments are made with respect to both legal tradition and individual judgment, and, at their best, they are always responsible. The nature of the responsibility is both personal and social. In an individual sense, the judgment is arrived at by a process of forming an opinion or evaluation by discerning and comparing; in a social sense, the judgment comes about through being responsive to social values and practices and the prescriptions of law.

There can be little doubt that considerations of discretion are everywhere to be found in our system of criminal justice. They inform legislatures' writing of our laws, actions of executive approval, and judicial interpretation of the statutes. Moreover, as the chapters of Part II demonstrate, acts of discretion interpenetrate each step in the criminal justice process and are complexly interwoven in such a manner as to provide a unifying principle of human action.

The first chapter, by Martin S. Greenberg and Chauncey E. Wilson, literally takes us to the threshold of the criminal justice system in that it deals with the inititation of the whole process as citizens exercise their discretion to report or not report crimes against themselves. The chapter is a useful and helpful start in understanding how discretion functions and why a citizen unlawfully aggressed against is literally "the gatekeeper of the criminal justice system."

"Discretion in Police Enforcement," by Thomas Gallager of the New York City Police Department, the chapter that follows, concerns itself with what may, or may not, happen once a citizen makes the judgment to report a crime. It is clear that police officers have—and must necessarily have—wide latitude in the decision-making process that characterizes every level of the criminal justice system as presently constituted.

In "Discretion in Jury Selection" Robert Buckhout and his associates direct our attention to the application of the principle of discretion in the selection of jury members. In doing so, they suggest how public prosecutors and defense attorneys, who operate with conflicting motivations and widely different objectives, seek to reconcile difference in the formation of a group of 12 persons who will be able to hear and weigh the trial evidence suitably. Through the use of empirical and experimental procedures, particularly a mock trial, the authors take us to the heart of the jury selection process and lay bare many of the dynamic factors, those forecast and those unforseen, that actually function in jury selection and deliberation.

Like "Discretion in Jury Selection," the chapter "When Psychologists Aid in the Voir Dire," by James D. Herbsleb and associates, is an important one, concerned as it also is with the many factors that enter into the selection of jury members, since the jury is widely regarded as one of the elements in the system of criminal justice that affords a defendant an opportunity to receive a fair hearing and to have a verdict that is equitable in relation to the evidence presented.

In their chapter, John C. Mowen and Darwyn E. Linder provide an interesting and insightful discussion of just how juries go about their business and seek to integrate the objective information, presented as evidence, with their subjective impressions. Offering much practical information, the contributors provide an integrating way of looking at jury functioning in terms of theories of signal detection and information integration. We come away from our reading of their material with a much better understanding of the roles of attitudes, beliefs, values, and personal factors as these enter into jury deliberations and the fashioning of a verdict.

For a number of years, the United States Parole Commission has undertaken a series of studies of the federal system of criminal justice that have looked at the short- and long-term consequences of indeterminate sentences. The chapter contributed by Peter B. Hoffman, the Director of Research for the Commission, and Barbara Stone-Meierhoefer, one of his research colleagues, sets forth the background of and the need for guidelines to sentencing and their application within the federal system. There is little doubt that the present tendency, not alone in the federal system but also among the states, is in the direction of determinate rather than indeterminate sentences. Several states have already adopted the principles involved, and other states are expected to follow; and at this time, the U.S. Congress has before it a modification of existing sentencing procedures looking toward the development of more specific guidelines.

Social psychologists in particular, but also the larger American public, have been concerned as to the consequences of enforced confinement in penal institutions of American citizens who, as a result of confinement, lose many civil liberties and are subjected to unusual forms of stress. Stanley L. Brodsky and Raymond D. Fowler, Jr., both of whom have done extensive research in this important area of concern, share with readers some of the current research findings and their implications and ramifications. At present, we know all too little about what persons confined to our penal institutions experience and what kinds of stress they are required to adjust to. The chapter provides a helpful view of the whole confinement effects.

The final chapter of Part II, by Charlan Nemeth, provides a perception, largely from social psychological experimentation, of the dynamics of jury decision-making. In doing so, it examines, among other things, the importance of the individual juror's background and personality characteristics as these have a bearing upon his role and status in the jury, considered as having a dynamic life of its own that is not different, in principle, from similar processes known to function in other small groups. Lawyers in particular, and thoughtful citizens who may themselves become members of a jury, are likely to find the chapter informative and insightful.

Martin S. Greenberg and Chauncey E. Wilson, in the chapter that follows, take us to the threshold of the criminal justice system, concerned as they are with the exercise of discretion by citizens in reporting crimes of theft. In their view, the average American citizen who is aggressed against is literally "the gatekeeper of the criminal justice system."

Indeed, the entire train of events with which the criminal justice system is concerned has its initiation in the exercise of discretion by the average citizen who is involved in any unlawful activity or becomes unwittingly a participant in it. Without the sensitivity, responsiveness, and reporting of crimes or other unlawful acts, the criminal justice system is not called into being.

The special value of this chapter is that it indicates the significant role that acts of discretion play at the very beginning of—indeed at the threshold of—the entire process of law enforcement.

1
Citizen Discretion and the Crime of Theft*

Martin S. Greenberg and Chauncey E. Wilson

Of the many roles that citizens perform in relation to the criminal justice system, none is more important than that of notifying authorities of a crime. It is no exaggeration to state that without citizen notification, the criminal justice system will become ineffective in preventing and controlling crime. The dependency of the criminal justice system on citizen notification is underlined by the findings of Black and Reiss (1967), which show that such notification accounts for about 85 percent of the crimes investigated by police. Since citizens' reports provide the primary impetus for police action, their decisions limit the number of people passing through the criminal justice system, and therefore control subsequent caseloads of prosecutors, probation officers, judges, and correction officers. Thus, citizens, in their role as victims and bystanders, represent the "gatekeepers" of the criminal justice system (Hindelang, 1976). Moreover, recent victimization surveys conducted jointly by the Law Enforcement Assistance Administration (LEAA) and the Census Bureau clearly indicate that citizens exercise their discretionary power to report or not report crimes. The reporting rate varies from a high of 91 percent for completed auto theft to a low of 15 percent for household larceny under $50 (LEAA, 1977). According to these surveys less than half the crimes committed in the United States are reported to the police.

In this chapter we will focus on one particular category of crime—the *crime of theft outside the home*. Unlike robbery, which involves the use of force, theft (or larceny) is a crime of stealth. In almost all cases the victim becomes aware of the crime only after its commission. The crime may involve direct contact be-

*This study was supported by PHS Research Grant No. MH27526-01, NIMH (Center for Studies of Crime and Delinquency).

tween the perpetrator and the victim, as in pocket-picking, or no direct contact, as when a person's coat is stolen from a coat room in a restaurant. We have chosen the crime of theft outside the home because victimization surveys have shown that this category constitutes the most prevalent type of crime, yet it is the second least likely offense to be reported, the least likely being larceny in the home. In 1975 it was estimated that there were over 15 million such victimizations, with only 26 percent reported to the police (LEAA, 1977). Another reason for examining citizen responses to theft outside the home is that it is one of the few categories of crime for which there exist experimental as well as survey data. In the following pages we will attempt to assess critically the empirical literature on citizen responses to the crime of theft and to identify issues in need of further research.

Bystanders and Victims

Current research on citizen responses to theft has focused on citizens' role as either bystander or victim. Essentially, two literatures have evolved, one focusing on bystander reactions and the other on victim reactions. In addition to differences in focus, the two literatures differ in a number of other significant respects. Bystander reactions have generally been studied by social psychologists employing an experimental paradigm, whereas victim reactions have been studied most often by sociologists relying upon the self-report or survey methodology. As a consequence of these differences in training and methodology, different sorts of variables have been examined with regard to bystanders and victims. Social influence variables have been of primary concern to those involved in bystander research, whereas demographic variables and characteristics of the crime (e.g., magnitude of loss) have been of primary concern to those investigating victim responses to theft.

We will discuss the literature in terms of three sequential stages. First, the individual must *detect* that some property is being taken or has been taken. Second, the individual must *label* this event as a theft. And third, the individual must decide on the appropriate course of *action*. This three-stage model will be used to examine reactions of bystanders and victims.

BYSTANDER REACTIONS

Detection

According to recent victimization surveys, most thefts occur during the day (53 percent), primarily in such settings as streets, parks, playgrounds (46 percent), schools (26 percent), and nonresidential buildings (14 percent) (LEAA, 1976). Despite the public character of these settings, many crimes of theft go undetected by those present. Thieves are able to complete such acts because of limitations inherent in human perception. Typically, individuals are bombarded by many more stimuli than they can possibly perceive. Research on perception has shown that attention to particular stimuli is a joint function of stimulus conditions and characteristics of the perceiver. Stimulus events that are dissonant or odd are more likely to stand out and, therefore, more likely to be noticed than stimuli that inconspicuously blend with the environment. For instance, if you are in a supermarket, your attention is more likely to be attracted by a loud crash or the sight of someone dashing up the aisle than by someone placing groceries in a cart. Similarly, in the street a person's attention is more likely to be drawn to the sight of a well-dressed man running than to one who is merely walking. Robbers themselves are often aware of this consideration. Thus, it has been noted that they sometimes prefer to commit their acts on a rainy day because few people will think it unusual for someone to be seen running in the street when it is raining (Letkemann, 1973).

With regard to perceiver characteristics, the perceiver's "set" is an important determinant of what stimuli are detected. Research on the influence of functional factors on perception has repeatedly shown that stimuli related to one's motivational state are more readily perceived than neutral stimuli (Erdelyi, 1974). Indeed, one of the major premises underlying the formation of citizen crime prevention programs is that by increasing citizen awareness of and concern about the crime problem, citizen vigilance, and hence crime detection, can be increased (Bickman and Lavrakas, 1976).

Laboratory and field experiments on the determinants of bystander reactions to a theft have been concerned less with detection and labeling than with the determinants of action once the theft has been noticed and appropriately defined. Consequently, researchers have invested considerable effort in arranging for experimental subjects to notice the theft. For example, in experiments on bystander reactions to a shoplifting incident, the usual procedure is for a confederate to commit a blatant theft in plain view of an "innocent" bystander. As an example of the elaborate precautions taken to facilitate detection, consider the procedure used by Gelfand, Hartmann, Walder, and Page (1973):

> The apparent shoplifter was a pleasant-appearing 21-year-old college coed whose actions were directed by means of radio communication with two observers concealed behind a one-way observation window which ran the length of the store and about 15 feet above floor level. When a lone shopper approached, the shoplifter, who carried a miniature radio receiver in her purse and wore a concealed earphone, was instructed by an observer to begin her shoplifting performance. She first attempted to attract the customer's attention by either dropping some small article, rattling a package, or reaching for an item located very close to the shopper. When notified by the observer that

the shopper was watching her, the shoplifter blatantly removed several items of merchandise and stuffed them into her handbag. . . . After placing the items in her handbag, the shoplifter hurried to the front of the store and out the door without paying the cashier. (p. 278)

Despite these elaborate precautions, only 28 percent of the subjects in this study were judged to have observed the theft.

As another illustration, consider the theft paradigm employed by Latané and Darley (1970). Columbia University freshmen signed up for a one-hour interview for which they would be paid two dollars. While subjects were seated in the waiting room, another "subject" walked over to the receptionist's vacant desk, removed some cash from an envelope lying on her desk, stuffed the cash into his jacket pocket, and returned to his seat. All of this was done in plain view of the subjects with no noticeable distracting stimuli being present. About a minute after the theft, the receptionist returned. After waiting 30 seconds, the receptionist sent the "thief" to his interview. After whether subjects mentioned the incident to the receptionist was noted, subjects were interviewed about their reactions to the theft. Latané and Darley reported: "Despite the smallness of the room, the absence of things to look at, and the blatant clumsiness of the theft, many subjects steadfastly claimed throughout the entire interview that they had not noticed the crime" (p. 72). These claims were all the more surprising given the observations of assistants who watched the scene from behind a one-way mirror. On the basis of subjects' startle reactions, they judged that most subjects actually did see the theft. How can one account for subjects' claims of failing to notice the theft, given the abundance of cues provided by the experimenter and the absence of distracting stimuli? Latané and Darley proposed an explanation based on conflict-avoidance motivation. A simple means of avoiding the conflict concerning what to do about the theft "was not to see the theft at all." Some subjects may have seen the beginning of the theft, and then, without consciously thinking, turned their attention away from what was happening. Still other subjects may have rationalized their inaction by pretending not to have observed the theft.

In order to facilitate bystander detection, Bickman and Rosenbaum (1977) devised a more successful procedure. In addition to the confederate-thief, they employed a second confederate who called the subject's attention to the theft. In their paradigm a "thief" stole several items from a checkout display while waiting on the checkout line. The second confederate alerted the subject to the theft by stating, "Say, look at her. She's shoplifting. She put that into her purse." Despite the very blatant attempt to ensure detection of the theft, it is somewhat surprising that only 78 percent were judged to have noticed the theft.

Another situational feature that may influence detection is the extent to which suspected shoplifters have characteristics that make them stand apart from others. Thus, college-age shoppers in a university bookstore were more likely to notice shoplifting by a middle-aged female conventioneer than by an apparent college coed (Bickman, 1975). Similarly, customers in two Salt Lake City drugstores (median age = 44 years) were more likely to detect a simulated shoplifting when the female suspect was dressed in hippie garb than when she was dressed more conventionally (Gelfand et al., 1973).

Detection can also be enhanced when bystanders commit themselves to maintaining surveillance over another's property. Moriarty (1975) staged a series of thefts (a portable radio) from an unattended blanket at a New York beach. In the commitment condition the confederate-victim said to the subject at an adjoining blanket, "Excuse me, I'm going up to the boardwalk for a few minutes . . . would you watch my things?", with the subject agreeing in each case. In the no-commitment condition the victim merely said, "Excuse me, I'm here alone and have no matches . . . do you have a light?" The victim then strolled away in direction of the boardwalk. A few minutes later a confederate thief walked up to the victim's blanket, picked up the portable radio, and quickly walked away. An observer stationed nearby noted whether or not the subject noticed the theft. Results showed that the theft was observed by all subjects in the commitment condition and by 71 percent of those in the no-commitment condition. The thief's sex was also varied but had no effect on detecting the theft.

A similar paradigm was employed to study responses to a library theft on a midwestern college campus (Shaffer, Rogel, and Hendrick, 1975). Victims asked half the subjects who were seated at the same table to watch their belongings for five minutes while they obtained a reference (request condition). The remaining half of the subjects were not asked to guard the victim's personal property (no-request condition). The thief appeared at the table two minutes after the victim left and began rummaging through the victim's belongings. Making noise to attract the subject's attention, the thief searched through all of the victim's books and folders and finally reached into the female victim's purse (or lifted the book that the male victim had been reading), and discovered approximately $20 in the victim's wallet (or the male victim's wristwatch, concealed beneath the open book). Then the thief glanced at the subject, hurriedly placed the money (or watch) into his pocket, and quickly walked away from the table. An observer noted that all subjects in the request condition noticed the theft compared to just 79 percent of those in the no-request condition. The results of this study and those reported by Moriarty (1975) suggest that neighborhood watch programs designed to increase citizens' commitment to watching over their neighbors' homes may have some utility insofar as detection of crime is concerned.

The difficulty encountered by several investigators in ensuring that bystanders notice a theft suggests that bystanders' inaction may be due in part to their all too frequent failure to detect the theft. The extent to which this failure derives from an inappropriate set or bystander motivation not to notice remains an unanswered empirical question.

Labeling

If bystanders are to take any action with regard to a theft, they must not only detect the event but they must label it as a theft. There currently exists very little empirical research on bystander inaction resulting from the failure to define an event as a crime. Gelfand et al. (1973) reported that older bystanders to a shoplifting more often cited "uncertainty" about the event as their reason for not reporting than younger bystanders (50 percent v. 2 percent). Similarly, female bystanders gave uncertainty as their reason more often than male bystanders (19 percent v. 3 percent). Moriarty (1975) reported that many bystanders to the theft of a portable radio from a beach blanket believed that the thief was really the victim's friend and therefore the event was not defined as a theft. In many theft situations bystander uncertainty is easily understandable. Most people assume that a typical thief will not commit a blatant theft, particularly when there is the possibility of detection. Further, most people assume that if detection is unavoidable, most thieves will provide false cues so as to convince observers that what they are seeing is not in fact a theft. More than one home has been burglarized by thieves disguised as "movers" or "repairmen."

What factors enter into a bystander's decision to label an incident as a theft? Common sense suggests a number of such factors. These include characteristics of the situation, such as the target's appearance, and behavior and perceiver characteristics, such as the bystander's training and set to perceive such events. The purpose of much of the instruction given to neighborhood watch groups is to foster the appropriate set and to educate citizens regarding suspicious events.

Of the various factors that can potentially affect bystander labeling, social influence appears to play a critical role. Stimulated by the seminal work of Leon Festinger (1954), social psychologists have demonstrated that in situations where they are uncertain about the correctness of their attitudes or beliefs, individuals often rely on the opinions of others as a source of confirmation. As Latané and Darley (1970) have shown in a series of experiments on bystander responses to noncrime emergencies, bystanders are powerfully influenced in their definitions of an emergency by the reactions of others around them. Applying this reasoning to a crime situation, Bickman and Rosenbaum (1977) experimentally demonstrated the influence that others have on one's interpretation of an event as a crime. Female subjects were placed in a small cubicle with a female confederate and were told that they would be observing a live telecast (in reality a tape) from a local supermarket. Their task was to record the reactions of shoppers to a display located near one of the checkout lines. Nine and a half minutes into the tape subjects observed a staged shoplifting of two packages of film from the display. The confederate, who either witnessed the theft or did not witness it (because she allegedly was searching for a missing contact lens), attempted one of three types of verbal influence. She either encouraged the subject to report the incident, discouraged the subject from reporting, or gave a noncrime interpretation to the event. When witnessing the theft, the confederate gave the following noncrime interpretation: "Oh, no! She's not shoplifting. I'm sure she'll pay for it. She probably told the clerk she put it in her purse." When not witnessing the theft, she said, "I didn't see it, but she couldn't be shoplifting." and then continued the same dialogue as in the witness condition. Results showed that subjects in the noncrime interpretation condition were significantly less certain that a crime had occurred in comparison with subjects in the encourage and discourage reporting conditions. Moreover, the reporting rate of subjects in the noncrime interpretation condition (14 percent) was no different from the reporting rate for subjects in the discourage reporting condition (8 percent).

In another study of the effect of social influence on the labeling of a shoplifting (Bickman and Green, 1977), less clear results were obtained. A staged shoplifting incident was presented to subjects while they waited in a supermarket checkout line. A confederate standing in line behind the subject remarked in half the cases, "Say, look at her. She's shoplifting. She put that into her purse." For the remaining half of the subjects, the confederate remained silent. When interviewed after their decision to report or not report the theft, 75 percent of the subjects said that they agreed with the confederate's interpretation, 23 percent said they were not sure if they agreed, and 2 percent disagreed with the confederate's interpretation. However, subjects who were exposed to the shoplifting interpretation were no more certain that it was a theft than subjects who were told nothing by the confederate. Bickman and Green explained this in terms of a ceiling effect generated by the blatantness of the theft.

As this literature survey shows, understanding the factors that influence bystanders' labeling of an incident as a theft or a nontheft is based more on common sense than on empirical investigation.

Choice of Action

Once having detected and appropriately labeled an incident as a theft, bystanders must decide on the appropriate course of action. Five possible courses of action can be identified. First, bystanders can notify the police. Second, bystanders can intervene directly—either verbally or physically. Thus, bystanders can request or order the thief to return the stolen property, or they can forcibly retrieve the stolen property and return it to its owner. Of course, bystanders can choose more than one option, such as combining the first two. Thus, bystanders can physically detain a suspect while simultaneously calling for the police. Third, bystanders can inform the victim or others of the theft. Fourth, bystanders can restructure their congitions about the situation. Examples of such restructuring include defining the event as a noncrime, minimizing the significance of the theft, or making the victim worthy of his fate. Fifth, bystanders may physically or psychologically leave the situation, or, of course, they may simply do nothing. In deciding among these options, we will assume like others (e.g., Piliavin, Rodin, and Piliavin, 1969; Bleda, Bleda, Byrne, and White, 1976) that bystanders are motivated to maximize their outcomes. In choosing among these alternatives, bystanders weigh the benefits and costs associated with each and choose the least costly alternative.

The decision to notify the police may produce such benefits as approval from the police, the victim, and others, as well as the self, for "doing the right thing." These benefits must be weighed against potential costs, such as legal and psychological costs resulting from having made a false accusation, time and effort spent giving testimony, and fear of reprisal from the thief. Consistent with this view are the findings of Gelfand et al. (1973), who noted that 41 percent of their subjects who failed to report a shoplifter gave as their reason the desire to avoid the costs associated with a countersuit and court appearances. The second option, direct intervention, while earning praise from self and others involves potential costs, such as being harmed by the thief and suffering embarrassment for falsely accusing someone. Informing the victim or others of the incident may earn the victim's gratitude as well as approval from self and others. However, these benefits have to be weighed against potential costs associated with embarrassment resulting from falsely accusing another and possible costs in terms of time and effort associated with testifying against the thief. If bystanders choose to restructure the situation cognitively, the need to take action in the form of notification or intervention is reduced. Important benefits associated with this option may include avoiding costs associated with notification and intervention (e.g., embarrassment, fear of reprisal, having to testify against the thief). However, in choosing this option bystanders may incur costs associated with falsifying reality. Others, including the victim, may subsequently challenge the bystander's definition of the situation. In addition, use of this option is liable to earn the disapproval of the victim. The fifth option of doing nothing or fleeing the situation provides immediate benefits in the form of avoiding confrontation with the thief, avoiding embarrassment at having falsely accused someone, and not having to suffer the costs of becoming involved with the criminal justice system. This option, however, is not without its own costs. Bystanders who choose this option may experience feelings of guilt and lowered self-esteem. The weighting of the benefits and costs associated with each option is no doubt a complicated matter and probably involves an interaction between bystanders' needs, self-concept, past experience, and the particular situation in which they find themselves.

Conspicuously absent from the experimental literature on reactions of bystanders to a theft are investigations of reporting to the police. Reactions typically studied include direct intervention (most often verbal) and informing a nonpolice authority of the theft. Most often the authority to whom the crime is reported is a store employee. This fact creates a particularly troublesome interpretative dilemma. The employee to whom the crime can be reported is simultaneously an *authority* and a *representative of the corporate victim.* In notifying the employee of the theft, are victims responding to the employee's status as authority or victim? Conceivably, bystanders may reason, "It's your company's merchandise that was taken so I thought that you should be told so that you can decide whether or not the police should be called." Bystanders may reason that it is the victim's decision to notify the police and that their role is simply to provide the victim with inputs relative to that decision. Clearly, then, notifying a representative of the corporate victim does not have the same cost/benefit implications as reporting to the police. If a bystander were on a checkout line in a supermarket and observed a shoplifting, to whom would the bystander report first—a policeman standing nearby or the cashier? This is an important empirical question that has yet to be answered.

Social Influence Exerted by Others. Reporting to store authorities can be enhanced or diminished by verbal advice from others present. The advice can take the form of defining the situation as a theft (Bickman and Green, 1977) or explicitly encouraging or discouraging reporting (Bickman, 1976; Bickman and Rosenbaum, 1977). For example, when subjects were explicitly encouraged to report by the statement. "We saw it. We should report it. It's our responsibility" (Bickman and Rosenbaum, 1977, Experiment 1), 72 percent reported. When, however, they were discouraged from reporting by the statement, "But it's the store's problem. They have security people here," only 32 percent reported. Similar advice given in Experiment 2 produced even a wider divergency in reporting (72 percent versus 8 percent). Presumably, encouragement to report increased the costs of doing nothing (e.g., increased sense of guilt) and increased the benefits for reporting (expected approval from self and others for doing the "right thing"). In a reverse manner, discouraging reporting by stating that "It's not our responsibility" may have decreased the costs of doing nothing (i.e., reduced feelings of guilt) and decreased the benefits of reporting (e.g., a member of the store's security force is likely to detect the theft).

Findings by Shaffer et al. (1975) suggest that the mere presence of others can affect bystander intervention. They found that bystanders were more likely to intervene to prevent a theft when they witnessed the theft alone than when one other person was present. Shaffer et al. reported that the presence of another person decreased the subject's sense of responsibility to intervene and thereby reduced the costs for nonintervention (e.g., reduced feelings of guilt). In the alone condition, subjects' feelings of responsibility were heightened, making it more costly to do nothing and more rewarding to intervene directly. Two experiments by Latané and Darley (1970), the first involving a theft from a receptionist and the second a theft of a case of beer from a beverage store, yielded marginal support for the effect of others' presence on reporting. In both experiments there was a tendency for bystanders who observed the theft alone to report more often than bystanders who observed the theft in the presence of another person. Anecdotal descriptions suggest that a number of bystanders may have chosen to restructure the situation cognitively:

> "It looked like he was only making change," said several subjects. "I thought he took the money by accident," said one charitable soul. A number of subjects seemed to feel some conflict between their responsibilities to the receptionist and to law and order on the one hand and to the "obviously" poor (but well dressed) college peer on the other. Some decided that not much money had been in the envelope after all. (Latané and Darley, 1970)

Social influence attempts to increase reporting of shoplifters via the mass media (Bickman, 1975) and signs advising reporting (Bickman and Green, 1977) have proved ineffective. Apparently, social influence is more effective when it is personal and face-to-face.

Social Influence Exerted by Victims. Social influence attempts by the victim appear to have a potent effect on bystander willingness to intervene to prevent a theft. Studies by Moriarty (1975) and Shaffer et al. (1975) show that when potential victims obtain a bystander's consent to watch their belongings, bystanders not only maintain better surveillance but are more willing to intervene than when no commitment is made. It seems likely that the commitment to guard another's belongings facilitates intervention by increasing the costs for nonintervention. Bystanders are liable to feel a greater sense of guilt for failing to abide by their commitment and, furthermore, may anticipate reprisal from an angry victim.

Influence Exerted by Thief Characteristics. Variations in the thief's characteristics have yielded mixed results. Although Gelfand et al. (1973) found that a thief dressed in hippie garb was more likely to be detected stealing, the thief was no more likely to be reported than one conventionally dressed. However, Steffensmeier and Terry (1973), using a similar paradigm, found that a hippie shoplifter was more likley to be reported than a "straight" shoplifter. The difference in results can be accounted for by any number of reasons, such as differences in populations studied and manipulations of the appearance of the shoplifter. In the Gelfand et al. (1973) study, for example, the conventional shoplifter wore a "medium length coat," whereas the "straight" shoplifter in the Steffensmeier and Terry (1973) study wore a "fur coat." Conceivably, wearing a fur coat implies more than merely being "straight." Given the conflicting findings, no firm conclusions can be drawn concerning the effect of the thief's appearance on reporting behavior.

With regard to the thief's sex, Moriarty (1975) found that, although bystanders were no more likely to intervene to prevent a theft by a female than by a male, the *quality* of the interaction was affected by the thief's sex. Subjects were more likely to use physical force in detaining the female thief, while they dealt with the male thief in a firm but far less aggressive manner. This is reflected in the fact that of those who intervened, 73 percent snatched the radio away from the female thief while only 17 percent did so when the thief was male. Presumably, bystanders had less to fear from a female thief than a male thief and were therefore more willing to take decisive action to prevent the theft. In the only other study that examined the implications of the thief's sex, Steffensmeier and Terry (1973) obtained an interaction between sex of the thief and sex of the bystander. A female thief was more likely to be reported than a male thief when the bystander was a male. In contrast, when the bystander was female, a male thief was more likely to be reported than a female thief. Additional data are needed in order to clarify the relationship between the thief's sex and bystander reactions. Other characteristics of the thief, such as the thief's age (Bickman, 1975) and the number of thieves involved in the theft (Latané and Darley, 1970), appear unrelated to bystander reporting.

Influence Exerted by Bystander Characteristics. Attempts to link bystander characteristics to intervention and reporting have yielded few insights. Reporting was not found to be related to bystander attitudes toward the store authority (Bickman, 1976), toward the thief (Bickman and Green, 1975; Gelfand et al., 1973), or toward shoplifting (Bickman and Rosenbaum, 1977). Studies that have investigated the relationship between bystanders' sex and reporting or intervention have produced inconsistent results. Of the seven studies that provide data on sex comparisions, four found no differences (Bickman, 1976; Bickman and Rosenbaum, 1977; Latané and Darley, 1970; Shaffer et al., 1975), one found that males reported *more* than females (Gelfand et al., 1973), another found that males reported *less* than females (Bickman and Green, 1977), and one reported an interaction between sex of the bystander and sex of the thief (Steffensmeier and Terry, 1973). Similarly inconsistent findings have emerged with regard to bystander age, education, and size of hometown where the bystander grew up (Bickman, 1976; Bickman and Green, 1977; Bickman and Rosenbaum, 1977; Gelfand et al., 1973).

Summary

Bystander reporting and intervention require that the theft be detected and labeled appropriately. The decision to report or intervene can be understood from a costs/benefits perspective. In deciding among the response options, it was assumed that bystanders choose the option that maximizes their expected benefits and/or minimizes their expected costs. Research indicates that bystander reporting and intervention can be affected by social influence exerted by others present and by potential victims. In contrast, investigations concerning the impact of thief and bystander characteristics have generally yielded inconclusive results. Our review of the literature further indicates that the experimental literature on bystander responses to a theft is extremely narrow in focus. Most of the research concerns reactions to shoplifting, and none involves reporting to the police. The failure to investigate reporting to the police stands in direct contrast to studies of victim responses.

VICTIM REACTIONS

The circumstances of theft victims differ from those of bystanders in two significant ways. First, victims' outcomes are directly affected by the thief's actions. Second, since larceny is a crime of stealth, detection is almost always confined to the period following commission of the act. The differences in circumstances have important implications for victim decision-making. Victims' decision-making is likely to have stronger emotional overtones, since the theft has been directed against them. As a consequence of their higher emotional arousal, victims may not be nearly so rational as bystanders in their review of options and calculation of benefits. Moreover, since victim detection is usually ex post facto, direct intervention *during* the theft is usually ruled out.

The special circumstances of victims can create a strong impetus to another option, that of *seeking a private solution* as distinct from notifying the police. Private solutions can take a number of forms. Victims may physically retrieve the stolen property, or they may attempt to ensure return of the property by employing threats of physical harm or by threatening to reveal the theft to others such as the police or the thief's parents. Alternatively, victims can offer the thief a financial reward for returning the stolen property with "no questions asked." If victims are less concerned with retrieving the stolen items and more concerned with preventing future thefts, they can offer the thief a financial reward in return for the promise not to commit further thefts against them (known as "paying protection money").

The search for a private solution may also take the form of increasing one's protective skills so as to avoid future victimization. Victims could learn judo, procure a weapon, purchase a watchdog, or install an alarm system. They can, of course, enlist the aid of others in their attempt to deal with the offender or to prevent future thefts. Thus, victims can hire a private detective or mobilize friends to search for the thief ("vigilante committees"), or they may hire a private guard or enlist the aid of friends in order to prevent future thefts (e.g., neighborhood watch organizations). Finally, rather than attempting to retrieve the stolen property from the thief, victims may attempt to obtain compensation indirectly by stealing from others (Reiss, 1976), as sometimes occurs in communities where stealing is considered normative.

In addition to seeking a private solution, victims can avail themselves of four other options: (1) notifying the police, (2) cognitively restructuring the situation (e.g., by blaming themselves, by believing that the thief will "get his due"), (3) physically or psychologically fleeing the situation, or, of course, (4) simply doing nothing. Thus, victims of repeated shopliftings may move their businesses elsewhere, and victims of locker room thefts may keep their valuables with them instead of continuing to use the lockers. The foregoing discussion suggests that victims' responses to a theft are directed towards two general goals—compensation or recovery of the stolen property and prevention of subsequent thefts. Table 1 presents the various response options and the goals that each is likely to

Table 1. Victims' Response Options and Goals Sought

Victim response options	Victim intention	
	Recovery of property (compensation)	Prevention of future thefts
1. Report to police	*	*
2. Seek private solution		
a. Physically retrieve property	*	
b. Use threats to retrieve property	*	
c. Offer reward	*	*
d. Increase protective skills		*
e. Enlist aid of others	*	*
f. Steal from others	*	
3. Cognitively restructure situation		
a. Blame self		*
b. Minimize harm	*	
c. Believe thief will get his/her due		*
4. Flee situation		*
5. Do nothing		

Note: Asterisk indicates that choice of particular response option is guided by intention indicated.

achieve. In choosing among the various response options, we will assume that victims generally choose the option(s) which they believe will maximize their outcomes. This does not necessarily mean that victims are typically correct in their selection of options. Because of their state of heightened arousal, or insufficient knowledge, or poor counsel from others, victims may act in ways that do not bring them optimal outcomes.

With the exception of the research program conducted by the present authors, research on victim reactions to a theft has been limited to the self-report or survey research methodology. This latter approach attempts to gain understanding of victim decision-making, not by manipulation of independent variables but by asking "real life" victims to reflect back on their decision-making following their victimization experience. As we have discussed elsewhere (Greenberg, Wilson, and Mills, in press), the survey methodology rests on several tenuous assumptions: (a) that victims know the reasons for their decisions, (b) that victims can accurately recall these reasons when asked to do so after an interval of weeks or months, and (c) that victims are willing to reveal these reasons to the interviewer. Quite likely, victimization surveys tell us more about what victims *believe* are the causes of their behavior than about the *"real"* causes of their behavior (Nisbett and Wilson, 1977). Despite these reservations, we nevertheless believe that retrospective reflections by victims can make some contribution to our understanding of victims' reactions to a theft.

None of the victimization surveys to date has examined the conditions under which victims detect and label their victimization experience. Instead, the surveys have focused exclusively on victims' decision concerning the appropriate course of action.

Survey Results

In 1965 the United States President's Commission on Law Enforcement and Administration of Justice was established to examine the causes of crime and delinquency and to make recommendations for their prevention. In response to this directive the Commission initiated the first national survey of crime victimization. The survey was conducted in the summer of 1966 by the National Opinion Research Center (NORC) of the University of Chicago (Ennis, 1967). A national sample of 10,000 households was taken to determine if any household member had been victimized in the preceeding 12-month period, if the crime had been reported to the police, and if not, why not. Results indicated that reporting of thefts was related to the magnitude of the theft, with 37 percent of petty larcenies (i.e., theft less than $50) being reported and 60 percent of grand larcenies (theft greater than $50) being reported. The principal reasons given for *not* notifying the police were that the "police would not be effective" and that the matter was "not of concern to the police." Together, these reasons accounted for approximately 88 percent of the reasons for not reporting.

Additional surveys conducted in Washington, D.C. (Biderman, Johnson, McIntyre, and Weir, 1967), Chicago and Boston (Reiss, 1967), and San Jose and Dayton (LEAA, 1974) produced rates of reporting essentially similar to those of the NORC study. In the Washington, D.C. survey, for example, the respective rates of reporting of petty and grand larceny were 31 percent and 70 percent. Similarly, the combined data for the San Jose and Dayton surveys show that victims reported 23 percent of petty larcenies and 62 percent of grand larcenies. Moreover, 74 percent of larcenies involving a loss of over $500 were reported to the police. Using much of the information gained from these surveys, the LEAA established in 1972 a continuing survey of victimization—the National Crime Panel. The Panel consists of two major components, the National Survey and the Cities Survey.

The National Survey. This survey is a continuing study involving interviews with a sample of approximately 150,000 individuals representing 60,000 households and 9,000 businesses in the 50 states and the District of Columbia. Data gathered for the years 1973, 1974, and 1975 (LEAA, 1976, 1977) indicate that for all three years crimes of theft constituted the single most prevalent type of personal crime, yet they were the one that was least likely to be reported. The percentages of reporting for the three years respectively were 22 percent, 25 percent, and 26 percent. Moreover, there were no systematic differences in reporting with regard to the victim's age, sex, or race. The 1973 survey—the only year for which there are complete data—shows that the major reason given for not reporting the incident to the police was "Nothing could be done—lack of proof" (32 percent), with "Not important enough" (28 percent) ranking second (LEAA, 1976).

The Cities Survey. This study consisted of interviews with members of 10,000 households in each of 26 cities, as well as representatives of approximately 2,000 commercial establishments in each city. The crime of theft was by far the most prevalent type of crime in all 26 cities. The rate of reporting ranged from a high of 36 percent (St. Louis and Washington, D.C.) to a low of 19 percent (Houston). Hindelang (1976) performed a detailed analysis of the data from 8 of the 26 cities (Atlanta, Baltimore, Cleveland, Dallas, Denver, Newark, Portland, and St. Louis) and found that completed thefts had a higher rate of reporting (45 percent) than attempted thefts (20 percent). While the victim's race was not related to reporting, the victim's sex was. Females were more likely to report (51 percent) than males (43 percent). In addition, victims between the ages of 12 and 19 had the highest rate of *nonreporting* compared with other age groups. The most prominent reasons given by victims for not reporting were the same as those found in the National Survey: "Nothing could be done—lack of proof" and "Not important enough." When victimizations were viewed in terms of the victim's prior relationship to the offender (i.e., stranger v. nonstranger), logically expected differences in reasons for nonreporting emerged. Stranger victims were more likely than nonstranger victims to give as a reason for nonreporting "Nothing could be done—lack of proof" (52 percent v. 26 percent), whereas nonstranger victims were more likely to cite as a reason "Personal or private matter" (21 percent v. 4 percent).

Additional surveys conducted on a more limited scale have produced findings that yield further insight into victim decision-making. In the first of these, Hindelang (1973) investigated the extent to which reporting by victims of commercial theft (i.e., shoplifting) was influenced by the age, sex, and race of the suspect, as well as by the total retail value of the merchandise stolen. Consistent with previous findings, only the last variable (theft magnitude) was positively correlated with reporting. Similar results concerning theft magnitude were obtained in a survey of residents of the Portland, Oregon metropolitan area (Schneider, Burcart, and Wilson, 1976). It was found in this study that the strongest predictor of reporting was crime seriousness, defined in terms of the dollar amount of the stolen property. The reporting rates for "low," (less than $10), "moderate," ($10–$250), and "high" ($250+) seriousness property crimes were respectively 25 percent, 49 percent and 84 percent. Property crimes in the *low seriousness* category were more apt to be reported if the victim (a) was more trusting of the police, (b) lived in an area where the police enjoyed good relationships with the community,* and (c) had participated in activities sponsored by the Crime Prevention Bureau antiburglary team. In contrast, property crimes in the *high seriousness* category were more likely to be reported if the victim (a) believed that the police would be able to catch the offender, (b) had lived in the city for a longer period of time, (c) had insurance on the stolen items, and (d) believed that the theft was committed by a stranger. While the correlations supporting these conclusions were all statistically significant, it should be noted that none exceeded .22.

Summary

Generally speaking, victimization surveys have yielded highly consistent findings. The rate of reporting theft victimizations to the police is consistent across geographical region and across time. The surveys further indicate that larceny is the most frequent category of personal crime and yet is the one least likely to be reported to the police. Characteristics of the victim appear to account for less of the variance in reporting than does the nature of the offense. It has been shown consistently that the greater the magnitude of the theft, the higher the incidence

*See Chapter 7 concerning this matter.

of reporting. The effect of the thief's characteristics has not been systematically explored, probably because theft victims rarely have an opportunity to observe the thief. In the one study that examined thief characteristics (Hindelang, 1973), no relationship was found between reporting to the police and the thief's age, race, and sex. The reasons given by victims for not reporting are highly consistent across studies. These include the belief that nothing could be done and that the theft was not sufficiently important to warrant the police's attention.

Still needed are studies of situational and social influences on victim decision-making. More needs to be known about the conditions under which victims detect and label their losses as a theft. In addition, data are lacking on the reasons why victims of personal theft *choose to report* to the police rather than not report. Further, little is known about the conditions under which victims prefer to settle the matter privately. Also needed are alternative methodologies for studying victim reactions. Given the likelihood that victims are not always able or motivated to recall accurately the reasons for their actions (see Greenberg, Wilson, and Mills, in press), it would seem wise for investigators to develop alternative research strategies that allow more direct access to the victim decision-making process. One such alternative strategy is described in the following section.

An Experimental Approach to Victim Reporting

Since naturalistic observation of victim reactions to a theft is unfeasible owing to the difficulty of forecasting victimizations, we have chosen an experimental approach in which we create our own victims. This approach seeks an understanding of victims' decision-making not in victims' self reports but in the systematic manipulation of variables presumed to affect such decision-making. The advantages of the experimental approach over the survey approach are many. They include random assignment of subjects, manipulation of the independent variables, and direct observation and quantification of victims' responses to the staged crime. In being able to standardize the stimulus event, manipulate independent variables, and record "victims'" immediate responses, the investigator is in a better position to test causal hypotheses. The experimental approach is not, however, without its disadvantages. In particular, the experimental investigation of reactions to criminal events in the laboratory poses formidable problems with regard to ethics and ecological validity. Yet, as shown below, the paradigm we have developed has been found to be highly involving, to arouse little or no suspicion, and to be noninjurious to participants.

Description of the Paradigm. In order to perpetrate the theft, we created a fictitious organization entitled "Industrial Research Associates of Pittsburgh." A suite of offices was rented in a middle-class retail section of the city. The "offices" were furnished with all the accoutrements one would expect to find in a research organization, such as desks, tables, chairs, file cabinets, as well as such human props as a "secretary," a "supervisor," and other "research participants." Participants were recruited from newspaper ads which read:

VOLUNTEERS–PAID

Adults needed for research on
work efficiency. $10 for $1\frac{1}{2}$
hours clerical work. Call . . .

Respondents were first screened for health problems (e.g., cardiac trouble, high blood pressure), and those who were free of such problems were given an appointment time. Shortly after participants arrived for their appointment, a second "participant" entered. He was, in reality, an experimental confederate who would subsequently play the role of "thief." The supervisor then entered, paid them the money promised in the ad, and once again questioned participants as to health problems, after reassuring them that the money could be kept regardless of how the question was answered. The supervisor explained that the organization was interested in investigating clerical efficiency in office settings and that they would be asked to complete some questionnaires and then work on a clerical task. After being seated in separate cubicles, they completed several brief questionnaires that assessed general demographic characteristics (e.g., age, occupation, education) and personality traits (shortened F Scale, need for approval scale).

The clerical task was then described. It consisted of transferring numbers from a card to a work sheet, adding the numbers, and inserting the completed work sheet and card in an envelope. Participants were told that immediately after completing each work sheet they should place the envelope containing the completed work in their "outbox" located directly behind them. They were further informed that in order to simulate real-life work conditions they would have an opportunity to earn additional money in the study. This was done by placing them in competition with the confederate and placing a monetary value of three dollars on each completed work sheet. They were told that at the end of the work period their productivity would be compared, and the person who produced less would pay the other an appropriate amount from funds with which they would be provided. Thus, if one participant completed ten sheets and the other six, the person with the smaller production would have to pay the other twelve dollars (a difference of four sheets at three dollars per sheet). Each was then given twenty dollars in small bills. They were thus led to believe that they could earn as much as forty additional dollars in the study. This would occur if they out-produced the other by seven sheets, since they would then win all of the other's money plus the twenty that they had in hand.

However, this possibility was quickly eliminated as the confederate stole 30 percent (on the average) of the participants' work from their outbox during the work period. In order to facilitate detection of the theft, participants were asked to check their work prior to its being scored by the secretary. The "evidence" of the theft consisted of several empty envelopes in their pile or completed work. After the work was picked up by the secretary and ostensibly scored, participants were informed over the intercom system that the confederate had completed seven more sheets than they did and at three dollars per sheet, they had lost their twenty dollars to the confederate. After they handed their money to the confederate, they were told that the study was completed and that prior to leaving they should go to the secretary's office to sign some additional forms.

The meeting in the secretary's office comprised the setting for assessing the dependent variable—the participant's willingness to report the theft to the police. Upon entering the secretary's office, few participants were aware that the empty envelopes were the result of a theft. Having not witnessed the theft, most participants either felt that they had made a clerical error or, at most, were mildly suspicious of the confederate. It remained for the secretary to confirm that their loss was the result of a theft committed by the confederate. When participants entered her office, the secretary casually asked, "Well, how did things go?" In 44 percent of the cases this question was sufficient to elicit a statement about the empty envelopes. Upon hearing this, the secretary volunteered to check the work sheets, which were located in another office. If the participant failed to mention anything about the empty envelopes, the secretary expressed surprise that the participant lost all of his or her money. She then offered to check the papers. Within minutes she returned with the evidence that permitted participants to label the event as a theft. The "evidence" consisted of four of the participant's completed sheets that were ostensibly found in the confederate's work pile. The secretary explained that her supervisor had left the office and that she was unable to provide any financial compensation.

She then proceeded to emit a series of prearranged prods designed to induce victims to phone the police. The first prod read, "The least I can do is get the police's number so you can file a complaint with them. They can be here in a few minutes." Prod two read, "I think you ought to seriously consider calling the police." Prod three read, "The police should definitely be notified. I'll dial and you can speak to them." In this way it was possible to quantify victims' willingness to report the event to the police on a six-point response scale ranging from a spontaneous request to call the police (scored six) to a failure to label the incident as a theft (scored one). A score of five was assigned if they agreed to call after prod one, a score of four if they agreed to call after prod two, a score of three if they agreed to call after prod three, a score of two if they resisted all prods.

The interaction was coded by an assistant who observed the sequence through a one-way mirror. The experiment was terminated immediately after participants agreed or failed to agree to call the police. For those who agreed to report the theft, no actual report was made, as the secretary's phone was not connected. Participants then received a lengthy debriefing by the supervisor, in which all of the deceptions and their rationale were revealed. In addition, they were paid a bonus of three dollars and asked to sign a consent form authorizing use of their data.

Because of the many ethical questions raised by this paradigm, it is necessary to review the precautions that were taken to ensure the well-being of participants. First, all respondents to the ad were screened for health problems. Second, participants were paid the money promised them immediately upon their arrival in order to prevent them from feeling coerced into remaining in the experiment. Third, after receiving payment, participants were asked once again about any health problems that they might have and were given an opportunity to leave with the money received. Fourth, the debriefing which participants received at the end of the study was extensive and done in a manner designed to increase their self-esteem. They were told about all of the deceptions, their necessity, and the importance of the research. If they appeared embarrassed by being taken in by the deception, it was explained to them that the procedure had been extensively pilot-tested and that almost all participants had been similarly taken in. In some cases it seemed advisable to achieve a friendly reconciliation between the participant and the confederate. Others were taken on a tour of the laboratory. All questions raised by participants were answered in a relaxed and unhurried manner. It may be added that almost all participants reacted to the revelations first with surprise and then with relief. Fifth, after being informed about all of the deceptions and after being paid the three-dollar bonus, participants were given an opportunity to withdraw their data from the analysis by refusing to sign a consent form authorizing us to use their data. Only four participants (2 percent) refused to sign the consent form. Sixth, pilot-testing of our paradigm was observed by an experienced clinical psychologist who observed the debriefing and participants' responses to it. His suggestions were incorporated into our debriefing procedure. Further, he was available to consult with those participants who it was felt left the experimental situation with some residual stress (this was deemed necessary in four cases). Seventh, after the study was completed and the results were analyzed, all participants received a three-page, single-spaced, feedback letter describing the purposes of the research and the nature of the findings. Finally, every effort was made to preserve the anonymity of the participants by identifying them by number only.

Independent Variables. Three independent variables were manipulated in a 2 X 2 X 2 factorial design. The variables consisted of magnitude of the theft ($20 v. $3), race of the thief (black v. white), and presence of the thief at the time of the report opportunity (thief present v. thief absent). The variable of theft magnitude was chosen in order to explore further survey results showing this to be an important predictor of reporting. We chose to look at the thief's race because the literature on racial stereotypes and the functioning of the criminal justice system (e.g., Chambliss and Seidman, 1971) suggests that blacks are more likely to be arrested and convicted and receive stiffer sentences than whites. We were interested in learning whether victims, as the gatekeepers of the criminal justice system, also take the suspect's race into account in their decision-making. The third variable, presence of the thief, was selected because survey results have shown that victims listed police ineffectiveness as one of the major reasons for failing to report their victimization to the police. In addition, we expected interactions among the three variables. Magnitude of the theft was manipulated by giving participants either $20 or $3 and then having them lose the money as a result of the theft of papers from their outbox. Race of the thief was manipulated by employing four college-age male confederates (two black and two white) to play the role of thief. Presence of the thief was manipulated by calling the participant in to see the secretary first (thief-present condition) or by calling the participant in second, after the thief had supposedly departed (thief-absent condition).

Participants. One hundred and twenty participants (94 females and 26 males) were randomly assigned to one of the eight experimental conditions ($n = 15$ per cell). There were 99 white and 21 black participants ranging in age from 16 to 66 ($M = 32.6$). In terms of occupation, 9 percent listed themselves as students, 40 percent held blue and white collar positions, 30 percent were unemployed, 20 percent described themselves as homemakers, and 1 percent were retired.

Results. Across all conditions, 31 percent agreed to call the police. This figure is comparable with reporting rates obtained in the National Survey (LEAA, 1976, 1977). Since need for approval was positively correlated with reporting ($r = .20$, $p < .02$), an analysis of covariance was used to analyze the data with the approval score serving as the covariate. None of the main effects was significant. However, there was a significant Magnitude of Theft X Presence of Thief interaction, $F(1, 112) = 4.03, p < .05$. As shown in Table 2, when the thief was present, reporting was unaffected by the magnitude of the theft. However, when the thief had left the scene, reporting was greater in the twenty-dollar condition than in the three dollar-condition. Unexpectedly, the *victim's race was related to reporting.* Black victims were more likely to call the police (67 percent) than white victims (23 percent), $t(118) = 2.86$, $p < .01$, regardless of the thief's race. This difference cannot be accounted for by socioeconomic class differences or by differences on other demographic dimensions. While there was no

Table 2. Mean Reporting Scores

Presence of thief	Magnitude of theft	
	$20.00	$3.00
Present	2.40	2.50
Absent	2.80	2.20

main effect for sex of the victim, there was a significant Sex of Victim × Presence of Thief interaction, $F(1, 112) = 6.37, p < .02$. As shown in Table 3, males were more likely to report when the thief was absent than when he was present, whereas the reverse was true for females. It is noteworthy that there was no race of thief main effect, nor was this variable involved in any of the interactions. It thus appears that the thief's race was not a significant factor in victims' decision to call the police.

Further insight into victims' decision-making is provided by the responses that "nonreporters" gave to the secretary's prods to call the police. Looking only at the *first reason* given by victims, we found that the most frequently mentioned reason was "Not important, not worth the time" (37 percent), followed by "Not a police matter" (24 percent), "Police ineffectiveness" (20 percent), "Concern for the thief's welfare," e.g., "I didn't want to get him in trouble" (10 percent), and "Fear of retaliation" (5 percent). Three percent mentioned some other reason.

Many victims expressed a strong sense of anger, not at having lost the money but at being taken advantage of, of being played for a fool. The state of anger often coexisted with a state of uncertainty about what to do. When confronted with this dilemma many victims looked to the secretary for advice. Consider the responses of two "reporters" to the secretary's final prod:

I really don't know what to say. What could they [the police] do, really? Where does he live? Exactly what do I have to do to call the police? I don't like to get robbed. I don't like someone to take advantage of me. [The participant then agreed to call the police.]

Table 3. Mean Reporting Scores

Presence of thief	Sex of victim	
	Male	Female
Present	2.25	2.51
Absent	3.00	1.56

You know if you want to call them its up to you. What does he owe me? Seems like a strange way to try and steal money. Do you have his name? I hate to be played for a fool. The police are going to think I'm crazy. What do you think I ought to do? I wonder where the guy is now. Okay, what the heck, go ahead and call them.

For others, the benefits of calling the police were offset by the fear of retaliation, as the following response indicates:

What would I say? What would I do? I don't want him to have it for free. It just irks you that somebody could be dishonest. I have to leave here and he may . . . don't leave me by myself here. [This victim refused to call the police.]

The victim's dilemma is further illustrated in the following remarks from a nonreporter:

I don't want to get started with any trouble with him. . . . What is this kid's address? I just don't want to start any trouble. They [the police] might think it's ridiculous. I hate to let him think he got away with it. . . . I don't want to get involved in a big thing and go to court, but I hate him to think he can get away with it. I think I'll just forget it. I'll feel bad whatever I do.

CONCLUSIONS

In this chapter we have highlighted the conflicting forces that affect citizens' responses to a theft. The nature of these forces and the ensuing arousal depends in part on the citizens' role as bystander or victim. For bystanders, there is a greater necessity for quick action, as their response can affect completion of the crime and apprehension of the suspect. Bystanders often must weigh the costs of involvement (e.g., time, effort, embarrassment, risk of injury) against the costs of noninvolvement (e.g., feelings of guilt, censure from the victim and others). For victims, the necessity for *quick* action is not nearly so acute as that for bystanders, since a victim's discovery of a theft usually takes place *after* the theft's completion, and often after the thief has fled the scene. The conflict for the victim is between the costs of taking action, such as enlisting the aid of the police and others, and the costs of inaction (e.g., not retrieving the stolen property). When faced with such a conflict, it has been shown that bystanders are particularly susceptible to social influence. Alternatively, for victims magnitude of the loss has been shown to play a pivotal role in their decision-making. However, victims too are susceptible to social influence by the *anticipated* responses of others. Many participants in our study looked to the secretary for advice, whereas others weighed the anticipated reactions of the police and the thief to their reporting the incident.

Much remains to be understood about the determinants of bystander and victim responses to a theft. For example, more data need to be collected concerning bystander responses to other forms of theft besides shoplifting. In addition, data are lacking on bystander willingness to inform legal authorities as opposed to representatives of the corporate victim (i.e., store authorities). Research on victim responses has provided little insight on conditions under which victims fail to detect and label an incident as a theft. Nor has victim research been informative concerning victims' preference for dealing with the theft via extralegal means.

Further research on the determinants of citizen reporting to the police can provide valuable inputs for programs involved in encouraging citizen reporting. It can be argued that increased reporting of larcenies will overtax the limited resources of the criminal justice system, and, in so doing, distract authorities from investigating the more serious crimes. While this argument certainly has merit, one must not overlook the fact that in order to allocate properly their limited resources, law enforcement officials need reliable information about the frequency, time, and place of occurrence of crimes. While the crime of larceny may not be so serious as other crimes, the sheer number and the cumulative dollar loss of such crimes merit the increased attention of researchers and citizens alike.

REFERENCES

Bickman, L., Bystander intervention in a crime: The effect of a mass media campaign. *Journal of Applied Social Psychology 5:* 296–302 (1975).

Bickman, L., Attitude toward an authority and the reporting of a crime. *Sociometry 39:* 76–82 (1976).

Bickman, L., and Green, S., Is revenge sweet? The effect of attitude toward a thief on crime reporting. *Criminal Justice and Behavior 2:* 101–12 (1975).

Bickman, L., and Green, S., Situational cues and crime reporting: Do signs make a difference? *Journal of Applied Social Psychology 7:* 1–18 (1977).

Bickman, L., and Lavrakas, P. J., *National Evaluation Program Phase 1 Report: Citizen Crime Reporting Projects.* Prepared for the National Institute of Law Enforcement and Criminal Justice (1976).

Bickman, L., and Rosenbaum, D. P., Crime reporting as a function of bystander encouragement, surveillance, and credibility. *Journal of Personality and Social Psychology 35:* 577–86 (1977).

Biderman, A. D., Johnson, L. A., McIntyre, J., and Weir, A. M., *Report of a Pilot Study in the District of Columbia on Victimization and Attitudes toward Law Enforcement* (Field

Surveys I, The President's Commission on Law Enforcement and Administration of Justice). Washington, D.C.: U.S. Government Printing Office (1967).

Black, D. J., and Reiss, A. J., Jr., *Studies of Crime and Law Enforcement in Major Metropolitan Areas: Patterns of Behavior in Police and Citizen Transactions* (Field Surveys III, Vol. 2, The President's Commission on Law Enforcement and Administration of Justice). Washington, D.C.: U.S. Government Printing Office (1967).

Bleda, P. R., Bleda, S. E., Byrne, D., and White, L. A., When a bystander becomes an accomplice: Situational determinants of reactions to dishonesty. *Journal of Experimental Social Psychology 12:* 9–25 (1976).

Chambliss, W. J., and Seidman, R. B., *Law, Order, and Power.* Reading, Massachusetts: Addison-Wesley (1971).

Ennis, P. H., *Criminal Victimization in the United States: A Report of a National Survey* (Field Surveys II, The President's Commission on Law Enforcement and Administration of Justice). Washington, D.C.: U.S. Government Printing Office (1967).

Erdelyi, M. H., A new look at the new look: Perceptual defense and vigilance. *Psychological Review 81:* 1–25 (1974).

Festinger, L., A theory of social comparison processes. *Human Relations 7:* 117–40 (1954).

Gelfand, D. M., Hartman, D. P., Walder, P., and Page, B., Who reports shoplifters? A field-experimental study. *Journal of Personality and Social Psychology 25:* 276–85 (1973).

Greenberg, M. S., Wilson, C. E. and Mills, M., An experimental approach to victim decision making. In V. J. Konecni and E. B. Ebbesen (eds.), *Social Psychological Analysis of Legal Processes.* San Francisco: W. H. Freeman, 1979.

Hindelang, M. J., Decisions of shoplifting victims to invoke the criminal justice process. *Social Problems 21:* 580–93 (1973).

Hindelang, M. J., *Criminal Victimization in Eight American Cities.* Cambridge, Massachusetts: Ballinger Publishing Co. (1976).

Latané, B., and Darley, J. M., *The Unresponsive Bystander: Why Doesn't He Help?* New York: Appleton-Century-Crofts (1970).

Law Enforcement Assistance Administration, *Crimes and Victims: A Report on the Dayton-San Jose Pilot Survey of Victimization.* National Criminal Justice Information and Statistics Service (1974).

Law Enforcement Assistance Administration, *Criminal Victimization in the United States— 1973.* National Criminal Justice Information and Statistics Service (1976).

Law Enforcement Assistance Administration, *Criminal Victimization in the United States: A Comparsion of 1974 and 1975 Findings.* National Criminal Justice Information and Statistics Service (1977).

Letkemann, P., *Crime as Work.* Englewood Cliffs, New Jersey: Prentice-Hall (1973).

Moriarty, T., Crime, commitment and the responsive bystander: Two field experiments. *Journal of Personality and Social Psychology 31:* 370–76 (1975).

Nisbett, R. E., and Wilson, T. D., Telling more than we know: Verbal reports on mental processes. *Psychological Review 84:* 231–59 (1977).

Piliavin, I. M., Rodin, J., and Piliavin, J. A., Good samaritanism: An underground phenomenon? *Journal of Personality and Social Psychology 13:* 289–99 (1969).

Reiss, A. J., Jr., *Studies in Crime and Law Enforcement in Major Metropolitan Areas* (Field Surveys III, The President's Commission on Law Enforcement and Administration of Justice). Washington, D.C.: U.S. Government Printing Office (1967).

Reiss, A.J., Jr., Personal communication. September 4, 1976.

Schneider, A. L., Burcart, J. M., and Wilson, L. A., III, The role of attitudes in the decision to report crimes to the police. In W. F. McDonald (ed.), *Criminal Justice and the Victim.* Beverly Hills, California: Sage (1976).

Shaffer, D. R., Rogel, M., and Hendrick, C., Intervention in the library: The effect of increased responsibility on bystander willingness to prevent a theft. *Journal of Applied Social Psychology 5:* 303–19 (1975).

Steffensmeier, D. J., and Terry, R. M., Deviance and respectability: An observational study of reactions to shoplifting. *Social Forces 51:* 417–26 (1973).

"Discretion in Police Enforcement" is a particularly timely statement by Thomas Gallagher of the New York City Police Department on the use of discretion in police enforcement of local laws and ordinances. In a time of shrinking budgets Gallagher indicates why the exercise of discretion at the level of the patrolman on the beat becomes a matter of great social importance, particularly because such discretionary acts are frequently not reviewed by higher authority.

The chapter provides the reader with an excellent view of the interplay between society's social needs and a police department's capacity to meet them in the give and take of everyday life. The treatment is compassionate and understanding, and the outcome is an increased awareness of the crucial role of the police officer working in a community, the demands made on him, and the significance of his discretionary judgments.

2
Discretion in Police Enforcement

Thomas Gallagher

DISCRETION IN POLICE WORK

Full Enforcement

Discretion, or prudent decision making, is part of our everyday life. The frequency of its use varies, depending on one's role in life. A labor mediator would use discretion more frequently than a short-order cook. A police administrator, whose subordinates continually interact with the public, must be concerned with discretion.

"A public officer has discretion whenever the effective limits on his power leave him free to make a choice among possible courses of action or inaction."[1] There is discretion in police work and it is necessary for effective police operations. Yet, in this period of enlightened police administration, there are still some police executives who deny its existence or fail to perceive the need for discretion.

"Given the massive amount of discretion that the police exercise and the extent to which it pervades all aspects of the police function, it seems incredible that there are those who cling to the notion that the police do not have discretion —or, if they do, should not."[2]

Those who resist discretion usually base their decision on an antiquated theory of a full enforcement policy, which means that police must enforce all laws, at all times, regardless of the consequences. They believe that anything less than full enforcement of all laws is a derogation of police responsibility. "A policy of 'full enforcement' implies that the police are required and expected to enforce all criminal statutes and city ordinances at all times against all offenders. It suggests that the police are without authority to ignore violations, to warn offenders when a violation has in fact occurred, or to do anything short of arresting the offender and placing a charge against him for the specific crime committed."[3] Support for their belief is found in the laws of many states, which mandate full enforcement by making it a crime for a police officer not to make an arrest for a violation not committed in his presence. Not satisfied with this hypocritical stance, lawmakers often attempt to legislate solutions too difficult to enforce, or unenforceable laws. "Ideally, the whole problem could be resolved by requiring legislative bodies to clarify their definitions of criminal conduct, to consider enforceability, to be more precise in their language, and to recognize the propriety of police discretion when they desire that it be used."[4]

Recently, there have been some encouraging legislative actions that, it is hoped, will trigger a more realistic approach by politicians to sensible law enactment. Outdated Blue Laws, especially in the area of Sabbath Law violations, have been repealed, prohibitions against sexual actions between consenting adults have been relaxed, and the decriminalization of the private use of small amounts of marijuana has been enacted by both state and federal legislation.

It is a recognized fact that modern-day police officers spend considerably more time servicing the needs of people than they do regulating their actions. "The police officer spends about 90% of his time in public service activities and only about 10% (or less) of his time in 'crook catching'."[5] The police officer, while providing service, must have flexibility in order to cope with the constantly changing situations he encounters. No two instances of traffic violations are exactly alike, each family dispute is unique, and the actions of a drunk or a disorderly group are equally unpredictable. "The exercise of discretion, suggests that the police are required, because of a variety of factors, to decide overtly how much of an effort is to be made to enforce specific laws. It recognizes that actions short of arrest may achieve the desired goal."[6] To address adequately the ever present, ongoing situations that a police officer is required to service, discretion is needed. We have come a long way in recognizing this fact. "It was only approximately 15 years ago that the existence of discretion in police work was first openly recognized."[7] However, we still have a distance to go before the use of police discretion is perfected, to ensure that it is accomplishing its goal—providing better service to the public.

Need for Discretion

Police services would be seriously affected if officers adhered to a policy of strict enforcement of all laws. This is especially true in larger cities where minor infractions of laws such as jaywalking, failing to curb a dog, having a dirty sidewalk, loud playing of a radio, and so forth, are constantly occurring. The simple fact is that it is impossible for police officers to enforce all laws. "Few police agencies have the number of personnel that would be required to detect the total amount of criminality which exists in a community and to prosecute all offenders. Rarely is consideration given to the relationship between the volume of what can be termed criminal acts and the resources available to deal with them."[8] Even if it were possible, it would be counterproductive. It is improper management of resources to have an officer constantly occupied by minor matters, which render him unavailable to rush a seriously injured person to a hospital or to respond to a call of a felony in progress.

Our form of government goes to great lengths to protect the rights of the innocent. As a result, even minor violations move slowly through the judicial process to ensure that all constitutional rights are safeguarded. It is not unusual for a police officer to spend more than one entire tour of duty processing paper work and waiting in court when a defendant in a traffic violation case pleads innocence. A felony criminal trial may consume more than a week of pretrial and courtroom appearances for one or more officers. Especially in times in fiscal constraints, it is impossible to hire officers in the numbers needed to provide all services and enforce all laws. "There are not enough agencies to handle every criminal violation. Nor would there be any justification for total coverage of the area of potential wrongdoing. A society can only pay so much for protection. It cannot put a policeman on every street corner."[9] The money is just not available. For example, in New York City, the annual budget for the Police Department exceeds one billion dollars. Approximately, 90 percent of that amount is spent on salaries and pensions. In 1975, when the city was on the verge of bankruptcy, it had to resort to laying off municipal employees. Many were fired, including 2,864 police officers. Similar occurrences happened in other cities.

Even if it were possible to pay the salaries of all the officers needed to ensure full enforcement of all laws, such enforcement still would not be achieved. The United States Constitution and state codes that guide police enforcement efforts are liberally sprinkled with such ambiguous terms as "without probable cause," "beyond a reasonable doubt," "unreasonable search and seizure," actions of a "reasonably prudent man." These phrases can be interpreted differently by individual officers. Quite often the Supreme Court of the land will split five to four in deciding a criminal issue. If learned justices differ on what is proper in a given set of circumstances, it is understandable why police officers will view situations differently. Given similar circumstances, some will make an arrest, while others will feel there are insufficient grounds for an arrest.

In recent years, there has been increased community involvement with police operations. For the most part, this involvement is advantageous. A policy of strict enforcement of all laws would be oppressive to the community. If actions of residents were being closely monitored for deviance, and officers took summary action in every instance, regardless of mitigating circumstances, we would soon have a community in disagreement with its police. Such style of policing would be more suited to a totalitarian state than a democratic nation. Community concerns must be considered in determining the enforcement approach.

Application of Discretion   •

An unusual factor about police discretion is that it is applied most often at the practioner level. "Unlike the military on which they claim to model themselves, police agencies allow their lowest-ranking officers to make some of their most important decisions."[10]   The higher one ascends the organizational ladder in a police department, the more frequently his decisions will be reviewed, thus diminishing the amount of discretion he exercises. Police operations at the street level are not a team or unit affair as is common in the military; most police jobs are handled by the individual officer alone or with a partner. Also, unlike the military, the ranking officer in police service is more an administrator than a commander of men. He usually responds after the fact and seldom personally directs the efforts of the people working under him, while it is rare for his military counterpart not to direct his underlings' efforts. Thus, there are major differences in the way military and police units function, which greatly influence who exercises discretion in the organization. "In discharging their routine order maintenance and law enforcement function, the police do not operate at all as a military or quasi-military organization, and analogies drawn between the two kinds of organizations, including those drawn by some police administrators, are quite misleading."[11]

It is ironic that the working street officer, who is very often the person least prepared to exercise discretion, is most often called upon to use it. He does not work under ideal conditions. Frequently he is under stress, either from the seriousness of the incident or the volume of work with which he is laboring.* He is expected to make a decision and, as previously indicated, often does not have a supervisor available to consult for advice.

Not only is the patrol officer overworked, but also he is, many times, the one in the police department who is least prepared to make decisions. As a rule, those persons who advance in a police department have received more formal education and have been exposed to varied aspects of policing, which help to develop discretion. Also, many departments have specialists in law and community affairs who have more technical training than the average patrol officer has for making discretionary decisions. Yet, since he is the most available, the least prepared person in the organization uses discretion most often.

---

*The 44th Pct. in New York City received 65,661 calls for service during 1976. Many more requests for police assistance are received while on patrol and are not reported to central radio. On a busy night a RMP team may handle more than 20 requests for assistance.

Control of Discretion

One of the responsibilities of management in any organization is to ensure that the objectives of the organization are fulfilled as efficiently and effectively as possible. To accomplish this, management establishes policy. Police departments are no exception. Most have very lengthy operation orders, manuals of procedure, and other department publications, clearly defining objectives and procedures. The one area where there is a noticeable lack of policy by police administrators is in the area of police discretion. This is a result of years of maintaining that the police should enforce all laws, which eliminates need for discretion in policing. It is difficult to set policy regarding enforcement policies you deny exist. It is a myth that discretion does not exist; it does exist in police work, and policy regarding its use is being established, but not by the administrators. Discretion policy is being made informally by the workers. "Top officers seem to have little to do with the making of enforcement policy. Some of the policy is made by officers of middle grade, but most of it is made at the bottom of the organization by ordinary patrolmen."[12]

An assembly plant would not function effectively if every worker were allowed to decide how to piece the product together. Bricklayers building a wall would not get far if they proceeded at their own speed without regard for the pace of the other bricklayers. In these instances, direction or policy has to be provided. The same is true for police work. Policy must be established by management in the area of police discretion. Managers are abrogating their responsibility by allowing workers to establish their own policy. Direction must be given regarding the type of policing that is in the public's best interest. This important area of responsibility should not be decided at random by each individual officer. Granted, there must be some allowance for flexibility to enable an officer to cope with the unpredictable, but the end result of all citizen-police contacts should be similar. "As a minimum, it would seem desirable that discretion be narrowed to the point that all officers in the same agency are operating on the same wavelength."[13]

A carefully thought-out policy must be established that would eliminate the personal prejudices from policing yet still allow officers to retain the amount of discretion needed to cope with changing situations. "It would be impossible to carry out the varied and often unpredictable tasks of the police without affording substantial discretion to officers at the operating level."[14]

What usually is needed is control of discretion, not its elimination. However, there are times when it must be eliminated. During disorders, it would be disastrous if officers acted independently. Clear direction must be given to the officers because intemperate action by even one officer could escalate the situation into a full scale riot.

FACTORS THAT AFFECT DISCRETION
The Charge

The single most important factor that affects police discretion is the seriousness of the act. As the gravity of the act increases, the amount of discretion decreases. It is common to find wide discretion in minor matters, such as enforcement of traffic regulations, violations of park regulations, controlling disorderly persons, and resolving family disputes. Usually such situations are resolved on the spot with the officer cautioning those involved. Sometimes a summons is issued for a future appearance by the defendant before a magistrate or hearing officer. Occasionally, the officer will make a summary arrest. The resolution of the matter is decided by the officer. Rarely is there a review of his decision. In fact, it would be unusual for a superior officer to know that discretion has been used.

In serious situations, such as robbery or burglarly, the latitude of discretion is very narrow. Usually, the only choice for the officer is to make an arrest. On rare occasions, such as burglary encountered during a large scale disturbance, the policy may be to disperse looters rather than attempt an arrest. The reasoning is that arrests may escalate the disturbance or risk causing unnecessary injury or possible deaths.

The Officer

The way an individual officer resolves a matter can vary from day to day. It is important to keep in mind that he is human and is also subject to pressures. If he has had a poor night's sleep or an argument with his wife or has just been admonished by a supervisor, he may be less understanding than he normally would be. His frame of mind at the time of the incident greatly influences his discretion.

A very important determiner of how the patrolman will act is the reaction of the citizen to his stop. A person who goes through a red light has a better chance of not receiving a summons if his reponse to being stopped is "I am sorry officer, I did not notice the light changing until it was too late to stop. It will not happen again." The citizen who chastises the officer with "Why don't you catch criminals? That light was green, what are you looking for—a payoff?" is more likely to receive a summons. A hostile person will normally trigger a negative reaction by the officer, while a reasonable reply is more likely to engender a favorable response.

A police officer is usually cast in an authoritarian role. Telling people what to do is familiar to him, since he is constantly regulating the actions of others. When he encounters someone who questions his judgment or starts telling him what he should do, the officer is on unfamiliar ground. Most officers do not like it, nor are they accustomed to it, and they may react negatively. This reaction greatly influences how the officer will use his discretion.

Peer Pressure

Most waking hours of a police officer's day are spent on his job or traveling to it. A married officer assigned to a radio car spends more time talking to his partner than he does communicating with his wife. Police officers frequently socialize with each other off duty because of their odd working hours. Even when going to work, many officers ride together to reduce expenses. With this constant exposure to fellow workers' views, it is little wonder that peer pressure influences his discretion. If he has doubts about how he acted in a police situation, he will most likely discuss it with fellow workers whose opinion he values. This is especially true of younger police officers whose approach to policing is still being formed.

Police officers, as a rule, are very defensive regarding their actions. They often view their efforts as being thwarted by a misguided citizenry, liberal judges, and unrealistic laws. Many think that the only way for the police to be effective is for them to "band together." Too often, they will make a discretionary decision based not on, "What do I believe is the best way?" but on, "What would other police officers expect me to do?"

Community

Community desires also influence the discretion exercised by a police officer. This is especially true in larger towns and cities where economic, racial, and religious factors subdivide the municipality into smaller groups with vested interests. A poor section of town may want relaxed enforcement of street gambling because some inhabitants see gambling as a potential means of escape from their way of life. On the other hand, they may want strict enforcement of such parking violations as blocking bus stops and fire hydrants because of their dependency on public transportation and the threat of fires in a crowded community. In another part of town, a more affluent group may be shocked by open gambling but may want relaxed parking law enforcement. The large number of automobiles and the limited amount of available parking often require them to park illegally. The average officer will gauge his enforcement efforts to keep them attuned to citizen desires. There is no doubt that community wishes influence a local chief's or commander's policy on enforcement. He is dependent on community support if he wishes to remain in his position.

The trend in recent years is toward more community involvement with police operations. In 1975 voters in New York City approved a law that mandates coterminous district boundaries for most city agencies. Prior to enactment of the law, agency boundaries were drawn up on the basis of how the agency believed it could best provide service. Sometimes these decisions were self-serving. Under provision of the new law, the Police, Sanitation, Park, and Highway departments along with most other smaller departments will have to change their boundaries to conform with the 55 planning boards that encompass the entire city. In addition, community boards were created to provide a vehicle for residents to have input into the delivery of services in their area. The law, which took effect on January 1, 1977, mandates that all changes be in effect by January 1, 1980. The Police Department made its first changes on January 1, 1978 in the borough of the Bronx. Every six months thereafter, precincts in a different borough were to change their boundary lines to conform to the planning board lines.

The average patrol officer is aware that his actions are under constant observation by members of the community. He knows they are omnipresent, watching from darkened rooms, parked automobiles, and public transportation. Officers are aware that failure to correct violations that the community wants corrected may be reported. As a result, a review of his actions will be conducted by a ranking officer. In order to avoid this close scrutiny, most officers are inclined to enforce laws in order to satisfy community wishes, thus limiting police discretion.

Media

The press, radio, and television industries wield tremendous power in our nation. In one form or another, they influence our lives daily. They also greatly influence police operations. The way they present a story is very important to police departments. "The police are constantly criticized for not meeting goals that cannot possibly be achieved. A newspaper editorial, for example, chides the local police for a rising crime rate. . . . in the case of crime, factors like the birth rate, unemployment, the sense of community that exists in a given neighborhood, and even the weather probably have much more to do with the incidents of crime than do the police."[15] In what could be called "media prerogative" they have the power to slant any story to be favorable or unfavorable to the police.

The media periodically embark on campaigns to arouse public interest about current problems. Targets such as an upsurge in crime, open vice operations, nonenforcement of parking regulations, and the condition of parks are frequently the objects of their crusades. Their intent is to raise public indignation to a point where public officials will be prodded to make greater attempts to solve a problem. Recently in New York City, one of the local newspapers printed daily an open letter to the Police Commissioner telling him of locations where flagrant violations of the parking regulations were occurring. Photos of the cars in violation were also printed, and the commissioner was asked what he was going to do to correct the condition.[16]

Most police officers react to such a series by narrowing their discretionary choices in traffic violation situations. They may take the articles personally, thinking that failure to take summary action would subject the department to possible ridicule. Other officers may be concerned that they will have to explain why they did not issue summonses for an obvious violation on their assigned post. In either circumstances, an officer will be issuing summonses where normally he might otherwise be inclined to overlook the violation.

Local commanders, aware of the cycle of media campaigns, often pressure their officers for recordable activity in areas where the media display an interest. They request summonses or arrests in minor situations in which the officer usually issues warnings or overlooks the violation. Thus the discretionary range of the officer is limited as a result of media pressure.

Education

"Few efforts to improve police operations in recent years have received such enthusiastic and widespread support as the general notion that police officers should be college educated."[17]   In 1967, the President's Commission on Law Enforcement and Administration strongly recommended higher educational requirements for police personnel.

Since that time, increasingly large numbers of police officers have attended college programs. Their attendance has been greatly encouraged by the Law Enforcement Education Program (LEEP) and increased educational benefits for veterans provided by the Veterans Administration. The Law Enforcement Education Program, a federal program providing financial assistance for employees of the Criminal Justice System, alone dispensed $40 million in aid in 1976. While there is a lack of empirical data on the benefits of college training for police officers, even the most outspoken critics of such programs will admit that they are not harmful. Most authorities in the field believe that college courses are quite beneficial.

. . . they see specific value in a program of studies that is heavily weighted with the liberal arts—the humanities, the sciences, and the arts—on grounds that such studies develop the ability of an individual to think, to be critical, and to be creative. They urge that students interested in policing major in sociology, psychology, or political science in their last two years of a four-year program and take courses on such subjects as urban government, constitutional law, systems of legal control (including the operations of the criminal justice system), minority groups, social conflict, deviant conduct and research methodology. Knowledge of these areas would, presumably, put policing in its proper perspective and help an officer to cope more effectively with the problems and people he confronts.[18]

Only after carefully controlled research studies will the benefit of college training for police officers be determined. It appears that college can better prepare officers for citizen contacts which frequently are difficult and require great understanding. Merely being exposed to the college environment requires one to mingle with persons of different races and cultures and can make him aware of different points of view. This heterogeneous contact should impact favorably on his use of discretion.

Police work, like most other jobs and professions, requires a period of time before the employee is considered proficient. Although an officer takes an oath of office and is given a shield, gun, and uniform, he is not thereby a skilled police officer. Even an extensive academy preparatory course will not fully qualify him as a police officer. He must undergo a period of on-the-job training, handle actual situations, and learn from his mistakes before he becomes a qualified police officer. All other variables being equal, the more experienced officer is better qualified and makes more effective use of his discretionary powers than the less experienced one. Formal education and experience usually have a positive bearing on discretion, although there are exceptions. We all know persons with graduate degrees who cannot make a decision and young high school graduates in many positions with innate good judgment and an excellent capacity for being decisive. However, these people are exceptions. Normally, college training and job experience will better prepare an officer for his assignment, enabling him to make more intelligent use of his discretionary powers.

Unusual Occurrences

Some police situations are so unique in nature that an unusual approach is necessary for their proper resolution. In these situations, discretion plays a major role because the officer is acting contrary to usual procedures. For example, it is an established fact that officers should take summary action against someone stealing a car. Under most circumstances, such an act would be a felony grade larceny. However, if the officer who observes the larceny is an undercover narcotics officer working on a major narcotics case, he may very well overlook the crime. To take action would reveal his identity, could seriously affect the outcome of the narcotics investigation, and could subject him to grave danger.

Accordingly, an officer who has infiltrated a subversive organization must use discretion to decide when to take police action and reveal his identity. He may choose to overlook a burglarly or robbery, depending on the extent to which the investigation has progressed and how vital his role is in its successful completion. Impulsive action by the infiltrating officer can ruin years of difficult, perilous work and allow a group of dangerous individuals to escape prosecution.

There are other instances when an officer may elect to overlook serious crimes that are not as clear-cut as those in which there is a covert police operation involved. Take the case of an officer involved in a riot or large scale disorder, similar to what occurred in New York City on July 13 and 14, 1977, during a 24-hour electrical failure. Lack of electrical power for lighting and for burglar alarms made it easier for persons to loot. In such a situation, an officer may decide to disperse looters rather than to arrest them. In his judgment, an arrest, while mandated by law, may be ill-advised. During the blackout, on occasion, officers found themselves outnumbered by looters by more than fifty to one. Making an arrest may be impractical, as it can spark violence with subsequent injury to innocent persons, including the police officer. It also would require the officer to leave his post for arrest processing and then more wide-scale thefts could occur. He must make an instant assessment and decide which course he will pursue. The upper echelon of the department must issue guidelines for police officers in such situations, which also allow for flexibility to enable an officer to cope with an unusual situation. The wise use of discretion by officers will permit a police department to be cognizant of the ever changing needs of the people they service.

The ultimate in police discretion occurs when an officer decides to fire his weapon in the line of duty. If a criminal is armed and poses a threat to the officer's or another's safety, the decision is almost automatic. There are other times, such as when shooting at a fleeing felon or believing that a person intends to grievously assault another, when the decision is not as clear-cut. "The language is quite general, leaving much room for the police officer to exercise discretion. This is highly significant, given that force— especially deadly force— constitutes the ultimate form of police authority."[19] Under any circumstances, it is not an easy decision to make. It is an awesome power to decide whether someone will live or die, and, very often, an officer must make the decision in seconds and live with it for the rest of his life.

ADVANTAGES OF DISCRETION

Conservation of Resources

A complaint common to most police departments is that of a shortage of personnel. The complexities of modern living have heaped additional responsibility on police officers without a commensurate increase in their numbers.   In recent years, officers have become involved in community affairs, crime analysis, intelligence gathering, organized crime matters, and coping with radical groups to an extent that would have seemed incredible 30 years ago.   Allowing officers to use discretion in adjudicating minor violations is not only practical but also allows a manager to use his resources more effectively.   It is an obvious waste to have an officer's day occupied with processing a minor violation through the court maze when it could have been handled more efficiently and effectively by a warning.   An officer in court does little to deter criminals or to reassure a citizenry upset by the lack of visible uniformed patrol officers.

The court system, as currently structured, could not function if police officers did not use discretion and strictly enforced all laws.   There are many instances of lengthy delays between the time when a person is charged with a criminal violation and the time when the matter is aired in court.   Some cases are dismissed, not because of the innocence of the defendant, but because an overburdened court has made a procedural mistake.   These conditions are exacerbated if the preliminary court stages are bogged down with cases that are kept out of court by officers exercising their discretion.

Strict enforcement of all laws would cause catastrophic inconvenience to the general public.   Salary reduction due to loss of work because of required court appearances, and the cost of fines, would have severe economic ramifications. While the matter is difficult to assess accurately because nonenforcement is rarely recorded, I would estimate that for every summons an officer issues, he overlooks ten others or chooses to process them by a warning.   In other minor violations such as noise complaints, sanitary code violations, and the like, the ratio of non-summons to summons may be even greater.   If all those not receiving summonses suddenly were issued summonses, it would certainly impact on police–community relations.   Police would be viewed as oppressive, controlling every movement of citizens, and would lose valuable public support.

Police officials too often fail to recognize that there are many in the communities which they serve who have an inherent distaste for authority—and especially police authority.   Joining with others of the same view and those whose beliefs are more firmly grounded in a support for our democratic processes, these people closely guard against the improper use of authority by the police.   It behooves law enforcement officials to refrain from unnecessarily creating a situation which annoys such individuals.   Such situations can be avoided through the exercise of proper discretion.[20]

There must be a realistic approach to policing. People will make mistakes, but often they are unintentional, or there are mitigating circumstances.   Proper use of discretion will allow for a "human touch" in policing.

PROBLEMS WITH DISCRETION

Difficulty in Reviewing

While discretion is necessary for effective police operations, it also presents some problems for the police administrator, largely because he rarely controls the use of discretion by his subordinates. "In view of the importance, complexity and delicacy of police work, it is curious that police administrators have seldom attempted to develop and articulate clear policies, aimed at guiding or governing the way policemen exercise their discretion on the street."[21] Since he does not accurately know to what extent discretion is used, the administrator is not in full control of his department. Rarely is he informed that discretion has been used by an officer. He knows it exists because of his own experience and feedback from officers, and occasionally it comes to light during the course of an investigation. However, he does not know with what frequency it occurs, under what circumstances, and who is applying it. Since discretion is usually not officially reported, the administrator does not have the opportunity to review the officers' actions. He thus loses a valuable opportunity to detect weakness and to make necessary training adjustments to correct the deficiencies.

Subjectivity

The use of discretion also holds the potential for abuse by the officer involved. As currently structured, it is a very subjective action. There are few guidelines for its use. As a result, the officer's personal feelings and prejudices often control its application. If discretion is not equally applied, it can be a source of discrimination and abuse of authority.

Corruption

Another abuse of discretion is that it can be used as a cover-up for corruption. An officer who takes money to overlook a traffic violation or to allow street gambling to function can explain his inaction as utilization of discretion. ". . . it enables a corruption-prone officer to make use of the unbridled discretion which he does in fact have in ways that will produce profits for himself—without having to account for his actions."[22] Such crimes by police officers are difficult to detect and even more difficult to prosecute. Mere observation of the violation is not sufficient to satisfy a successful corruption investigation. The corrupt officer must be caught in the act, and corroborating evidence be present. Discretion makes investigation of corruption complaints more difficult.

Citizen Dissatisfaction

The use of discretion may cause resentment on the part of some of the citizenry. Consider, for example, residents of a building near a park who call the police to complain about loud noises. If the responding officer resolves the matter with a warning, it may correct the problem, but can be a source of irritation to those who complained about the noise. A warning may be construed as "doing nothing." Many persons are influenced by television shows and movies where, by the end of the story, the officer takes action and "always gets his man," thus pleasing everyone. In real life officers frequently do not successfully investigate violations and often make mistakes or err in their judgment. The only way to be free from mistakes is to make no decision. Discretion extends the range of an officer's decision-making and may thus arouse some citizen dissatisfaction.

ENSURING PROPER DISCRETION

Recognition

The first step needed to ensure the proper use of discretion is for the chief administrator to admit that it exists and to recognize that it is vitally needed. ". . . there is today a steadily growing recognition of police discretion and increasing support for the contention that it is not only necessary and desirable, but should be openly acknowledged, structured, and controlled."[23] Without this recognition of discretion it is difficult for an administrator to exert influences on its uses. His influence is needed if he is to direct the operations of his department effectively. The administrator should not set rigid guidelines on discretion, as they would be as harmful as no guidelines at all. Rather he should determine what the goals of the organization are and then set general guidelines, allowing each officer to determine how he is going to achieve those goals. "A rule that structures discretion says to the officer: 'Within the area in which you have discretionary power, let your discretion be guided by these goals, policies, and principles, and follow these procedures that are designed to minimize arbitrariness.'"[24] It is not unreasonable for citizens to expect equality in enforcement from the guardians of the law. As many departments are currently structured, it is not unusual to find disparity in the way officers resolve matters. This should not be; each citizen should receive "equal treatement under the law." While methods used may be different, the end results should be generally the same.

Review

To ensure that discretion is being used properly, its use must be reviewed. "The real answer is to adopt practical administrative means for directing discretion, preferably by shared controls and by reviewing its exercise internally."[25] Superior officers must follow up on assignments handled by their subordinates. They should determine the resolution of the matter and why. On-the-job training should be given when they uncover violations of department guidelines. Superior officers should also provide feedback to the chief on misuses of discretion and trends they uncover.

It is easier to check on discretion when there is some type of formal reporting of its use. Some departments have officers issue formal warning notices to traffic violators whom they do not issue a summons or arrest. A duplicate copy of that notice provides the opportunity to review the officer's actions.

The use of forms to report an officer's field actions can also provide the basis of a review of his discretion. For example in New York City a "Stop and Frisk" report is prepared by officers when they stop and temporarily detain someone who they believe is committing a crime. If investigation reveals no wrongdoing on the part of the citizen, he is released, and a "Stop and Frisk" report is filed by the officer. A check of these forms will give insight into police street operations and the manner in which officers are using their discretion.

Reports from others in the criminal justice system provide a very good source of information for reviewing the discretionary actions of officers. Judges and prosecutors are well-situated to report on police discretion, especially its misuse. The media and citizens' comments may also give insight into the use of discretion by officers.

Controls

Formal controls are needed to regulate the discretionary actions of police officers. For instance, there is always concern when a police officer fires his weapon. Not only may he be deciding if someone lives or dies, but also he may be placing innocent persons in jeopardy. The threat is greater in larger municipalities where the population density compounds the danger. The working police officer usually takes a dim view of these controls, but they are necessary. In New York City since 1973, the Police Department has imposed restrictions on the use of firearms and established a Firearm Discharge Review Board to review shooting incidents. The guidelines contained in Interim Order 118, issued August 27, 1973, are more restrictive than the New York State Penal Law, the authority that determines when a police officer may fire his weapon in New York State. Clearly stated in the order is department policy concerning the use of firearms. If lives of innocent persons are endangered, the firing of warning shots and the use of a weapon are prohibited. Furthermore, the order limits the use of a weapon from or at a moving vehicle, as a means to summon assistance, or as a means of controlling animals. All members are held accountable regarding their use of discretion. Review of the shooting incidents is a very effective way of controlling discretion. Since the order's inception, the number of shooting incidents has been decreased (from 803 in 1972 to 448 in 1975), and the number of persons killed or shot has been reduced (from 247 to 169). These statistics substantiate the value of formal controls.

During the electrical blackout in New York City mentioned earlier, there was wide-scale looting. In a 24-hour period on July 13 and 14, 1977, over 3,000 persons were arrested for looting without the police resorting to shooting one criminal. This remarkable feat is directly related to the guidance provided by Interim Order 118 over the previous four years.

Definitive setting of policy by a police administrator can also be found in Interim Order 27, issued by the New York City Police Commissioner on August 5, 1977. Many police departments have experienced instances of overreaction by their officers to citizen observers at the scene of police incidents. This overreaction often escalates if the officers sense that the observers do not approve of their actions. Most arrests of observers at police scenes are ultimately dismissed, often resulting in costly lawsuits for the municipality, and may foster ill feelings for the police. Mindful of this, the Police Commissioner directed that speech alone, even though crude and vulgar, the requesting and making note of shield numbers or names of officers, the taking of photographs, and remaining in the vicinity of a stop or arrest, are not, by themselves, sufficient grounds for an arrest. He directed officers to refrain from making such arrests and held his commanders responsible for the order's being obeyed.

Thus the development of discretionary policy is possible. It must be clearly delineated. Although it will be unpopular with many officers, it is vitally needed. "The development of overall law enforcement policies must be made at the departmental level and communicated to individual officers. This is necessary if the issues are to be adequately defined and adequately researched and if discretion is to be exercised consistently throughout the department."[26]

Selection

Selection of proper candidates for police service will assist an administrator in his quest for the proper use of discretion. "Complexities inherent in the policing function dictate that officers possess a high degree of intelligence, education, tact, sound judgment, physical courage, emotional stability, impartiality, and honesty."[27]   Entrance examinations should be designed to test an applicant's intelligence, judgment, stability, and level of maturity. "Existing selection requirements and procedures in the majority of departments, aside from physical requirements, do not screen out the unfit."[28]   Interviews should be conducted, preferably by a psychiatrist or a psychologist, to determine if there are any flaws in the potential police officer. An extensive background investigation must be conducted on each candidate. "No department should admit any person into the police service until his background has been comprehensively investigated."[29] School records should be examined, neighbors interviewed, medical records scrutinized, previous employers spoken to, all with a view of detecting something that would make the applicant unfit to be a police officer. Any doubt about his suitability should be decided in favor of the department.

Training

There should be a formal training period of at least 12 weeks, during which the recruit should be exposed to police work. "... a recruit should be acquainted with the multiplicity of police functions, should learn the methods (informal as well as formal) the police use for intervening in incidents and for disposing of their business, and should be instructed in how to use his discretion in choosing among them."[30]   Following his training period, a recruit should be placed on probation to evaluate his performance. "A reliable evaluation cannot be made in a few months. For this reason, a probationary period should be eighteen months in length, and certainly no less than one year."[31]   During the training period the new officer should be closely observed, and his suitability to perform police duties should be monitored. Proper use of executive discretion is needed in eliminating marginal candidates from police service. If not eliminated, they often become sheltered by civil service laws which make removal difficult.

Training must not end once the recruit leaves the academy setting. "New laws are enacted and old ones amended; the enforcement needs of a community change, and new concepts of police technology and department policy emerge. These facts dictate that training be a continuing process."[32]   Daily roll-call training and frequent in-service training should stress current problems and highlight weaknesses. Discretion and its use will always be an appropriate topic for police training.

FUTURE DIRECTION

Shift from Past to Present

The beat officer of the past represented the ultimate of discretion in a police officer. He provided the intimate, personal, police–citizen contact and police presence frequently desired by the law-abiding segment of a community. He was familiar with his beat and knew the activities and behavior patterns of its residents. He knew those persons who belonged in his neighborhood and those who did not, and gauged his enforcement efforts accordingly. Most violations of laws were handled informally. Even serious crimes such as burglarly or grand larceny may not have been processed by prescribed procedures if he believed the violator had "roots in the community" and could be redeemed. He was not averse to directing a well-placed kick to the rear of some youth who he felt was "headed for trouble."

This style of policing has many weaknesses, one of which is that it is inefficient: "... it is a highly expensive form of coverage, geographically restrictive in nature, and can be wasteful of manpower."[33]   The demands of modern policing have mandated a shift from foot to motorized patrol. Because of the increased calls for service and an ever spiraling crime pattern, it is not practical or economically feasible to rely on foot patrol: "... it is rather obvious that the strategic deployment, throughout a city, of officers in radio-equipped vehicles is the most efficient way in which to create the kind of police readiness."[34]   However, in this transition the personal touch has been lost to policing. "The most significant weakness in American motor patrol operations today is the general lack of contact with citizens except when an officer has responded to a call. Forced to stay near the car's radio waiting an assignment, most patrol officers have few opportunities to develop closer relationships with persons living in the district."[35]

Citizen Involvement

The future direction of policing appears to lie in more citizen involvement, which is already happening in some of the larger cities, where groups are often formed to push for community demands. People are no longer content to sit back and let others control their destinies. In the not too distant future, communities will tell the police where they want enforcement emphasis placed. Naturally, this will limit a police officer's discretion. He will be aware of what is of concern to the community, and what is not, and guide his enforcement actions accordingly.   As stated earlier, such discretion will rarely be applicable to serious crimes; it will be applied to a myriad of minor violations, only a small portion of which are susceptible to enforcement because of manpower constraints. Instead of deciding himself what laws he is going to enforce, the individual officer will be increasingly influenced by what the people want.

Citizen desires will not be directly transmitted to the enforcement agent, but will be channeled through the organization managers. These managers must be carefully selected. "Police agencies must be led by articulate, well educated, up-to-date professional administrators who are informed as to new management theory, conscious of behavioral science application, and solicitous of the well-being of every citizen."[36]

Discretion is a valuable tool that can provide a more humanistic type of police service. It must be guided by the formation of department policy and intelligently applied by the officers in the field.

FOOTNOTES

1. Davis, Kenneth· C., *Discretionary Justice.*   Baton Rouge, Louisiana: Louisana State University Press (1969), p. 4.

2. Goldstein, Herman, *Policing a Free Society*. Cambridge, Massachusetts: Ballinger Publishing Company (1977), p. 106.
3. Blumberg, Abraham S., and Niederhoffer, Arthur (eds.), *The Ambivalent Force: Perspectives on the Police.* Waltham, Massachusetts: Xerox College Publishing (1970), p. 148.
4. Goldstein, *Policing a Free Society*, p. 108.
5. President's Commission on Law Enforcement and Administration of Justice, *Task Force Report: The Police.* Washington, D. C.: Government Printing Office (1967).
6. Blumberg and Niederhoffer, *The Ambivalent Force*, p. 140.
7. Goldstein, *Policing a Free Society*, p. 93.
8. Ibid., p. 142.
9. Miller, Frank, Dawson, Robert O., Dix, George E., and Parnas, Raymond I. (eds.), *The Police Function.* Mineola, New York: The Foundation Press, Inc. (1971), p. 58.
10. Goldstein, *Policing a Free Society*, p. 101.
11. Wilson, James Q., *Varieties of Police Behavior.* Cambridge, Massachusetts: Harvard University Press (1968), p. 80.
12. Davis, *Discretionary Justice*, p. 38.
13. Goldstein, *Policing a Free Society*, p. 112.
14. Ibid., p. 111.
15. Ibid., p. 14.
16. *New York Daily News*, December 13 to 20, 1976.
17. Goldstein, *Policing a Free Society*, p. 283.
18. Ibid., p. 290.
19. Ibid., p. 97.
20. Blumberg and Niederhoffer, *The Ambivalent Force*, p. 155.
21. President's Commission on Law Enforcement and Administration of Justice, *The Challenge of Crime in a Free Society.* Washington, D.C.: Government Printing Office (1967), p. 103.
22. Goldstein, *Policing a Free Society*, p. 200.
23. Ibid., p. 94.
24. Davis, Kenneth C., *Police Discretion.* St. Paul, Minnesota: West Publishing Company (1975), p. 145.
25. Miller, Dawson, Dix, and Parnas, *The Police Function*, p. 62.
26. President's Commission on Law Enforcement and Administration of Justice, *Task Force Report: The Police*, p. 19.
27. Ibid., p. 125.
28. Ibid.
29. Ibid., p. 129.
30. Goldstein, *Policing a Free Society*, p. 275.
31. President's Commission on Law Enforcement and Administration of Justice, *Task Force Report: The Police*, p. 132.
32. Ibid., p. 139.
33. Ibid., p. 54.
34. Goldstein, *Policing a Free Society*, p. 50.
35. President's Commission on Law Enforcement and Administration of Justice, *Task Force Report: The Police*, p. 54.
36. Cromwell, Paul F., Jr., and Keefer, George. *Police-Community Relations* St. Paul, Minnesota: West Publishing Company (1973), p. 22.

REFERENCES

Blumberg, Abraham S., and Niederhoffer, Arthur, *The Ambivalent Force: Perspectives on the Police.* Waltham, Massachusetts: Xerox College Publishing (1970).

Cromwell, Paul F., Jr., and Keefer, George, *Police-Community Relations.* St. Paul, Minnesota: West Publishing Company (1973).

Davis, Kenneth C., *Discretionary Justice.* Baton Rouge, Louisiana: Louisiana State University Press (1969).

Davis, Kenneth C., *Police Discretion.* St. Paul, Minnesota: West Publishing Company (1975).

Goldstein, Herman, *Policing a Free Society.* Cambridge, Massachusetts: Ballinger Publishing Company (1977).

Miller, Frank, Dawson, Robert O., Dix, George E., and Parnas, Raymond I., *The Police Function.* Mineola, New York: The Foundation Press, 1971.

President's Commission on Law Enforcement and Administration of Justice, *The Challenge of Crime in a Free Society.* Washington, D.C.: Government Printing Office (1967).

President's Commission on Law Enforcement and Administration of Justice, *Task Force Report: The Police.* Washington, D.C.: Government Printing Office (1967).

Wilson, James Q., *Varieties of Police Behavior.* Cambridge, Massachusetts: Harvard University Press (1968).

Leon Friedman's chapter, which follows, provides convincing evidence of the essential role of the public prosecutor in the American criminal justice system. Standing as he does between those who seek redress and the grand jury that must determine whether such redress is to be permitted, the public prosecutor plays one of the critical roles in the American legal system.

The public prosecutor has within the range of his discretion the responsibility for determining whether presentment should be made to a grand jury or whether it should not move forward. The merit of Leon Friedman's contribution is that it provides a historical overview of the background and changing functions of the public prosecutor and of the extent to which his discretionary decisions are reviewable by our appellate courts.

3

Discretion and Public Prosecution

Leon Friedman

"The prosecutor has more control over life, liberty, and reputation than any other person in America."[1] So wrote Attorney General (later Supreme Court Justice) Robert H. Jackson in 1940. His candid analysis of the range of prosecutorial discretion in our criminal justice system is still the starting point for any serious discussion of the subject.

> His discretion is tremendous. He can have citizens investigated and, if he is that kind of person, he can have this done to the tune of public statement and veiled or unveiled intimations. Or the prosecutor may choose a more subtle course and simply have a citizen's friends interviewed. . . . He may dismiss the case before trial, in which case the defense never has a chance to be heard. . . . [A] prosecutor stands a fair chance of finding at least a technical violation of some act on the part of almost anyone. . . . It is in this realm—in which the prosecutor picks some person whom he dislikes or desires to embarrass, or selects some group of unpopular persons and then looks for an offense, that the greatest danger of abuse of prosecuting power lies.[2]

Prosecutors in continental Europe are professional civil servants owing their allegiance to and under the responsibility of the judiciary rather than the executive department. In theory they have no discretion—they must prosecute all cases that the evidence allows to the fullest extent possible. And they have little if any role in the decision on sentencing. Recent studies have cast some doubt on the lack of discretion in the European systems,[3] but there is no question that American prosecutors have far greater decision-making power, and that the American system permits—indeed requires— that crucial decisions at all stages of the process be left in the hands of the public prosecutors with little if any supervision, control, or standards to guide them.

The reasons for this wide range of discretion are varied and complex:

1. *Separation of Powers.* Unlike the European systems, in the American system we consider the lack of control of prosecutors by the courts to be a virtue rather than a shortcoming. Each arm of government is supposed to be separate and distinct, with no control by one over the other. The power to prosecute belongs to the executive department. Under the Constitution, the President must execute the laws; that is, he must prosecute those who disobey them. If the different phases of the process—investigation, charging, granting immunity, prosecuting, plea bargaining—were supervised by the courts, the commingling of functions would raise serious due process problems. In addition, since many prosecutors are elected or chosen through the political process, they are, for good or bad, subject to popular pressures. Thus the democratic process that we all applaud requires some flexibility in what has been looked upon as a political office.

2. *Range and Vagueness of the Laws.* A wide range of penal laws are in force, which reach many phases of the day-to-day lives of citizens. These include prohibitions against intoxication, certain kinds of sexual behavior, almost any form of gambling, and more recently certain drug offenses—crimes that many people do not consider immoral. The tax laws prohibit any intentional falsification of returns, however small. Licenses or permits are necessary for many business activities, and the failure to secure the right document may lead to criminal charges. Bad check and non-support laws exist in every jurisdiction. In the business field, laws against securities violations, price-fixing, market-sharing, conflict of interest, or trading with the enemy are in force. Many Americans are unclear about what conduct is forbidden and may regularly violate such laws, in part because they do not feel their conduct is morally reprehensible. In addition, some of the criminal statutes are so loosely written, vague, or ambiguous on the one hand, or so complex and incomprehensible on the other, that it is often difficult to determine what behavior they cover. Legal prohibitions exist against many types of inchoate crimes (conspiracy, attempts, solicitation, aiding and abetting) and existing legal rules make these crimes applicable to what appears to laymen to be innocent behavior. All of this gives a prosecutor the opportunity to apply the criminal codes selectively.

3. *Lack of Institutional Controls.* In theory there are a number of institutional controls over a prosecutor that can limit his discretion. In practice they are seldom if ever applied. The grand jury, consisting of 23 citizens, is supposed to investigate a crime, call witnesses in front of it, question them, and determine whether to indict. In fact, it is the prosecutor who makes such decisions. In the rare cases in which a grand jury does not indict, it is usually because a prosecutor does not want any action taken. Any honest prosecutor will admit that the grand jury takes direction from him. Even if an exceptional grand jury asserted

itself against a prosecutor, he could always bring the matter before a second grand jury, since the double jeopardy clause does not apply to grand jury actions.[4] The fiction of an independent grand jury in fact plays into a prosecutor's hands. Since in theory the grand jury is reviewing what a prosecutor does, and itself consists of ordinary citizens who would protect other citizens being investigated, it seems permissible to grant a grand jury enormous powers of investigation. But those powers are being usurped by the prosecutor, giving him even more power than he had previously. A prosecutor's discretion is also limited in theory by a magistrate who can decide in a preliminary examination that a prosecution lacks merit. But the legal rules allow the preliminary examination to be eliminated if the grand jury has returned an indictment. Even when a grand jury has not acted, magistrates will not dismiss an indictment if there is any legal evidence presented that could lead a jury to convict even if the magistrate is himself dubious about the evidence. Thus there are no effective institutional controls over a prosecutor's decision to bring a criminal action.

4. *Discretion as Mercy.* Discretion is a two-way street. In the same way that discretion may be used to prosecute someone based on little if any evidence, discretion may also be applied not to prosecute someone, despite the fact that he is clearly guilty of a crime. Our criminal justice system encourages its participants to use their discretion mercifully—that is, in favor of the defendant—at all stages. Thus a district attorney may decide not to prosecute a youthful offender for stealing a car because it was his first offense, because he was under the influence of others, because the car was returned, and so on, even though technically the offender is just as guilty as the others. Other offenders may not be prosecuted because the evidence was secured illegally, or the offender had a compassionate reason for doing what he did, or he has already been punished in other ways (by losing his job, having his reputation tarnished). Still others may not be prosecuted because they have agreed to testify against their co-conspirators. We applaud prosecutors who take such actions. But they can do so only if they are given wide latitude in their decision to prosecute. Thus we have established and maintained a system that gives prosecutors great discretion at both ends of the spectrum.

The prosecutor's powers are enormous and almost unreviewable. If he decides to investigate a particular individual, he does not have to give any reason for doing so. Jonathan Goldstein, the former United States Attorney for New Jersey, developed an enviable reputation for his prosecution of fraud and white-collar crime. He has publicly stated that his investigations often began on a "hunch." If he heard about a particular municipal contract being signed, he might subpoena all the bank records of the participants without their knowing about it. (The Supreme Court has held that bank records of a depositor are owned by the bank, and therefore the depositor has no right to complain if bank records about him are subpoenaed.) Phone records and credit card records might also be secretly subpoenaed. Thus a prosecutor can build up an enormous file on a person and on his business and political activities. The prosecutor also decides whom to call before a grand jury, whom to grant immunity to, and whom to cite for contempt if he feels their answers are inadequate. Since the grand jury's powers are so sweeping and far-ranging, the courts seldom if ever put limits on what is done in the grand jury's name.

If a prosecutor decides not to bring a case, his decision is not reviewable. In the early days of the civil rights drive in the deep South, civil rights workers tried to force the federal government (particularly Robert F. Kennedy, as Attorney General) to bring federal criminal action against Mississippi sheriffs and police officers who were violating the rights of blacks and civil rights workers. They offered an impressive number of affidavits by the victims of these crimes, showing that civil rights violations had occurred. Nevertheless, the courts refused to order Kennedy to do anything.[5] Similarly, some of the victims of the state troopers who used excessive force in their recapture of Attica prison in 1971 tried to obtain a federal court order requiring prosecution of the state troopers. They were refused relief.[6]

The reluctance of the courts to order prosecution is understandable. After all, the prosecutor is in charge of the case when it reaches the courts. If he does not want to bring a prosecution, it is doubtful that he will enthusiastically press the charges. Thus the case is likely to be lost anyhow. Only in rare instances is it possible to appoint a special prosecutor, as when a conflict of interest is present. In addition, ordering a prosecutor to bring a case is inconsistent with the mercy we want him to show wherever possible.

The only time the courts have become involved in the decision not to prosecute is if the decision is based upon racial or other class-motivated grounds. In 1976 the NAACP brought a case against Attorney General Edward Levi charging that the FBI would not fully investigate charges of police brutality against blacks in Arkansas. This "the plaintiffs claim, was arbitrary and racially discriminatory conduct by federal officials." The federal judge hearing the case held that the complaint stated a good cause of action and that the plaintiffs "should be afforded an opportunity to support these allegations."[7]

However, even if the plaintiffs won such a case, the most they would receive is a court order requiring the prosecutors to exercise their discretion in a racially neutral manner. The courts would still not order a prosecutor to bring a particular case against a particular individual because of the impossibility of supervision and the other reasons noted above.

The same reasoning is applied if an individual complains that a prosecutor should have brought one charge rather than another, or that he should have granted immunity to one defendant rather than another co-defendant, or that he should have allowed one defendant rather than another to plead guilty. In each of these situations the courts are asked to review not *whether* to bring a prosecution but *how* it should be brought. The courts will not review the technical, day-to-day details of how a prosecutor does his job—what charges he brings, whom he selects to make a deal with, whether the person should be treated as an adult or a juvenile offender,[8] or whether multiple offender charges should be brought against anyone.[9] The matter was put directly by Chief Justice (then Circuit Judge) Warren E. Burger in a case in the District of Columbia:

> few subjects are less adapted to judicial review than the exercise by the Executive of his discretion in deciding when and whether to institute criminal proceedings or what precise charges shall be made, or whether to dismiss a proceeding once brought.[10]

There are two qualifications to this judicial hands-off policy. If the prosecutor's decision in these areas is made only on racial or class-motivated grounds, it can be challenged. In 1962, the Supreme Court considered a case in which the defendant complained of the fact that he alone had been charged as a multiple offender by the prosecutor despite the fact that five other individuals in exactly the same position as his were not treated the same way.[11] The Supreme Court answered his contention as follows:

> the conscious exercise of some selectivity in enforcement is not in itself a federal constitutional violation. Even though the statistics in this case might imply a policy of selective enforcement, it was not stated that the selection was deliberately based upon an unjustifed standard such as race, religion, or other arbitrary classification.[12]

Obviously if a prosecutor applied a habitual offender law only against blacks, Catholics, or Italians, his actions could be challenged on traditional equal protection grounds, in the same way that racially based decisions by a school administrator could be challenged.

In addition, the Supreme Court has recognized that a prosecutor's actions based upon vindictiveness may be reviewed by the courts. In *Blackledge v. Perry*,[13] the defendant, a prison inmate, had been accused of assault with a deadly weapon—a misdemeanor. He was found guilty in a lower North Carolina court by a judge sitting without a jury. He appealed his conviction, an action that would allow him to have a full jury trial in a superior court. Before his trial took place, the local prosecutor secured a grand jury indictment against him for assault with a deadly weapon with intent to kill—a serious felony—based upon the same conduct that gave rise to his first trial. He argued that the prosecutor had behaved vindictively; that is, that he had brought the more serious charges to punish the defendant for having taken the appeal. The Supreme Court said:

> A person convicted of an offense is entitled to pursue his statutory right [to appeal] without apprehension that the State will retaliate by substituting a more serious charge for the original one, thus subjecting him to a significantly increased potential period of incarceration. . . .

> Due process of law requires that such a potential for vindictiveness must not enter into North Carolina's two-tiered appellate process.[14]

Lower courts have begun to apply the *Blackledge* case to a number of different situations. In a California federal case, an illegal alien was charged with unlawful entry into the United States—a misdemeanor. Since he had illegally entered the United States a number of times, he could have been charged as a multiple offender—a felony, punishable by a maximum of two years in jail. He insisted on a jury trial for the misdemeanor. The United States Attorney then charged him as a multiple offender. His conviction on the more serious charge was reversed by a federal court of appeals.[15] The court said:

> the prosecution bears a heavy burden of proving that any increase in the severity of the alleged charges was not motivated by a vindictive motive. We do not question the prosecutor's authority to bring the felony charges in the first instance . . . nor do we question the prosecutor's discretion in choosing which charges to bring against a particular defendant. . . . But when, as here, there is a significant possibility that such discretion may have been exercised with a vindictive motive or purpose, the reason for the increase in the gravity of the charges must be made to appear. . . .

> On the record before us there is absolutely no evidence that justifies the increase in the charges brought against the [defendant].[16]

In a similar case, a postal worker was accused of obstructing the passage of the mail—a misdemeanor.[17] The United States Attorney already possessed evidence that the worker had thrown away mail that had postage due, which could have given rise to more serious charges. However, the government did not press for a felony indictment until the postal worker insisted on being tried by a District Court judge instead of by a U.S. Magistrate as the government wanted. Again the more serious charges were dismissed by the court on the ground of vindictiveness. In another case, a defendant refused to accept a plea bargain offered him by the prosecutor, who promptly secured a harsher indictment against him. Those new charges were dismissed.[18]

In a case growing out of Richard Nixon's transfer of his governmental papers to the National Archives, one of the persons involved, Frank DeMarco, Jr., was accused of filing false papers in connection with the gift which allowed Nixon to take a substantial tax deduction.[19]   DeMarco filed a motion to transfer the venue of the case to California where he lived. The Watergate Special Prosecutor objected to the transfer, since it would mean that the two individuals involved in the crime would not be tried together. One of the prosecutors told DeMarco's lawyer that if the case were transferred, more serious charges would be brought against DeMarco. He insisted on the change of venue, and additional charges were brought. The judge promptly dismissed them.

The *Blackledge* principle is rarely applied. It comes into play only when the prosecutor has an option on the charges to bring and presses more serious charges at a later time in retaliation for the exercise of a defendant's constitutional rights.[20]   But the more serious problem remains: what can be done to challenge the prosecutor's decision to bring any charges at all?

We have had a long history in this country of what now appear to be politically motivated trials.[21]   A prosecutor may bring criminal charges on the flimsiest of grounds against representatives (often the leaders) of opposition groups to suppress their polictical activities or at the least to shed unfavorable light on their political efforts. Opponents of the existing regime, or dissident groups challenging the existing order, or even specific individuals who oppose one or more policies of the government, have been targets of elusive and ambiguous criminal laws, which focus primarily on their open political actions. The following examples are familiar to most students of American law and politics:

1. In the period from 1798 to 1800 the Federalist party used the Alien and Sedition Acts to indict a number of their political opponents in the Jeffersonian-Republican party merely for voicing criticism of the government.

2. Union members in the early part of the nineteenth century were indicted for organizing other workers, striking, or picketing in violation of common law conspiracy laws.

3. In the period before the Civil War it was made a crime in all the southern states to be a member of an abolition society or to suggest that owners had no property rights in slaves.

4. Eight anarchist leaders were indicted for conspiracy to murder after the Haymarket bombing of 1886 when eight policemen were killed. Five of the defendants were not even present at the meeting where the bombing occurred, but all were tried and found guilty, since they had advocated the use of violence in labor disputes.

5. During World War I, leading members of the IWW and the Socialist party

were indicted for interfering with the recruitment of men for the Army because they said in public speeches that the war was a capitalist war and was not in the interests of the working man.

6. In 1941, the leaders of a Minneapolis teamster union, leaders of a dwindling Trotskyite faction, were indicted under the recently enacted Smith Act for conspiring to plot the violent overthrow of the government. The indictments were instigated by national teamster leaders who had important influence with the Roosevelt administration and applauded by the Communist party, to whom the Trotskyites were anathema.

7. During the civil rights drive of the early 1960s, many black activists and their supporters were casually arrested by southern authorities on charges of disturbing the peace for distributing voter registration information or protesting or demonstrating in any way.

8. During the Vietnam war, Benjamin Spock and four others were indicted for conspiring to counsel young men not to enter the armed forces. The charges were based entirely on their meetings and printed manifestos opposing the war and supporting young draft resisters. The prosecutions grew out of a dispute between the Justice Department and General Lewis Hershey of the Selective Service System, who insisted that action be taken.[22]

It is doubtful that a single one of the criminal charges outlined above would hold up under the current state of the law. Except for the Haymarket affair, no one was accused of violence against persons or property, and the defendants' open political activity was the basis of the charges. There is little question that the primary offense of the defendants was that they were political opponents of the party in power, and the government saw some political gain for itself in bringing the cases. The vagueness and overbreadth of the criminal laws and the existing legal rules granting prosecutors such broad discretion allowed the prosecutors to select a politically unpopular group of defendants for criminal action.

Such political prosecutions are not the only danger that arises from unfettered prosecutorial discretion. A prosecutor may bring criminal charges against someone because of personal animosity. The authorities may use the criminal law to favor one economic group against another. Or cases can be brought based on racial or ethnic prejudice. Legal rules are necessary to check all of these abuses.

In recent years, state and federal courts have begun to fashion standards to check into abuse of prosecutorial discretion and to set up barriers to selective enforcement of the law. The legal building blocks for the new rules have been available for some period of time. As long ago as 1886 the Supreme Court considered the discriminatory administration of an ordinance in the case of *Yick Wo v. Hopkins.*[23] San Francisco had passed an ordinance requiring a license for the operation of laundries in wooden buildings in the city. The administrative board passing on the licenses granted them to 69 out of the 70 white applicants but to only 40 out of 240 Chinese applicants. One of the persons denied a license was prosecuted, and after he was convicted, complained that he was the object of racial discrimination by the authorities. The Supreme Court ordered him released. The Court held that the law was being applied discriminatorily:

> Though the law be fair on its face and impartial in appearance, yet, if it applied and administered by public authority with an evil eye and an unequal hand, so as practically to make unjust and illegal discrimations between persons in similar circumstances, material to their rights, the denial of equal justice is still within the prohibition of the Constitution.[24]

Although the decision of the Supreme Court was directed to the actions of the licensing board, the principles enunciated could be applied as well to other prosecutorial decisions. But there are problems in applying *Yick Wo* to prosecutors. If a person is admittedly in violation of the law, why should the courts protect him only because other persons are not being prosecuted? How thorough must the discrimination be? How can you prove that the prosecutor was motivated by racial or religious discrimination or any other "evil eye" or "unequal hand"?

It is only in recent years that the courts have tried to answer these questions. The first cases involved outright racial discrimination, such as that involved in *Yick Wo*. In a 1959 California case, a black defendant arrested on gambling charges claimed that the police were enforcing the laws almost completely against blacks and were ignoring whites who were also gambling. The trial judge accepted the argument in these words.

> I take great exception to what I term a discriminatory pattern of enforcement of the gambling laws of this city. It is my opinion they are enforced mostly against members of the Negro race. If I were to take the [Chief of Police's] figures as they speak to this, it would leave me to believe that Negroes, who constitute 10 percent of the population of this city, are responsible for 90 percent of the gambling in this city. I refuse to believe that as the truth.[25]

On appeal the superior court reversed the dismissal of the charges because no proof was offered to show the discrimination charged. The appeal court said, however:

> Beyond doubt, where the laws have been enforced in a discriminatory manner, with the intent and purpose to deny the equal protection of the law to any persons or group of persons, a discriminatory enforcement of a statute fair on its face when established by adequate proof may invalidate an otherwise proper conviction.[26]

In a later case growing out of the Watts riot,[27] the defendants were convicted of violating a section of the Los Angeles Municipal Code prohibiting fixing any sign to private property. The defendants had written "B - - -, B - - -, B - - -" which authorities said stood for "Burn, Baby, Burn." There was evidence that there were hundreds of violations of the law, but only two complaints had been brought in the past six months. Thus, the defendants claimed, the law was discriminatorily applied against them because the authorities did not like the black-militant slogan associated with the sign. The California Supreme Court acknowledged that if the defendants could prove such discriminatory enforcement of the law, they would have a defense to the charges.

The New York courts were arriving at the same conclusions. In one of the first cases that thoroughly discussed the issue of selective enforcement, the defendant had been accused of violating the state's Sunday closing laws. While he admitted the crime, he claimed that many other stores in Utica stayed open on Sunday, but only his discount drug store and one other cut-rate store were prosecuted. The Appellate court said that the defendant had a valid defense to the charges:

> The claim of discriminatory enforcement does not go to the question of the guilt or innocence of the defendant, which is within the province of the jury. The question is whether in a community in which there is general disregard of a particular law with the acquiescence of the public authorities, the authorities should be allowed sporadically to select a single defendant or a single class of defendants for prosecution because of animosity or some other illegitimate reason. The wrong sought to be prevented is a wrong by the public authorities. To allow such arbitrary and discriminatory enforcement of a generally disregarded law is to place in the hands of the police and the prosecutor a power of the type frequently invoked in countries ruled by a dictator but wholly out of harmony with the principle of equal justice under law prevailing in democratic societies. The court is asked to stop the prosecution at the threshold, not because the defendant is innocent, but because the public authorities are guilty of a wrong in engaging in a course of conduct designed to discriminate unconstitutionally against the defendant.[28]

The court acknowledged that the defendant had a heavy burden in proving discrimination. It pointed out that a prosecutor might have legitimate reasons for selectively enforcing the law, "when the meaning or constitutionality of the law is in doubt and a test case is needed to clarify the law or to establish its validity."[29] A prosecutor might also want to seek a "striking example of a few examples . . . to deter other violators, as part of a bona fide rational pattern of general enforcement."[30] It is only when the selective enforcement was designed "to discriminate against the persons prosecuted, without any intention to follow it up by general enforcement against others, that a constitutional violation may be found."[31]

In a later New York case, *People v. Walker*,[32] the defendant was charged with various violations of the Multiple Dwelling Law because of the manner in which she maintained a building. She claimed that she was being prosecuted by the Department of Buildings for exposing corruption by certain building inspectors who had demanded a bribe from her. The New York Court of Appeals held that such retaliatory prosecution could not be permitted, and proof of such charges could lead to a dismissal. Eventually she was able to prove her charges, and her case was dismissed.[33]

The federal courts were also examining the problem of selective enforcement. In Portland, Oregon a special agent of the Internal Revenue Service instigated an indictment for tax evasion against a local lawyer who had been active in the National Lawyers Guild and had vocally opposed American policy in Cuba and Vietnam. The report of the agent recommending criminal action contained statements that the lawyer was a suspected Communist, that he had organized a chapter of the Lawyers Guild in Portland, and that he often wrote letters to the editor opposing American policy in Southeast Asia and elsewhere. The agent recommended that the lawyer be indicted for income tax fraud because he had taken a much larger depreciation allowance than the law allows—a deviation from the tax laws that rarely if ever has led to criminal prosecution.

A federal appeals court threw out the conviction. The majority did not consider the lawyer's action to amount to willful violation of the law. One of the judges went further:

I regard what I have recited above [about the background to the prosecution] as a scandal of the first magnitude in the administration of the tax laws of the United States. It discloses nothing less than a witch-hunt, a crusade by the key agent of the United States in this prosecution, to rid our society of unorthodox thinkers and actors by using federal income tax laws and federal courts to put them in the penitentiary.[34]

In a case in the District of Columbia, a motorist was stopped by the police for alleged traffic violations. They took no action against him. Two days later the motorist complained to the police department about the conduct of the police who had stopped him. The city lawyer told the motorist that if he would drop his complaint, the city would not press any traffic violations against him. The motorist nevertheless continued with his complaint, and the city instituted criminal action against him for the original traffic violation. The Court of Appeals dismissed the charges, since it found that the government's action was improper:

> prosecutors have broad discretion to press or drop charges. But there are limits. If for example, the Government had legitimately determined not to prosecute appellant and had then reversed its position solely because he filed a complaint, this would clearly violate the first amendment. The Government may not prosecute for the purpose of deterring people from exercising their right to protest official misconduct and petition for redress of grievances.[35]

With the rise of public protest over the Vietnam war, the problem of selective enforcement of the law came into the courts with greater frequency. One of the first cases involved a group of Quakers who held a peace worship service in the Pentagon.[36]   They were prosecuted for making loud and unusual noises in government buildings. In their defense they showed that an Army band had played in exactly the same place where they had held their service and no action had been taken against the players. There were 16 other meetings in the same place with no complaint from the authorities. The court of appeals threw out the prosecution.

In another case, arising in Hawaii, the government prosecuted a young man for refusing to answer questions for the 1970 census. He was a vocal opponent of the census and had urged other citizens not to cooperate with the census takers. He held press conferences, distributed leaflets, and appeared on radio shows protesting against snooping by the government into a citizen's private life. He and three associates were investigated by the government as "hard-core resisters," and eventually criminal charges were brought. The court of appeals threw out his conviction: "We conclude that Steele demonstrated a purposeful discrimination by census authorities against those who had publicly expressed their opinion about the census."[37]

The most important case dealing with selective enforcement grew out of a prosecution for draft evasion.[38]   Jeffrey Falk was an active member of a draft counseling organization and a vocal critic of the government's policy on the draft and the war. He was one of thousands of individuals who had sent their draft cards in to the Attorney General in protest against the war in December 1967. He also sent his draft registration card to a federal judge in November 1968. In May 1970 he was ordered to be inducted into the army but refused to appear. He was then indicted (in October 1970) for draft evasion and in three separate counts for his failure to possess his draft cards. At his trail he was acquitted of the draft evasion charge but convicted of the three non-possession counts. He appealed the convictions, claiming that he was singled out for prosecution because of his draft-counseling and antiwar activities.

Falk made an impressive showing that the law was being applied particularly against him. He cited published figures showing that approximately 25,000 persons had handed in their draft cards but only a handful were prosecuted for non-possession, usually when they destroyed their cards at the same time. Official publications of the Selective Service System stated that there was an agreement between the Justice Department and Selective Service that non-possessors would not be prosecuted, but would be handled administratively. Finally, almost three years had elapsed from the time he first sent in his card to the time when he was indicted for non-possession.

At his trial, Falk offered to show that the government was well aware of his draft-counseling activities and his protest actions against the Vietnam war. The Assistant U.S. Attorney handling the case told the court that the indictment had been approved not only by his superiors in Chicago but by the Department of Justice itself.

The Seventh Circuit Court of Appeals, sitting en banc, reversed the convictions. Citing the *Crowthers*, *Steele*, and *Dixon* cases, the court found that Falk had made out a prima facie case of discriminatory enforcement of the law for the purpose of inhibiting his exercise of first amendment rights. The court reviewed all the factors in Falk's favor:

> To summarize, the combination in this case of the published government policy not to prosecute violators of the card possession regulations, Falk's status as an active and vocal dissenter to United States policy with regard to the draft and the Vietnam War, the Assistant United States Attorney's statement that officials ranging from an Assistant Attorney to the Department of Justice in Washington participated in the decision to prosecute Falk, the untimely delay in bringing the indictment and the government's stated policy to prosecute only those who refuse induction while absolving those who submit to the will of the authorities, lead us to conclude that the district court erred in refusing a hearing on the offer of proof.[39]

The *Falk* case established the defense of selective enforcement as an accepted part of the law. The fact that an important federal court of appeals sitting with all its members participating would recognize such a defense made it eminently respectable.

A series of cases followed *Falk* and considered the elements of the selective enforcement defense. One of the most important was the Second Circuit decision in *United States v. Berrios*.[40] In that case a teamster union official was indicted for violating a federal law that prohibited a person convicted of a felony within five years from holding union office. Berrios had been convicted of arson within the five-year period. Berrios claimed that he had been indicted because he had supported Senator George McGovern for president in 1972, against the wishes of his union superiors. He had also led a strike against the Marriott chain, which had close personal and family ties to President Nixon. His lawyer offered to show that there were many unprosecuted violations of the law in question. The trial judge then ordered the government to produce its file seeking authorization to proceed with the prosecution. On appeal the Second Circuit held that the defense was entitled to see all evidence in the government's files relevant to the defense of selective prosecution. The court established the standards of the defense as follows:

> To support a defense of selective or discriminatory prosecution, a defendant bears the heavy burden of establishing, at least prima facie, (1) that while others similarly situated have not generally been proceeded against because of conduct of the type forming the basis of the charge against him, he has been singled out for prosecution, and (2) that the government's discriminatory selection of him for prosecution has been invidious or in bad faith, i.e., based upon such impermissible considerations as race, religion or the desire to prevent his exercise of constitutional rights.[41]

The final important case in this area was decided in 1975 by the California Supreme Court.[42]   Six members of the United Farm Workers were prosecuted for malicious mischief, reckless driving, driving without a license, and violating a court order. All these charges were based upon their activities as union organizers in Kern County, California. The defendants charged that the law enforcement officials had adopted a policy of using the criminal laws selectively against anyone associated with the UFW for the purpose of discouraging them from engaging in union activities. The California court said that the defendants could not be prosecuted if they proved their claims:

> in order to establish a claim of discriminatory enforcement, a defendant must demonstrate that he has been deliberately singled out for prosecution on the basis of some invidious criterion. Because the particular defendant, unlike similarly situated individuals, suffers prosecution simply as the subject of invidious discrimination, such defendant is very much the direct victim of the discriminatory practice. Under these circumstances, discriminatory prosecution becomes a compelling ground for dismissal of the criminal charge, since the prosecution would not have been pursued except for the discriminatory design of the prosecuting authorities.[43]

Following *Falk* and *Berrios*, there has been an explosion of cases in which claims of selective enforcement have been made. Many of them do not involve politically active individuals but others who claim they were unfairly picked out for prosecution. "Skitch" Henderson, the famous band leader, was prosecuted for income tax evasion because of the fraudulent donation of his musical scores to a university library, for which he claimed a large income tax deduction. The charges against him were precisely the same as those made against President Nixon, but only Henderson was criminally charged. The court said that was not enough to prove selective enforcement, since others were prosecuted for the same crime.[44]

The three major television networks claimed that a minor antitrust suit brought against them was the result of the Nixon administration's unhappiness with the way in which the President was portrayed on television.[45] A butcher prosecuted under the federal Meat Inspection Law claimed that he was being prosecuted only because he was Italian, and that the law was not generally enforced. His case was eventually dismissed because the government refused to produce its file on the case.[46] A customs official was prosecuted for illegally wiretapping and bugging a suspected drug dealer. He claimed that members of the Drug Enforcement Authority did the same thing but were not prosecuted. He also claimed that he had been selected because he was in Customs, which was part of the Treasury Department, while DEA officers were part of Justice, which was involved in a bureaucratic squabble with the other executive department. The claim was rejected, since the defendant could not prove that DEA agents committed the same crime but were not prosecuted.[47] In a similar case, a Connecticut state trooper was indicted for assaulting an FBI agent. He claimed that the agent was drunk and the federal government was trying to cover up the misconduct of one of its agents. The government answered this claim by showing that it regularly enforced the law in question. Besides, the government said, there was no "arbitrary, invidious or unjustifiable standard, such as race, religion, color or the desire to prevent his exercise of a constitutional right."[48]

The most troublesome cases have been in the tax area. Tax evasion laws are generally applied in this country. But suppose special resources are applied to check the tax returns of organized crime figures to see if criminal charges can be brought against them. Or a political enemy's returns may be examined to see if there is any basis for a prosecution. Or a prominent person in the community may be selected for tax evasion charges although lesser known individuals would have been ignored for doing the same things. How should a court react to these situations?

James Scott was the leader of the "Tax Rebellion Committee" and a self-styled national tax resistance leader. He was quite vocal in his opposition to the income tax. When he was prosecuted for income tax evasion, he claimed that, like Mr. Steele, he had been selected for prosecution because he was a prominent and vocal opponent of the tax laws. But, unlike Steele, he could not show that the laws were generally not enforced. Thus his claim was rejected.[49]

Another accused tax evader claimed that charges were brought against him because he had become involved in a personal fight with the District Director of Internal Revenue. Even if that were true, the court said, "the defendant failed to allege, or make a substantial showing that prosecutions are normally not instituted for the offenses with which he was charged."[50]

A prominent anti-Vietnam war leader in Minnesota, William Ojala, refused to file any tax returns from 1969 to 1971 as a protest against the war. When he was running for reelection as a state representative, the press reported on his failure to file returns. Shortly thereafter, he was indicted by the federal government for failure to file his returns. He claimed that there were 51,000 tax delinquency investigations in Minnesota from 1969 to 1971. About 4,000 possible tax violations were brought to the attention of the IRS Intelligence Division. But only nine cases of failure to file were prosecuted. Ojala claimed that he was selected because of his antiwar policies and because of his prominence within the state. He also claimed that the IRS moved more swiftly than usual to bring him up on criminal charges. The court rejected his claim. It said that prosecuting a person because of his prominent position in the community was a proper use of the tax laws. "It makes good sense to prosecute those who will receive the media's attention. Publication of the proceedings will enhance the deterrent effect of the prosecution and maintain public faith in the precept that public officials are not above the law."[51] Furthermore, the public announcement that he had disobeyed the law required swift action. Other cases had held that it is proper to pay special attention to tax delinquencies by attorneys, accountants, and other professionals.[52]

The law of selective enforcement is now firmly established in American law. Although the courts have retreated from the ready acceptance of the defense that followed the Falk case, they have now established legal standards for testing the defense and institutional procedures for determining whether it is validly invoked. The acceptance of the defense should not seriously interfere with the legitimate activities of prosecutors. A defendant must show a general policy of non-enforcement of a particular law. Even then, if a prosecutor can show some valid reason for applying the law, the courts will approve his actions. Thus if he resurrects a law that had been generally ignored and announces that it will be enforced again, the courts will probably decide that a legitimate law enforcement purpose is being served. If he carefully selects a case to test a new law, that will be considered permissible. In short, almost any activity that shows an intent to enforce the law on a wide scale will pass muster.

As for proving improper motive, the defendant has the burden of showing either that the prosecution was based on improper classification by the government or that it acted to chill his exercise of constitutional rights. The courts will not readily accept such claims, since they start with a premise that the government usually acts in good faith.

Nevertheless we have advanced far from the days when a prosecutor's actions were considered unreviewable. He was the last government official whose discretion became subject to check. Yet he was the one, as Robert Jackson said almost 40 years ago, who had the greatest control over our day-to-day lives.

FOOTNOTES

1. Jackson, Robert H., The federal prosecutor. *Journal of American Judicature Society 24:* 18, 19 (1940).
2. Ibid.
3. See Goldstein, Abraham S., and Marcus, Martin, The myth of judicial supervision in three "inquisitorial" systems: France, Italy and Germany. *Yale Law Journal 87:* 240 (December 1977); Davis, Kenneth, *Discretionary Justice in Europe and America* Urbana, Ill. (1976).
4. In the nineteenth century, the grand jury played a truly independent role—investigating political corruption and setting itself apart from the prosecutor. There are a number of reported cases in which the grand jury would exclude the prosecutor from their operations. But in this century that independence has disappeared. The legal rules became more complex and beyond the scope of most lay grand jurors. A prosecutor can assert his point of view because of his superior knowledge of the law. In addition, grand jurors were more selectively chosen and came to reflect the law-and-order position of the prosecutor. In general, the population has simply become more pliant when dealing with persons in authority.
5. *Moses v. Kennedy*, 219 F. Supp. 762 (D.D.C. 1963).
6. *Inmates of Attica v. Rockefeller*, 477 F.2d 375 (2d Cir. 1973). In the summer of 1977, a group representing "battered wives" brought an action against New York City police personnel and Family Court personnel for refusing to apply the criminal law against husbands who beat up their wives. A New York Supreme Court Justice stated that "this court has the power to compel the Police Department defendants to perform the duty imposed upon them by law to exercise their discretion, and to exercise it in a reasonable, non-arbitrary manner" [*Bruno v. Codd*, 46 L.W. 2042 (N.Y. Sup. Ct. July 6, 1977)]. No prosecutors were involved in the case since the police rarely made arrests that could lead to prosecution.
7. *NAACP v. Levi*, 418 F. Supp. 1109 (D.D.C. 1976).
8. See *Woodward v. Wainwright*, 556 F.2d 781 (5th Cir. 1977). See also *United States v. Partyka*, 561 F.2d 118 (8th Cir. 1977).
9. *Martin v. Parratt*, 549 F.2d 50 (8th Cir. 1977).
10. *Newman v. United States*, 382 F.2d 479, 480 (D.C. Cir. 1967).
11. *Oyler v. Boles*, 368 U.S. 448 (1962).
12. Ibid., at 456.
13. 417 U.S. 21 (1974).
14. Ibid., at 28.
15. *United States v. Ruesga-Martinez*, 534 F.2d 1367 (9th Cir. 1976).
16. Ibid., at 1369.
17. *United States v. Lippi*, 435 F. Supp. 808 (D.N.J. 1977).
18. *Hayes v. Cowan*, 547 F.2d 42 (6th Cir. 1976).
19. *United States v. DeMarco*, 401 F. Supp. 505 (C.D. Calif. 1975).

20. If a prosecutor can offer any plausible reason for bringing more serious charges at a later time, the courts will generally accept them. See *United States v. Partyka*, 561 F.2d 118 (8th Cir. 1977), where the court accepted the prosecutor's argument that more serious charges were brought because an informer's identity had been revealed, and it was no longer necessary to protect him.
21. See Friedman, Leon, Political power and legal legitimacy: A short history of political trials, *Antioch Review 30:* 157 (Summer 1970).
22. Mitford, Jessica, *The Trial of Dr. Spock* (New York, 1969).
23. 118 U.S. 356 (1886).
24. Ibid., at 373-74.
25. *People v. Winters*, 342 P.2d 538, 540 (Super. Ct. L.A. Cty 1959).
26. Ibid., at 540.
27. *People v. Gray*, 254 Cal. App 2d 256 (1967).
28. *People v. Utica Daw's Drug Company*, 225 N.Y.S. 2d 128, 133 (4th Dept. 1962).
29. Ibid., at 136.
30. Ibid.
31. Ibid.
32. 252 N.Y.S. 2d 96 (1964).
33. *People v. Walker*, 271 N.Y.S. 2d (1966).
34. *Lenske v. United States*, 383 F.2d 20, 27 (9th Cir. 1967) (Madden, J. concurring).
35. *Dixon v. District of Columbia*, 394 F.2d 966, 968 (D.C. Cir. 9168).
36. *United States v. Crowthers*, 456 F.2d 1074 (4th Cir. 1971).
37. *United States v. Steele*, 461 F.2d 1148, 1152 (9th Cir. 1972).
38. *United States v. Falk*, 479 F.2d 616 (7th Cir. 1973).
39. Ibid., at 623.
40. 501 F.2d 1207 (2d Cir. 1974).
41. Ibid., at 1211.
42. *Murguia v. Municipal Court for Bakersfield Judicial District*, 124 Cal. Rptr. 204, 540 P.2d 44 (1975).
43. 540 P. 2d at 51-52.
44. *United States v. Henderson*, 386 F. Supp. 1048 (S.D.N.Y. 1974).
45. *United States v. National Broadcasting Co. et al.*, No. 72-819-RJK (C.D. Calif. November 26, 1974).
46. *United States v. Cammisano*, 433 F. Supp. 964 (W.D. Mo. 1977).
47. *United States v. Kelly*, 556 F.2d 257 (5th Cir. 1977).
48. *United States v. Carson*, 434 F. Supp. 806, 809 (D. Conn. 1977).
49. *United States v. Scott*, 521 F.2d 1188 (9th Cir. 1975). See also *United States v. Oaks*, 527 F.2d 937 (9th Cir. 1975).
50. *United States v. Bourque*, 541 F.2d 290, 293 (1st Cir. 1976).
51. *United States v. Ojala*, 544 F.2d 940, 944 (8th Cir. 1976).
52. *United States v. Swanson*, 509 F.2d 1205 (8th Cir. 1975).

Robert Buckhout and his colleagues at Brooklyn College, City University of New York, examine the role of discretion in the selection of jurors. In their treatment, it is clear that conflicting aspirations and forces operate — prosecutors seek jurors who will convict, and defendants' lawyers look for jurors who will acquit their clients. What is known about how such conflicting motivations and objectives are reconciled and a group of jurors is qualified to sit on a particular jury?

Using an experimental model and a mock trial procedure, the authors provide a statement of the dynamic properties of jury groups, the emergence of juror roles, and the effect of such roles upon the prospective course of jury behavior and trial outcome, as determined by empirical observation and experimental study.

4
Discretion in Jury Selection[1]

Robert Buckhout, Jeffery Licker,[2]
Murray Alexander, John Gambardella,
Paul Eugenio, and Bill Kakoullis

INTRODUCTION

In recent years a great deal of research has been directed toward the jury selection process with a focus on the voir dire, that phase of a jury trial in which potential jurors are questioned about their attitudes, prejudices, and backgrounds
(Schulman, et al., 1973). Lawyers selecting for either side rely on experience,
intuition, superstitution, body-language, appearance cues, and prejudices to
choose jurors in an arena where they can rarely check the accuracy of their predictions (Tate, 1974). Many lawyers will cite Clarence Darrow, who is alleged to
have said that he looked for emotional jurors—especially women—so that an appeal to the emotions could influence their verdict. The bottom line of course is
that prosecutors look for jurors who will convict; defense attorneys look for
jurors who will acquit. Zeisel and Diamond (1976) report that in a study of
jurors rejected by attorneys, both sides were "somewhat" effective in rejecting
prospective jurors who were detrimental to their interests; but, defense attorneys
were better at challenging jurors who were found later to have had a predisposition to convict the defendant than prosecutors were in rejecting jurors prone to
acquit. The authors wrote a detailed account of the jury selection process in the
John Mitchell–Maurice Stans conspiracy trial, in which social science survey data
were used by the defense along with lawyer intuition to select a jury that ultimately acquitted the defendants. Christie (1975) reports that there are some
data which show that lawyers and psychologists are very imprecise in predicting
a juror's verdict on the basis of observation alone.

This recent entry of social scientists into the jury selection process creates a
familiar conflict between psychology and the law. Going beyond the well-

documented ethical debate (Etzioni, 1974) is the question of whether a social scientist's measures have a degree of predictive validity that is sufficiently superior to the lawyer's intuition to justify the costs. It can be argued that the weight of evidence, lawyer skills, characteristics of a defendant, and so forth, are all more important than personality of jurors as determinants of as simple a measure as a verdict. Indeed Saks (1976a, b) goes so far as to dismiss the concept of personality-determining attitudes altogether; apparently *they* (jurors) all look alike to him. He presents data showing that the amount and strength of trial evidence accounted for a higher proportion of the variance of a "certainty of guilt measure" than did attitudes of the jurors. Saks goes on to question the claims made by the advocates of scientific jury selection through attitude and personality assessment, feeling that while it may help in a close case, it doesn't matter who is on the jury if the evidence against the defendant is very strong or very weak.[3]

The truth about this controversy may be that neither the research data nor inadequately quantified trial experiences can give a definitive answer at this time. Psychological research with mock juries has always been limited by the lack of real motivation by "jurors," inadequate sampling, and short-cut experimental designs that rely on individual reactions to case summaries rather than group-deliberated jury verdicts (Foss, 1975). Quantitative analyses of real voir dires or real juror attitudes are rare. The main practitioners of scientific jury selection—Richard Christie and Jay Schulman—have simply been too busy winning cases (e.g., the Gainesville 8 trial; the Joan Little trial) either to write or critically evaluate the predictive validity of their techniques (Christie, 1975; Bush, 1976). It is Christie's belief that even in cases where the evidence against the defendant is weak or nonexistent (as in many political cases), defendants are prosecuted, juries do deliberate, and the attitudes and personalities of the jurors are relevant. Attitudes can determine how jurors will react to evidence—indeed, how they may vote without any evidence.

In the application of such selection techniques (Kairys, 1975), the usual pattern involves conducting a survey of registered voters in the community (from whom jurors are called), factor analysis of the attitudinal items, assignment of factor scores to each individual, profile analysis[4] of the distribution of factor scores according to the demographics of the sample, and the use of a simplified courtroom index to classify jurors as information comes in during the voir dire. The factor scores usually consist of *authoritarianism*, a direct measure of *guilt* (if the defendant is known), and, on occasion, a unique factor peculiar to the case.[5] Potential jurors are ranked according to the degree to which they match the desired profile. To a great extent the lawyer seeks to eliminate people with a high probability of bias toward their side. In an adversary system, where both the defense and the prosecution can accept or reject jurors, the people chosen for the jury are evaluated on how well they may function in a coalition within the larger group. Thus, theory and practice converge on a model that will predict the interaction of a personality type in the setting of a group charged with deliberating to arrive at a unanimous decision on guilt or innocence.

The authoritarian personality (Adorno et al., 1950) has been studied empirically in mock jury research for many years; many lawyers have a rather good intuitive grasp of the typology. Mitchell and Byrne (1973) found that there was a significant interaction between authoritarianism and attitude similarity on certainty of defendant's guilt and recommended severity of punishment. The higher the F-scale score, the more severe was the recommended sentence. The F scale is considered a good predictor of authoritarianism; however, according to Boehm (1968), it is not relevant to jury research. She reports that, "Few of the items measure attitudes specifically relevant to the jury decision making process." It is for this reason that she set out to devise a test which would correlate with the F scale and Rokeach's Dogmatism scale and also be relevant to the jury decision process. Boehm developed the Legal Attitudes Questionnaire (LAQ) scale—a simple forced-choice test yielding three scores: authoritarianism, equalitarianism, and antiauthoritarianism. The highest of these three scores defines the label placed on the person.

Boehm defines the authoritarian trait as a right wing (law and order) philosophy, with a trend toward punitiveness and rigidity. Antiauthoritarian items express left-wing sentiments and imply blame on society for antisocial acts. The equalitarian items endorse traditional liberal, nonextreme positions on legal questions and virtually parrot the United States Constitution.

Boehm tested jurors with the LAQ in a mock trial setting, finding that "those who go against the trend (of acquittal) and convict on the evidence provided in a 'not guilty' case are more authoritarian than those who follow the trend." In her study both authoritarians and antiauthoritarians were inclined to distort the evidence; however, authoritarians tended toward toughness, while antiauthoritarians tended to be more lenient in response to the same evidence. Those findings essentially replicated those of Jurow (1971), Mitchell and Byrne (1971, 1973), and Vidmar and Crinklow (1973). Saks (1976a), however, points out that only 38 percent of the jurors in Boehm's study showed any change from pre- to post-verdict.

A study by Vidmar (1972) considered the differences in verdicts obtained when jurors in a simulated murder case were confronted with (a) a verdict choice of guilty or not guilty or (b) a range of verdicts, with two manslaughter verdicts and a second degree murder verdict between the two extremes. This study is especially relevant for states like New York, where murder case jurors often must vote guilty or not guilty of first degree murder, as opposed to other states where the jury has the option of several levels of guilty verdicts. Vidmar found that, "although jurors having at least a moderate penalty option seldom choose a verdict of not guilty, over half of the jurors faced with only a 'severe' penalty option choose not guilty."   Once again, all of these jury studies did not use group deliberations, which would have made the studies more generalizable to real juries.   Secondly, there may have been a great loss in retention by jurors who had to read a transcript as compared to jurors in a live or videotaped trial in which both the senses of vision and audition are used.

Alexander and Licker (1975) found that the LAQ, as a predictor of individual verdicts regarding the evidence in an ambiguous murder trial, separated their sample group significantly—with authoritarians voting guilty more often than equalitarians.   Equalitarian jurors also showed a significant tendency to shift toward a more lenient verdict during deliberation when faced with the counter arguments of a confederate who vigorously argued for acquittal.   The authoritarian score from the LAQ was significantly correlated with severity of verdict ($r = .41$) but *not* with recommended sentence.   These findings suggest that a measure of authoritarianism—made more relevant to the legal context—may be more useful in predicting behavior in group deliberations than in ascertaining gut reactions to a criminal case, the evidence, or the defendant.

EXPERIMENTAL DESIGN

A 2 X 2 factorial design based on deliberation condition (all authoritarians or all equalitarians) and pre-verdict (guilty or not guilty) was employed.   In order to ensure controversy during deliberations, each jury consisted of three jurors voting guilty and three jurors voting not guilty on the pre-verdict.

As Table 1 indicates, deliberation conditions 1 and 2 represent jurors who have the same (pure) personality type.   We structured these juries to have three jurors with initial verdicts of guilty and three jurors with initial verdicts of not guilty. Conditions 3 and 4, on the other hand, have a mixture of three equalitarians and three authoritarians each.   Each jury also contains three guilty and three not guilty jurors, the only difference lying in the fact that in condition 3 the authoritarians had voted guilty and the equalitarians had voted not guilty, whereas in condition 4 the equalitarians had voted guilty and the authoritarians had voted not guilty.[6]

METHOD

Subjects

Serving as mock jurors in a simulated murder trial were 295 Brooklyn College students, who received experimental credit in their Introductory Psychology course for their participation.   Age of the sample group averaged 21 years; 49

Table 1.   Jury Deliberation Conditions

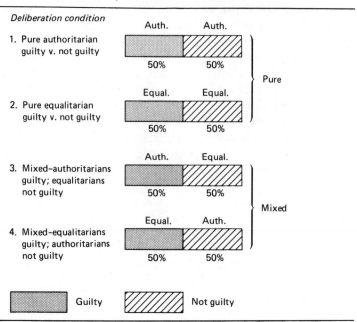

percent were women, 51 percent were men; 77 percent of the sample were white, 13 percent black, 10 percent others.

Apparatus

Dependent measures were derived from a package of five questionnaires to be completed by the subjects:

1. The Legal Attitude Questionnaire (Form II), which measures attitudes toward law enforcement, legal procedures, and the overall judicial system. The LAQ scale (Boehm, 1968) is structured so that subjects answering it are required to make a series of forced-choices, both an affirmative (+) and a negative (−) response to a three-part question. Each answer is coded to yield an authoritarian, equalitarian, or antiauthoritarian score (Appendix A).

2. A biographical questionnaire recording standard demographic data (see Appendix B).

3. A pre-deliberation verdict measure, requiring jurors to vote guilty or not guilty based on their impressions *then*. Included was a four-point scale of confidence in their verdict, ranging from "not sure" to "absolutely sure" (see Appendix C).

4. A final verdict ballot on which jurors recorded guilty or not guilty (see Appendix C).

5. An after-verdict, asking jurors to record which of five verdicts (first degree murder, second degree murder, reckless manslaughter, negligent manslaughter, and not guilty) they *would* have chosen *if* the judge had permitted that range of verdicts (see Appendix C).

The Trial

Adapted from Vidmar (1972), a murder trial was enacted by volunteer actors and recorded on $\frac{1}{2}$-inch videotape for playback on a SONY 3600 videotape recorder. The tape is 32 minutes long, included initial standard judge's instructions, presentation of prosecution and defense cases, summations, and the final charge to the jury by the judge (Weg, 1973). What follows is a capsule description of the case:

The case of Charles Young,
accused of murder in the death of Duncan Barnes

On December 10, 1971, at approximately 10:00 P.M., the defendant, Charles Young, entered the shop of the mother of the victim, located at 502 Fourth Avenue, New York, for the purpose of robbery. The victim, 24-year-old Duncan Barnes, lived in the rear of the shop with his mother and brother. The living area consisted of a sitting room, kitchen, and bedrooms. The sitting room was separated from the rest of the shop by what is called a half-door, with curtains on the store side extending to the floor. A bell would ring in the living area when the street door of the shop was opened.

On the occasion of the incident, Mrs. Ethel Barnes was sitting in the sitting room with the deceased son Duncan and his brother Thomas. The store bell having rung, the mother entered the shop. She saw that Young was carrying a revolver and screamed; to the others in the sitting room. At about this point, a customer, Steve Wilson, entered the store. He quickly saw that a robbery was in progress and dove for a counter on the right side of the store. From this point on, the events and sequence of events are unclear. A struggle ensued between Young and the victim, Duncan Barnes. Three shots were fired from Young's revolver. One bullet wounded the victim in the hand, another wounded him in the arm, and a third entered his head, causing the fatal wound. Young fled the shop, but was apprehended a short time later.

In the trial, the jurors hear the testimony of the witnesses, the defendant, and a forensic pathologist who aids the defendant's case. The judge instructs the jury on burden of proof, reasonable doubt, and the specifics of a charge (indictment) of first degree murder.

In the murder trial, the question of the attempted robbery is undisputed. However, the trial testimonies of Young, Mrs. Barnes, Duncan's brother, and the customer, Steve Wilson, differ. The only available physical evidence consists of two bullet holes found in the curtains that separate the store from the rear living quarters.

The following witnesses gave testimony:

Mr. Steve Wilson (A customer who came in): Saw Mr. Young holding a gun, ran behind the counter, heard three shots, but did not see the bullets strike. First two, a pause, and then the third; he saw nothing.

Brother of Duncan Barnes: Said he saw the men struggle. His brother was trying to take the gun away from the defendant; the defendant shot twice, ran to the door, turned around, and deliberately shot the victim in the head. In cross-examination, when asked if he could have been confused, he said it was possible.

Mrs. Ethel Barnes (Duncan's mother): Says she was with her son behind the curtains. She came out, heard the defendant say that "this is a robbery." She screamed, seeing Young shoot through the curtains, hitting the victim. Duncan ran out, struggled with Young, but she fainted at the critical time of the fatal shot. During cross-examination, she also admits it is possible she could be confused.

Young: Admitted he came into the store to rob it, but said he knew nothing about guns. He just bought it earlier in the day and didn't know it was loaded. When asked if he intended to use it, he said only to scare them. He said that when Mrs. Barnes screamed, Duncan ran out and began struggling. His hand actually hit the trigger when Duncan grabbed his wrist. He accidently pulled the trigger again when he hit against the counter. He took no money.

Forensic Pathologist: Bullets probably did not go through the curtains before hitting the victim. He gave the opinion that it is possible but improbable that the bullets went through the curtains first.

Basically, the mock trial is ambiguous in terms of evidence and is not skillfully presented by either trial attorney. Our experience has been that the trial generally evokes division and high interest among jurors and frequent "hung" verdicts. This was a valuable asset of the trial, since our purpose was to study how personalities operate in reaching decisions.

Procedure

Subjects first met as a large group (the jury pool) and were administered the Legal Attitudes Questionnaire. Each juror was assigned a number to assure his anonymity. Before viewing the tape of the mock trial on TV monitors, subjects were told that they must not take notes or talk to the other jurors while viewing the trial, and that they would be broken up into juries later. While the jurors were viewing the trial, the LAQ's were being scored. Each juror was labeled as an authoritarian, equalitarian, or antiauthoritarian, based on the highest of the three scores achieved on the LAQ. We eliminated the use of antiauthoritarians, since they were rarely found in our subject pool.[7] After viewing the trial, subjects were asked to give a pre-verdict based on their judgment at that point, and were administered demographic questionnaires. Experimenters randomly selected juror numbers from pools of authoritarian guilty or not guilty and equalitarian guilty or not guilty, in order to satisfy the four conditions of the design. Subjects were told to select a foreperson and to reach a unanimous decision. They were also told that they would be taped, and that the tape would only be used to evaluate the group dynamics. Some juries were actually taped; however, all jury rooms included a microphone and taping equipment. The juries were allowed one hour for deliberation; if they were undecided, the foreperson was told to get a verdict vote from each juror, and at that point the jury was labeled "hung." At the conclusion of deliberations, the jurors took a final vote and recorded their verdict. They then filled out the after-verdict questionnaires and were debriefed.

RESULTS

In Table 2 we present the percentage of convictions, acquittals, and hung juries in each of the four conditions. While there are differences among the four conditions, several interesting trends appear. There was a significant difference between the two pure conditions (authoritarians v. authoritarians and equalitarians v. equalitarians). The pure equalitarian juries were more prone to acquittal then the pure authoritarian juries ($\chi^2 = 36.02, p < .01$). There was also a significant difference between the two mixed conditions—the defendant was less likely to be acquitted in a mixed jury (condition) where equalitarians started out feeling that he was guilty. This condition also yielded the highest number of "hung" juries—a result that avoids conviction but necessitates a new trial for the defendant.

Table 2. Final Jury Verdicts

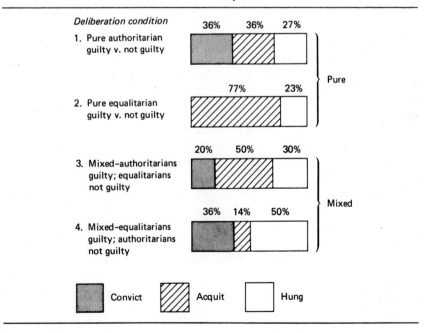

Table 3. Analysis of Mean Verdict as a Function of Deliberation Condition and Pre-verdict

Source	df	ms	F
(A) Deliberation Condition	1	0.332	2.36
(B) Pre-verdict	1	0.121	0.86
A × B	1	1.409	9.999 $p < .01$
Residual	44	0.141	
TOTAL	47	0.171	

In Table 3 we present a 2 × 2 ANOVA of mean jury verdicts (the average of all votes in the jury) as a function of deliberation conditions (pure v. mixed) and pre-verdict (authoritarians v. equalitarians voting guilty initially). As the table indicates, there were no significant differences for the main effects; however, there was a significant difference for the interaction effect of the two variables (see Figure 1). Condition 4 (equalitarian guilty) juries had an average verdict that was significantly more guilty than all other juries ($p < .01$).

In Table 4 we present a 2 × 2 ANOVA of the deliberation shift measure (pre-verdict–final verdict) as a function of deliberation conditions and pre-verdict of guilt. There was a significant deliberation shift as a function of deliberation condition ($p < .01$), with "pure" juries shifting more than "mixed" juries. A significant interaction ($p < .01$) was influenced by the pure equalitarian juries shifting more than any other juries.

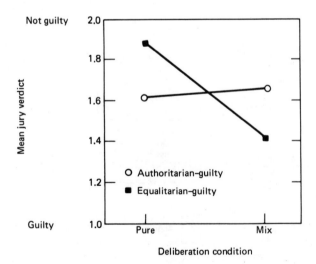

Figure 1. Final verdict as a function of deliberation condition and initial verdict.

Table 4. Analysis of Deliberation Shift as a Function of Deliberation Condition and Pre-verdict

Source	df	ms	F
(A) Deliberation Condition	1	0.328	2.313 $p < .01$
(B) Pre-verdict	1	0.089	0.630
A × B	1	1.302	9.196 $p < .01$
Residual	44	0.142	
TOTAL	47	0.169	

Table 5. Analysis of After-verdict as a Function of Deliberation Condition and Pre-verdict

Source	df	ms	F
(A) Deliberation Condition	1	2.257	8.961 $p < .01$
(B) Pre-verdict	1	0.217	0.861
A × B	1	1.292	5.129 $p < .05$
Residual	44	0.252	
TOTAL	47	0.319	

Table 6. Analysis of Sentence as a Function of Deliberation Condition and Pre-verdict

Source	df	ms	F
(A) Deliberation Condition	1	4.968	3.472 $p < .10$
(B) Pre-verdict	1	0.166	0.116
A × B	1	15.656	10.943 $p < .01$
Residual	44	1.431	
TOTAL	47	1.779	

In Table 5 we present a 2 × 2 ANOVA of after-verdict as a function of deliberation conditions and pre-verdict. There was a significant main effect as a function of deliberation condition ($p < .01$), with "pure" juries showing an after-verdict that indicated less guilt that the "mixed" juries. A significant interaction ($p < .05$) was influenced by condition 2 jurors, who gave an after-verdict indicating higher levels of guilt than jurors in all other conditions.

Table 6 shows a 2 × 2 ANOVA of sentences as a function of deliberation condition and pre-verdict. "Mixed" juries tended to give higher sentences than "pure" juries ($p < .10$). A significant interaction was influenced by condition 2 and 3 juries giving very long sentences ($p < .01$).

Table 7. Distribution of Juror's Pre-verdicts, Final Verdicts and After-verdicts as a Function of LAQ Scale Classification

	Pre-verdicts		Final verdicts		After-verdicts	
	Auth	Equal	Auth	Equal	Auth	Equal
Guilty: First Degree Murder	46%	52%	45%	33.1%	6.6%	10.5%
Guilty: Second Degree Murder	*	*	*	*	24.1%	22.2%
Guilty: Reckless Manslaughter	*	*	*	*	36.0%	33.3%
Guilty: Negligent Manslaughter	*	*	*	*	30.7%	30.7%
Not Guilty	54%	48%	55%	66.9%	0.7%	3.3%

In Table 7 we present the percentage distributions of individual pre-verdicts, final verdicts, and after-verdicts ("if possible") by personality type. As shown in this table, when jurors were given a final verdict choice of "guilty of first degree murder" or not guilty, 45 percent of authoritarians voted guilty, while only 33 percent of the equalitarians voted guilty. However, when all were given a choice of five alternative verdicts, there was no real difference in verdict choice, with an extremely small percentage of all jurors voting either guilty or not guilty.

To test how sentences were recommended as a function of LAQ classification, we computed a t test on the average sentence assigned by individual authoritarians and equalitarians. Authoritarians gave significantly longer sentences to the defendant than equalitarians ($t = 3.012, p < .01$).

Table 8 presents the distribution of the certainty of final verdict after deliberation as a function of LAQ scale classification. This table shows almost equal percentages of authoritarians and equalitarians falling into the middle categories, while there were significant differences in the extreme categories. A greater percentage of authoritarians indicated that they were not sure of their final verdict, and a greater percentage of equalitarians indicated that they were absolutely sure of their final verdicts.

Table 8. Distribution of Post-sure as a Function of LAQ Scale Classification

Post-sure	Authoritarian	Equalitarian
Not Sure	16.2%	6.7%
Somewhat Sure	16.2%	17.3%
Very Sure	39.0%	38.7%
Absolutely Sure	28.7%	37.3%

DISCUSSION

In a previous study we concluded that the authoritarian juror is "rigid" or resistant to change as a function of deliberation, and when he does change his verdict, he is more prone to change from not guilty to guilty. On the other hand, the equalitarian juror was labeled as more "flexible" or prone to change in the face of persuasive arguments during deliberations, and that change was more likely to go from guilty to not guilty. While the results of this study confirm our previous results, they indicate that interpersonal dynamics owing to the makeup of the jury may well be as important as, if not more important than, the mere personality label. Obviously, the pure authoritarian or pure equalitarian jury represents an ideal jury in the eyes of the prosecutor or the defense attorney, respectively. Such ideal situations, in an adversary system where both sides have a chance to select members of the jury, occur rarely. True to form, the pure juries lived up to the ideal expectations of them. That is, the pure authoritarian juries convicted more often than the equalitarian juries. Further, individual authoritarians convicted more often than equalitarians. It was when we got into the mixed-jury phase of the experiment that the more interesting results emerged.

In a mixed-jury situation where the defense attorney would be most happy (a set of equalitarian jurors who begin deliberation holding for a not guilty verdict), we find that the juries go on to acquit about 50 percent of the time. (Our direct observations of some juries showed that equalitarians were very persuasive advocates.) This represents a very good set of odds in comparison to the usual high rate of convictions with real juries in real situations. At least in the present experiment, this type of mix produced more than four times as many acquittals as the other type of mix (an unusual jury composition), in which the equalitarians start feeling that the defendant was guilty and the authoritarians were carrying the burden for the defense attorney—arguing in favor of not guilty. In that condition—lamentable from the defense attorney's point of view—the authoritarians were not so successful in persuading their fellow jurors to vote to an acquittal. Only 14 percent of the juries came in with an acquittal. The meaning of these jury outcomes will of course be interpreted differently by a prosecutor. If the prosecutor were looking at the same set of data, he would probably be initially happy with the last mixed condition in which the equalitarians started out feeling that the defendant was guilty.

We have to be cautious in our reading of these results, since the overall percentage of convictions among any of the juries studied was small. This low percentage came primarily from the fact that there were so many hung jury verdicts—a tribute to the type of evidence presented. A common criticism of this type of research (mock juries) is that simulated juries tend never to reach decision because it doesn't mean so much to the participants. (Diamond and Zeisel, 1974, found that parallel juries differed markedly from real juries in the type of verdict they reached when they saw the same case as the real jurors.) While we generally agree with this point, we would also note that, in some cases, the evidence which reaches juries is very ambiguous. We made no attempt in this research to sample from a population of cases that realistically would probably produce a very small percentage of hung jury verdicts. Rather we deliberately chose an ambiguous case, kept constant for all jurors, whose evidence could be interpreted in a variety of ways. Most attorneys who have viewed this case and offered their opinions feel that it is a natural hung-jury-verdict case. Thus the thrust of the results shows that in such a situation, the personality of the individual jurors, considered in combination with their fellow jurors, can be a major determinant of the results of jury deliberations.

The ideal "prosecution" juries (all authoritarians) reacted to the evidence by voting about equally for acquittal and conviction, with one-third being hung. The average verdict was more toward conviction than in the case of the "defense" juries (all equalitarians). The ideal defense juries, in fact, acquitted the defendant more than any other group, and were hung on a verdict in the remaining 23 percent of the deliberations. (They did not convict—a testimonal to how scientific jury selection can aid a defendant *if* everything goes his way on the voir dire.) The equalitarian is believed to be flexible and more persuadable than the authoritarian. Our results reflect this behavior of the equalitarian personality in a trial where the burden of proof was not effectively met to support a first degree murder conviction. Generally, the equalitarians who started out voting guilty listened to their fellow equalitarians, and shifted to not guilty. The authoritarians showed little change after talking to their own kind.

Of course, attorneys do not always have their way, so the rest of our experiment dealt with realistic mixtures of authoritarians and equalitarians. In condition 3 the mixture was fairly typical, authoritarians who started out voting guilty while equalitarians were voting not guilty. But here the equalitarians were successful in persuading many authoritarian jurors to shift to a not guilty verdict, leading to 50 percent acquittals in all. In condition 4 we simulated the jury in which the selection process fails; the attorney picks the right personality but the wrong verdict. Authoritarians are in the awkward position (for them) of arguing for acquittal; equalitarians are arguing for conviction. In this awkward position there was little change in verdicts, but when there was a change, authoritarians tended to switch their verdict toward guilt. The conviction rate now jumped to 36 percent; there were only a few acquittals, and most of the juries were deadlocked.

Obviously the present experiment studied only one type of group dynamic situation. It compared pure juries with mixed juries where the ratio of one type of personality to another was 50-50. In addition, we had the constraint of a three to three initial vote. Whether the same principles of interactive personality dynamics apply in a majority v. minority deadlock, we do not know. All the evidence from prior research suggests that such majorities tend ultimately to persuade the minority to give in to the pressure and go the way of the majority. We have only the scantiest evidence as to what percentages of various types of splits in initial verdicts occur among real juries. At least at this stage we have been able to demonstrate quite clearly the advantage to be gained in selecting jurors on the basis of a measure of their degree of authoritarianism—a variable that has traditionally been found to be relevant in judicial settings.

FOOTNOTES

1. Reprints may be obtained from the senior author at the Center for Responsive Psychology, Brooklyn College, C.U.N.Y., Brooklyn, New York 11210. This research was supported (in part) by a grant from the Faculty Research Award Program of the City University of New York.
2. Now at the Law School, State University of New York, Buffalo, New York.
3. Christie, R., Personal communication.
4. Typically, factor scores are broken down using the Automatic Interaction Detection (AID) sub-routine of the OSIRIS package.
5. The "authoritarianism" factor has shown up in every survey conducted by Christie and Shulman and the senior author. The 8-9 item scale is a hybrid between Boehm's LAQ scale and the older F scale.
6. Since we showed the trial to a large audience at one time, the fitting of jurors into the design involved the acceptance of a few people who met the rigid criteria, and the rejection of many who did not on any given testing day. Having had prior experience with this trial (Weg, 1973; Licker, Alexander, et al., 1975), we felt that the goal of having a 3 : 3 tie vote was worth the sacrifices of precision made in this selective sampling. Our prior research had demonstrated that we would have had an excess of not guilty voters had we not been selective.
7. They would likely be rejected in real jury pools as well because of the high likelihood that they would be characterized as anti-capital punishment, defense-oriented, or anti-establishment—and thus far from the normative values of jury selection officials.

REFERENCES

Adorno, T., et al., *The Authoritarian Personality*. New York: Harper & Brothers (1950).

Alexander, M., and Licker, J., Jury selection: Finding rigid and flexible jurors and deciding if they are needed. Report No. CR-18, Center for Responsive Psychology Report Series, Brooklyn College, C.U.N.Y., Brooklyn, New York 11210 (July 1975).

Boehm, V., Mr. Prejudice, Miss Sympathy, and the authoritarian personality: An application of psychological measuring techniques to the problem of jury bias. *Wisconsin Law Review*, 734–43 (1968).

Buckhout, R., Jury without peers. In M. Reidel and P. A. Vales (eds.), *Treating the Offender: Problems and Issues*. New York: Praeger Publishers (1977).

Bush, N., The case for the expansive voir dire. *Law and Psychology Review 2:* 9–26 (1976).

Christie, R., Probability vs. precedence: The social psychology of jury selection. Columbia University, unpublished manuscript (1975).

Diamond, S., and Zeisel, H., A courtroom experiment on juror selection and decision-making. *Personality and Social Psychology Bulletin 1* (1): 276–77 (1974).

Etzioni, A., Creating an imbalance. *Trial 10:* 28 (1974).

Foss, R. D., A critique of jury simulation research. Paper presented at the American Psychological Association Meeting, Chicago, Illinois (September 1975).

Jurow, G. L., New data on the effect of "death qualified jury" on the process of guilt determination. *Harvard Law Review*, 607–11 (1971).

Kairys, D. (ed.), *The Jury System: New Methods for Predicting Prejudice*. The National Jury Project and National Lawyers Guild (1975).

Mitchell, H. E., and Byrne, D., Minimizing the influence of irrelevant factors in the courtroom: The defendant's character, judge's instructions and authoritarianism. Unpublished paper (1971).

Mitchell, H. E., and Byrne, D., The defendant's dilemma: Effects of juror attitudes and authoritarianism on judicial decision. *Journal of Personality and Social Psychology 25:* 123–29 (1973).

Saks, M. J., Social scientists can't rig juries. *Psychology Today 9* (8): 48–57 (1976a).

Saks, M. J., The limits of scientific jury selection: Ethical and empirical. *Jurimetrics Journal 17* (1): 3–22 (1976b).

Schulman, J., Shaver, P., Colman, R., Emrich, B., and Christie, R., Recipe for a jury. *Psychology Today*, 37–84 (May 1973).

Tate, E., Hawrish, E., and Clark, S., Communication variables in jury selection. *Journal of Communication 24* (3): 130–39 (1974).

Vidmar, N., Effects of decision alternatives on the verdicts and social perceptions of simulated jurors. *Journal of Personality and Social Psychology 2:* 211–18 (1972).

Vidmar, N., and Crinklaw, L. D., Retribution and utility as motives in sanctioning behavior. Paper presented to the Midwestern Psychological Association Convention (April 1973).

Weg, S., The effects of jury size and decision rule on jury verdicts. Paper submitted in partial fulfillment of the requirements for the degree of Master of Arts (1973).

Zeisel, H., and Diamond, S. S., The jury selection in the Mitchell–Stans conspiracy trial. *American Bar Foundation Research Journal 1976* (1): 151–74 (1976).

APPENDICES

A. Legal Attitudes Questionnaire
B. Demographic Questionnaire
C. Pre-deliberation, Final, and After-verdict Questionnaire

APPENDIX A

The Legal Attitudes Questionnaire (L.A.Q.):

LEGAL ATTITUDES QUESTIONNAIRE (FORM II)

On the following page are ten groups of statements, each expressing a commonly held opinion about law enforcement, legal procedures and other things connected with the judicial system. There are three statements in each group.

Put a plus (+) on the line next to the statement in a group that you agree with most, and a minus (−) next to the statement you agree with least.

An example of a set of statements might be:

__+__ A. The failure of a defendant to testify in his own behalf should not be taken as an indication of guilt.

_____ B. The majority of persons arrested are innocent of any crime.

__−__ C. Giving an obviously guilty criminal a long drawn-out trial is a waste of taxpayer's money.

In this example, the person answering has agreed most with statement A and least with statement C.

Work carefully, choosing the item you agree with most and the one you agree with least in each set of statements. There is no time limit on this questionnaire, but do not spend too much time on any set of statements. Some sets are more difficult than others, but please do not omit any set of statements.

SET I

_____ A. Unfair treatment of underprivileged groups and classes is the chief cause of crime.

_____ B. Too many obviously guilty persons escape punishment because of legal technicalities.

_____ C. The Supreme Court is, by and large, an effective guardian of the Constitution.

SET II

_____ A. Evidence illegally obtained should be admissible in court if such evidence is the only way of obtaining a conviction.

_____ B. Most prosecuting attorneys have a strong sadistic streak.

_____ C. Search warrants should clearly specify the person or things to be seized.

SET III

_____ A. No one should be convicted of a crime on the basis of circumstantial evidence, no matter how strong such evidence is.

_____ B. There is no need in a criminal case for the accused to prove his innocence beyond a reasonable doubt.

_____ C. Any person who resists arrest commits a crime.

SET IV

_____ A. When determining a person's guilt or innocence, the existence of a prior arrest record should not be considered.

_____ B. Wiretapping by anyone and for any reason should be completely illegal.

_____ C. A lot of recent Supreme Court decisions sound suspiciously Communistic.

SET V

_____ A. Treachery and deceit are common tools of prosecutors.

_____ B. Defendants in a criminal case should be required to take the witness stand.

_____ C. All too often, minority group members do not get fair trials.

SET VI

_____ A. Because of the oppression and persecution minority group members suffer, they deserve leniency and special treatment in the courts.

_____ B. Citizens need to be protected against excessive police power as well as against criminals.

_____ C. Persons who testify in court against underworld characters should be allowed to do so anonymously to protect themselves from retaliation.

SET VII

_____ A. It is better for society that several guilty men be freed than one innocent one wrongfully imprisoned.

_____ B. Accused persons should be required to take lie-detector tests.

_____ C. When there is a "hung" jury in a criminal case, the defendant should always be freed and the indictment dismissed.

SET VIII

_____ A. A society with true freedom and equality for all would have very little crime.

_____ B. It is moral and ethical for a lawyer to represent a defendant in a criminal case even when he believes his client guilty.

_____ C. Police should be allowed to arrest and question suspicious looking persons to determine whether they have been up to something illegal.

SET IX

_____ A. The law coddles criminals to the detriment of society.

_____ B. A lot of judges have connections with the underworld.

_____ C. The freedom of society is endangered as much by overzealous law enforcement as by the acts of individual criminals.

SET X

_____ A. There is just about no such thing as an honest cop.

_____ B. In the long run, liberty is more important than order.

_____ C. Upstanding citizens have nothing to fear from the police.

APPENDIX B

MAKE NO MARKS ON THESE FORMS PLEASE

Please mark your answers on the computer sheet
next to the corresponding numbers.

JUROR NUMBER (3) _____ (4) _____ (5) _____

Do you read any of the following:

(13)	The New York Daily News	Yes = 1	No = 0
(14)	The New York Times	Yes = 1	No = 0
(15)	New York Post	Yes = 1	No = 0
(16)	Wall Street Journal	Yes = 1	No = 0
(17)	Village Voice	Yes = 1	No = 0
(18)	Amsterdam Times	Yes = 1	No = 0
(19)	Other	Yes = 1	No = 0

(20) Sex: Male = 1   Female = 2

(21) What is the principal occupation of the head of your household?

Professional = 1   Housewife = 4
White Collar = 2   Other   – 5
Blue Collar = 3

Would you please tell me your age at your last birthday. (22) _____ (23) _____

(24) Would you tell me your race?

White   = 1   Asian American = 4
Black   = 2   Other   = 5
Hispanic = 3

(25) What is your religion?

Catholic   = 1   Other = 4
Protestant = 2   None = 5
Jewish   = 3

(26) What was the last year of school completed by your father?

Elementary   = 1   College Graduate = 4
Some High School   = 2   Graduate Degree = 5
High School Graduate = 3

(27) Can you tell me approximately what your family's annual income level is?

$3,000–$6,000   = 1 $16,000–$25,000 = 4
$6,000–$11,000 = 2   over $25,000   = 5
$11,000–$16,000 = 3

(28) Can you tell me if you are married or single? Married = 1   Single = 2

(29) In what political party are you registered?

Democrat   = 1   Conservative = 3   Not Registered = 5
Republican = 2   Other   = 4

THANK YOU VERY MUCH

APPENDIX C

#3 Pre-Deliberation Verdict

JUROR NUMBER ____

Based on what you saw, please check GUILTY or NOT GUILTY.
Based on your first impressions:

GUILTY   NOT GUILTY

In your opinion, how sure are you of your verdict.

NOT SURE   SOMEWHAT SURE   VERY SURE   ABSOLUTELY SURE

#4 Final Verdict

JUROR NUMBER ____

GUILTY   NOT GUILTY

#5 Follow-Up to the Jury Study

JUROR NUMBER ____

We want to thank you for participating. You probably now realize that we had to restrict you in rendering a verdict in this case to the requirements of New York State Law—which only allows a juror to say GUILTY or NOT GUILTY.

Can you now tell us how sure you are that your final verdict reflects how you really feel about the defendant.

PLEASE CIRCLE ONE NUMBER   1   2   3   4
                                 Not Sure   Absolutely Sure

Assume that you were a juror in a state which allows a jury to choose from a range of verdicts. Which of the following would have been your final verdict?

1. GUILTY OF FIRST DEGREE MURDER: Defendant acted "intentionally" with the conscious objective of bringing about death.
2. GUILTY OF SECOND DEGREE MURDER: Defendant acted "knowingly" with the awareness that his conduct would bring about death.

3. GUILTY OF RECKLESS MANSLAUGHTER: Defendant consciously disregarded a substantial and unjustifiable risk that his behavior could result in circumstances that would lead to death.
4. GUILTY OF NEGLIGENT MANSLAUGHTER: Defendant should have been aware, but failed to perceive, that his behavior could result in circumstances that would lead to death.
5. NOT GUILTY

Assume that the defendant has been found Guilty as charged for First Degree Murder. What sentence should the judge have imposed on the defendant, based on what you now feel about this case?

PLEASE CIRCLE:	Suspended sentence	9	18
	1 year	10	19
	2 years	11	20
	3 years	12	21
	4 years	13	22
	5 years	14	23
	6 years	15	24
	7 years	16	25
	8 years	17	Life

"When Psychologists Aid in the Voir Dire" addresses itself to both the legal and the ethical considerations involved in the complex relationships and activities associated with the selection of jury members.

Such activities and relationships, as the authors call to our attention, are complex precisely because social scientists, in their capacity to advise and aid in the selection of jurors, have to be responsive both to legal practices and to ethical considerations of their professions. Social psychologists, in particular, need to be both sensitive and responsive to the principles of ethics of the American Psychological Association, and one of the important merits of this chapter is to show how psychologists aiding in the voir dire can meet both their legal and ethical responsibilities. In doing so, the contributors direct our attention to the pertinent judicial decisions and relate them to specific ethical principles, developed by the American Psychological Association, that have a bearing on the professional aid such psychologists can render to the judicial system.

5

When Psychologists Aid in the Voir Dire: Legal and Ethical Considerations*

James D. Herbsleb, Bruce Dennis Sales, and John J. Berman

Under our system of administering criminal law, the jury is a feature of the very highest importance. The selection of the jury is not a mere gesture. The rhetorical remark of a British statesman that "The whole machinery of the state, all the apparatus of the system, and its varied workings, end in simply bringing twelve good men into a box," carried a real truth. . . .[1]

In the 46 years since this quotation appeared in a federal court opinion, the jury has retained its central importance. But even this hallowed institution has been unable to remain static in the dynamic flux of our society. A technology based on social science research and methodology is now being created and used to aid the attorney in conducting the voir dire—that part of the trial where the actual jurors are chosen from the larger available pool.

Before going further, it should be helpful to the reader to consider briefly how juries are chosen from the larger pool of potential jurors who are called to the courtroom on a particular day. Jurors are not chosen from the panel of prospective jurors; rather, they are rejected. After this process has taken place, the first 12 people remaining become the sworn jury. Counsel can exclude individuals by means of causal and peremptory challenges. A specific basis of partiality or some other statutory violations must be proved before a juror can be excluded by a challenge for cause. After all challenges for cause have been ruled upon,

*The preparation of this chapter was partially supported by a grant from the National Institute of Mental Health, Center for Studies of Crime and Delinquency, MH 13814-03-04.

counsel are allotted a limited number of peremptory challenges, which are "exercised without a reason stated, without inquiry, and without being subject to the court's control."[2]

The aim of social science technology is to increase the effectiveness with which the peremptory challenges are exercised (Suggs and Sales, 1978). Such technologies, however, raise new and important legal and ethical issues, which deserve detailed consideration. Before considering them, it is important to understand the general structural characteristics of these new technologies. Since it is not the intent of this chapter to present a detailed description of these techniques, and since more detailed critiques of them are presented elsewhere (Berman and Sales, 1977; Suggs and Sales, 1978), only a brief account will be given.

One can divide the social science techniques in this area into those conducted outside and those conducted inside the courtroom. There are essentially two techniques employed outside the courtroom. One is a survey intended to provide predictability about jurors' predispositions from knowledge about demographic characteristics; the other is an investigation of prospective jurors' predispositions by contacting their acquaintances (see generally, Kairys, Schulman, and Harring, 1975).

The survey consists of asking a random sample of the population from which jurors are selected (usually registered voters) a series of questions designed to ascertain respondents' (1) demographic characteristics (e.g., age, sex, religion), (2) attitudes toward the central issues of the case (e.g., the facts in the case, the litigants, the legal issues in question), and (3) attitudes toward issues that are not directly relevant to the case but which might correlate with the central issues. The purpose of the survey is to determine which demographic characteristics and/or attitudes toward related issues best predict (i.e., correlate highest with) attitudes toward the central issues. Having demographic predictors is advantageous, for as soon as a prospective juror indicates his religion, age, and so on, one knows how most people with this set of characteristics feel about the central issues in the case. Having predictors consisting of attitudes toward issues indirectly relevant to the case is advantageous in that the lawyer can ask about these issues without the prospective juror's or opposing attorney's knowing exactly what a particular reponse might mean about that juror's predisposition toward the central issues.

The second out-of-court technique is the juror investigation. It is conducted by establishing an information network constructed by contacting the defendants and the friends, families, and supporters of the defendants. Each of these in turn contacts several other people, who in turn contact several other people, and so on. When the list of prospective jurors becomes available, it is passed along the network with the hope that most of the veniremen will be known by someone in the network who will be able to report on their probable predispositions. Schulman (1973) estimated that a network of approximately 400 people ought to be adequate to produce information on 70 to 80 percent of the prospective jurors.

The in-court techniques used to aid in the voir dire have in common the fact that they all consist of the social scientist's rating each prospective juror on some dimension during the voir dire. However, the aspects or dimensions of the jurors that have been rated have varied considerably, depending on the nature of the trial, and what seems to have been even more important, the area of professional expertise of the social scientist.

One of the frequently used dimensions has been authoritarianism (Christie, Reference Note 1). This is so because the social science techniques have been frequently been used in defense of political dissidents. That is, since authoritarian jurors by definition ought to be more submissive to authority, especially the authority of the government, social scientists have been eager to identify authoritarians and exclude them from the jury. A second approach has rated prospective jurors on their degree of legal development. Tapp and Keniston (Reference Note 2) propose that people who are at the highest degree of legal development will make the fairest jurors. It is noteworthy that they are interested in a "fair" juror not a "favorable" one.

The final technique discussed is one in which the verbal, paralinguistic (i.e., pitch and tone of voice, pauses, and so forth), and kinesic (i.e., body language) behaviors of prospective jurors are rated by the scientists (Suggs and Sales, 1978). The use of this technique is based on research in communication which shows that people's nonverbal behavior can often be a better clue than their verbal behavior to what they are really thinking and feeling. The goal of these ratings, therefore, is less like the other in-court procedures, which attempt to measure jurors' stable personality traits, and more like the out-of-court procedures that attempt to measure jurors' attitudes and reactions to the sides and issues in a particular trial.

After the questioning has been completed and before the peremptory challenges are exercised, all the information that has been collected on each juror must be combined. This is accomplished at a meeting attended by representatives from each of the data-gathering teams (i.e., survey, juror investigations, and in-court ratings), as well as the litigants and their attorneys. Each person at the meeting gives his/her assessment of each prospective juror, and discussion continues until a consensus can be reached about who is a desirable juror and the rank order of desirability.

With this admittedly brief but hopefully sufficient background, the remainder of the paper will pose and attempt to answer a number of legal and ethical questions raised by the use of social science techniques to aid in the voir dire.

For example, does the use of these techniques by one party violate the right of the adversary to a trial by an impartial jury? Should the information gained pursuant to these techniques be discoverable? Can a social scientist be subject to criminal sanctions for engaging in a juror investigation? Is it ethical for a psychologist engaged in this practice to accept remuneration as a provider of psychological services? Does this practice lead to the violation of the subjects' freedom of participation? What must the psychologist do to protect the confidentiality of the data he obtains?

Is the constitutional right to trial by an impartial jury violated when one party uses social science techniques for exercising peremptory challenges and the other does not?

As of this writing, there is no convincing evidence that the use of social science techniques to direct the exercise of peremptory challenges results in a more favorable jury than does the unaided exercise of these challenges by an attorney (Berman and Sales, 1977; Suggs and Sales, 1978). It seems clear that such evidence would be required in support of a successful constitutional challenge to the practice.[3]

The Supreme Court has held that deliberate discrimination against recognized groups, e.g., women[4] and blacks,[5] is constitutionally impermissible. But challenges to jury selection systems that have not been based on this explicit type of discrimination have failed where the defendant was unable to show a significant difference in viewpoint between those selected and those rejected.[6] The Court has further held that "tentative and fragmentary" evidence of this difference will not suffice.[7] There are also indications that the Court will be even more reluctant to inquire into the bases of peremptory challenges than it was to overturn the jury selection systems in the cases mentioned above.[8] We must conclude that the one-sided use of social science techniques to aid in the voir dire is not constitutionally impermissible in the absence of evidence demonstrating its effectiveness.

If convincing evidence should ever become available that these techniques have the capability of affecting verdicts, their constitutionality would be drawn much more seriously into question. A firm basis would then exist for the claim that where these techniques are used, the jury drawn is not impartial. Despite the aforementioned reluctance of the courts to examine the bases of peremptory challenges,[9] it would seem that the availability of a technique capable of securing conviction- or acquittal-prone juries would be sufficiently threatening to the fundamental right to trial by an impartial jury to warrant some remedial action. We suggest that discovery of juror information (discussed below) is the least disruptive and most effective remedy.[10]

Should jury information be discoverable?

Discovery is a procedure whereby a party to a court action may be required to disclose certain evidence to the adversary.[11] The purpose is generally seen as the elimination, to some extent, of the element of surprise, in order to promote a search for the truth as opposed to creating a sporting event.[12]

An overwhelming number of state and federal cases can be cited in support of the proposition that information on prospective jurors is not subject to discovery.[13] Typical of these cases is *United States v. Falange*,[14] where the prosecutor obtained information on prospective jurors from the FBI, from credit bureaus, and from city and state police departments. This information served as the basis for the exercise of the prosecutor's peremptory challenges. Falange was convicted, and his appeal charged that the investigation was designed to secure a jury favorable to the prosecution. The court rejected this argument, saying, "The fact that some members of the panel were challenged does not mean that those who were not were biased or prejudiced."[15]

A similar approach was taken by the court in *United States v. Costello*.[16] In this case, the prosecution obtained the income tax returns of the prospective jurors, and used this information to place each juror in one of four categories, from most to least favorable. The prosecution used five of its six peremptory challenges to eliminate two class II jurors and three class III jurors. The jury which eventually sat in the case consisted of eight class I jurors (most favorable to prosecutor), two class II jurors, two class III jurors, and no class IV jurors. Costello was convicted by this jury, and his appeal charged that the jury was "specially conditioned" to convict. The court held that Costello had not been denied the right to trial by an impartial jury, since the exercise of peremptory challenges is a rejective process which can lead only to the rejection of unduly biased jurors, not to the selection of a "specially conditioned" jury.[17]

The logic of *Falange* and *Costello* seems to typify most state and federal decisions which have addressed the issue of the discoverability of juror information.[18] The argument may be summarized as follows: There is no authority which requires the court to allow discovery of juror information, and since its value is merely speculative, the interest of justice does not require that the court use its discretion to grant a motion requesting discovery.[19]

The use by one party of juror information may be seen merely as a special case of the generally recognized fact that counsel are never perfectly equal in abilities and resources.[20] Viewed from this perspective, exercising peremptory challenges is just one small facet of the task an attorney undertakes when he tries a case. If we assume that attorneys vary to some extent in the skill with which they exercise peremptory challenges, there is no evidence to show, nor would there seem to be any a priori reason to assume, that the difference in effectiveness between highly skilled and relatively unskilled attorneys is any less than the difference in effectiveness between an attorney using social science techniques and one not using these techniques. Since the inequality of counsel is simply accepted as inevitable in our legal system,[21] it can be argued that the mere possibility that some type of inequality may be created by the use of social science techniques is insufficient to require any form of remedial action.

This is especially convincing in view of the fact that inequalities in counsel will pervade every aspect of a trial, from the planning of strategy to the closing arguments. Social science techniques are employed only in the very limited capacity of providing a source of information for the exercise of peremptory challenges. The great range of styles and abilities among attorneys can create differences which dwarf any that may be created by the use of these techniques.

Despite the overwhelming weight of authority which can be cited in support of the proposition that juror information is not subject to discovery, a legal basis for requiring its discovery can be found. The modern trend seems to be toward an expansion of criminal discovery; as noted in *Dennis v. United States*,[22] "[t]hese developments are entirely consonant with the growing realization that disclosure, rather than suppression, of relevant materials ordinarily promotes the proper administration of criminal justice."[23]

This trend was noted in *People v. Aldridge*,[24] where the prosecutor had in his possession a dossier on the prospective jurors that allegedly contained information about the jurors' adverse contacts with the law and information indicating whether a juror was "prosecution minded." The court held that the principle of fairness entitled the defendant to discovery of the juror information. In support of its holding, the court reasoned that "[s]ince jurors are so important to our system of criminal justice, nondisclosure of information upon which defendant may exercise peremptory challenges places a premium upon 'gamesmanship' to the subversion of the trial's search for truth."[25] The court indicated in dictum that the prosecution would also be entitled to discovery of juror information in the possession of the defense, and that such discovery by either party should be limited by the "work product" doctrine (discussed below).

A case with similar import was *Losavio v. Mayber*,[26] a suit brought by the public defender's office to gain access to the police records of prospective jurors, which were routinely furnished to the district attorney's office for use during voir dire. In holding that such records must be furnished to the public defender's office if they are furnished to the district attorney's office, the court reasoned that "[the petitioners] were seeking no more from these records than what was provided to the district attorney. As thus framed, the request of the petitioners is eminently reasonable, just and fair."[27]

The basic concept of fairness furnished the basis for the holdings in both *Aldridge* and *Losavio*. If we add to this the requirement that "justice must satisfy the appearance of justice,"[28] a very powerful argument for the discoverability of juror information begins to emerge. The Supreme Court has repeatedly recognized the importance of avoiding even the appearance or likelihood of bias in a trial.[29] In *Taylor v. Louisiana*,[30] the Court recently held that a state jury selection system which tended drastically to reduce jury participation by women[31] violated the defendant's right to trial by an impartial jury. The Court recognized the importance of the appearance of justice in its explanation of its holding: "Community participation in the administration of the criminal law . . . is not only consistent with our democratic heritage, but is also critical to public confidence in the fairness of the criminal justice system."[32]

It seems at least possible, if not likely, that the use of social science techniques will lead the public to doubt the fairness of a trial where these techniques are used. This seems especially true because the techniques have been used in a number of trials with strong political overtones which have received national publicity[33] (Shapley, 1974).

It may be instructive to note the effects of a University of Chicago "jury bugging" experiment on the public.[34] Although done with the prior consent of the court and opposing counsel, this scientific intrusion into the workings of a jury trial caused widespread public disapproval.[35] A number of state and federal laws to prohibit such conduct were passed within two years after the public disclosures of the experiment.[36] It does not seem likely that scientific practices *designed to affect the outcome* of a jury trial, rather than merely to observe it, will produce less of an effect on the public. Articles discussing these techniques and their implications are appearing in proper publications.[37] All of this suggests that the one-sided use of social science technology may seriously undermine public confidence in the potential for a just verdict.

Finally, it may be argued in support of the discoverability of juror information that the failure of research to provide convincing evidence of the efficacy of social science technology should not be taken as evidence that such techniques have no effect. In fact, there have been no systematic evaluations of these techniques. Even if an evaluation of a technique were conducted, and it did not demonstrate the efficacy of the technique, it would still be serious scientific error to assume the truth of the null hypothesis. The failure to find an effect can be due to any number of deficiencies in methods, measurement, or design. Given the great difficulty of doing this type of research, it would not be surprising if a rather powerful effect were to go undetected.

The major arguments favoring the discoverability of juror information obtained by the application of social science techniques may be summarized as follows: Allowing discovery of such information puts both parties on an equal footing for the intelligent, informed exercise of peremptory challenges, and preserves our basic value of fairness. Since the effectiveness with which this information can be used is an unknown quantity, allowing discovery will prevent possibly grave miscarriages of justice while causing no significant disruption of the present voir dire system.

Here is where the superiority of the arguments favoring discoverability becomes apparent. Even though discovery does not seem to be constitutionally required because of the lack of evidence showing its efficacy, it does not follow from this proposition that the information should not be discoverable. If we examine and balance the possible consequences of the alternatives, it becomes immediately apparent that refusing to allow discovery serves no higher purpose, except perhaps to preserve more completely the image of a trial as a sporting event. Allowing discovery, as already mentioned, will prevent the victimization of either party at the hands of a subtly biased jury. If discovery is not allowed, many litigants may suffer from the injustice of this "jury stacking" before its efficacy is definitely established.

Furthermore, allowing discovery tends to bolster public confidence in the jury system as one in which the verdict depends on the evidence adduced at trial, and not on the notoriety or financial status of the litigants. While not constitutionally mandated, discovery will certainly be consistent with the goal of selecting a jury that represents a cross section of the community,[38] because it will prevent either litigant from unilaterally eliminating all jurors of a particular point of view. Finally, if we assume that juror behavior can be predicted, providing juror information to both sides carries the potential of actually improving our present jury selection system by allowing jurors prejudiced in either direction to be more effectively eliminated.

Should the work-product doctrine prevent or limit the scope of discovery of juror information?

A legal concept known as the work-product doctrine has been interpreted as either barring all discovery of juror information[39] or acting as a limitation upon discoverability.[40]   The standard promulgated by the American Bar Association (ABA) reads as follows: "(a) Work Product. Disclosure shall not be required of legal research or of records, correspondence, reports or memoranda to the extent that they contain the opinions, theories or conclusions of the prosecuting attorney or members of his legal staff."[41]   The Commentary points out that protecting the attorney's thought processes is necessary to preserve the adversarial nature of a trial,[42] and it was to this end that the doctrine was formed.

The Commentary then clarifies the scope of the work-product doctrine by presenting examples showing the distinction to be drawn between opinions and facts: "[T]o the extent that the material or information is comprised of opinions of lawyers, *e.g.*, as to the truthfulness of a witness, as contrasted with knowledge of some facts, *e.g.*, what a witness has said, then the material or information is work-product under subsection (a)."[43]   The question to be answered here, then, is whether the jury information generated by social scientists is considered factual or whether it is more akin to a lawyer's opinion. Another excerpt from the Commentary directly addresses this issue: "The following would be protected [from disclosure] : . . . memoranda between personnel in the office on legal questions, evidence, prospective jurors, or other aspects of the case except medical, scientific, and expert's reports. . . ."[44] It is the aspect of protecting lawyers' opinions on prospective jurors that has been addressed by the courts which have held the work-product doctrine to bar all discovery of juror information; these cases were concerned with some form of information generated by the legal staff.[45] They should be distinguished from those cases where social scientists have gathered jury information.

In light of the above discussion, it would seem reasonable, in order to protect the opinions of lawyers, that there should be no discovery of the final product of the juror evaluation process because the attorneys have a substantial input into this process at the point at which all the various types of information are combined. But before this point is reached, the data seem to be "scientific" or "experts' reports" rather than opinions of lawyers.

Although the data may more aptly be termed "opinions" of social scientists rather than "facts" (to return to the original distinction), the ABA Commentary clearly indicates that expert opinions are to be treated as facts, not as opinions of lawyers: "Since material and information are work product only to the extent that they reflect the mental processes of the prosecuting attorney and his legal staff, the opinions, theories and conclusions of lab technicians or other experts would remain discoverable. . . ."[46] In light of this analysis, we conclude that the final rank-ordering of jurors, accomplished by combining all the information and discussing its import with the attorneys and litigants, is protected from discovery by the work-product doctrine. On the other hand, all the information that the social scientists bring to this meeting (i.e., survey results, information gained from juror investigations, and in-court ratings) falls outside the scope and purpose of this doctrine, and should be discoverable.

The possibility exists, of course, that a court order requiring the disclosure of these data may be seen as an invitation to gamesmanship. The data can be presented in such an obscure or inadequately labeled form as to be of little benefit to the recipient. It is hoped that the ethical standards of the social scientists (APA, 1977a) will prevent intentional or negligent obfuscation of their data. Judges should be aware of this possibility when framing disclosure orders.

What legal and ethical problems may the social scientist encounter when using social science techniques to aid in the voir dire?

A. Can criminal sanctions be imposed on a social scientist for conducting juror investigations?

As indicated by the quotation with which we introduced the chapter, the institution of the jury trial is not one that the law takes lightly. A jury cannot properly fulfill its function and render a verdict based soley on the evidence developed at trial if corrupt influences, i.e., bribes, threats, or illicit attempts at persuasion, enter into the decision-making process. As one may suspect, the sanctity of the jury is protected by a number of state and federal statutes. When a social scientist undertakes a jury investigation, he runs the risk that his actions may be construed as falling within those proscribed by one of these statutes. This is not so remote a possibility as it may at first seem; the overt acts of the investigator are quite similar in a number of ways to the acts that may be performed by one seeking subtly to influence a juror. When a uniform rule (i.e., a criminal law) is applied to both sets of actions, there is no guarantee that the rule will distinguish perfectly between them.

In our discussion of jury-tampering laws, we will focus on the federal statutes as interpreted by the federal courts. Each state also has statutes that protect juries in the state court systems,[47] but because of the wide diversity of these statutory schemes, it is impractical to attempt here an analysis of state law. Suffice it to say that although the state statutes are similar to the federal laws in general import, anyone who intends to undertake a jury investigation will be well-advised to examine carefully all of the applicable laws in the particular jurisdiction.

The federal criminal contempt statute[48] may be brought to bear on social scientists who engage in "[m]isbehavior . . . in [the court's] presence or so near thereto as to obstruct the administration of justice."[49] Courts have held persons in contempt for communicating with sworn jurors, even though no wrongful intent was shown.[50] Furthermore, a defendant was held in contempt for employing a detective agency to shadow sworn jurors during a trial, even though no juror had been contacted, nor was any juror even aware that he had been shadowed.[51] In at least one decision a defendant was held in contempt for attempting to bribe a prospective juror (one who is not summoned or sworn);[52] but more recent decisions seem to indicate that actions toward jurors who have not yet been summoned are not within the "presence" of the court or "so near thereto" to come within the statute.[53] Although it is cetainly not impossible, it seems unlikely that this statute will be applied today to hold social scientists in contempt for gathering jury information, unless some communication with the sworn jurors has occurred in or near the courtroom.

The statute more likely to pose problems for the social scientist defines obstruction of justice: "Whoever corruptly . . . endeavors to influence, intimidate, or impede . . . any grand or petit juror . . . in the discharge of his duty . . . shall be fined not more than $5,000 or imprisoned not more than five years, or both."[54] This section has been held to apply to prospective as well as sworn jurors,[55] and unlike criminal contempt, the acts need not occur in or near the presence of the court.

The term "endeavors" has been given a rather broad interpretation; an incomplete or ineffective act may be an endeavor.[56] For example, in *Caldwell v. United States*,[57] Caldwell offered a third party a sum of money to talk to the jurors during the course of a trial to see how they felt about the case. There was no evidence that Caldwell wanted the third party to do any more than solicit the jurors' opinions; furthermore, there was no evidence introduced that the third party ever accepted any money or contacted any juror. Nevertheless, Caldwell's conviction for obstruction of justice was affirmed, the court holding that his actions constituted a corrupt endeavor within the meaning of the statute.[58]

In *United States v. Roe*,[59] Roe was a friend of Crouse, who was the defendant in a criminal action. Roe telephoned the husband of a juror sitting in the Crouse case, mentioning that Crouse was a good person and offering to help the juror's husband with a business problem by contacting a third person. Although the offer of help was not expressly conditioned on any action of the juror or her husband, Roe was convicted of obstructing justice. In affirming this conviction, the appellate court said:

> Neither do we think the fact that the effort to influence was subtle or circuitous makes any difference. If reasonable jurors could conclude, from the circumstances of the conversation, that the defendant had sought, however cleverly and with whatever cloaking of purpose, to influence improperly a juror, the offense was complete.[60]

Despite the fact that the specific intent to impede the administration of justice is an essential element of the offense of obstructing justice,[61] *Roe* suggests that the jury is given a wide range of discretion in drawing inferences about intent from the defendant's actions.

We now have a background against which we may examine the actions of a social scientist conducting a jury investigation. As long as no juror is contacted, there seems to be no problem. But suppose that as social scientists are establishing their network, one of the people contacted becomes suspicious of the investigators' motives and of the propriety of their actions. This does not seem unlikely if we consider the fact that social scientists usually rely on friends of the defendant or other nonprofessionals who are not trained in the skills and techniques of gathering this type of information. In this situation, the probability of these people acting inappropriately or "looking suspicious" as they attempt to obtain information, is substantial. If a person who is contacted by the network does become sufficiently suspicious, he may contact the prospective juror to inform him that persons of questionable character and motives are conducting an investigation into his personal affairs. The prospective juror in turn may well feel threatened or intimidated by the knowledge that someone is "checking up" on him. The authors have personally observed such an occurrence.

In light of the wide range of discretion granted to the jury to infer intent from a defendant's actions[62] and the broad interpretation given the phrase "corrupt endeavors" in the obstruction of justice statute,[63] anyone engaged in jury investigations is well advised to take all possible precautions against causing a juror to be contacted. One important precaution is to advise carefully everyone in the information network not to contact prospective jurors or members of their families because of the legal dangers involved. Since social scientists do not have direct contact with all members of the network, the warning must be "passed down the line" as the network is being formed. The reader may recall that the information network is created when friends and supporters of the defendant are contacted and asked to contact several other people who, in turn, contact several more people, etc. Thus, the warning must be passed on through a long chain of people if it is to reach everyone who will be contacted by the network.

Since the probability is quite small that an oral warning will survive these successive transmissions intact, it is strongly recommended that a written precautionary statement also be prepared. The statement should explain the legal constraints on contacting jurors and their families, and should state that the investigation has the court's approval (if, in fact, it has), that the information will be used only to exercise challenges, and that provisions have been made (if, in fact, they have) for the confidentiality of the information. Everyone who is contacted in the process of conducting the juror investigation should be given a copy of this statement.

Despite the necessity for such a precautionary statement, the persons contacted may become even more suspicious of someone who tells them not to contact the prospective juror. To allay these suspicions, arrangements may be made to allow persons to contact the clerk of the court or some other official who will vouch for the legitimacy of the social scientists' actions.

B. What ethical problems arise from the general social implications of using social science techniques to aid in the voir dire?

A number of ethical standards promulgated by the American Psychological Association (APA) can bear on the actions of psychologists applying social science techniques to aid in the voir dire (APA, 1977a). Principle 1, section e reads as follows: "As practitioners, psychologists know that they bear a heavy social responsibility because their recommendations and professional actions may alter the lives of others. They are alert to personal, social, organizational, financial, or political situations or pressures that might lead to misuse of their influence" (APA, 1977a, p. 2).

As previously noted, social science techniques have generally been utilized either in controversial trials with strong political overtones, where the services have been donated, or where the party can afford the great expense.[64] Since the estimated cost of buying this service is well beyond the means of most people, it can be seen as working to the exclusive benefit of the notorious and the rich. If the techniques are indeed effective, have social scientists widened the gap between justice for the privileged and justice for the unprivileged? The rich already have the best in attorneys and investigators, and we may now be giving them the best in juries. Psychologists who are engaged in the voir dire as practitioners (rather than as researchers) should be sensitive to this issue, and should consider the possibility that their influence is being misused in response to political or financial pressures. Although researchers are apparently not affected by the section discussed above, they should not be oblivious to the social consequences of their actions.

Principle 3, section c, reads as follows: "In providing psychological services, psychologists avoid any action that will violate or diminish the legal and civil rights of clients or of others who may be affected by their actions" (APA, 1977a, p. 3). Assume that a psychologist can and does help a defendant obtain an acquittal-prone jury as opposed to a fair, open-minded one. By so doing, has the psychologist diminished the rights of the public (through the state, which acts as their representative) to a fair trial? In addition, shouldn't the social scientist be concerned with the possibility that he is undermining an important justification for our trial process—its fundamental fairness?

If the social science techniques are effective, then in those cases where the defendant's acquittal is attributable to the intervention of these techniques, the responsibility for the defendant's release rests squarely on the shoulders of the social scientists. One may argue that they are responsible for any crimes the defendant may commit as a consequence of his acquittal. At the very least, the social scientists must concede that their actions carry the potential for profoundly affecting a number of lives, and they should be cognizant of this fact.

A psychologist employed by the prosecution creates a more obvious example of a situation in which a person's legal rights may be diminished. If the psychologist can and does secure a conviction-prone jury, the legal right of the defendant to trial by an impartial jury has been at least somewhat diminished if not entirely abrogated.

It should be noted that all the ethical problems raised thus far in this section can exist only where one side employs social scientists and the other does not, and where jury information is not discoverable. If this is not the situation, then the differential advantage, which is the source of the problems, disappears.

C. Is it ethical for a psychologist to provide the use of social science techniques to aid in the voir dire as a service, and to accept remuneration for these activities?

Principle 6 of the "Ethical Standards of Psychologists" (APA, 1977a) as well as Standard 1 of the "Standards for Providers of Psychological Services" APA, 1977b) throw some doubt on the propriety of the actions of psychologists who engage in aiding in the voir dire as a service. Principle 6 provides, in part, that "psychologists who find that their services are being used by employers in a way that is not beneficial to the participants . . . have the responsibility to make their observations known to the responsible persons and to propose modification or termination of the engagement" (APA, 1977a, p. 5). Standard 1 provides, in part, "Psychologists shall limit their practice to their demonstrated areas of professional competence" (APA, 1977a, p. 5).

Since the effectiveness of social science techniques for the voir dire has never been convincingly demonstrated (Berman and Sales, 1977; Suggs and Sales, 1978), it may be argued that no psychologist can claim professional competence in this area, and in the absence of any indication that these services are benefiting his clients, he should refrain from providing these services for remuneration. Principle 6 requires that psychologists propose modification or termination of services once their ineffectiveness becomes apparent, but is it ethically consistent for a psychologist to agree to provide a service he knows to be of only dubious value?

The above argument loses much of its force when it is realized that demonstrating the effectiveness of various types of psychological techniques and services is no easy task, and that an absence of evidence does not necessarily indicate ineffectiveness. Perhaps the real ethical issue regarding the effectiveness of the psychologist's techniques boils down to a matter of honest representation to the client of what the psychologist can and cannot do for him. There seems to be little reason for withholding services from a client who wants them, as long as the psychologist is scrupulously honest in offering only what he can in fact provide, which, in this case, is a technique with some face validity but no demonstrated effectiveness. A client who is so informed is then in a position to make an informed, intelligent choice. Results cannot be guaranteed, but if the psychologist represents his services honestly, there seems little justification for depriving a client of his freedom of choice.

D. Does a psychologist who is using social science techniques to aid in the voir dire violate the ethical standards requiring freedom of subject participation?

Perhaps the most serious ethical problem in applying social science techniques to the voir dire concerns freedom of subject participation, since many social scientists aiding in the voir dire do so primarily for research purposes and only secondarily to aid the attorney. Principle 6 provides that "psychologists . . . freely acknowledge that clients, students, or participants in research have freedom of choice with regard to participation" (APA, 1977a, p. 4). Principle 9, section e, provides that subjects must be free to decline *and to withdraw* from research, and that "the obligation to protect this freedom requires special vigilance when the investigator is in a position of power over the participant, as, for example, when the participant is a student, client, employee, or otherwise is in a dual relationship with the investigator" (APA, 1977a, p. 7).

Jurors are not free to decline participation in a trial for which they have been summoned; they are required by law to serve, and are subject to legal sanctions if they fail to do so. If jury research is being conducted at the trial for which they are called, jurors become unwitting subjects. From this standpoint, the freedom-of-participation problem is even more severe in jury research than in situations involving students, clients, or employees because the degree of compulsion is much greater. To complicate the problem further, any attempt on the part of the researchers to contact the subjects and attempt to obtain their consent is ill-advised, in light of the jury-tampering laws discussed earlier in this chapter. Thus, the researcher is in an apparent double-bind: he is ethically obligated to respect the jurors' freedom of participation, yet he has no readily available legal means of obtaining their consent.

One possible solution to this dilemma, employed in the past, is to have the court announce the presence of the social scientists and ask jurors if they object. If objections are voiced, the judge orders the social scientists to discontinue their research; if no objections are voiced, it is assumed that the jurors are participating voluntarily. While this device accords the jurors some degree of freedom of choice, it is not without problems.

First, many of the data on the jurors are likely to have been gathered already by this point. It does little good to ask for the subjects' consent when a major portion of the research has already been completed. Second, should a person who objects to participating in this research be required to voice his objection publicly in the courtroom? Social constraints and pressure to conform seem to make it more difficult for a subject to decline in this situation than when a subject declines privately with only the researcher present. Third, this procedure allows a subject to decline at only one point in the research, which is inadequate to protect his continuing right to withdraw at any time.

A more adequate solution, which requires the cooperation of the court and the psychologists, entails sending a description of the proposed research to each prospective juror along with his summons. Included in this description is sufficient information to allow the jurors to make an intelligent, informed choice about whether to participate. At the very least, it should include a description of the type of information the social scientists are seeking, a description of their methods, information as to the use that will be made of the data and who will have access to it, and the plans that have been made to protect its confidentiality.

The juror should also be informed that he may decline participation before the research begins and that he may also withdraw at any subsequent time. In order to allow the juror to exercise this right effectively, withdrawing or declining should be made as simple and easy as possible; perhaps the juror can simply contact the bailiff or clerk, or any other person the court cares to designate. The person can then make the juror's wishes known to the social scientists. This procedure avoids the objections mentioned above by asking for consent before the research begins, by providing for a relatively simple and private means for withdrawal by a subject, and by protecting the subjects' continuing right to withdraw. Although this procedure demands more of the researcher, something along these general lines is necessary to protect the subjects' rights, as psychologists are ethically bound to do.

E. What is a psychologist who is involved in using social science techniques to aid in the voir dire ethically required to do to protect the confidentiality of his data?

Principle 5 states that:

> safeguarding information about an individual that has been obtained by the psychologist in the course of his teaching, practice, or investigation is a primary obligation of the psychologist. Such information is not communicated to others unless certain important conditions are not [sic] met. . . . b. Information obtained in clinical or consulting relationships, or evaluative data concerning children, students, employees, and others are discussed only with persons clearly concerned with the case. Written and oral reports should present only data germane to the purposes of the evaluation and every effort should be made to avoid undue invasion of privacy. (APA, 1977a, p. 4)

In addition, Principle 9, section j, provides that when there exists a possibility that other persons may gain access to the data, subjects must be made aware of this possibility and of the plans to protect confidentiality (APA, 1977a).

At a minimum, all the social scientists involved in the data gathering, the attorneys with whom they are working, and their clients will have access to the juror information, since all of these persons are involved in the final step of combining the data. Of these people, only the psychologists are ethically bound to maintain confidentiality. One possible solution is for psychologists to condition their offer of services (or agreement to engage in research) on the attorneys' and clients' agreement to be contractually bound to keep all information confidential. This arrangement (or whatever other plan is adopted) should be outlined in the research description sent to the prospective jurors.

The most difficult problem concerning confidentiality is created by the possibility that the court may order disclosure of all jury information to opposing counsel. If this happens, the psychologist loses all control over the fate of his data. It should be borne in mind that the identities of the individual subjects are a vital part of such data; anonymous or group data are of no practical use during voir dire, and do not satisfy a disclosure order.

A solution to this problem, once again, requires the cooperation of the court. Counsel for the litigant who is employing the psychologist can request a pretrial hearing, the object of which is to settle the issues of discovery and confidentiality of the data. Opposing counsel would be given the opportunity to move that he be given access to the jury information, and if the court should grant the motion, the issue of confidentiality would be raised. Counsel can request that the court require opposing counsel to keep the information confidential, and that contempt of court be the sanction.

After this motion is ruled upon, the psychologist will have a definite idea of who will have access to the data, and how its confidentiality will be protected. He can then include this information in the research description sent to prospective jurors, who will thereby be given a more realistic idea of the nature of that to which they are asked to consent.

CONCLUSION

One measure of the viability of a legal system is its ability to respond effectively to those innovations that create new stresses in the legal framework. An ideal response harnesses that creativity to further the ends of justice. The novel use of social science techniques to aid in the voir dire presents the legal system with an opportunity to approach this ideal.

The alternatives are clear. We can retain the well-entrenched rule disallowing the discovery of juror information, and fail to acknowledge that the assumptions upon which it is based are crumbling in the face of new technology. The alternative recognizes that justice is best served by the elimination of biased prospective jurors from the jury panel. By allowing both attorneys access to jury information, it can reasonably be expected that biased jurors will be more effectively eliminated than when no such information is available to either party.

If juror information remains nondiscoverable, social science techniques will work only to the advantage of those with the money or influence to employ them. Requiring disclosure of such information will, on the other hand, augment the ability of the law to secure impartial juries beyond the bounds of its present ability to do so. It is to be hoped that the legal system will take this opportunity to demonstrate its viability by harnessing the new technology to the higher ends of justice and equality.

Commensurately, social scientists who are the creators and practitioners of this new technology should share in the responsibility for determining the ends it will serve. Each time the technology is employed, an ethical decision needs to be made about whether or not higher social and ethical values have been taken into consideration. Such decisions should not be made by default. Social scientists should consider the full consequences of their actions before they bring their potentially powerful technology to bear on our legal system.

FOOTNOTES

1. *Gideon v. United States*, 52 F.2d 427, 429 (8th Cir. 1931).
2. *Swain v. Alabama*, 380 U.S. 202, 220 (1965).
3. *Contra*, Note, The constitutional need for discovery of pre-voir dire juror studies. *S. Cal. L. Rev. 49:* 597 (1976).
4. *Taylor v. Louisiana*, 419 U.S. 522 (1975).
5. *Smith v. Texas*, 311 U.S. 128 (1940).
6. *Fay v. New York*, 332 U.S. 261, 291-92 (1947); *United States ex rel. Chestnut v. Criminal Court*, 442 F.2d 611 (2d Cir. 1971).
7. *Witherspoon v. Illinois*, 391 U.S. 510, 517 (1968).
8. See *Swain v. Alabama*, *supra* note 2 (affirming a conviction despite the fact that the prosecution used its peremptory challenges to eliminate all blacks from the jury).
9. Id.
10. See Note, The constitutional need for discovery of pre-voir dire juror studies. *S. Cal. L. Rev. 49:* 597, 625-26 (1976).
11. See *Fed. R. Crim. P.* 15, 16. See generally ABA, *Project on Standards for Criminal Justice: Standards Relating to Discovery and Procedures Before Trial* (approved draft, 1970) [hereinafter cited as *ABA Project*].
12. Id., Commentary to Standard 1.2.
13. See, e.g., *United States v. Falange*, 426 F.2d 930 (2d Cir.) *cert. denied*, 400 U.S. 906 (1970); *Hamer v. United States*, 259 F.2d 274 (9th Cir.) *cert. denied*, 359 U.S. 916 (1958); *United States v. Costello*, 255 F.2d 876 (2d Cir.) *cert. denied*, 357 U.S. 937 (1958); *Best v. United States*, 184 F.2d 131 (1st Cir. 1950) *cert. denied*, 340 U.S. 939 (1951); *Slinker v. State*, 344 So.2d 1264 (Ala. Cr. App. 1977); *People v. Quicke*, 71 Cal.2d 502, 78 Cal. Rptr. 683, 455 P.2d 787 (1969); *People v. Brawley*, 1 Cal.3d 277, 82 Cal. Rptr. 161, 461 P.2d 361 (1969); *People v. Darmiento*, 243 Cal. App.2d 358, 52 Cal. Rptr. 428 *cert. denied*, 386 U.S. 1010 (1966); *People ex rel. Keller v. Superior Court*, 175 Cal. App.2d 830, 1 Cal. Rptr. 55 (1959); *Crawford v. State*, 257 So.2d 898 (Fla. App. 1972; *Monahan v. State*, 294 So.2d 401 Fla. App. 1974); *Robertson v. La. State*, 262 So.2d 692 (Fla. App. 1972); *State v. Holmes*, 347 So.2d 221 (1977); *Commonwealth v. Smith*, 350 Mass. 600, 215 N.E.2d 897 (1966); *People v. McIntosh* 400 Mich. 1, 252 N.W.2d 779 (1977); *People v. Heard*, 58 Mich. App. 312, 227 N.W.2d 331 (1975); *People v. Stinson*, 58 Mich. App. 243, 227 N.W.2d 303 (1975); *People v. Martin*, 57 Mich. App. 84, 225 N.W.2d 174 (1974); *Commonwealth v. Von Smith*, 457 Pa. 638, 326 A.2d 60 (1974); *Commonwealth v. Galloway*, 238 Pa. Super. 69, 352 A.2d 518 (1975); *Commonwealth v. Showalter*, 231 Pa. Super. 278, 332 A.2d 456 (1974); *Commonwealth v. Foster*, 219 Pa. Super. 127, 280 A.2d 602 (1971); *Enriquez v. State*, 429 S.W.2d 141 (Tex. Crim. App. 1968).

14. 426 F.2d 930 (2d Cir.) *cert. denied*, 400 U.S. 906 (1970).
15. Id. at 933.
16. 255 F.2d 876 (2d Cir.) *cert. denied*, 357 U.S. 937 (1958).
17. Id. at 884.
18. See cases cited note 13 *supra*.
19. Some courts have held that it is not within the discretion of the trial court to order disclosure of jury information. See *People ex rel. Keller v. Superior Court*, 175 Cal. App.2d 830, 1 Cal. Rptr. 55 (1959) (holding that it is not within the jurisdiction of a trial court to order discovery of juror information); *State v. Holmes*, 347 So.2d 221 (La. 1977) (holding that the trial court abused its discretion in requiring disclosure of jury information).
20. This approach was taken in *Hamer v. United States*, 259 F.2d 274 (9th Cir.) *cert. denied*, 359 U.S. 916 (1958). The court held that the trial court did not err when it refused to order disclosure of the prosecutor's "jury book," saying that "[p]erfect equality of counsel can never be achieved." Id. at 281.
21. Id. at 281.
22. 384 U.S. 855 (1966).
23. Id. at 870.
24. 47 Mich. App. 639, 209 N.W.2d 796 (1973).
25. Id. at 801.
26. 178 Colo. 184, 496 P.2d 1032 (1972).
27. Id. at 1034.
28. *Offutt v. United States*, 348 U.S. 11, 14 (1954) (holding that a judge who had engaged in a verbal battle with an attorney over the entire course of a trial could not summarily sentence that attorney for contempt).
29. *Turner v. Louisiana*, 379 U.S. 466, 474 (1965) (holding that a jury which was in the custody and constant company of two deputies who were also the chief prosecution witnesses could not try the case); *In re Murchison*, 349 U.S. 133, 139 (1955) (holding that a judge could not adjudicate a contempt charge which arose from conduct before that judge); *Tumey v. Ohio*, 273 U.S. 510, 523 (1927) (holding that a judge compensated only for convictions could not adjudicate the case).
30. 419 U.S. 522 (1975).
31. The jury selection system provided that no woman could be called for jury duty unless she had previously filed with the clerk a written declaration of willingness to serve. Id.
32. Id. at 530.
33. Social science techniques were employed, e.g., in the Angela Davis trial (a black militant was accused of conspiracy in the murder of a judge); the Harrisburg 7 (Father Philip Berrigan and others were charged with conspiracy to raid draft boards and to kidnap Henry Kissinger); the Wounded Knee trials (arising out of the armed occupation by American Indians of Wounded Knee, South Dakota in 1973); the Attica trials (resulting from the Attica, New York prison riot of 1974); the Joan Little trial (a black woman killed a white jailer who she claimed was trying to rape her); the Fred Hampton trial (arising out of a police raid on the Black Panther Party headquarters in Chicago, in which two party members were killed); the Mitchell–Stans trial (in which former Attorney General John Mitchell and Maurice Stans wer accused of perjury, obstruction of justice, and conspiracy). Note, Peremptory challenge–divining rod for a sympathetic jury? *Cath. Law. 21:* 56 (1975). Note, The Constitutional Need for Discovery of Pre-Voir Dire Juror Studies. *S. Cal. L. Rev. 49:* 597, 603-5 (1976).
34. See Ruebhausen and Brim, Privacy and behavioral research. *Colum. L. R. 65:* 1184 (1965).

35. Id.
36. E.g., 18 U.S.C.A. §1508 (1964); *Mass. Ann. Laws* ch. 272, §99A (Supp. 1964).
37. See, e.g., Schulman, Shaver, Colman, Emrich, and Christie, Recipe for a Jury. *Psychology Today*, at 37 (May 1973).
38. See, e.g., *Smith v. Texas, supra* note 5; *Taylor v. Louisiana, supra* note 4; *Swain v. Alabama, supra* note 2.
39. See, e.g., *People ex rel. Keller v. Superior Court, supra* note 13; *People v. Heard, supra* note 13, *Commonwealth v. Von Smith, supra* note 13.
40. See, *People v. Aldridge, supra* note 24.
41. *ABA Project, supra* note 11, Standard 2.6.
42. Id., Commentary to Standard 2.6.
43. Id.
44. Id.
45. See cases cited in note 39 *supra.*
46. *ABA Project, supra* note 11, Commentary to Standard 2.6.
47. See, e.g., *Cal. Penal Code* §95 (West) (prescribing a $5,000 fine or imprisonment for corruptly influencing a juror); *Ill. Ann. Stat.* ch. 38, §32-4 (Smith-Hurd) (any person who communicates directly or indirectly with a person whom he believes has been summoned as a juror has committed a Class A misdemeanor); *Neb. Rev. Stat.* §§28-703, 28-737 (prescribing penalties of up to $500 or one to five years imprisonment for corrupting or influencing a juror); *N.Y. Penal Law* §§215.15, 215.25 (McKinney) (bribing a juror is a Class D felony; communicating with a juror with the intent to influence him is a Class A misdemeanor).
48. 18 U.S.C.A. §401 (1964).
49. 18 U.S.C.A. §401(1) (1964).
50. *Kelly v. United States*, 250 F.947 (9th Cir. 1918).
51. *Sinclair v. United States*, 279 U.S. 749 (1929).
52. *United States v. Russell*, 255 U.S. 138 (1921).
53. See *United States v. Welch*, 154 F.2d 705 (3rd Cir. 1946) (construing 28 U.S.C.A. §385 predecessor of 18 U.S.C.A. §401); *United States ex rel. May v. American Machinery Co.*, 116 F. Supp. 160 (E.D. Wash. 1953).
54. 18 U.S.C.A. §1503 (1964).
55. *Osborn v. United States*, 385 U.S. 323 (1966).
56. E.g., Id., *Caldwell v. United States*, 218 F.2d 370 (D.C. Cir. 1954).
57. *Supra* note 56.
58. Id. In reaching its decision, the court held that the following instructions to the jury were proper:

    If you find beyond a reasonable doubt that the defendant offered Robert C. Fraction a sum of money for the purpose of obtaining information as to the feelings and opinions of the jurors sitting in the Louis case, prior to the verdict, then you are instructed, as a matter of law, that such act was a corrupt endeavor to influence, obstruct, or impede the due administration of justice in this court, and that is all the Government must prove in order to establish the defendant's guilt.... Id. at 371.

59. 529 F.2d 629 (4th Cir. 1975).
60. Id. at 632.
61. *United States v. Ryan*, 455 F.2d 728, 734 (9th Cir. 1972).
62. Id.
63. *Caldwell v. United States, supra* note 56.

64. The cost has been estimated to be as high as $150,000 on the open market. Kahn, Picking Peers. *Wall Street Journal*, at 18, col. 6 (August 12, 1974).

REFERENCE NOTES

1. Tapp, J. L., and Keniston, A., Jr., Wounded Knee—Advocate or expert: Recipe for a fair juror. Paper presented at meeting of the American Psychological Association, Washington, D.C. (September 1976).
2. Christie, R., Psychohistory of conspiracy trials. Paper presented at meeting of the American Psychological Association, Washington, D.C. (September 1976).

REFERENCES

American Psychological Association, Ethical standards of psychologists (1977a).
American Psychological Association, Standards for providers of psychological services (1977b).
Berman, J., and Sales, B. D., A critical evaluation of the systematic approach to jury selection. *Criminal Justice and Behavior 4:* 219–40 (1977).
Caldwell v. United States, 218 F.2d 370 (D.C. Cir. 1954).
Dennis v. United States, 384 U.S. 855 (1966).
Kairys, D., Schulman, J., and Harring, S. (eds.), *The Jury System: New Methods for Reducing Prejudice.* Philadelphia: National Jury Project and National Lawyers Guild (1975).
Losavio v. Mayber, 178 Colo. 184, 496 P.2d 1032 (1972).
People v. Aldridge, 47 Mich. App. 639, 209 N.W.2d 796 (1973).
Schulman, J., A systematic approach to successful jury selection. *Guild Note*, 1973, *2*, 13–20.
Shapley, D., Jury selection: Social scientists gamble in an already loaded game. *Science 185:* 1033–34, 1071 (1974).
Suggs, D., and Sales, B. D., The art and science of conducting the voir dire. *Professional Psychology* (in press).
Taylor v. Louisiana, 419 U.S. 522 (1975).
United States v. Costello 255 F.2d 876 (2d Cir.), *cert. denied*, 357 U.S. 987 (1958).
United States v. Falange 426 F.2d 930 (2d Cir.), *cert. denied*, 400 U.S. 906 (1970).
United States v. Roe 529 F2d 629 (1975).

Juries have the task of integrating subjective impressions, as well as objective information, into a final decision. John C. Mowen and Darwyn E. Linder assume that they function psychodynamically much like a single individual, and therefore their decisions are the final combination of a two-component process which is amenable to understanding and prediction.

Explaining this integrating procedure, they apply the theories of signal detection and information integration. Measuring the consequences of manipulating criterion levels of guilt or innocence, relative to the sensitivity of jurors to the weight of presented evidence, is illustrated by means of practical examples and an experimental study.

Using both these theories in this manner, the authors believe, will account satisfactorily for individual juror attitudes, beliefs, and personal evalutions of situational factors.

6
Discretionary Aspects of Jury Decision Making

John C. Mowen and Darwyn E. Linder

Discretion is defined as the power of free decision, individual judgment, and undirected choice (Merriam-Webster, 1961). As applied to the criminal justice system, it refers to areas of choice in which a criminal justice official is able to make a decision dictated by his or her own judgment and conscience (Black, 1968). While the decision is made within the confines of rules and principles of law, the discretionary judgment involves the application of the individual's own beliefs, attitudes, and personal perception of the situation and circumstances.

Even though writers such as Shaver, Gilbert, and Williams (1975) have discussed the use of discretion in the criminal justice system from the perspective of the police, prosecution, courts, and corrections, little attention has been given to an analysis of jury discretion. At first glance the role of discretion in jury decision-making may seem minimal. After all, the role of the jury in America is to determine the facts and apply the law to them. However, the fact-finding process itself involves the use of discretion in determining the credibility of a witness. In addition, the psychological integration of facts into weight of evidence against the defendant involves the interpretation of the importance of various pieces of evidence. Finally, the jury has the inherent power to ignore and nullify laws. In the general verdict of guilty or not guilty, the jury does not have to give reasons or explanations for the finding. Such a power to abrogate laws, though controversial, represents jury discretion at its maximum. The jury, then, has choice in several aspects of the decision-making process, from the nullification of laws to the interpretation of the relative importance of the evidence in the case.

In this chapter we propose that two theories, when utilized together, account for the general jury decision-making process. Discretion in jury decision-making is represented in the theories by components that allow for the influence of at-

219

titudes, beliefs, and situational factors in the decision. We will first present the Theory of Signal Detection as a model within which the final jury decision may be analyzed. The model, however, fails to account for how the jury determines the total amount of evidence against the defendant. Information integration theory was developed to explain the process of combining disparate pieces of information to arrive at a judgment and is, we argue, well suited to fill this explanatory gap. Jury decision-making, as well as discretion, is discussed in terms of each model, and an empirical study is presented that provides support for the application of the Theory of Signal Detection to jury decision-making.

In this chapter it will be assumed that the jury functions much as a single individual. Therefore, the same factors that have been shown to influence an individual will be assumed to influence a group. Such an assumption has been made previously (e.g., Fried, Kaplan, and Klein, 1975) and is an important step in simplifying and bringing into investigatory focus a complex process. In addition, previous research has shown that mock jury decisions can be predicted with good accuracy from the preliminary decisions of the individual jurors (Bray, 1974; Davis et al., 1975). Thus we believe that the ecological validity of the model will not be severely tarnished by our concentration upon the factors influencing individual decisions.

THE THEORY OF SIGNAL DETECTION

The Theory of Signal Detection (TSD) evolved from statistical decision theory and psychophysics; its lineage can be traced from Blackwell to Thurstone to Fechner (Swets, 1973). An important catalyst to its development was the need to understand the process of detecting electromagnetic signals; for example, how can one explain the decrement in performance of radar operators attempting over long periods of time to locate a signal (enemy aircraft) amid the noise (clouds, etc.) appearing on the radar scope?

A two-component model, TSD views the precision of the observer in distinguishing signal from noise (d') as independent of the observer's criterion or bias (B) in reporting the presence or absence of a signal. An observer's sensitivity is related to his general ability to discriminate the "blip" of the aircraft from various false readings on the scope. The observer's criterion represents the amount of certainty which he must have in order to indicate that the "blip" is a signal. The presence of the criterion biasing a decision is exemplified by the radar operator who will tend, when uncertain, to state that a "blip" is a signal in order to avoid letting an enemy aircraft pass undetected. The theory assumes that observers make mistakes and that the judgmental factors of the perceived prior probability of a signal and of the relative rewards and costs of making certain types of mistakes influence the type of error made. The error of stating that a signal occurred when it was absent is called a "false alarm," while the error of stating that no signal occurred when it was present is called a "miss." Correct responses are labeled either a "hit" or a "correct rejection," giving the 2 × 2 response matrix presented in Figure 1. When certain assumptions are met, d' is independent of B. Thus manipulations of the a priori probability of a signal, or of the response payoff matrix, have been found to affect B while leaving d' constant.

Swets (1973) has described succinctly the history, computational procedures, and applications of TSD. He noted that TSD has been successfully applied to the study of vigilance, perceptual defense, recognition memory, attention, learning, personality, speech, and other topics. In each case an organism attempts to detect a stimulus under circumstances where the signal probability or the benefits and costs of the stimulus-response outcomes may influence the decision to report a stimulus as either a signal or a noise.

TSD AND JURY DECISION-MAKING

We propose that the tasks facing a juror and a radar operator are conceptually similar. Each makes a binary decision under uncertainty. While the radarman must determine if a "blip" indicates an enemy aircraft or only a cloud, a juror must decide if the amount of evidence presented by the prosecution is sufficient to indicate the defendant's guilt. The juror utilizes the underlying continuum of "evidence against the defendant" to detect guilt, much as the radar operator uses the amount and quality of light on the radar scope to determine if the stimulus was signal or noise. This analysis assumes that a defendant's "guilti-

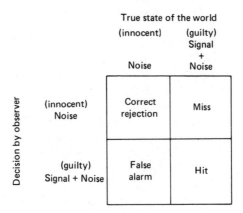

Figure 1. The 2 × 2 response matrix utilized in the Theory of Signal Detection to analyze the decisions of observers.

ness" lies on a unitary dimension labeled "evidence against the defendant." The idea that the dichotomy of guilt and innocence is artificial has previously been submitted by Feinberg (1972). He suggested, for pedagogical purposes, that the ability to defend oneself is a continuum and that factors such as an alibi, a good lawyer, and so on, generate a differential ability to defend. Feinberg's analysis, however, would lead one to conclude that a defendant must prove his innocence. To avoid this misconception, we have labeled the continuum "evidence against the defendant," indicating that the prosecution must prove guilt.

We have, then, a relatively tight formal analogy between TSD and jury decision-making. A juror (observer) is confronted by a trial (the stimulus) that can vary from a small amount of evidence against the defendant (only noise present) to a very great amount of evidence (an unmistakable enemy plane "blip"), and must decide whether the defendant is innocent or guilty.

Factors Affecting A Jury's Criterion For Guilt

If the isomorphism between TSD and jury decision-making exists, factors affecting a jury's criterion and sensitivity should be identifiable. In fact, the trial seems structured to ensure that the jury sets a high criterion for finding guilt. When the guilt threshold is set very high, an increased amount of evidence is required to convict, resulting in a lower probability of conviction. If the observer in Figure 1 makes many fewer "guilty" decisions, the number of false alarms will be reduced, but so will the number of hits, while both correct rejections (an innocent person found not guilty) and misses (a guilty person set free) will increase. One principal way of setting the criterion is through reasonable doubt instruction. As shown by Kerr et al. (1976), if the instruction sets a lax standard for guilt (i.e., criterion is set low), an increased number of guilty verdicts results. Conversely, setting severe standards for guilt results in a lower number of guilty verdicts. [In the Kerr et al. study, the lax criterion was that "a reasonable doubt must be a substantial one," and the stringent criterion was that "essentially any doubt about the defendant's guilt qualified as a reasonable one" (p. 285)]. In TSD terminology, setting a high criterion for guilt decreases the probability that an innocent person will be found guilty (a false alarm).

Note that the bias in the American jury system to avoid the false alarm differs from that of the radarman. Our judicial system abhors making a false alarm, while for the radar operator it only scrambles the jet interceptors with time and money lost. Conversely, a miss for the radarman results in potential catastrophe with an enemy plane undetected, and for the jury results in freeing a guilty individual. Such variations in criteria are based upon the differential reward-cost structure operating in the two situations. For the jury, the cost of convicting an innocent person is higher than the cost of letting a guilty person go free.

Conversely, the cost of scrambling the jets is low for the radarman, while the cost of missing an enemy plane is high.

Manipulation of the 2×2 payoff matrix affects the jury's criterion in additional ways. The perceived severity of the sentence that the defendant will receive if found guilty may affect the criterion. For example, much more evidence may be required to convict if the death penalty rather than life imprisonment results from a guilty verdict. The death penalty is, of course, assumed to increase the cost of false alarms. The heinousness of the crime may work conversely, however. Hendrick and Shaffer (Reference Note 1) found that a heinous crime increases the probability that a jury will find the defendant guilty. Such a crime may cause the costs of a miss to be perceived as highly noxious, thereby lowering the criterion for guilt. The relative impact of a conviction on the defendant may also affect the costs of either type of error. For example, the cost of convicting an individual with a job and family may be greater than for an individual without such socially approved responsibilities. Another case was the requirement to find the "smoking gun" in order to impeach Richard Nixon. The costs to the defendant and potentially to the United States of impeaching a President were so great that no evidence short of a "smoking gun" would suffice to find guilt.

Another factor that can affect the placement of the criterion is the prior probability of a signal's occurring, and several variables may operate similarly in the courtroom. Pretrial publicity may act to create an a priori expectation of the defendant's guilt (see Hoiberg and Stires, 1973). The use of character witnesses seems directed at convincing the jury that, despite the evidence, the likelihood that the defendant committed the crime is low. The physical attractiveness of the defendant may act similarly to create an expectation among jurors that a particularly attractive individual would not have resorted to crime (Sigall and Ostrove, 1975; Landy and Aronson, 1969; Reynolds and Sanders, Reference Note 2.) Finally, the prior probability of a previously convicted offender committing a second crime will probably be perceived as greater than the probability of an individual committing his first offense, resulting in a greater likelihood for conviction because a lower criterion is set (see Doob, 1976).

Factors Affecting A Jury's Sensitivity

Factors affecting a jury's ability to detect a guilty individual also exist in the courtroom. The trend to allow jurors to take notes and for juries to request information while deliberating is clearly related to increasing sensitivity. The method and quality of the presentation of the respective cases by the prosecution and defense attorneys can also affect sensitivity. The adversary system of

American courtroom procedure is a method of ensuring a high-quality presentation of the prosecution and defense cases. Also of critical importance is the quality of the police investigation. A sloppy investigation will result in a lack of evidence or evidence of poor reliability, which can be harmful to both defense and prosecution cases. The ability of the judge to control the courtroom and to ensure the proper execution of the trial procedings can also affect the sensitivity of the jury. Finally, studies investigating the impact of varying the order of the testimony (e.g., Walker et al., 1972) may identify factors influencing the sensitivity of the simulated jury.

Note that all of the above factors are external to the jury. An appropriate analogy is a comparison of the sensitivity of the radar operator who must work with a vintage 1950 radar and an operator working with a 1970 radar. Because of superior equipment, the latter operator will be more sensitive in distinguishing signal from noise. Similarly, properly presented cases, good police investigation, and proper handling of the courtroom by the judge increase the resolution of the process of presenting the evidence of the case. However, factors internal to the jury may also affect sensitivity. The intelligence of the individual panel members, the mix of dominant and submissive individuals, and perhaps the mix of personality types can influence the jury's ability to distinguish signal from noise.

The importance of analyzing jury decision-making in terms of TSD can be demonstrated by the following example. Suppose court officials decided that their goal was to maximize the percentage of correct judgments made by juries. To do this, they could try to have each jury set a criterion that placed equal importance on avoiding either a false alarm or a miss. This procedure, however, would result in an increase in the number of innocent individuals found guilty. Paradoxically, then, if criminal justice officials decided that the percentage of correct responses should be increased by eliminating, to the extent possible, the discretionary aspects of jury decision-making, the probability of false alarms (convictions of innocent persons) occurring would increase. To satisfy their goal, officials must ensure that the criterion remains fixed while the sensitivity of the process is increased.

Figure 2 may help to clarify this example. The two matrices are composed of hypothetical innocent and guilty verdicts crossed by the hypothetical true state of the world. In matrix A note that the number of false alarms is very low and that the number of misses is quite high. When the calculations are made of sensitivity (d') and bias (B) (see Hochhaus, 1972), one finds that $d' = 1.70$ ($d' = 0$ if the matrix is random) and that the criterion is set at 3.31, revealing a bias to avoid finding an innocent person guilty ($B = 1$ if no such bias existed). In matrix B note that the number of false alarms and the number of misses are equal, indicating that $B = 1$, and that no bias exists to avoid either type of error. The

Matrix A		
	True state of world	
	Innocent	Guilty
Innocent	47	22
Guilty	3	28
		100

Matrix B		
	True state of world	
	Innocent	Guilty
Innocent	40	10
Guilty	10	40
		100

Verdicts

Figure 2. Frequencies of verdicts in the 2 × 2 response matrix. Matrix A reveals a criterion set to avoid a false alarm. Matrix B reveals a criterion set to maximize the proportion correct.

sensitivity is equal to 1.68, indicating the same ability to discriminate noise from signal + noise as in matrix A. Also, note that the percentage correct has increased from 75 percent in matrix A to 80 percent in matrix B. The point of the example is that, in moving the criterion, the sensitivity remained essentially unchanged, the proportion of correct responses increased from 75 percent to 80 percent, and the probability of finding an innocent person guilty increased from 6 percent to 20 percent. Thus, moving the criterion to a point at which the types of errors are balanced increases the probability of finding an innocent person guilty, while increasing the overall proportion of correct verdicts. Such an example reveals the importance of conceptualizing jury decision-making in the form of a two-component process. Increases in the total percentage correct can result from either increasing sensitivity or changing the criterion so that the two types of errors are equally weighted. Because the bias to avoid convicting innocent persons is essential to the American system of justice, gains in accuracy must be achieved by increasing the sensitivity of the process, which is not necessarily measured by increases in the percentage of correct verdicts.

Two Alternative Models Resembling TSD

Prior to the discussion of the application of information integration theory to determining the weight of the evidence, two conceptual models bearing some similarity to TSD should be mentioned. Fried, Kaplan, and Klein (1975) introduced a decision theory model that resembles TSD. Their approach assumes that a juror determines a verdict by calculating the probability that the defendant is guilty as well as the ". . . values or utilities for voting for conviction or acquittal given the true states of the world" (p. 58). Within the model a matrix of utilities is developed that gives the value for each of the four decision outcomes. The matrix is quite similar to the one developed in Figure 1. The utilities are combined to form a criterion or standard of reasonable doubt that must be surpassed by the perception of the probability of guilt in order to convict. The probability of guilt is determined by assessing the evidence presented in the trial and closely approximates the concept in the TSD formulation of determining the weight of the evidence against the defendant. The formation of a decision criterion by assessing the mattix of utilities for outcomes also closely approximates the process of setting the decision threshold in TSD by analyzing the reward-cost outcome matrix. Thus the Fried et al. model resembles the TSD formulation in these two important respects. Their model, however, does not contain a parameter relevant to the sensitivity or accuracy of jurors in decision-making, nor does the model utilize the jurors' view of the prior probability of guilt in explaining jury decision-making. In summary, the decision theory model of Fried, et al. contains components strongly resembling those of TSD, but offers a less differentiated view of jury decision-making.

A second model similar to the TSD approach was developed by Thomas and Hogue (1976). As in TSD, the model assumes that jurors calculate an apparent weight of the evidence and that a decision criterion exists which the weight of the evidence must surpass in order to convict. As structured, the model, with but one exception, can account for all of the influences on jury decision-making with which TSD deals. The model is unable to develop an index of juror sensitivity. The approach, though, has strength in that with some simplifying assumptions, it can empirically identify movements in a juror's criterion. Thus while lacking the overall explanatory ability of TSD, the model developed by Thomas and Hogue can be empirically tested in a trial setting in a more stringent manner than can currently be done with TSD.

Determining the Weight of the Evidence

The Theory of Signal Detection gives promise of adequately explaining the factors influencing the final binary decision of the jury. However, one component of the decision task which the jury faces diverges substantially from that encountered by the radio operator. To determine the amount of evidence against the defendant, the jury must integrate a complex set of stimuli presented over a period of days or even weeks. Conversely, the radar operator in a brief period of time, lasting only a few seconds, must determine the intensity of the signal. TSD, then, provides only a partial explanation of jury decision-making. Another theoretical model is required to explain how the jury determines the weight of the evidence against the defendant.

In order to determine the weight of evidence, the jury must integrate the information provided by the witnesses and by the quality and force of the lawyer's arguments. In other words, the amount of evidence is a total of all of the evidence presented during the trial for and against the defendant. Information integration theory (Anderson, 1971) explicitly addresses the question of how individuals or groups combine information in order to reach a decision. We propose that in order to determine the amount of evidence against the defendant, the jury utilizes an information integration process. Only after the jury determines the weight of the evidence is TSD utilized to reach the final decision.

INFORMATION INTEGRATION THEORY

Norman Anderson and his colleagues have applied information integration theory to an astonishing variety of areas over the past 15 years, in experimental as well as social psychology. Theoretical formulations to which integration theory has been applied in social psychology include judgments of motivation and ability, moral judgements, attitudes and opinions, impression formation, and group decision-making. Integration theory has even been applied to jury decision-making (Kaplan and Kemmerick, 1974).

Based on a simple but highly flexible algebraic judgment model, integration theory distinguishes between the scale value and weight of a piece of information and then describes alternative methods of how the pieces are integrated into a judgment. The scale value (s) of an informational stimulus refers to its location on a judgmental dimension. For example, the scale value of a highly attractive individual would be 8 or 9 on a scale of attractiveness with 10 as the very attractive boundary. The weight (w) of an informational stimulus refers to its psychological importance in the final decision. In other words, in the overall judgment the weight indicates how much a particular scale value counts.

The basic theoretical model (Anderson, 1971) is:

$$R = C + \Sigma W_i S_i$$

In the equation, R is an overt response on a scale, C is a scaling factor to allow for an arbitrary zero point, W is the weight, and S is the scale value. The first term of this summational model, $W_0 S_0$, is the initial attitude or opinion of the individual prior to receiving the informational stimuli. In an attitude change experiment, S_0 can be conceived of as the target person's initial position, and W_0 represents his personality characteristics, persuasibility, strength of opinion, and so on. The quantity S_i gives the scale values of the communications, and W_i gives the importance of each communication in the final judgment. The weight of each communication is influenced by such factors as the communicator's status, reliability, and expertise.

Anderson (1971) specified several basic integration rules. One stated that "... the total effect of a communication to be the product of its weight and value" (p. 175). A second rule specified that when two communications are combined, they follow some form of an averaging rule.

Integration Theory And Determining The Weight Of Evidence

If the task of determining the weight of evidence in a jury trial is viewed as analogous to an impression formation task, information integration theory is directly applicable. In impression formation tasks, the subject is provided information, often in the form of a series of adjective traits. It is hypothesized that each piece of information is given a scale value and a weight and then combined with other information to yield a value on a unitary trait dimension. The jury is faced with a similar task. Information is given in the form of witness testimony and of the attorneys' arguments. In processing the information, the jury assigns a scale value and a weight to the testimony of each witness and integrates the information, probably via an averaging process, to obtain a stimulus value on the unitary dimension of evidence against the defendant. The averaging model, in which each piece of evidence has different scale value and weight, is presented in the simple algebraic expression below:

$$E = \frac{W_0 S_0 + \Sigma W_e S_e}{W_0 + \Sigma W_e}$$

The quantity E is the judgment of the amount of evidence, S_0 is the preexisting scale value of the impression of the evidence, S_e are the scale values assigned to the pieces of evidence, and W_0 and W_e are the respective weights.

The scale value of the tesitmony of a witness represents the extent to which the information given is indicative of guilt. For example, in a murder case if a witness testifies that he saw the defendant pull the trigger of the pistol and saw the victim fall from the impact of the bullet, the scale value of this evidence will be very high. However, the importance of this information in the final judgment is determined by the weight assigned to it. The characteristics of the source of information are, in theory, independent of the content of the information, and such source characteristics function to weight the evidence provided. If the source person was a known liar, turned state's evidence to avoid prosecution, or was nearly blind, and so forth, his credibility would be low and his information would be given little weight. Another example of a factor influencing the weighting of evidence occurs when inadmissible evidence is presented in the courtroom. In asking the jury to disregard the testimony, the judge may be viewed as telling the jury to assign it a weight of zero so that it will not influence their final judgment.

The jurors may also have an initial opinion regarding the guilt of the defendant. Such an initial opinion will enter the final judgment and have a scale value and weight. For example, pretrial publicity will result in jurors' having formed some opinion of the defendant's guilt. Another factor which may influence a juror's initial opinion is the fact that the defendant was brought to trial. Jurors are aware that prosecutors will not bring a person to trial unless good evidence of guilt exists. The judicial instructions to presume the defendant innocent may be viewed as an attempt to influence the weighting of the scale value for this piece of evidence.

DISCRETION IN JURY DECISION-MAKING

A model of jury decision-making has been proposed in which evidence or information is first integrated into a judgment of the amount of evidence against the defendant. The final binary decision is made by comparing this judgment to the amount of evidence necessary to convict, in a manner proposed by the theory of signal detection. From this general model the discretionary components of jury decision-making may be derived. Because the model of decision-making proposed consists of two components, sources of discretion are viewed as occurring in both the integration phase and in the binary decision phase.

Discretion In Determining The Weight Of The Evidence

The process of determining the amount of evidence against the defendant was hypothesized to consist of the jury's assigning a scale value and a weight to the information provided by each witness and lawyer. In such a judgmental process, we propose that determining the scale values of each piece of testimony is relatively impervious to the influence of an individual's own beliefs, attitudes, and idiosyncracies, and thus relatively free of influence of discretionary processes. We do propose, however, that the process of weighting of information is influenced by discretionary forces. The factors previously hypothesized to influence the weighting of information are those related to the introduction of attitudes and beliefs in the decision. In particular, attitudes regarding the believability of certain types of witnesses (e.g., minorities or ex-convicts) should function to influence the weighting of the evidence and, therefore, involve the application of discretionary judgment.

To test empirically the hypothesis that the weighting of information is viewed as influenced by personal values and beliefs while the determination of the scale value of the information is not, an experiment was performed. College students were asked to play the role of jurors and were given information on an individual charged with first degree murder. The evidence against the defendant was held constant in the two conditions of the study. In one condition a key piece of evidence was supplied by the deceased's twin brother, who possessed poor eyesight (80-20 when corrected). In the other condition the evidence was furnished by an impartial observer (a respected store owner). Subjects in independent groups rated the witnesses' testimony on two dependent variables—"How indicative of guilt was the testimony?" (a measure of scale value) and "How much weight would you give to this evidence in your decision?" (a measure of the weighting of the scale value). The results revealed that the evidence against the defendant was rated as about equal in the two conditions ($t < 1$), and that the evidence supplied by the impartial observer would be rated as having more weight, $t(25) = 1.75$, $p < .05$, one-tailed. These results support the hypothesis that factors related to discretion, such as the characteristics of the witness, should influence the weighting of the scale value, but not the scale value itself.

Discretion In The Binary Decision Task

In assessing the role of discretion in the jury's decision task of determining guilt or innocence, it is necessary to determine how beliefs and attitudes interact with the decision process. As noted previously, two factors determine the decision—the jury's sensitivity and the criterion for the amount of evidence necessary to convict. Sensitivity refers to the ability of the individual to discriminate noise and signal + noise and is independent of the judgmental factors of the reward-cost matrix of the decision and of the prior probability of either signal or noise occurring. In the theory of signal detection the observer's discriminatory ability is considered to be a perceptual process, not influenced by judgmental factors. In the jury's task, sensitivity refers to the ability of the jury to assess accurately the weight of the evidence against the defendant. The sensitivity of a jury was noted previously to depend upon such external factors as the quality of the police investigation. Internal factors were also noted, such as the collective intelligence of the jury. Such factors are largely unrelated to the role of attitudes and beliefs in personal judgment. Thus the sensitivity of the jury is hypothesized to be unrelated to discretion in decision-making.

In contrast, in TSD setting the criterion is conceptualized as specifically influenced by judgmental factors. As applied to the jury, then, discretion in the binary decision task involves the influence of the reward-cost outcome matrix and the perception of the prior probability of the signal. When discretion is conceptualized in this manner, some of the court rules and procedures as well as tactics of attorneys appear focused upon reducing (or increasing) the influence of discretion in jury decision-making. This conceptualization is illustrated by the judicial instructions for the jury not to consider the potential sentence—a factor influencing the reward-cost matrix. Similarly, prosecutors may attempt to influence the reward-cost matrix by emphasizing the heinousness of the crime through lurid photographs. Another example of a trial procedure designed to minimize discretion is the rule that the prosecution cannot itself introduce the defendant's prior record into evidence. Such a rule helps to reduce the likelihood that subjective prior probabilities will spuriously influence setting the criterion.

In summary, discretion in jury decision-making is hypothesized to occur when personal attitudes and beliefs enter into the decision process. Thus, within the model of jury decision-making developed in this chapter, discretion occurs in determining the importance of individual items of testimony utilized in assessing the total weight of the evidence and in setting the criterion for the amount of evidence required to convict.

In the introduction to this chapter, we briefly discussed the extreme use of discretion in which the jury acts "lawlessly" to nullify a law. Within the model developed in this chapter, such behavior results from the placement of a criterion so high as to make it extremely difficult for the prosecution to gather enough evidence to surpass the threshold for guilt. Kalven and Zeisel (1966) discussed four reasons for the nullification of laws by juries: (1) the penality was too severe; (2) enforcement of the law was not being applied evenhandedly; (3) the jurors themselves sometimes committed the same crime (e.g., gambling or hunting violations); (4) the jurors resented laws regulating their behavior on social or moral grounds (e.g., victimless crimes). In each case a high threshold for guilt seems to exist. In the first case an extremely severe sentence should lead to the perception of even greater costs for convicting an innocent person than would normally be the case. In the last three instances the criterion is raised because the costs of releasing a guilty individual are low. One, the inequity of charging some individuals and not others makes the cost of releasing a guilty person low. Two, the juror knows that he is not a threat to society for having committed the offense; so the individual being tried should not be a threat, with a resultant extremely low cost for a "miss." Finally, in a victimless crime, the harm is borne predominantly by the defendant himself, thereby lowering the cost of a miss to society.

AN EMPIRICAL TEST OF THE TSD MODEL

Research by Kaplan and his colleagues has demonstrated the utility of applying information integration theory to jury decision-making. However, except for the theoretical article developed by Mowen and Linder (Reference Note 3) and the related work of Fried et al. (1975) and Thomas and Hogue (1976), TSD has not previously been applied to jury decision-making. In this section we will reanalyze a study reported by Vidmar (1972), which investigated the dynamics behind the jury's verdict in the Algiers Motel trial. The reanalysis reveals that certain aspects of the study's results support hypotheses derived from TSD. A conceptual replication of the Vidmar study is then presented, which gives additional support for the TSD model.

Vidmar (1972) conducted a study inspired by the infamous Algiers Motel incident (see Hersey, 1968), in which three young blacks were killed during the Detroit riots of 1967. A white policeman was brought to trial for the death of one of the men. In his final instructions to the jury, the judge gave the jurors the verdict alternatives of guilty of first degree murder or not guilty, omitting the middle ground verdicts of second degree murder and manslaughter. Such instructions are unusual, though legal, and represent another example of judicial discretion. The jury returned with a verdict of not guilty, despite considerable evidence against the defendant. A number of questions of a psychological nature arose from the trial. Did omission of the middle ground verdict alternatives lower the probability of the jury finding the defendant guilty of something? And does varying the number of decision alternatives influence the type of decision reached by the jury?

The experimental approach utilized by Vidmar consisted of having simulated jurors (college students) read a trial summary weighted so that the average juror viewed the defendant as guilty of either manslaughter or second degree murder. The four decision alternatives—first degree murder (1st), second degree murder (2nd), manslaughter (MS), and not guilty (NG)—were then arranged into seven conditions defined by the seven combinations of guilty verdicts and not guilty (see Table 1). In analyzing the results of the study, Vidmar focused entirely on the three two-choice conditions (1st v. NG, 2nd v. NG, and MS v. NG). For these conditions the results revealed that the probability of a guilty verdict de-

Table 1. Frequency of Verdicts as a Function of Experimental Condition in Vidmar (1972)

		Condition #						
		1	2	3	4	5	6	7
Possible Verdicts	1st	11			2	7		2
	2nd		20		22		11	15
	MS			22		16	13	5
	NG	13	4	2	0	1	0	2

Note: Blank cells indicate that the verdict alternate was not allowed for subjects under the condition.

creased as one moved from MS v. NG to 2nd v. NG to 1st v. NG. Vidmar identified a mechanism possibly responsible for such results in his introduction: "One might hypothesize that in the instance of a choice between a guilty verdict which carries too severe a penalty or a not guilty verdict, jurors will say 'the penalty is too severe even though the defendant is guilty, and hence I will find him to be not guilty'" (p. 212).

As explained by Vidmar, the effects found in the comparison of the two-choice conditions closely match the effects that excessive penalties have on the criterion for the amount of evidence required for guilt. With high penalties the jurors will not want to risk finding an innocent man guilty of the crime. TSD, then, accounts for Vidmar's interpretation of these results. However, Vidmar failed to consider that in addition to variations in the penalty for the various two-choice cases, there are also variations in the amount of evidence required to prove guilt. Proof of MS requires evidence of a wrongful killing; proof of 2nd requires evidence of malice, and proof of 1st requires evidence of premeditation. Thus the decrease in the number of 1st verdicts could have resulted from the fact that proof of 1st requires additional evidence, not from a penalty perceived as excessive. Thus TSD does not provide the only explanation for the patterns of results Vidmar obtained, and, while the model is not contradicted by the data, it is not unambiguously supported.

Other aspects of the results of the study, however, offer much stronger support for the TSD analysis. TSD may be applied to the situation of multiple decision alternatives in the following manner. The evidence required to convict of MS, 2nd, and 1st may be viewed as forming a Guttman scale. To prove 1st, the prosecution must prove both 2nd and MS, and in order to convict of 1st the jury must determine that the killing was wrongful, with malice, and premeditated. Thus the verdict alternatives are aligned on a scale of evidence against the defendant, with each separate verdict alternative having a different criterion for the amount of evidence necessary to convict. As usual, these criteria may be affected by differential reward-cost outcome matrices or by variations in the probability of the signal.

In Table 1, the verdict of 1st was paired with either one, two, or three other verdicts (i.e., 1st-NG, 1st-MS-NG, 1st-2nd-NG, 1st-2nd-MS-NG). Analyzing the likely costs of finding either an innocent person guilty or a guilty person innocent of 1st across the three sets of conditions leads to a straightforward prediction based upon the following reasoning. With no other verdict alternatives available, the cost of finding an innocent person guilty of 1st is high, and particularly so for the verdict of 1st because of the severe punishment associated with it. However, with no other guilty alternatives available, the cost of not convicting a guilty person is also great, because a murderer can possibly be set free. With the cost of releasing a guilty person and of convicting an innocent person both high in the two-choice case of 1st–NG, the two types of costs will balance. The criterion will then be set to require a middle range of evidence to convict of 1st. For the three-choice alternatives of 1st–2nd–NG and 1st–MS–NG, the costs of failing to convict a person guilty of 1st are lower because he can still be convicted of a lesser charge. This results in the cost of convicting an innocent person of 1st becoming relatively greater than the costs of failing to convict a guilty person of 1st. The result is a higher threshold for guilt, consequently making it more difficult for the prosecution to obtain a conviction of 1st in the three-choice conditions than in the two-choice condition. With four choices an additional guilty alternative is available, which will further increase the relative cost of convicting an innocent person of 1st. This analysis leads to the prediction that a linear trend should exist such that the probability of finding a person guilty of 1st degree murder should be greatest in the two-choice condition and least in the four-choice condition with the three-choice conditions falling in between.

The prediction can be tested by utilizing the Vidmar data. His data were entered into a 2 X 3 matrix, given in Table 2. The columns represent the two-choice, three-choice, and four-choice conditions (with conditions 4 and 5 from Table 1 collapsed for the three-choice conditions). The top row shows the number of 1st verdicts, and the second row shows the frequency of all other verdicts. The statistical analysis consists of first testing for a linear trend and then for a quadratic component. The test for linear trend was significant, ($X^2 = 10.2$, $df = 1$, $p < .001$, and the quadratic component was not significant, ($X^2 = .24$, $df = 1$), supporting the hypothesis that reducing the number of decision alternatives increases the probability of a 1st verdict.

Attention can also be focused on the influence of the number of decision alternatives on obtaining an acquittal. In order to avoid the confounding element of type of guilty charge, we will deal only with conditions having MS as the least severe guilty alternative. Again an analysis of the reward/cost structure of the

Table 2. Analysis of the Effects of the Number of Verdict Alternatives Available on the Frequency of First Degree Murder Verdicts

	2-choice condition	3-choice conditions	4-choice conditions
Frequency of 1st	11 (45%)	9 (19%)	2 (8%)
Frequency of other verdicts	13 (55%)	39 (81%)	22(92%)

Note: Conditions 4 and 5 shown on Table 1 were collapsed to form the 3-choice condition above.

decision outcomes allows for a straightforward prediction. In the two-choice condition of MS/NG, the costs of finding an innocent person guilty and of a guilty person innocent balance themselves in a manner similar to those for 1st degree murder. In three-choice cases, however, with the alternative of 2nd or 1st also available, we propose that the perceived costs of finding an innocent person guilty will decrease. The reason is that with 1st or 2nd or both available (i.e., in the four-choice condition), a verdict of MS will be perceived as a less severe outcome in a manner analogous to a perceptual contrast phenomenon. Thus members of the jury will respond as though they felt that "Well, the defendant could have been convicted of 1st (2nd), so a conviction of MS is not so severe." If our hypothesis is correct, a linear trend should be found such that as the number of decision alternatives increases, the probability of a NG verdict will decrease even with the least severe guilt alternative held constant as MS.

Again the data from the Vidmar study were entered in a 2 X 3 matrix with the two rows consisting of (1) NG verdicts and (2) all other verdicts. However, a visual inspection revealed that no differences existed. It was apparent that so much evidence was brought against the defendant that nearly all the simulated jurors found the defendant guilty when MS was given as an alternative. With such a ceiling effect the hypothesis could not be tested. A test can be made, though, by utilizing 2nd degree murder as the least severe guilt alternative. Thus condition 2 (2nd v. NG) was compared to condition 4 (1st and 2nd v. NG). The comparison was made utilizing the Fisher Exact Probability Test because two of the cells contained expected frequencies of less than five (Siegel, 1956). The exact probability that the observed distribution, or one more extreme, could occur was $p = .055$, supporting the hypothesis that as the number of decision alternatives increased, the probability of a NG verdict decreased, even with the least severe guilty alternative held constant. However, full support for the model required that we obtain similar results with MS as the least severe guilty alternative. Thus, an experiment was conducted in which the strength of the evidence was lowered in order to avoid the ceiling effect found in the Vidmar study. In addition, two trials were utilized in order to obtain some data on the generalizability of the results.

THE EXPERIMENT

Serving as simulated jurors were 675 students in introductory psychology. Subjects listened to audio-taped summaries of and reached verdicts on two trials—a version of the Vidmar (1972) trial with some evidence removed and a trial summarized from Norris (1965). The contents of the trials were recorded on audio cassette tape by a single narrator, and subjects reached their verdicts individually, without a group decision process. The experimental sessions were run with groups of from 6 to 31 subjects, with an average of 20. Because of the high cost of using large numbers of subjects, only four conditions from the Vidmar experiment were utilized (1st-NG, 2nd-NG, MS-NG, and 1st-2nd-MS-NG). The subjects were randomly assigned to one of the four verdict conditions in each trial, and the order of the presentation of the trials was counterbalanced across sessions.

Subjects were introduced to the experimental situation by being instructed to imagine that they were in a courtroom with a judge, witnesses, and so on. They were also reminded that in the future they would probably serve as jurors. They then heard the cassette tape recordings of the trials (lasting 7 and 14 minutes, respectively) and recorded their verdicts on forms supplied by the experimenter. After all simulated jurors had reached a verdict, the second trial was played. The experimental situation appeared to elicit a high level of involvement, and subjects indicated great interest in the study, evidenced by the fact that only two failed to complete the experimental questionnaire. Subjects were given the definition of "reasonable doubt" and the definitions of the verdict alternatives and were instructed not to consider the possible sentence in reaching a verdict. At the conclusion of the experiment all subjects were asked if they were aware that the commission of a homicide while committing another felony is automatically considered to be first degree murder. Individuals who were aware of this fact and who indicated that it affected their verdict were discarded from the analysis of the Vidmar trial (88 total). In this trial the defendant allegedly committed a homicide while performing an armed robbery.

RESULTS AND DISCUSSION OF THE EXPERIMENT

In each trial the two predictions developed from TSD were supported; the results are presented in Table 3. For the prediction that as the number of verdict alternatives increased, the probability of a guilty verdict would increase, the respective one-tailed tests of significance were: Trial $1-X^2 = 31.4$, $df = 1$, $p <$ .001; Trial $2-X^2 = 2.94$, $df = 1$, $p < .05$. Thus with the least severe guilt alternative of manslaughter held constant, adding the verdicts of first and second degree murder increased the chances that the defendant would be found guilty, from 68 percent to 87 percent in Trial 1 and from 70 percent to 79 percent in Trial 2. The prediction that as the number of verdict alternatives increased, the probability of a verdict of first degree murder would decrease was also supported in each trial: Trial $1-X^2 = 46.6$, $df = 1$, $p < .001$; Trial $2-X^2 = 31.4$, $df = 1$, $p < .001$. The frequency of 1st verdicts decreased from 30 percent to zero (Trial 1) and from 67 percent to 32 percent (Trial 2) as the number of alternatives increased from two to four.

The support obtained for each of the predictions derived from TSD has

Table 3. Frequencies and Percentages of Verdicts in the Experiment

Verdicts Available to Jurors

		1st–NG	2nd–NG	MS–NG	1st–2nd MS–NG
Verdict Chosen	1st	40 (30%) / 103 (68%)			0 (0%) / 56 (32%)
	2nd		83 (56%) / 108 (70%)		48 (34%) / 30 (17%)
	MS			100 (68%) / 116 (70%)	73 (52%) / 50 (29%)
	NG	93 (70%) / 54 (34%)	64 (44%) / 46 (30%)	48 (32%) / 50 (30%)	18 (13%) / 37 (21%)

Note: Frequencies above diagonals are for the Vidmar trial replication. Frequencies below diagonals are for the second trial, extracted from Norris (1965).

theoretical and practical importance. Although other explanations of the results of the Vidmar study are possible (see Larntz, 1975),* the findings can be interpreted to provide evidence that the reward/cost decision matrix can be influenced by the types of other decisions available. TSD, a theoretical formulation of considerable explanatory power, has therefore been shown empirically to account for some aspects of jury decision-making.

On the practical side, the results imply that the discretion of the judge to select the number of verdict alternatives may have important consequences for the defendant. By adding decision alternatives, the probability of a guilty verdict increased by an average of 14 percent in the two cases, but 1st verdicts decreased by about 30 percent for both trials when 2nd and MS were added to 1st and NG as possible verdict alternatives.

The results of the experiment reveal the utility of applying TSD to jury decision-making. The theory's distinction between sensitivity and criterion setting has potential importance in developing court procedures that maximize the overall probability of convicting those who are guilty while concomitantly avoiding the serious error of convicting a larger proportion of innocent defendants. This

*Larntz (1975) was able marginally to fit Vidmar's (1972) study with a mathematical conditional probability model. The model was applied to the data obtained in the two trials and was found not to fit with $p < .01$ in each case.

point is an important one in understanding the application of TSD to jury decision-making. Merely moving the criterion to a point at which the two types of errors are given equal weight will not, in theory, influence the sensitivity of the jurors. However, it will increase the number of innocent individuals found guilty, as was shown by the example presented earlier in the chapter.

There is an additional advantage when the information integration approach is used in combination with TSD. To conceptualize discretion in jury decision-making as occurring in setting the criterion in the final judgment and in determining the weight of the items of evidence is a first step in the process of more clearly defining an elusive concept. In previous work, discretion has generally been treated as a broad concept, and no attempt has been made to define it precisely. Until the term is narrowed and related to specific behaviors or components of a theory or model, research on discretion in jury decision-making will be difficult. Our attempt to define discretion in terms of the judgmental aspects of setting decision thresholds and of determining weighting of evidence, though somewhat arbitrary, fulfills the function of narrowing the concept to the point at which the variables influencing it can be specified, and its impact on decision-making identified. Future research in this area should focus on additional factors that influence weighting evidential information and setting the criterion.

REFERENCE NOTES

1. Hendrick, C., and Shaffer, D., Murder: Effects of number of killers and victim mutilation on simulated jurors' judgments. Unpublished manuscript, Kent State University.
2. Reynolds, D. E., and Sanders, M. S., The effects of the defendant's attractiveness, age, and injury on severity of sentence given by simulated jurors. Paper delivered to Western Psychological Association (May 1973).
3. Mowen, J. C., and Linder, D. E., The theory of signal detection as an analogy to the jury decision making process. Presented at the Rocky Mountain Psychological Association Convention, Phoenix, Arizona (April 1976).

REFERENCES

Anderson, N. H., Integration theory and attitude change. *Psychological Review 78:* 171–206 (1971).

Black, H. C., *Black's Law Dictionary* (4th ed.). St. Paul, Minnesota: West Publishing Co. (1968).

Bray, R., Decision rules, attitude similarity, and jury decision making. Unpublished doctoral dissertation, University of Illinois at Urbana, (1974).

Davis, J. H., Kerr, N. L., Atkin, R. S., Holt, R., and Meek, D., The decision processes of 6- and 12-person mock juries assigned unanimous and two-thirds majority rules. *Journal of Personality and Social Psychology 32:* 1–14 (1975).

Doob, A. N., Evidence, procedure, and psychological research. In G. Bermant, C. Nemeth, and N. Vidmar (eds.), *Psychology and the Law.* Lexington, Massachusetts: Lexington (1976).

Feinberg, W. E., Teaching the Type I and Type II errors: The judicial process. *The American Statistician 26:* 21–23 (1972).

Fried, M., Kaplan, K. J., and Klein, K. W., Juror selection: An analysis of voir dire. In R. J. Simon (ed.), *The Jury System in America.* Beverley Hills, California: Sage Publications (1975).

Hersey, J. R., *Algiers Motel Incident.* New York: Knopf (1968).

Hochhaus, L. A table for the calculation of d' and B. *Psychological Bulletin 77:* 375–76 (1972).

Hoiberg, B. C., and Stires, L. K., The effect of several types of pretrial prublicity on the guilt attributions of simulated jurors. *Journal of Applied Social Psychology 3:* 267–75 (1973).

Kalven, H., and Zeisel, H., *The American Jury.* Chicago: University of Chicago Press (1966).

Kaplan, M., and Kemmerick, G. D., Juror judgment as information integration; Combining evidential and nonevidential information. *Journal of Personality and Social Psychology 30:* 493–99 (1974).

Kerr, N. L., Atkin, R. S., Stasser, G., Meek, D., Holt, R. W., and Davis, J. H., Guilt beyond a reasonable doubt: Effects of concept definition and assigned decision rule on the judgments of mock jurors. *Journal of Personality and Social Psychology 34:* 282–94 (1976).

Landy, D., and Aronson, E., The influence of the character of the criminal and victim in the decisions of simulated jurors. *Journal of Experimental Social Psychology 5:* 141–52 (1969).

Larntz, K., Reanalysis of Vidmar's data on the effects of decision alternatives on verdicts of simulated jurors. *Journal of Personality and Social Psychology 31:* 123–25 (1975).

Norris, H., *A Casebook of Complete Criminal Trials.* Detroit: Citation Press (1965).

Shaver, K. G., Gilbert, M. A., and Williams, M. C., Social psychology, criminal justice and the principle of discretion: A selective review. *Personality and Social Psychological Bulletin 1:* 471–84 (1975).

Siegel, S., *Nonparametric Statistics for the Behavioral Sciences.* New York: McGraw-Hill (1956).

Sigall, H., and Ostrove, N., Beautiful but dangerous: Effects of offender attractiveness and nature of the crime on juridic judgment. *Journal of Personality and Social Psychology 31:* 410–14 (1975).

Swets, J. A., The relative operating characteristic in psychology. *Science 182:* 990–1000 (1973).

Thomas, E. A. C., and Hogue, A., Apparent weight of evidence, decision criteria, and confidence ratings in juror decision making. *Psychological Review 83:* 442–65 (1976).

Torgenson, W. S., *Theory and Methods of Scaling.* New York: John Wiley & Sons, Inc. (1962).

Vidmar, N., Effects of decision alternatives on the verdicts and social perceptions of simulated jurors. *Journal of Personality and Social Psychology 22:* 211–18 (1972).

Walker, L., Thibaut, J., and Andreoli, V., Order of presentation at trial. *The Yale Law Journal 82:* 216–26 (1972).

The chapter that follows, by Peter B. Hoffman and Barbara Stone-Meierhoefer, provides the reader with a clear statement of some new guidelines to sentencing. In recent years, both in several states and in the federal system, increasing attention has been given to the development of standards or guidelines for the sentencing of convicted persons so that determinant rather than indeterminant periods of confinement can be equitably followed by state court and federal judges.

The research reported in the following chapter is that undertaken under the auspices of the U.S. Parole Commission, some of which serves as a basis for pending legislation in the U.S. Congress looking toward a codification of the laws and practices now scattered throughout the U.S. Code. The authors address themselves to the legal and ethical issues. Also they provide a series of guidelines for sentencing and indicate the conditions under which those guidelines may be applied to particular kinds of infractions of both state and federal laws. The result is a helpful overview of the issues and problems that confront those who believe in sentences of determinant length for specific crimes.

7
Application of Guidelines to Sentencing

Peter B. Hoffman and Barbara Stone-Meierhoefer

Sentencing decisions lie at the very heart of the criminal justice system. Next to the determination of guilt or innocence, a determination waived by the substantial proportion of defendants who plead guilty, the sentencing decision is probably the most important decision made about the criminal defendant in the entire process. In most jurisdictions, the sentencing judge has broad discretion in determining both type and duration of sentence. In the federal system, for example, a judge generally has discretion to impose a fine, a period of probation, a suspended sentence, any period of imprisonment up to the statutory maximum for the offense, or some combination of the above. If a period of imprisonment with a maximum term exceeding one year is imposed, the judge may set a minimum term of one-third of the maximum imposed, a lesser minimum, or no minimum at all. Within the limits of the minimum term, if any, and the maximum (less institutional good time earned), the determination as to the actual period to be served in confinement is made by the paroling authority.

A major concern with sentencing practice in the United States today involves what is commonly termed "sentencing disparity." Actually, this problem is more properly characterized as one of unwarranted sentencing variation, as critics of "sentencing disparities" do not generally claim that all individuals should receive identical sentences, but rather that there should be justifiable reasons for the differences in sentences imposed. The literature on sentencing is filled with case examples of widely disparate sentences imposed upon defendants with extremely similar offenses and backgrounds. Unwarranted disparity may occur in

Note: Adapted from an article of the same title which appeared in the *Law and Psychology Review*, Volume 3, 1977 (reprinted with permission). The views expressed in this paper are the personal views of the authors and do not necessarily represent those of the United States Parole Commission, its individual members (specifically Commissioners Dorothy Parker and Joseph Nardoza), or the Department of Justice.

sentences imposed by different judges or in those imposed by the same judge from one time to the next. Few dispute the existence or extent of this problem, found by the President's Commission on Law Enforcement and Administration of Justice (1967) to be pervasive.[1]   The National Advisory Commission on Criminal Justice Standards and Goals (1973) declared the state of the sentencing process in this country to be nothing less than appalling.[2]   American sentencing practices have recently been characterized by one critic as ". . . so arbitrary, discriminatory, and unprincipled that it is impossible to build a rational and humane prison system on them."[3]   Another critic, a federal district court judge, has bluntly concluded that the discipline of sentencing presently constitutes ". . . a vast wasteland in the law."[4]

The existence of unwarranted disparity in sentencing poses problems, both ethical and practical. From an ethical standpoint, the problem is obvious: unwarranted sentencing disparity is antithetical to our cherished concepts of fairness and justice. Frequently quoted is an excerpt from an opinion by Justice Potter Stewart, written while he was an appellate judge:

> Justice is measured in many ways, but to a convicted criminal its surest measure lies in the fairness of the sentence he receives. . . . It is an anomaly that a judicial system which has developed so scrupulous a concern for the protection of a criminal defendant throughout every other stage of the proceedings against him should have so neglected this important dimension of fundamental justice.[5]

The practical problems posed by unwarranted sentencing disparity are equally clear. Inequity in sentencing (real or perceived), it has often been argued, is likely to be dysfunctional for efforts at rehabilitation.[6]   Knowledge of disparate sentencing practices may interfere with the orderly administration of justice as attorneys attempt to alter schedules to bring their clients before judges perceived as lenient.[7]   Moreover, appellate judges—where precluded from direct review of sentences—may be encouraged to distort substantive law to provide what they feel is the required relief.[8]

Three primary factors appear to contribute jointly to the problem of unwarranted sentencing disparity. The first involves the lack of clearly articulated and accepted sentencing goals, priorities, and criteria; the second concerns the substantial discretion provided sentencing judges and paroling authorities [which in most jurisdictions share the sentencing function] in the absence of such goals and criteria; while the third involves the procedures under which this discretion is presently exercised.

The functions of criminal sanctions have generally been defined as including deterrence (primary and secondary), retribution, incapacitation, rehabilitation, and maintenance of respect for law (community condemnation).[9]   Unfortunately, legislatures customarily have been silent as to either the appropriateness or the primacy of these purposes, and as to how situations in which these purposes appear to conflict are to be resolved. For example, federal law merely mandates that the court in passing sentence consider ". . . in its opinion the ends of justice and best interests of the public. . . ."[10] Nor is legislative guidance provided as to the factors or types of information to be considered at sentencing or the importance to be attached to them. Again, federal statute provides only that "No limitation shall be placed on the information concerning the background, character, and conduct of a person convicted of an offense which a court of the United States may receive and consider for the purpose of imposing an appropriate sentence."[11]

Consequently, a federal judge is left to act at sentencing without any standards to guide the exercise of his discretion other than the attitudes and values he brings with him or develops on the bench. Whether factors relating the circumstances of the present offense, the defendant's prior record, social background, "attitude or remorse," or type of plea are given primary weight, some weight, or no weight at all, is left totally to the discretion of the individual sentencing judge. Thus, sentencing policy-making in addition to, and as distinguished from, individual case decision-making, in effect, has been delegated to each of the over 350 federal district court judges.

Nevertheless, sentencing judges and paroling authorities as a rule have not attempted to fill this legislatively created gap by formally articulating sentencing principles and criteria, nor have sentencing procedures been designed to highlight the operational criteria in effect. The United States Parole Commission is an exception to this rule, which will be discussed later. Reasons for judicial sentencing decisions in the federal system are not generally articulated, nor are they required. Multijudge sentencing panels are used only in a few scattered districts, while appellate review of a sentence within the statutory maximum is simply unavailable. It is not difficult to see how this lack of guided, reasoned, and reviewable discretion permits claims of arbitrary and capricious decision-making and unwarranted decision disparity.

Moreover, without the articulation of underlying sentencing policy, it is questionable whether the mere provision of procedural reforms such as sentencing panels, written reasons, and/or appellate review is sufficient to produce the desired effect. A panel approach has been the rule among parole boards, yet criticisms of disparate parole decision-making are by no means rare.[12] There is some evidence that merely providing written reasons in each case does not appreciably reduce disparity, and that the reasons given tend to be rather rote generalizations.[13] Similarly, without clearly articulated policy and meaningful sentencing reasons at the trial court level, appellate review is likely to be ineffective.[14]

244 Part II. Discretion in the System of Criminal Justice

MANDATORY SENTENCES

In reaction to this morass, there has recently been increased interest in legislatively eliminating or severely curtailing judicial sentencing discretion through the establishment of what are termed mandatory penalties.

Mandatory sentencing proposals appear to have three basic forms. One approach simply specifies a legislatively prescribed penalty for each statutory offense (e.g., burglary first degree shall be punished by eight years in prison) or offense/prior record combination (e.g., first degree burglary shall be punished by twelve years in prison if the offender has one or more prior felony convictions). No provision would be made for consideration of mitigating or aggravating factors. On its face, no judicial sentencing discretion would be allowed. This approach has been recommended by the American Friends Service Committee.[15] Several state death penalty statutes passed in reaction to the United States Supreme Court decision in *Furman v. Georgia*[16] were of this form.[17]

A second type of legislative solution involves what has been termed presumptive sentencing.[18] In this variation, the legislature prescribes a sentence for each statutory offense (or offense class), but permits judicial discretion to vary from the prescribed sentence by a given amount (e.g., sale of narcotics shall be punishable by four years imprisonment $\pm$ one year) or upon a finding of specific aggravating or mitigating factors (e.g., the offender acted under duress). Recently enacted California legislation contains presumptive sentences for terms of imprisonment that may be imposed.*

A third form of mandatory sentencing proposal specifies not what the penalty must be, but rather what it may not be (e.g., persons convicted of felonies involving the possession or use of a weapon shall not receive probation or a term of less than two years imprisonment). In this case, judicial discretion is retained to impose any penalty not expressly prohibited. We wish to stress that there may be considerable variation within the forms described from one proposal to the next. The essence of all these proposals, however, is that the present abuses of sentencing discretion may be rectified by strict legislative limitation of such discretion.

While the image of "mandatory" sentences may appeal to the desire of the lawmakers and citizenry to make punishments more certain—and while it appears generally agreed that legislators ought to give more attention to specifying the underlying rationale and priorities for the imposition of criminal sanctions— a number of troublesome problems are presented by both the mandatory and the presumptive sentencing approaches.

*State of California Penal Law SB 42, effective July 1, 1977. This legislation, while setting presumptive sentences when imprisonment is imposed, does not provide guidance for the judge's discretion regarding whether or not to impose imprisonment, fine, suspended sentence, or probation in the first place.

First, it appears unlikely that any legislative body will be able to specify in advance and with sufficient detail all of the possible factors and combinations of factors that would be necessary to make a strict mandatory sentencing (no discretion) scheme comport with present notions of desired equity and justice in sentencing. For example, a criminal act labeled assault may encompass a wide range of behaviors with different degrees of harm and/or culpability. Likewise, both the sale of marijuana to grade school children for profit and the gift of a small quantity of marijuana by a 16-year-old to a 17-year-old friend might, in some jurisdictions, constitute "distribution of marijuana to a minor." It is our belief that present conceptions of equity in sentencing do not call for identical sentences for each statutory crime, but rather for justifiable reasons for variations in sentences. As recently noted by the Supreme Court in *Woodson v. North Carolina:*

> This court has previously recognized that "[f] or the determination of sentences, justice generally requires consideration of more than the particular acts by which the crime was committed and that there be taken into account the circumstances of the offense together with the character and propensities of the offender." Consideration of both the offender and the offense in order to arrive at a just and appropriate sentence has been viewed as a progressive and humanizing development.[19] [Citations omitted.]

While the Supreme Court's holding in this case [that failure to consider the character and record of the individual offender and the circumstances of the particular offense constituted an infirmity of constitutional magnitude] was specifically restricted to the imposition of capital penalties, it would appear that the underlying logic remains valid in relation to other sentencing dispositions.

Although this problem is not quite as acute in presumptive sentencing proposals (which provide for limited sentencing discretion), there is little reason to believe that a truly limited sentencing range will be able to accommodate the more unusual cases—the very cases for which sentencing discretion is necessary in the first place. On the other hand, if the discretionary ranges are set wide enough to handle such cases, it is likely that the intended effect on disparity will be minimal. Similarly, it is unlikely that narrowly drawn legislative statements of mitigating or aggravating factors, which may be used to override the presumptive sentence, will be sufficient to anticipate in advance all the appropriate exceptions; yet broadly drawn standards will provide only minimal discretionary control.

As Kress et al. point out, a central flaw in presumptive sentencing proposals is that the legislature must make before-the-fact, speculative judgments as to what will constitute "typical" offense behaviors and criminal histories, as to what punishments are appropriate, and as to what specific factors may alter such punishments by particular amounts. Thus, they conclude:

[If] the legislature makes its decision only on the basis of theoretical argument and the skimpy factual information it now possesses, it will inevitably draw unrealistic conclusions which will insure the wholesale discretionary avoidance of the legislative mandate by police, prosecutors, and judges which has rendered so many prior reform efforts nugatory.[20]

Second, while legislatively prescribed terms of either form may begin with relatively modest penalty lengths, there is an underlying potential for unanticipated escalation. Recently passed California legislation, for example, provides a penalty of four years ± one year for rape or sale of heroin, with additional enhancements for specific aggravating factors of up to three years. However, up to one-third of the term can be remitted on the basis of institutional conduct ($\frac{3}{12}$ for good behavior and an additional $\frac{1}{12}$ for programming). Thus, for an individual with no prior prison commitments (even though he may have numerous convictions not resulting in prison terms) the maximum possible penalty for rape or narcotics sale—no matter how heinous or aggravated—would appear to be 64 months (60 + 36 – 32), provided the offender maintained good institutional adjustment. It is theorized that a legislative tendency to react to dramatic incidents (e.g., a particularly brutal rape or large-scale narcotics conspiracy) may produce a potential for equally dramatic increases in the entire penalty structure in such a system, especially if public attention is directed towards these cases in close proximity to election time.* As Frankel has commented:

Many of our criminal laws are enacted in an excess of righteous indignation, with little thought or attention given to the long number of years inserted as maximum penalties. Written at random, accidential times when particular evils come to be perceived, the statutes are not harmonized or coordinated with each other. The resulting jumbles of harsh anomalies are practically inevitable.[21]

Although proponents of legislative sentencing may contend that the increased ability to calculate future prison costs under a fixed sentencing scheme will deter legislators from wholesale increases in penalties,[22] this has not been demonstrated; and it appears to us equally likely that, given more immediate political considerations, such deterrent effect will be minimal.

---

*Between the time the legislation described here was enacted and its effective date (July 1, 1977), several amendments were adopted which appear to allow both for increased judicial discretion and tougher enhancements to the base term.

There is also the question of whether the legislative process will be unduly cumbersome in relation to the monitoring of sentencing practice and the modification of presumptive or mandatory sentences that experience may dictate (particularly if downward modification is recommended).* Although harsh application of outmoded mandatory sentences may result in considerable injustice, it is questionable whether the types of persons who become defendants and prisoners can engender the same degree of sympathy and public concern that may be generated for those perceived as innocent victims.

Third, there appears to be a substantial possibility that the real impact of mandatory or presumptive sentencing schemes would be to promote hidden disparity. That is, although it might appear on the surface that penalties were being fairly administered (i.e., similar sanctions rendered for similar statutory offenses), the net effect would be that sentencing discretion would to a greater extent be turned over to the prosecutor (who could effectively control the sanction by the offense charged or arrived at through plea negotiation). As noted by Heinz et al., the resultant danger is obvious:

> To rely on prosecutorial discretion to provide differentiation in the treatment of these very different cases would be neither safe nor principled—it would, in fact, be to admit the need to import individualized justice back into the system.[23]

It is to be remembered that as one moves toward the intake point in the criminal justice system (from judge to prosecutor to police), the exercise of discretion tends to become less visible and, thus, less subject to control.*

There is also the possibility that with mandatory sentences, there will be less rather than more certainty in the application of punishments. As the Supreme Court pointed out in *Woodson*, American juries have persistently refused to convict a significant portion of persons charged under mandatory death penalty statutes. Similar arguments have been made in relation to the effects of mandatory sentences for narcotic offenders.[24] Thus, it is argued, if discretion to accommodate mitigating factors is removed from the sentencing stage, juries and/or judges may react to penalties deemed too harsh by more frequently letting offenders go free entirely.

SENTENCING GUIDELINES

A different approach to structuring sentencing discretion, favored by the writers of this paper, involves what may be termed a "guidelines model." In this ap-

---

*For example, one may look at the resilience of laws governing private sexual relationships among consenting adults, which, although rarely if ever enforced, appear quite resistent to legislative repeal.

*See Chapter 3 for further discussion of this point at the level of initial discretion-making.

Table 1. Adult Guidelines for Decision-Making

[Guidelines for Decision-Making, Customary Total Time to be Served before Release (including jail time)]

OFFENSE CHARACTERISTICS: Severity of Offense Behavior (Examples)	OFFENDER CHARACTERISTICS: Parole Prognosis (Salient Factor Score)			
	Very Good (11 to 9)	Good (8 to 6)	Fair (5 to 4)	Poor (3 to 0)
LOW				
Escape [open institution or program (e.g., CTC, work release)–absent less than 7 days] Marihuana or soft drugs, simple possession (small quantity for own use) Property offenses [theft or simple possession of stolen property] less than $1,000	6–10 months	8–12 months	10–14 months	12–18 months
LOW MODERATE				
Alcohol law violations Counterfeit currency (passing/possession less than $1,000) Immigration law violations Income tax evasion (less than $10,000) Property offenses [forgery/fraud/theft from mail/embezzlement/interstate transportation of stolen or forged securities/receiving stolen property with intent to resell] less than $1,000 Selective Service Act violations	8–12 months	12–16 months	16–20 months	20–28 months
MODERATE				
Bribery of a public official (offering or accepting) Counterfeit currency (passing/possession $1,000 to $19,999)	12–16 months	16–20 months	20–24 months	24–32 months

16–20 months	20–26 months	26–34 months	34–44 months

Drugs:
  Marihuana, possession with intent to distribute/sale [small scale (e.g., less than 50 lbs.)]
  "Soft drugs," possession with intent to distribute/sale (less than $500)
Escape [secure program or institution, or absent 7 days or more—no fear or threat used]
Firearms Act, possession/purchase/sale (single weapon: not sawed-off shotgun or machine gun)
Income tax evasion ($10,000 to $50,000)
Mailing threatening communication(s)
Misprison of felony
Property offenses [theft/forgery/fraud/embezzlement/interstate transportation of stolen or forged securities/receiving stolen property] $1,000 to $19,999
Smuggling/transporting of alien(s)
Theft of motor vehicle (not multiple theft or for resale)

HIGH

Counterfeit currency (passing/possession $20,000 to $100,000)
Counterfeiting (manufacturing)
Drugs:
  Marihuana, possession with intent to distribute/sale [medium scale (e.g., 50 to 1,999 lbs)]
  "Soft drugs," possession with intent to distribute/sale ($500 to $5,000)
Explosives, possession/transportation
Firearms Act, possession/purchase/sale (sawed-off shotgun(s), machine gun(s), or multiple weapons)
Mann Act (no force—commercial purposes)
Theft of motor vehicle for resale

Table 1. Adult Guidelines for Decision-Making

[Guidelines for Decision-Making, Customary Total Time to be Served before Release (including jail time)]

OFFENSE CHARACTERISTICS: Severity of Offense Behavior (Examples)	OFFENDER CHARACTERISTICS: Parole Prognosis (Salient Factor Score)			
	Very Good (11 to 9)	Good (8 to 6)	Fair (5 to 4)	Poor (3 to 0)
Property offenses [theft/forgery/fraud/embezzlement/ interstate transportation of stolen or forged securities/receiving stolen property] $20,000 to $100,000				
VERY HIGH				
Robbery (weapon or threat)	26–36 months	36–48 months	48-60 months	60–72 months
Breaking and entering [bank or post office—entry or attempted entry to vault]				
Drugs:				
Marihuana, possession with intent to distribute/ sale [large scale (e.g., 2,000 lbs. or more)]				
"Soft drugs," possession with intent to distribute/ sale (over $5,000)				
"Hard drugs," possession with intent to distribute/ sale (not exceeding $100,000)				
Extortion				
Mann Act (force)				
Property offenses [theft/forgery/fraud/embezzlement/ interstate transportation of stolen or forged securities/ receiving stolen property] over $100,000 but not exceeding $500,000				
Sexual act (force)				

GREATEST

Aggravated felony (e.g., robbery, sexual act, aggravated assault) — weapon fired or personal injury

Aircraft hijacking

Drugs:

"Hard drugs," possession with intent to distribute/ sale (in excess of $100,000)

Espionage

Explosives (detonation)

Kidnapping

Willful homicide

(Greater than above — however, specific ranges are not given owing to the limited number of cases and the extreme variation in severity possible within the category.)

NOTES: 1. These guidelines are predicated upon good institutional conduct and program performance.
2. If an offense behavior is not listed above, the proper category may be obtained by comparing the severity of the offense behavior with those of similar offense behaviors listed.
3. If an offense behavior can be classified under more than one category, the most serious applicable category is to be used.
4. If an offense behavior involved multiple separate offenses, the severity level may be increased.
5. If a continuance is to be given, allow 30 days (1 month) for release program provision.
6. "Hard drugs" include heroin, cocaine, morphine, or opiate derivatives, and synthetic opiate substitutes. "Soft drugs" include, but are not limited to, barbiturates, amphetamines, LSD, and hashish.
7. Conspiracy shall be rated for guideline purposes according to the underlying offense behavior if such behavior was consummated. If the offense is unconsummated, the conspiracy will be rated one step below the consummated offense.

proach, a collegiate body (e.g., a sentencing commission, appellate court, or paroling authority) is given the task of formulating explicit sentencing policy under broad standards set by the legislature.* This policy formulation would involve the identification and articulation of the primary factors to be considered at sentencing and the customary weights to be given to them. For each combination of major decision elements, an explicit policy would be provided. The individual sentencing judge would be obligated to apply the guidelines to each case. However, discretion to render a decision departing from the guidelines would be retained, provided that adequate reasons for such departure were specified on the record. Thus, each defendant would be told at sentencing how his or her case was assessed against the guidelines, and if the sentence imposed departed from the guidelines, of the reasons therefor. By focusing on departures from customary policy, this system should avoid the trivialization of reasons that is alleged to occur when such reasons are required without the articulation of underlying sentencing policy. Moreover, a guidelines system would facilitate the provision of appellate review of sentences. In contrast to jurisdictions in which such review is currently allowed, appellate review under a guideline model would have a very specific focus. That is, two sequential questions would be asked. First, were the guidelines properly applied? Second, if the decision was outside the guidelines, were the reasons given for departure sufficient; or if the decision was within the guidelines, did substantial reasons exist that made compliance with customary policy unreasonable?

An operating example of a guideline model is provided by the decision-making practices of the United States Parole Commission (formerly the U.S. Board of Parole). Faced with similar criticisms of its decision-making practices in the late 1960s and early 1970s (i.e., that its decisions were arbitrary, capricious, and disparate),[25] the Board launched a pilot project, commencing in 1972, which included hearings conducted by two-man panels of hearing examiners, provision of written reasons in cases of parole denial, an administrative review process, and the *use of decision guidelines*. From this pilot project, revised decision-making procedures incorporating these features were developed and expanded to all federal parole decisions in October 1974.[26]

Designed to guide and structure the Board's broad discretion, the guideline model was developed as a result of a three-year study of parole decision-making, funded by the Law Enforcement Assistance Administration and conducted by the Research Center of the National Council on Crime and Delinquency in a collaborative effort with Board members and staff.[27] The guideline matrix used by the Parole Commission is in the form of a two-axis chart (see Table 1). On the vertical axis, the severity (gravity) of the subject's present offense behavior is considered. Six categories of offense severity (from low to greatest) are desig-

---

*Though we are not in favor of mandatory or presumptive sentences, we do agree that the legislature ought to be more specific in establishing sentencing principles.

nated.* For each category, the Commission has listed examples of common offense behaviors that are to be placed in the category, arrived at by consensus judgment of Commission members.[28] Not all possible offense behaviors are listed. Severity ratings for offense behaviors not listed are to be determined by comparison with similar offense behaviors that are listed, or by interpolation or extrapolation therefrom. On the horizontal axis, four categories of parole prognosis (from very good to poor) are defined. An actuarial device, termed a salient factor score (see Table 2), was empirically developed and is used as an aid in making prognosis assessments.[29]

For each combination of offense (severity) and offender (parole prognosis) characteristics, a decision (guideline) range is provided. This decision range specifies customary paroling policy in terms of the number of months to be served before release (subject to the limitations of the judicially imposed sentence), assuming the prisoner has demonstrated good institutional behavior. For example, an adult parole applicant with a low moderate severity offense (e.g., forgery/fraud of less than $1,000) and good parole prognosis (e.g., a salient factor score of 6-8) might expect to serve between 12 and 16 months before release under this explicit policy. A very high severity/poor risk case, on the other hand, (e.g., armed robbery, salient factor score 0-3) might expect to serve 60 to 72 months, in the absence of exceptional circumstances. For greatest severity cases (e.g., murder, kidnapping) there are no upper guideline limits presently specified. Consequently, decisions in such cases must be based upon extrapolation from the guideline time ranges specified for very high severity cases with similar prognosis and institutional characteristics.

Decisions outside the guidelines, either above or below, may be rendered for "good cause," provided that the reasons for the departure from customary policy are specified. Cases of especially aggravating or mitigating offense factors, clinical judgment (supported by specifics) that the prisoner is a better or poorer parole risk than the actuarial device indicates, or exceptionally good or poor institutional program achievement are examples of cases in which decisions outside the guidelines may be rendered.[30] During the period October 1974 through September 1976 approximately 83 percent of decisions ($N = 23,500$) at initial parole hearings fell within the Commission's guidelines.*

*In determining the appropriate severity rating, the Commission may look beyond the offense of conviction to consider mitigating or aggravating factors [*Lupo v. Norton*, 371 F. Supp. 156 (D. Conn. 1974); *Zannino v. Arnold*, 531 F 2d 687 (1976); *Billiteri v. United States Board of Parole*, Docket No. 75-6120, Slip Op. 5285 (CA2, August 30, 1976)].

*It is to be noted that the above figures consider only discretionary decisions as outside the guidelines. Since the Commission may not parole a case below the judicially set minimum sentence (if any), nor may it hold a prisoner past his maximum sentence (mandatory release date), there are certain cases in which the Commission's discretion is limited by the sentence structure (i.e., a minimum sentence longer than the guideline range, or a maximum sentence

Furthermore, the guideline model itself is periodically considered for revision (at six-month intervals) by Commission policy. At such reviews, the Commission may utilize feedback from previous months to examine the adequacy of the reasons given for departure from the guidelines and to determine whether there are recurring patterns of circumstances for which additional policy can be specified. Also, the Commission may consider whether any modification of the predictive device, offense behavior classifications, or the guideline ranges themselves appears warranted.

Recent legislation (the Parole Commission and Reorganization Act of 1976) has codified this administratively developed system. Among the prominent features of this legislation are: (1) a comparatively specific mandate concerning the major elements to be considered in parole determinations (i.e., institutional conduct, offense severity, and parole prognosis); (2) a requirement that the Parole Commission establish explicit guidelines for parole selection, and that decisions departing from the guidelines be made only for "good cause" and be accompanied by specific reasons for such departure; and (3) statutory provision for an administrative review (appeal) process.

Legislation proposing a number of similar innovations for federal sentencing practices was introduced during the 94th Congress (1975) in both Senate (S 2699) and House (HR 1665). In these proposals, a United States Commission on Sentencing would be established to formulate explicit sentencing guidelines under broad legislative standards. Judges would be required to apply the guidelines to each case and to provide written reasons for decisions departing from the guidelines. Appellate review in relation to guideline usage would also be authorized.

At this point, it is important to note that it is not the allocation of the sentencing function (to judge, sentencing tribunal, parole board, or some combination thereof) that is most critical, but rather the methods under which sentencing decisions are rendered. As Von Hirsch notes: ". . . the decision to have sentencing norms does not compel selection of a particular agency to set them."[31] Although an argument can be made that, given the application of guidelines, all sentencing functions should be returned to the trial court, there appear to us to be even stronger arguments for an opposite position. Among the arguments in favor of placing sentencing discretion (even with guidelines) in a separate agency (e.g., a sentencing tribunal or parole board) are the following: (1) a centralized "corporate" body will inherently provide greater consistency than is possible with numerous individual decision-makers; (2) sentencing is an essentially part-time function for judges; full-time parole board or sentencing tribunal members would develop greater proficiency and expertise in this complex area; and (3) a

---

shorter than the guideline range). Decisions controlled by the limits of the sentence are counted as within the guidelines.

Table 2. Salient Factor Score (Revised 4/1/77)

Register Number ----------------------- Name ---------------------------------------

ITEM A --

No prior convictions (adult or juvenile) = 3
One prior conviction = 2
Two or three prior convictions = 1
Four or more prior convictions = 0

ITEM B --

No prior incarcerations (adult or juvenile) = 2
One or two prior incarcerations = 1
Three or more prior incarcerations = 0

ITEM C --

Age at first commitment (adult or juvenile) :
    26 or older = 2
    18 - 25 = 1
    17 or younger = 0

*ITEM D --

Commitment offense did not involve auto theft or
   checks(s) (forgery/larceny) = 1
Commitment offense involved auto theft [X], or
   check(s) [Y], or both [Z] = 0

*ITEM E --

Never had parole revoked or been committed for a
   new offense while on parole, and not a probation
   violator this time = 1
Has had parole revoked or been committed for a
   new offense while on parole [X], or is a probation
   violator this time [Y], or both [Z] = 0

ITEM F --

No history of heroin or opiate dependence = 1
Otherwise = 0

ITEM G --

Verified employment (or full-time school attendance)
for a total of at least 6 months during the last 2
years in the community = 1
Otherwise = 0

TOTAL SCORE ---

* NOTE TO EXAMINERS:
    If item D or E is scored 0, place the appropriate letter (X, Y or Z) on the line
    to the right of the box.

centralized sentencing agency would be less subject to local community pressures. It is to be noted that attacks presently leveled at indeterminate sentences do not necessarily require the return of all sentencing discretion to the trial judge. It could be argued that a system in which judicial sentences of imprisonment were reviewed within 120 days by a parole board or sentencing tribunal, which would then fix a tentative release date (subject to satisfactory institutional conduct), would contain the advantages noted above without the liabilities of "indeterminacy."

However, given our tradition, it is unlikely that much support can be generated for vesting all sentencing functions in a separate specialized agency. A middle position, which appears to us more feasible, would be to retain the initial determination as to type of sentence (e.g., probation or imprisonment) in the trial court, while vesting the determination of the actual length of time to be served in custody for those persons imprisoned in a smaller specialized agency (e.g., a parole board).

CONCLUSION

While proposals for sentencing guidelines appear far from perfected, it is our opinion that the guideline concept provides a model superior to either present practice or legislatively determined (mandatory or presumptive) sentencing. Given the wide variability in offense behaviors and offense characteristics among individuals enmeshed in our criminal justice system, it is our belief that retention of considerable discretion in sentencing will be both necessary and desirable. As Davis has succinctly argued:

> Discretion is a tool, indispensable for individualization of justice. . . . Rules alone, untempered by discretion, cannot cope with the complexities of modern government and modern justice. . . . Let us not oppose discretionary justice that is properly confined, structured and checked; let us oppose discretionary justice that is improperly unconfined, unstructured, and unchecked.[32]

It is our position that a guideline model, such as used by the United States Parole Commission, can substantially structure, control, and confine discretion without the liability of either removing individual case consideration or papering over the problem by transferring discretionary power to parts of the system where it will be less visible. Moreover, a guideline model would appear to have the flexibility to allow for development and modification as experience and/or changes in social attitudes dictate, yet, as opposed to legislatively determined sentences, provide a safeguard against hasty or emotional policy shifts engendered by the unusual but "dramatic" incident.

FOOTNOTES

1. President's Commission on Law Enforcement and Administration of Justice, *Task Force Report: The Courts.* Washington, D.C.: U.S. Government Printing Office (1967), p. 23.
2. National Advisory Commission on Criminal Justice Standards and Goals, *Corrections.* Washington, D.C.: U.S. Government Printing Office (1973), p. 142.
3. Morris, N., *The Future of Imprisonment.* Chicago: University of Chicago Press (1974), p. 45.
4. Frankel, M. E., Lawlessness in sentencing. *Cincinnati Law Review 41:* 1, 54 (1972).
5. *Shepard v. United States,* 257 F. 2d 293, 294 (CA6 1958).
6. See, for example, Bennett, J. V., Of prisons and justice. Senate Document No. 70, 88th Cong., 2d sess. (1964).
7. President's Commission, *Task Force Report: The Courts,* pp. 23–24.
8. Frankel, M. E., *Criminal Sentences: Law Without Order,* New York: Hill and Wang (1973), p. 82. (See Note 1.)
9. Appellate review of primary sentencing decisions. *Yale Law Journal 69:* 1453, 1455 (1960).
10. 18 U.S.C. 3651, 4205(b).
11. 18 U.S.C. 3577.
12. See, for example, Citizen's Inquiry on Parole and Criminal Justice, Inc., Summary report on New York parole. New York: 84 Fifth Avenue, Room 300 (1974).
13. Rubin, S., Disparity and equality of sentence—A constitutional challenge. *F.R.D. 40:* 55, 57 (1966).
14. Hoffman, P. B., and DeGostin, L. K., An argument for self-imposed explicit judicial sentencing standards. *Journal of Criminal Justice 3:* 195, 197 (1975). See also, Appellate review of primary sentencing decisions, (Note 9) p. 1461.
15. American Friends Service Committee, *Struggle for Justice.* New York: Hill and Wang (1971), p. 144.
16. 408 U.S. 238 (1972).
17. For example, the North Carolina and Louisiana death penalty statutes [described in *Woodson v. North Carolina,* 44LW 5267 (June 29, 1976) and *Roberts v. Louisiana,* 44LW 5281 (June 29, 1976)].
18. See, for example, Fogel, D., "*. . . We are the Living Proof . . .*" *The Justice Model for Corrections.* Cincinnati: The W. H. Anderson Co. (1975) pp. 245–60.
19. *Woodson v. North Carolina* (note 17), 5274.
20. Kress, J. M., Wilkins, L. T., and Gottfredson, D. M., The trial court judge: An endangered species? Paper presented at the American Congress of Corrections, Denver, Colorado (August 1976).
21. Frankel, *Criminal Sentences* (note 8), p. 9.
22. Fogel, *Justice Model for Corrections,* (Note 22) pp. 258–60.
23. Heinz, A. M., Heinz, J. P., Senderowitz, S. J., and Vance, M. A., Sentencing by parole board: An evaluation. *Journal of Criminal Law and Criminology 67:* 1, 20 (1976).
24. American Bar Association Project on Minimum Standards for Criminal Justice, Sentencing alternatives and procedures. New York: 33 Washington Square West (1968), p. 150.
25. See, for example, Davis, K. C., *Discretionary Justice: A Preliminary Inquiry.* Baton Rouge: Louisiana State University Press (1969), pp. 52–55.
26. 28 C.F.R. § 2.1–2.58. [Most recently published as 42 *Federal Register* 151:39809–39822 (August 5, 1977)].
27. Gottfredson, D. M., Wilkins, L. T., Hoffman, P. B., and Singer, S. M., The utilization of

experience in parole decision-making: Summary report. Washington, D.C.: U.S. Government Printing Office, Doc. No. 2700–00277 (November 1974).

28. Hoffman, P. B., Beck, J. L., DeGostin, L. K., The practical application of a severity scale. In W. E. Amos and C. L. Newman (eds.), *Parole: Legal Issues/Decision-Making/ Research*. New York: Federal Legal Publications (1975), pp. 169–83.

29. Hoffman, P. B., and Beck, J. L., Parole decision-making: A salient factor score. *Journal of Criminal Justice 2:* 195–206 (1974). A recent revision of the salient factor score (April 1977) containing seven items is shown in Table II. See Hoffman, P. B., Meierhoefer, B. S., and Beck, J. L., Salient factor score and releasee behavior: Three validation samples. U.S. Parole Commission Research Unit, Report 15 (August 1977).

30. Hoffman, P. B., Federal parole guidelines: Three years of experience. United States Board of Parole Research Unit Report 10 (November 1975).

31. Von Hirsch, A., *Doing Justice*. New York: Hill and Wang (1976), p. 104.

32. Davis, *Discretionary Justice*, (Note 25) pp. 25–26.

In recent years, particularly against a background of increasing concern for the civil rights of Americans confined in prisons, there has been a developing interest in further understanding of the social and personal consequences of such long-term confinement. It is this issue that Stanley L. Brodsky and Raymond D. Fowler, Jr., address, drawing on research findings and judicial decisions.

The chapter directs the reader's attention to the role of violence in prison settings, to the effects of crowding and loss of personal privacy, and to such stresses as a high noise level and enforced idleness. In doing so in relation to current knowledge and prison practice, the authors take the reader into the social and cultural climate of the confinement institution and provide a picture of the known and suspected effects of confinement upon the psyche and person of those serving sentences. The result of their inquiry provides a picture of possibilities for significant changes in present conceptions and practices.

8
The Social Psychological Consequences of Confinement

Stanley L. Brodsky and Raymond D. Fowler, Jr.

Not all confinement is experienced negatively. For example, submarines, monasteries, compact cars, Boeing 747 jets (tourist section only), tuberculosis wards, trips through Lion Safari Country, and times in one's own room can provide confinement experienced positively, voluntarily sought out, and associated with personal development or goal-achievement. In contrast, this chapter addresses the psychology of involuntary confinement and attends to processes and events that occur when individuals are incarcerated without choice or free will. The involuntary nature of prisons and of incarceration separates them qualitatively from most other life experiences.

Historically, psychologists have been primarily involved in clinical activities in corrections. In the last half dozen years, several academic programs have emerged, preparing psychologists for applied, academic, and research careers in criminal justice and corrections.* Furthermore, there has been a series of class action suits since 1970 in which psychological evaluation and knowledge of prison functions and effects have played key roles. Indeed, orders issued by judges at the federal district, appeals, and supreme court levels have drawn heavily on psychological knowledge. Such knowledge has become central to the setting of standards, formulation of programs, and allocation of societal resources (e.g., *Laaman v. Helgemoe*, 1977; *Bowring v. Godwin*, 1977).

Historically, the psychological focus has been a search for psychopathology of individual inmates. Psychologists have played Cassandra, crying of illness, and

---

*These programs are offered by The University of Alabama, Brigham Young University, The California School of Professional Psychology, Florida State University, Hahnemann Medical College, John Jay College, Middle Tennessee State University, The University of Nebraska.

predicting psychopathological doom. The goal of much research and professional activity has been a search for the so-called criminal personality, a concept no longer credibly acknowledged. Indeed, this search for the criminal personality and for the differentiation of psychopathology among inmates was the rationale for development of classification and diagnostic centers in corrections. Following World War I, the coming together of psychological assessors and correctional needs led to a massive organizational and professional effort to classify inmates, by intelligence and personality. This effort is part of an individual-blame model, believing that there are criminogenic illnesses or disorders. The assumption that there must be something wrong with the confined individuals or they would not have committed their crimes is at odds with existing knowledge of massive base rates in crime surveys in Philadelphia (Wolfgang, Figlio, and Sellin, 1972) and literature analyses of prison psychodiagnoses (Brodsky, 1973).

In the field of psychological criminology, a fundamental shift in attention is occurring. Instead of searching for internal causes, investigators have redirected their search toward the dynamics and analyses of crime-producing situations and prison processes. The prison itself becomes the object of study and the object of attribution of blame. Research has been addressed to the effects of incarceration, critical environmental factors within prisons, correctional officer socialization and activities, and programmatic emphasis that lead to differential types of prison patterns and prisoner behavior (Hawkins, 1976; Monahan, 1976).

Certain behaviors appear to be caused by being in prison. The term "cause" is used guardedly because cause and effect relationships are as difficult to assess in prisons as in other settings. Certainly many behavior problems may be enhanced, or may arise from synergistic processes between preexisting tendencies and situational influences. Let us start by examining violence.

VIOLENCE

There is substantial reason to believe that the rate of violence in prison settings is anywhere from two to one hundred times the rate of that in free-world settings. The rate of known violence in American society is 188 violent crimes (murder, rape, assault) per 100,000 people (Megargee, 1976). In some prison settings examined by the authors, the incidence of assault victims is as much as every other person. In a recent discussion with seven randomly chosen inmates at the Baltimore City Jail, all of them reported to us that they had personally engaged in fights in the institution. Similarly, the rates of physical assault and sexual assault at one Alabama prison studied by the present authors, indicated that virtually everyone had at some time personally engaged in either aggressive, self-defensive, or victim roles in violent acts; virtually everyone was armed with a knife.

Why this level of violence? Some interpretations use frustration-aggression theory, noting the thwarting of goals of self-satisfaction, efficacy, and worthwhileness. Anxiety-based explanations observe that anxiety is very great and is seen in U-shaped curves. The highest levels of anxiety are experienced toward the beginning and toward the end of prison terms, with lowest levels in the middle. Anxiety becomes transformed into hostile actions in correctional settings as part of a lessening of emotional controls and an acquisition of antisocial values and behaviors.

CROWDING AND PRIVACY

Overcrowding and lack of privacy occur particularly in prison settings, and seem to be associated with negative behavior changes among inmates. These phenomena are of special interest because they have been attacked in a series of prison class action suits and because they have been the subject of several psychological studies. The first issue is the extent of the crowding. The Baltimore City Jail and the Tuscaloosa (Alabama) County Jail were inspected by the authors as part of suits that alleged that the crowded conditions caused significant psychological harm to the inmates. Our testimony confirmed that this was true for substantial numbers of the prisoners, observing that the square footage per prisoner, or population density, ranged from 21 to 32 square feet per person.

In a study of prisoners at a federal correctional institution, in which the overall population density was 69.1 square feet per inmate, Megargee (1977) found a correlation of $-.52$ between square feet of living space available per inmate and number of disciplinary violations for misconduct and disruptive behavior. Generally, laboratory research with college students has not demonstrated harmful effects of crowding. However, Megargee posits that the long-term restrictions on personal space are indeed toxic with prison populations:

> Chronic high-density living conditions are associated with negative behavior when the crowding is involuntary and when there is little hope for relief in the foreseeable future. In such conditions the adverse effects of crowding are probably exacerbated by the individuals' feelings of powerlessness. (p. 296)

D'Atri and Ostfeld (1975) reported that inmates living in close confinement in dormitories in three Massachusetts correctional facilities experience significant and hazardous rises in both systolic and diastolic blood pressure levels. In their cross-sectional study, they found a progressive rise in blood pressure after the first 30 days of confinement, as part of a long-term maladaptive pattern. In such correlational studies of crowding as well as clinical observations, there is reason to believe that with crowded conditions anxiety, psychological maladjustment, and sensitivity to loss of privacy do indeed accelerate.

NOISE

The National Clearinghouse for Criminal Justice Planning and Architecture (1977) has recently completed a thoughtful analysis of noise in jail and prison settings. It had been observed that regular conversation can occur only at ambient noise levels that are at or below 60 decibels (dB). The use of telephones, for example, becomes difficult at noise levels of 70 dB, and if individuals are going to speak in a normal voice, the amount of noise must be 66 dB or less. The noise levels at the Manhattan House of Detention, also known as "The Tombs," averaged between 75 and 80 dB in the recreation areas. In normal conditions, with television sets on, the noise levels in the officers' bridge averaged 75 dB with peaks over 80 dB. During meal times, and in areas in which there were openings and closings of cell doors, the transient peaks rose to 94 dB. The noise levels were cited in a federal district court ruling to close down "The Tombs" for constitutional reasons. The noise levels were not only held by the district judge to be "intolerable," but the judge ruled that they represented a "gross tax on the mental health" of the inmates.

IDLENESS

If crowding and noise represent two vehicles of prison pathology, idleness is clearly the third. In prisons all over the country, inmates sit about, often locked in their cells, for 17 to 22 or 23 hours a day. Even in institutions that claim to have "full-employment," large numbers of inmates loiter in industrial shops, watching other inmates work. We suggest that individuals need to have some constructive or positive activity as affirmation of their self-worth as human beings. Prolonged idleness and long periods of time without any product to represent one's value lead to a deterioration in self-concept, restlessness, and impaired personal functioning. Federal courts have ruled that there must be opportunities for participation in correctional work assignments, vocational training, educational programs, or treatment programs. In *James v. Wallace* (1976), Judge Frank M. Johnson stated that these elements are four of eleven fundamental constitutional rights for inmates, and that any inmates who have the ability to benefit from such programs, and are interested, *must* have such opportunities provided to them.

MEDIATING FACTORS

Subjective perceptions, personal opinions, and perceived distress in correctional settings are as important as the objective data provided on blood pressure, square footage, and rates of violence. Much of what goes on in prisons is perceived by residents as being arbitrary. No consistent rationale or basis for prison events is understood. This applies to rules that govern the prison as well as to the very cause of imprisonment. Over a period of time, a shift in attribution occurs. Instead of individuals' assuming responsibility for their crimes and seeing themselves as perpetrators, their views shift, and they see themselves as victims of an unjust society acting in a criminal way.

The low-trust, high-control syndrome is important to note in this context. A pervasive underlying process in correctional settings is low-trust, high-control of others (Brodsky, 1977). Correctional officers and inmates alike simply do not trust the other group, and indeed often trust few of their own colleagues. A continuing effort is made to maintain control over one's own life and the lives of other persons. Because of this distrust and effort to control, manipulation is the fundamental motive attributed to others. Suicide attempts by inmates are interpreted frequently by officers as being manipulative in nature. Homosexual rapists or rape victims are sometimes dismissed or ignored by officers. Minimum empathy is available among individuals who perpetually distrust the other persons with whom they live and work. A corollary rule for prisoners is "Don't squeal"; never tell anything to people in authority. Although it is regularly broken, the basic implicit rule for inmates is not to report events to guards.

A perceived zero sum game is part of the low-trust, high-control process. It is believed that there are just so many interpersonal, physical, and organizational resources available. Every time an inmate makes a gain in correctional institutions, it is felt as a loss by the officers, and vice versa. In one penal institution, when a plan was put forward to build a swimming pool for the inmates, the guards protested and picketed. Their rationale was that it would interfere with their ability to control the inmates. In actuality, the availability of recreation resources probably would have made it easier to control inmates; indeed the resources for swimming might have been available for the officers themselves during some time periods. This zero sum perception operates in other ways as well. Every time there is increased inmate freedom, officers experience it as a limitation in their own work and freedom. The mirror image works equally well in prisoners' perception of guard power and roles. Zero sum judgments in correctional settings truly are the prisoners' dilemma.

One antecedent condition for harmful events in corrections is the rigid exclusion of outsiders. The geography of prisons' locations, the walls themselves, and the decisions of officials to maintain privacy and secrecy, all contribute to such exclusion. Indeed, problems as seen by reformers, inmates, and concerned citizens, have been dealt with by denying or closing off their existence. As Bergan Evans has observed, "What can't be cured, must be obscured." Burns (1969) has described this process in corrections as part of a miniature totalitarian state, characterized by a single party ideology and a single party leader, complete control of communications and the economy, impermeable barriers between the institution and the outside, and an underground.

The concerns of inmates are present in correctional officers as well. Officers themselves have increasing psychological difficulties over time in ways which parallel those of inmates. They are at the bottom of a military hierarchy and in a graceless position. They have received a bad press in the newspapers, and in many correctional texts as well. Their occupational roles may be described as representing a no-win situation; except in minimum security prisons, they only reinforce negative actions—they punish and control. Haney, Banks, and Zimbardo (1973) generated powerful arguments from the Stanford prison experiment, to indicate that correctional officers are occupationally socialized to roles of brutality and harm. In their simulated prison, normal and well-adjusted college students were malevolently transformed to assume controlling, coercive, and psychopathological roles. Brodsky (1974), in his analysis of officer roles and activities, identified an occupational bill of rights for correctional officers. This list of rights assumes that every person has a need to see personal improvement and growth. For many individuals, occupational self-improvement is the central source of growth. Thus, one occupational right for correctional officers is to see personal improvement through occupational growth. Still another is to have a "piece of the action," and yet another important element is to have a sense of contributing positively and in a worthwhile manner to societal interests.

TOWARD POSITIVE CHANGE IN CORRECTIONAL SETTINGS

We have observed few individuals who show extraordinary and remarkable personal growth in correctional settings. It is easy and inaccurate to offer a blanket condemnation of corrections as being pathology-producing and negative. In one study by Osterhoff (1973), 15 percent of all Minnesota state reformatory inmates through the first 18 months after imprisonment showed improvement in their psychological well-being, as evaluated by the Minnesota Multiphasic Personality Inventory.

The issue of psychological survival in prisons has been addressed recently by Toch (1977), who has studied positive coping skills of inmates and nonstressful aspects of correctional environments. Toch asked inmates what the best possible prison would be for them, what correctional characteristics would be easiest, would be most profitable personally, and what could have made them happier while they served time. Conversely, the inmates were also queried about the worst possible prison, and the institutional characteristics they hated the most, which would make them most miserable. Individual prison environments were studied through the use of a "self-anchoring scale" and through the Prison Profile Inventory (PPI), a 56-item comparison scale.

The principal features of the best institutions as seen by contented inmates were programs that facilitated self-improvement, and "fellow inmates who are 'my brothers.'" The discontented inmates at this same prison—Coxsackie in New York—attended much more to the characteristics of correctional officers. They described inmate participation in selection of officers and understanding officers from one's own environment as most valued events in the best possible prisons.

When 234 youthful inmates were compared to 229 older inmates on the PPI, officer behaviors and quiet housing and conversation differentiated the groups. The item sets that discriminated best were:

Guards who are consistent
Guards who are friendly

Housing that keeps out the noise
Housing that lets people rap

The pursuit of safety and maintenance of sanity in prison environments are never simple. As Toch (1977) observes:

Diminished structure can signify painful ambiguity for one man and relaxation of tension for another. One man's social stimulation is another's lack of privacy; it may be a third's impaired safety. And safety is best secured by threatening an aggressor's prized freedom. (p. 189)

Still, prison environments do differ remarkably, and the profiles of Toch (1977), demonstrate great contrasts in the amount of freedom, initiative, privacy, and activity within prisons of the same nominal custody levels. The unfolding task is somehow to engineer these positive traits into our correctional institutions in ways that are both just and accountable.

There have been many cases of individual inmates maturing in what would be toxic settings to most people. Two examples will be considered. Ahmed A. had been an impulsive, hyperactive youth. As a late adolescent and young adult, he was involved in civil rights activities and then criminal pursuits, particularly distributing drugs and operating illegal businesses. When incarcerated in a state prison, Ahmed found himself greatly restricted in his range of possible actions. He began to develop his powers to manipulate and change other people. Seeing a vacuum in the authority structure of the Black Muslim group in the prison, he assumed a position of leadership. He was soon selected by his fellow inmates as minister of the Muslims and quickly transformed the group into a powerful influence. The group provided protection for black inmates, then a minority in the prison, gave him an opportunity to negotiate with prison authorities, and created considerable safety for him, since he was guarded at all times. He developed his abilities to speak, to influence other peoples' behavior, and to lead.

Despite his diminutive size, within a short time he became the acknowledged leader of the entire prison, and little could occur without his approval. His fundamental transformation was from an insecure, diffuse, unhappy, and ineffective individual into a person who had managed to mobilize his intellectual and personal resources in highly effective, goal-directed ways. Furthermore, the skills acquired persisted and were evident in his effectiveness in college as well. Before his incarceration, he had performed poorly in undergraduate studies on several occasions. His inability to focus on any task over time caused him to fail his courses or get into trouble, and then to be expelled from school. He is now completing a degree with good grades at a difficult and competitive university.

Hector M. came from a family associated with organized crime in the Northeast, and had never considered any alternative to a career in crime. While traveling to visit a relative in the South, he was arrested for robbing a motel. During his incarceration, he discovered that he had considerable talent for art. He began painting and soon was teaching other inmates to paint. He found that he had an ability for quiet leadership in a culturally appreciative and active group of prisoners. His intelligence, artistic skill, and considerable leadership ability resulted in inmates' respecting him as a trustworthy and high-status person. His goals were to continue his art career and to obtain a teaching position. He has done so, and is functioning well as an art teacher and an administrator of a community arts program.

But for each successful prisoner, there are many who come with adequate functioning and who depart with major deficits in their ability to cope or succeed. Nevertheless, it is important to consider individuals who grow in an oppressed setting. The case histories described here identify individuals who were verbally and interpersonally fluent and above average in intelligence. It has been observed that "men, like bullets, go furthest when they are smooth." This is surely true in prison settings for such verbally smooth individuals. Both of these men were also physically attractive and reported experiences in childhood of being extremely important to their parents, highly regarded, and treated with great affection.

CLASS ACTION SUITS

The class action suit is of critical importance because it represents a formal mechanism for introducing minimum standards of mental health care and allowable psychological harm in correctional settings. It has been found unconstitutional to replace the brains and hearts of confined citizens with the functional equivalent of pats of butter left sitting in the sun too long. Do individuals deteriorate psychologically during the time they are in prison? The evidence, based on a series of studies and a series of court rulings in at least half a dozen class action suits, is powerfully and strongly yes. The Osterhoff (1973) study, which identified 15 percent of individuals as improving, identified over 50 percent of reformatory inmates as deteriorating over the 18-month period involved.

Rehabilitation has not been established as a right of inmates in any of the cases heard in federal courts. In fact, it has been specifically ruled out by the decision of the Fifth Circuit Court in *James v. Wallace.* However, Judges Frank M. Johnson and Hugh Bouns have ruled that prison systems cannot create situations in which it is impossible for individuals to rehabilitate themselves or in which individuals lose skills as a result of incarceration.

In the case of *Palmigiano v. Garrahy* (1977) in the United States District of Rhode Island, the judge cited an 18-year-old who was repeatedly gang-raped on a number of occasions over a period of years. Finally, he suffered a "nervous breakdown." Shortly afterward, he was denied parole for the sole stated reason that he needed psychiatric counseling (which had never been provided). This represents the prototypical Catch 22. That is, an individual who is caused mental anguish or suffering as a result of the incarceration is then punished further because of the incarceration harm that he has suffered. Indeed, it is fundamentally the issue of mental health deterioration about which the class action suits have revolved.

In the case of *Bowring v. Godwin* (1977), the United States Fourth Circuit Court of Appeals decided for the first time that a right to treatment was required for individuals confined in correctional settings. This right to mental health treatment was qualified by the observation that it had to be treatment which would work and treatment which could not be delayed until after the prisoner was released. By contrast, in the Fifth Circuit the claim that prisoners deteriorated was dismissed by Judge Coleman, who stated that "everyone deteriorates and there's nothing anyone can do about it." This statement of the Fifth Circuit is reminiscent of Roman Hruska's classic misstatement, in the Senate confirmation hearing of Judge Harold Carswell, of the need to have mediocrity represented in the Supreme Court.

It is becoming clear that individuals have a right to be confined in conditions that will not deteriorate or harm their mental health or well-being. This is an important rule, with far-reaching implications. After all, mental health services in corrections typically attempt to repair the damage caused by living in an oppressive, crowded, and fundamentally harmful environment.

REFERENCES

Bowring v. Godwin, 555 F. 2nd 44, 47–48 (4th Circuit, 1977).
Brodsky, Stanley L., *Psychologists in the Criminal Justice System.* Urbana, Illinois: University of Illinois Press (1973).

Brodsky, Stanley L., A bill of rights for the correctional officer. *Federal Probation 38*(2): 38–40 (1974).

Brodsky, Stanley L., The ambivalent consultee: The special problems of consultation to criminal justice agencies. In S. C. Plog and P. I. Armed (eds.), *Principles and Techniques of Mental Health Consultation.* New York: Plenum (1977), pp. 135–49.

Burns, Henry, A miniature totalitarian state: Maximum security prison, *Canadian Journal of Corrections 11*, 153–164, (1969).

D'Atri, David A., and Ostfeld, Adrian. Crowding: Its effects on the elevation of blood pressure in a prison setting. *Preventive Medicine*, 1975, *4*, 550–566.

Haney, Craig, Banks, Curtis, and Zimbardo, Philip, Interpersonal dynamics in a simulated prison. *International Journal of Criminology and Penology 1:* 69–97 (1973).

Hawkins, Gordon, *The Prison: Policy and Practice.* Chicago: University of Chicago Press (1976).

James v. Wallace, 406 F. Supp. 318 (M.D. Alabama, 1976).

Laaman v. Helgemoe, C.A. No. 75-258 (U.S. District Court for New Hampshire, 1977).

Megargee, Edwin I., The prediction of dangerous behavior. *Criminal Justice and Behavior 3:* 1–23 (1976).

Megargee, Edwin I., The association of population density, reduced space, and uncomfortable temperature with misconduct in a prison community. *American Journal of Community Psychology 5:* 289–98 (1977).

Monahan, John (ed.), *Community Mental Health and the Criminal Justice System.* New York: Pergamon (1976).

National Clearinghouse for Criminal Justice Planning and Architecture, Noise in jails: A constitutional issue. *Transfer* Number 19, 4 pp. (1977).

Osterhoff, William E., MMPI changes in the youthful offender during incarceration. Doctoral dissertation, The University of Alabama (1973).

Palmigiano v. Garrahy, (U.S. District Court for Rhode Island, 1977).

Toch, Hans, Prison environments and psychological survival. In Bruce Dennis Sales (ed.), *Perspectives in Law and Psychology: Volume 1. The Criminal Justice System.* New York: Plenum pp. 161–90 (1977).

Wolfgang, Marvin E., Figlio, Robert M., and Sellin, Thorsten, *Delinquency in a Birth Cohort.* Chicago: University of Chicago Press (1972).

The chapter that follows, by Charlan Nemeth, a social psychologist long interested in the dynamics of small groups, offers a picture of the factors that enter into jury decision-making by drawing upon a body of research to which she has herself made significant contributions.

The contribution is concerned with small group process as manifested in juries, addressing itself to such important factors as the background and makeup of individual jury members, their personality characteristics, and the roles they take as functioning jury members. Particular attention is directed to the importance of jury decisions made by members of the group who establish both minority and majority positions.

The nature of the deliberative process that jury members engage in, and the factors that influence its direction and outcome, are examined in the light of what is presently known from the general study of small groups and from the particular attention that jury members, jury deliberations, and juror interactions have received.

9
Group Dynamics and Legal Decision-Making*

Charlan Nemeth

Why should a lawyer want or need to know anything about group decision-making? Outside of academic interest, are there implications for the administration of justice? Are there practical gains to be made from such an understanding? The position of this chapter is a clear "yes" to the latter two questions.

Most lawyers quite reasonably assume that winning a jury trial, for example, requires knowing whom to challenge and then persuading most of the final jurors to adopt a given judgment. The "who" is often assumed to be based on demographic data; i.e., the age, sex, race, occupation, and so forth, of the given individual. Such categories are often related to particular attitudes which can be of relevance in determining sympathy to a given defendant, to the specifics of a situation or motive, to understanding the complexities involved, and so on. But the "who" can also be important for understanding the group dynamics that will occur once those 12 individuals are behind closed doors and have to reach a consensus. Some "whos" are more persuasive than others, and their vote may be considerably more important than their numbers.

One of the main points to remember is that the decision of a jury is not simply a composite of the decisions in the minds of each individual. This group of 12 is just that—a group. Together, they will reflect on and discuss the information; they will try to piece together the evidence; they will attempt to re-create the situation; they will compare and contrast their memories, their visions, and their judgments. And, ultimately, they must try to form a consensus, to agree on a verdict. In this process, there will necessarily be influence except for the rare

*Preparation of this manuscript was supported in part by USPHS Grant No. 7 ROI MH31401-01 to the author, support which is gratefully acknowledged.

situation where all are in agreement on the first ballot. And the form of the in-fluence processes will dictate the final verdict.

Let's start with the process implicitly assumed by the notion that winning a case depends on convincing a majority of the jurors. This influence process is termed conformity and describes movement toward the position held by the majority on the jury. Thus, one assumes that members of an initial minority will, over the course of discussion, change their judgments in the direction of the initial majority, and that it is by this process that verdicts can be achieved.

As it turns out, this is the process that describes the vast percentage of trial cases. Kalven and Zeisel (1966), for example, showed that verdicts tend to be the position that was initially favored by the majority of jurors. If the majority favored "guilty"—i.e., 7 to 11 of the 12 jurors voted "guilty" on the first ballot —86 percent of the cases studied rendered a verdict of "guilty." If the majority favored "not guilty," 91 percent of the cases ended with a "not guilty" verdict. Thus, the power of the initial majority opinion is evident.

One can then ask why such a process should be so powerful. Is it the case that this process is automatic? Does it always occur, and, if not, when not? Does it depend on the size of the initial majority? Does it represent thoughtful reconsideration of viewpoints by the minority?

Social psychologists have concentrated on this specific form of influence for a number of years, and we will look at an important early series of studies by Solomon Asch (1955) for some understanding of this process. In this early series, Asch demonstrated that conformity is not necessarily a simple or rational process by which a majority convinces a minority of the truth of a particular judgment. Rather, the process appears to be heavily determined by two power-ful assumptions: (1) that a majority is likely to be correct, and (2) that disap-proval and rejection may follow from holding a minority position or not agreeing with the majority. More anecdotally, some people follow a unanimous majority that disagrees with them because they think "they all can't be wrong, and I'm right," or because they don't want "to stick out like a sore thumb" or to have others "think I'm crazy." Another general point is that conformity appears to relate more to the unanimity of the majority than it does to sheer size of the ma-jority. We will develop these propositions a little later in this chapter.

To show how this process operates and the bases on which it rests, let's start by describing the original study by Asch (1951). In this study, a single indi-vidual was brought into an experimental room with seven to nine other indi-viduals. Unknown to the "naive" person, these seven to nine individuals were paid accomplices of the experimenter and were asked to make specific judgments.

All individuals were seated and shown a series of cards. On the left was a card showing a standard vertical line of a given length. On the right was a card show-ing three vertical lines of unequal length, one of which was equal to the stan-dard. Each person was asked to judge which of the three comparison lines was equal to the standard. The "naive" person was last to respond. According to prearranged instructions, the seven to nine experimental accomplices, who deliberately were first, all agreed on a comparison line that was incorrect. If the "naive" person, however, was alone, Asch found he/she was highly correct, making fewer than 1 percent errors. What did he/she do when faced with the judgments of seven to nine people which disagreed with his/her own sensory information? Asch found that approximately 35 percent of the judgments made in this setting were in agreement with the deliberately erroneous majority and in disagreement with the naive perceiver's own senses. Since that original series of studies, hundreds of studies have confirmed the power and replicability of this phenomenon.

When the power of the phenomenon and its replicability were noticed, many people were both concerned and eager to understand why an individual would abdicate the information from his/her own senses and follow a majority's erroneous judgment. Basically, two reasons were found to fit both the experimental data and the self-reports. The first reason, termed "informational influence," refers to "influence to accept information obtained from another as evidence about reality" (Deutsch and Gerard, 1955).

This type of explanation stems in part from the theorizing of a social psychologist, Leon Festinger (1950), who pointed out that when there is no physical way of determining the truth or falsity of a position, people rely on others to determine the correctness of their perceptions or opinions. Thus, one might expect that if the individual in Asch's study had had a ruler by which he/she could judge the correctness of the lines, the conformity process might not have occurred.

However, most situations do not have a clear physical referent for obtaining information about the truth or falsity of one's position. In such cases, people look to others' judgments to determine such truth or falsity. In general, the more stable the contrary opinion held by others is, the more conformity is evidenced. Thus, if the majority is unanimous in its judgment and in disagreement with the naive individual, conformity is very high (approximately 35 percent in the original Asch situation). When that unanimity is broken, conformity drastically decreases. For example, the presence of one supporter—i.e., one person who judges the correct comparison lines—causes a decrease in conformity to approximately 5 percent. Further, unanimity appears to be more important than numbers per se. Asch's studies showed an increase in conformity as the size of the majority increased from one to three, but no increase thereafter. Putting the two pieces of information together, one may hypothesize that being one person in disagreement with five people on a six-person jury will lead to more conformity with the majority than being two people in disagreement with 10 people on a 12-person jury. One will expect more independence of the minority in the latter situation (Asch, 1951, 1952, 1955).

While this search for opinion validation is an important reason for conformity, other research has pointed to the importance of "normative influence," i.e., anticipation of rewards for agreement or avoidance of punishment from others for disagreement. Thus, some people conform because they don't want to appear different or don't want to incur disapproval. As a result, some research shows that conformity is higher when judgments are public rather than private.

A related finding is that the lower one's status is (with aspirations for improving one's status), the higher the conformity. Thus, a study by Harvey and Consalvi (1960) showed greatest conformity in small groups among second-ranking persons and least conformity among leaders. An implication of this for jury behavior is the expectation of least conformity from the foreman of the jury. Thus, if there is an 11:1 split, it is unlikely that the lone individual will hold out, but the likelihood should be increased if that individual is confident or has high status. In a jury, the foreman has status, and, interestingly, it appears that his/her confidence may have helped to elect him/her to that position.

Evidence from studies by Strodtbeck et al. (1957) shows that the person elected as foreman most actively participates in the deliberation and is the person judged to be the most influential. Considering demographic characteristics, the foreman is most likely to be male, middle-aged, and from a managerial or professional occupation (Strodtbeck et al., 1957; Strodtbeck and Mann, 1956). However, lest we assume that women, the young, and the "avant-garde" will not be placed in such a position, there is also evidence pointing to the importance of the person's behavioral style for election to foreman. Specifically, the person who chooses the head seat at a rectangular table is most likely to be elected to the foreman position (Strodtbeck and Hook, 1961; Nemeth and Wachtler, 1974).

Speculating for a moment, people may assume that such an act is one of "taking charge"; it clearly is seen as an act of confidence. And the jurors appear willing to let that person "take charge" in the sense of being foreman. Since any type of person can behave in such a manner, one is advised to look for cues as to the probability of such behaviors rather than to assume it from demographic categories. A confident woman may be more likely to be elected foreman than a less confident man. Yet, available evidence (Nemeth, Endicott, and Wachtler, 1976) shows that males are much more likely to take the head seat than are females.

Until now, we have considered the powerful process of conformity as the only means of achieving consensus. Thus, we have concerned ourselves with the likelihood of resistance to conformity, resulting possibly in a "hung" jury. In so doing, we have pointed to behavioral styles and categories of persons likely to resist conformity, as well as to size of the factions in determining the likelihood of conformity. But there are possibilities other than a verdict that represents the position initially held by the majority or one where a jury "hangs." While less frequent, there is also a group consensus around the position initially held by a minority of individuals. This process is called minority influence.

The prototype for minority influence in a jury setting is the movie "Twelve Angry Men," starring Henry Fonda as the lone juror holding out for a verdict of "not guilty," eventually convincing the other 11 who favored a "guilty" verdict. According to the statistics compiled by Kalven and Zeisel (1966), such influence is relatively rare, comprising less than 10 percent of the cases. However, it may occur in highly controversial cases, ones where deeply held convictions are involved. These may be some of our most important cases.

Some of our own research (Nemeth, 1977) points to the fact that, much as in the Fonda movie, minorities holding the "not guilty" position are more likely to be effective in swaying the majority to their position than are minorities holding the "guilty" position. At one level, it is intuitively obvious that it is easier to convince someone that he/she has a "reasonable doubt" than to convince the person beyond such a doubt. Not so obvious is the fact that minorities holding the position of "not guilty" are less likely to give in; they are more likely to demonstrate behavioral styles of consistency and confidence that are found to be effective strategies for minorities.

In considering what kinds of behaviors aid the minority in their influence attempts, we have to rely on relatively few studies in this newly researched area. One of the variables found to be highly important in minority influence is the unwillingness of the minority to capitulate. An early study by Moscovici, Lage, and Naffrechoux (1969) demonstrates this fact and also illustrates the paradigm often used in studies of minority influence. In their study, four naive individuals were placed amid a six-person group with two experimental accomplices. These people were simply asked to indicate what color they saw on a slide as well as its subjective brightness. The slides were of a pure blue color, and people alone ordinarily had no trouble reporting they saw this color. When faced with two individuals who repeatedly said that they saw "green," approximately 8 percent of the responses by naive individuals were "green." In another experimental variation, the two "minority" individuals said that they saw "blue" on one-third of the trials and "green" on two-thirds of the trials. Under such circumstances, the minority influence was reduced to essentially zero. Thus, the importance of consistency and maintenance of position was underscored.

Other experiments, e.g., Nemeth, Swedlund, and Kanki (1974), point out that the process is more subtle than simple repetition; the important point is to be perceived as consistent, a perception that does not necessarily require repetition. However, these studies also point to the importance of maintenance of position by the minority in order to affect influence.

Other studies, e.g., Nemeth and Wachtler (1974), point to the importance of specific acts of confidence that aid the minority in its influence attempts. In one study, the act of taking the head seat at a rectangular table was studied. We previously discussed this action as one that increases the likelihood of a person's election as foreman. In fact, this action is one that is interpreted as an act of confidence and, even without the status of foreman, significantly affects the degree of influence exerted. In our study, five-person groups deliberated a personal injury case. One individual was a paid confederate who memorized prearranged arguments and gave them from memory. He also held a highly deviant position, espousing a judgment of $3,000 when the other individuals held positions of around $15,000. What varied was the seated position occupied by this individual and whether he chose it or was assigned to it.

Results indicated a significant decrease in monetary judgments by those exposed to this consistent minority of one when he chose the head seat. Having been persuaded by this minority, the other individuals reported a change in their judgment, after the deliberation, in the direction of the "minority" position. In other words, they significantly decreased the amount that they felt was proper compensation for the injuries incurred. Further, on a totally new personal injury case, the individuals reported significantly lower judgments of compensation. When the "minority" person chose a side seat, or when he was assigned to either a head or a side seat, there was essentially no influence. People reported judgments at the end of the deliberation which were similar to those that they had held prior to deliberation.

Lest one underestimate the importance of such initial acts of confidence, they can set the tone for the ensuing deliberation. Even with arguments held constant, they can affect perceptions of the person and the likelihood of accepting his/her judgment.

In the studies that we have conducted on minority influence, the pattern that emerges is of a consistent and confident minority which is initially not taken very seriously (Nemeth, 1977). After a period of insistence and noncapitulation, the majority starts to reconsider its position. If one person starts to waver and the changes his/her viewpoint, the process often "snowballs"; i.e., others in the initial majority start to change their position. Moreover, it appears that the abdication of the majority position by some of its members greatly aids the minority position. This raises question about the majority position, and our speculation is that abdication by a "majority" member is *more* helpful to the "minority" than if that person had initially been part of the "minority." Thus, a jury member originally sympathetic to the other side but likely to waver or change his/her mind may be of more help than another member sympathetic to one's own position.

Another finding of potential interest for lawyers choosing the jury is the fact that size of the minority does not seem to relate to its potential effectiveness. We earlier mentioned that a lone "minority" member might be particularly susceptible to conformity, and that therefore having an ally is of importance for resistance to conformity. However, if the minority member resists conformity and argues his/her own position consistently and confidently, having an ally is not necessarily a help—though it also appears not to be a hindrance.

In one study (Nemeth, Wachtler, and Endicott, 1977), we found roughly equivalent influence by a minority of one, two, three, or four when faced with a six-person majority. However, the perceptions of the minority differed as a function of size. The larger the "minority," the *more* likely it was to be assumed to be correct; however, the larger the "minority," the *less* confident it was seen to be. The latter finding becomes interesting in that the data point to a potential asset of being in the minority, or alone for that matter. We have speculated that people essentially know the conformity process; they know that it is difficult for an individual to remain consistent in a position when alone and faced with a strongly unanimous majority that disagrees with him/her. Thus, when such resistance occurs, people are likely to assume that the individual really believes his/her position, a perception that will aid him/her in influence attempts. In this study, size of the minority led to a trade-off. The larger the number, the greater the perceived correctness but the less the perceived confidence. Both perceptions together predicted influence. Thus, size of the minority may not be so important from the point of view of influence, *given* that the minority maintains its position. However, size may be important for achieving such maintenance of position.

The significance of such research on minority influence, from a practical point of view, is that it points to the importance of behavioral style rather than numbers per se. Thus, it recognizes that maintenance of position, behaviors indicating confidence, and so on, are important for influence, perhaps more important than numbers. The lawyer may thus be better off with one strong and persuasive person than with the same person with an ally who is likely to waver.

One may well ask how it is possible to detect such persuasive and committed persons. The best guess would be by use of the demographic variables that are found to relate to choice of foreman and high participation in jury deliberations. Such persons tend to be male, highly educated, and from high status occupations. In fact, one such individual was found to be highly influential in the recent Mitchell-Stans case. (Zeisel and Diamond, 1976). In that trial, 138 jurors were excused for "cause," and the Court allowed the defense 23 peremptory challenges (20 for the jury and 3 for the alternate jurors), and the prosecution 11 challenges (8 for the jury and 3 for the alternates). In Zeisel and Diamond's report, the comparison between initial panel and final jury did not differ significantly in terms of race, sex, or age. What did change were education and occupation. The original panel had 45 percent of its members with some college education; the jury had only 8 percent—i.e., one juror with one year of college.

White collar occupations rose from 35 percent in the original panel to 76 percent on the jury. Several weeks into the trial, however, it happened that one of the jurors fell ill, and an alternate juror, Andrew Choa, took her place. The first ballot showed eight votes for the prosecution and four (one being Choa) for the defense. The final verdict was "not guilty." Both defendants were acquitted on all counts.

The contrast between educational and occupational backgrounds of Choa and the other jurors is quite apparent and we assume not irrelevant. Anecdotal reports offered by Zeisel and Diamond confirm the influence of this alternate juror. However, we also assume that his influence was not simply a function of his background but, rather, his behavioral style and also because of the unavailability of a competitor with such characteristics.

If we draw on our own research with minority influence, it will not come as a surprise that we set forth a cautionary note with regard to the selection of jurors based on demographic characteristics alone. Such characteristics are helpful, particularly in the absence of other information, for determining the likelihood of position and the likelihood of influence. Yet, they need to be mediated by behavioral styles that foster influence, and such behavioral styles can also be deduced directly from the jurors available to attorneys. Nonverbal cues, such as answering quickly and maintaining eye contact, are available to the attorney and provide important information for the potential maintenance of position and perceived confidence. Thus, too casual usage of juror categories can be not only prejudicial but also impractical. A confident and consistent female may be more influential than a less emphatic male. However, if one had no other information, choosing a male over a female might be advantageous from an influence point of view. But is even this true?

Some recent information indicates that the sex differences reported in research some 20 years ago may no longer be valid (Nemeth, Endicott, and Wachtler, 1977). In the fifties, several studies (e.g., Strodtbeck and Mann, 1956; Strodtbeck et al., 1957) showed women to participate less than men and to show solidarity, tension release, and agreement in their comments, whereas men gave more suggestions, information, and opinions. More recent studies (e.g., Nemeth, Endicott, and Wachtler, 1977) indicate few differences between males and females. They did not differ in verdict or persuasibility. But, interestingly, both males and females *believed* that males were more influential, rational, strong, independent, confident, aggressive, and more of a leader in these groups than females. Thus, the stereotypes still prevail, among both males and females. But they seem not to correspond with verdict, style, or persuasiveness. Such results caution the potential lawyer in using outmoded categories for prediction.

As complex as are the processes determining which faction will prevail, a third process is also possible—compromise. In many criminal cases, this process may be less evident in that the decision is often dichotomous, i.e., "guilty" or "not guilty." However, the charge may be lessened on some occasions, thus allowing for compromise; another form of compromise may be to find "guilty" on one count and "not guilty" on another count. In civil cases, this process is undoubtedly more frequent.

The available literature on the role of compromise indicates that such a process is often the result of a negotiation rather than actual influence processes. In other words, it may be the only way to find a resolution though none of the parties finds it the appropriate decision. Sometimes, it *is* a process of actual influence; i.e., the parties come to believe that compromise is the correct position. On the basis of available evidence, this appears to occur when the situation is highly ambiguous, when no one is very sure of his/her position, and when the persons have equal abilities and competencies.

The model used for the investigation of such a process of influence is taken from studies by Sherif (1935). Searching for an ambiguous stimulus, Sherif utilized a phenomenon known as the autokinetic effect. Briefly, this refers to the fact that a stationary point of light, in an otherwise totally dark room, appears to move to the naive perceiver. Sherif found that individuals at first see variability in its movement; e.g., they may start out by saying that the light is moving 2, 4, 6, and 8 centimeters. They then tend to establish their own subjective reference point, e.g., 2 or 4 centimeters. Thus, there is a convergence of judgments by the person through a series of estimates.

Sherif, however, was interested in the ways in which such subjective reference points would be modified when several individuals made their judgments public. He placed individuals together after each had established his/her own reference point. The results showed that the norms or reference points began to converge. In many cases, this new convergence was near the average of the individual reference points.

In considering the elements of such a model where convergence or compromise is often found to occur, one finds ambiguity in the stimulus situation, a plurality of individuals rather than a majority and minority. There are also no clear commitment or status differences between individuals with regard to the judgments made. Thus, one may speculate that highly complex cases where all people feel relatively inexpert and where little moral commitment is likely to be evident are most likely to produce a compromise verdict. A good guess is that compromise is more likely to occur in civil rather than criminal cases, the latter being more likely to invoke moral commitments and clear factions.

GROUP DYNAMICS AND DUE PROCESS

In the preceding discussion, we have concentrated on group dynamics in terms of prediction of verdict outcome—who is likely to be persuasive, which faction

is likely to succeed. Group dynamics, however, has another place in the interface between psychology and law. This is in the determination of due process
and as an implementation of the values held by us as a society.

In the allowance of particular procedural changes, for example, the appellate
courts must often decide on whether or not a defendant's right to due process
has been violated. This cannot be decided by a demonstration that the verdict
may be significantly changed, since we cannot prejudge the outcome. What we
do ask for is a process that is fair and impartial, one where opinions are confronted and considered.

In the last decade, one such procedural issue which came before the Supreme
Court of the United States was the issue of jury unanimity. The cases were
Johnson v. Louisiana, and *Apodaca, Cooper and Madden v. Oregon*. The appellants charged that due process and equal protection under the law had been
violated by their convictions under statutes that allowed nonunanimity of verdict. Johnson was convicted on a 9:3 vote by a 12-person jury; Apodaca was
convicted by a 11:1 verdict, Cooper by a 10:2 verdict, and Madden by a 11:1
verdict.[1] The Court ruled that appellants' constitutional rights had not been
violated by such nonunanimous jury convictions. The Court's decision in this
case was a nonunanimous 5:4 vote.

In making its ruling, the Court described some of the elements that we value in
our conception of jury decision-making. And in so doing, it offered a theory
of social influence, of interactions between majority and minority in disagreement. Let us first see the assumptions of group dynamics from the Court opinion, delivered by Mr. Justice White in *Johnson v. Louisiana*:

> We have no grounds for believing that majority jurors, aware of their responsi-
> bility and power over the liberty of the defendant, would simply refuse to
> listen to arguments presented to them in favor of acquittal, terminate dis-
> cussion, and render a verdict. On the contrary it is far more likely that a juror
> presenting reasoned argument in favor of acquittal could either have his ar-
> guments answered or would carry enough other jurors with him to prevent
> conviction. A majority will cease discussion and outvote a minority only after
> reasoned discussion has ceased to have persuasive effect or to serve any other
> purpose—when a minority, that is, continues, to insist upon acquittal without
> having persuasive reasons in support of its position.[2]

Thus, we receive a picture of conscientious individuals who, aware of their
responsibilities and duties, will consider all viewpoints and outvote a minority
that they don't need for a verdict only when "reasoned discussion has ceased
to have persuasive effect."

The dissenting justices, however, raise a different theory of majority/minority interactions and voice additional concerns. Justice Douglas, with Justices Marshall and Brennan concurring, offers this alternative view:

> Nonunanimous juries need not debate and deliberate as fully as most unanimous juries. As soon as the requisite majority is attained, further consideration is not required either by Oregon or by Louisiana even though the dissident jurors might, if given the chance, be able to convince the majority ... the collective effort to piece together the puzzle of historical truth ... is cut short as soon as the requisite majority is reached in Oregon and Louisiana. ... It is said that there is no evidence that majority jurors will refuse to listen to dissenters whose votes are unneeded for conviction. Yet human experience teaches that polite and academic conversation is no substitute for the earnest and robust argument necessary to reach unanimity.[3]

Here we see concerns about cutting the deliberation short if unanimity is not required. Further, the justices raise an important distinction between deliberation that is "earnest and robust" and the "polite and academic."

It should be pointed out that both majority and minority justices would be concerned if a majority outvoted a minority as soon as the requisite votes were achieved. Values of reasoned discussion and full consideration of all viewpoints are obviously cherished by both sets of justices. They differ, however, in their theory about whether or not this consideration will be achieved or hindered by the allowance of nonunanimity. Further, the dissenting justices point to full consideration in terms of "earnest and robust" discussion.

Still another important issue was raised in these cases concerned with non-unanimity of verdict, and that is the symbolic function of the jury. Specifically, the issue of community confidence in the jury was raised by Justice Stewart, with Justices Marshall and Brennan concurring:

> Community confidence in the administration of criminal justice cannot but be corroded under a system in which a defendant who is conspicuously identified with a particular group can be acquitted or convicted by a jury split along group lines. The requirements of unanimity and impartial selection thus complement each other in ensuring the fair performance of the vital functions of a criminal court jury.[4]

Here we see concerns over the appearance as well as the fact of due process, a recognition of the relationship between the community and the administration of justice.

The issue in these cases was essentially one of group dynamics. What will be the nature of the deliberations, what changes may result, from the allowance of nonunanimity of jury verdict? The issue is not simply a statistical one of whether or not the verdict might have been different. It is an issue surrounding the "robustness" of the deliberations, the likelihood of the majority outvoting the minority, and the subjective judgments regarding the administration of justice.

In a series of studies, we investigated the nature of simulated jury deliberations under the requirement of unanimity v. nonunanimity (Nemeth, 1977; Nemeth, Endicott, and Wachtler, 1976). Having videotaped the entire deliberations, we analyzed votes, each comment uttered, as well as subjective impressions of the jurors and the deliberation process.

The two were companion studies in that the same variable, i.e., unanimity/ nonunanimity, was under investigation. In the first set of studies, however, we specifically created groups that would split 4:2 on the first ballot in order systematically to study majority/minority interactions of juries deliberating the same case. In the second study, we used closely simulated courtroom situations and investigated majority/unanimity instructions in both civil and criminal cases. Here, however, we had no control over the initial split of opinion.

In the first set of studies, we pretested 753 undergraduates at the University of Virginia on a criminal case involving a charge of first degree murder. Of those who indicated a clear position of "guilty" or "not guilty," we created 37 groups of six persons each, where there would be a clear 4:2 split initially. Of these, 19 were groups in which the majority of four favored "guilty," and the remaining 18 groups consisted of the majority favoring "not guilty." Half of each type of group was required to deliberate to unanimity; the other half was required to deliberate to a two-thirds majority. All deliberated the same case.

In the second study, we utilized case presentations constructed by the University of Virginia Law School for its trial court practice course. The cases were tried in an actual courtroom with a local presiding judge. Live witnesses appeared with information from scripts, and the trial was conducted according to normal procedure. Seven cases were tried, three criminal and four civil. For these trials, which lasted approximately two hours each, we brought the jury of 12 individuals who heard the case and then deliberated in two groups of six persons. One group was required to deliberate to unanimity, the second was required to deliberate to a two-thirds majority.

The parallel findings of these studies offered some directly relevant information to the justices' concerns in the *Johnson v. Louisiana* and *Apodaca et al. v. Oregon* cases. With regard to final verdict, both sets of studies showed no statistically significant difference between the "guilty" and "not guilty" verdicts reached by groups required to deliberate to unanimity and those required to deliberate to a two-thirds majority. Groups required to deliberate to unanimity did tend to "hang" more often.

There were, however, considerable differences between unanimity and nonunanimity requirements on the deliberation process itself. While there were some differences between the studies, there tended to be longer "functional" deliberation times under requirements of unanimity. In one analysis of the comments uttered during deliberation, we kept a running count of the comments made pro-prosecution and pro-defense. When the number of comments favoring one position over the other reached a point of seven, we found that we could predict the final verdict nearly every time. Less than halfway through the deliberation, the outcome could be determined.

In our studies, this functional deliberation time—i.e., the amount of time needed before the verdict could be predicted—tended to be less when unanimity was not required. In other words, we could predict the outcome sooner when two-thirds majority rule was required. This "operational definition" of deliberation time may well relate to the distinction between robust argument and academic conversation. If placed together with other information in these studies, unanimity is more likely to lead to "robust argument" than to "academic conversation." The number of comments favoring each side stays fairly equivalent for a long period of time rather than being quickly one-sided so that a verdict can be determined at a very early stage of discussion.

Another finding of direct relevance to the justices' concerns is the fact that the majority does tend to outvote the minority when unanimity is not required —not necessarily as soon as the requisite votes are achieved but short of full consensus. In our studies, the requirement of unanimity led to voice vote of six persons in agreement. This was seen in the videotapes of the deliberations. Under requirements of a two-thirds majority, very few deliberated to full consensus, i.e., six persons in agreement. Many stopped at 4:2, the minimal requirement, whereas others deliberated until a 5:1 voice vote was achieved. Few deliberated until a 6:0 vote was reached.

Several consequences resulted from this tendency not to deliberate to full consensus. The first is that fewer opinions were changed during the course of deliberation when unanimity was not required. Individuals also reported less agreement with the verdict. And, lastly, individuals reported less confidence that justice had been administered when unanimity was not required.

The full array of the complex data can be found elsewhere (Nemeth, 1977), but the above summary results lend credence to the dissenting justices' concerns. Our available data indicate the deliberation is not so robust when unanimity is not required, the deliberation is likely to stop short of consensus, fewer opinions will change during the course of deliberations, and the individuals themselves will feel less sure that justice has been administered. Such consequences are relevant to the elements of jury decision-making that we hold dear, not just for the adjudication process itself but for its symbolic function to the community as well.

Tribe (1971) has very ably argued that this symbolic function may be one of the most important functions for the jury. He writes:

> rules of trial procedure in particular have importance largely as expressive entities and only in part as means of influencing independently significant conduct and outcomes. . . . (They) can serve a vital role as . . . a reminder to the community of the principles it holds important . . . that remind him (the defendant and the public about the sort of society we want to become and, indeed, about the sort of society we are.

Thus, the ritual of robust deliberation to full consensus may be deeply ingrained in our notions of justice and relate to the confidence with which the public regards our system of justice. This is of considerable importance even if the procedural change to nonunanimity did not appreciably alter verdict outcome.

From the above account, it is clear that group dynamics concerns itself with process as well as with outcome. To that extent, an understanding of influence processes and group dynamics can help us to implement values that we wish to preserve in our system of justice, since it is the fair process that we ensure rather than a specific outcome.

Apart from theories that help us to implement values relating to justice, the literature on group dynamics is also a practical aid to the attorney placed in an adversarial role. Quoting from a famous social psychologist, Kurt Lewin, "nothing is so practical as a good theory."

While there are dynamics that we may wish to preserve, there are also dynamics that favor one position over the other. As dealt with earlier in this chapter, they concern the "whos" in interaction, the numbers and solidarity of members in each faction as well as the nature of the case, and the decision rule (e.g., unanimity). It should be clear that the decision is not made at the end of closing arguments. That is only the beginning of a complicated process of influence and decision-making that will render the practical outcome.

FOOTNOTES

1. In Oregon, a 10:2 vote is needed (except for first degree murder, where the unanimity of the 12 persons is required). In Louisiana, a 9:3 vote is required for cases where the punishment is necessarily at hard labor; where punishment may be at hard labor, the case is tried before five persons, who must be unanimous; where the punishment may be capital, unanimity of 12 is required.
2. *Johnson v. Louisiana* 92 S. Ct. at 1624.
3. *Johnson v. Louisiana* 92 S. Ct. at 1647, 1648.
4. *Johnson v. Louisiana* 92 S. Ct. at 1627.
5. *Apodaca, Cooper and Madden v. Oregon*, 406, U.S. 404, 1972.

REFERENCES

Asch, S. E., Effects of group pressure upon the modification and distortion of judgment. In H. Guetzkow (ed.), *Groups, Leadership and Men.* Pittsburgh, Pennsylvania: Carnegie Press, (1951) pp. 177-90.

Asch, S. E., *Social Psychology.* Englewood Cliffs, New Jersey: Prentice Hall (1952).

Asch, S. E., Opinions and social pressure. *Sci. American 193:* 31-35 (1955).

Deutsch, M., and Gerard, H. B., A study of normative and informational social influences upon individual judgment. *J. Abnorm. Soc. Psychol. 51:* 620-36 (1955).

Festinger, L., A theory of social comparison processes. *Hum. Relat. 7:* 117-40 (1950).

Harvey, O. J., and Consalvi, C., Status and conformity to pressures in informal groups. *J. Abnorm. Soc. Psychol. 60:* 182-87 (1960).

Kalven, J., Jr., and Zeisel, H., *The American Jury.* Boston: Little Brown and Co. (1966).

Moscovici, S., Lage, E., and Naffrechoux, M., Influence of a consistent minority on the responses of a majority in a color perception task. *Sociometry 32* (5): 365-80 (1969).

Nemeth, C., Interactions between jurors as a function of majority vs. unanimity decision rules. *J. Applied Soc. Psychol. 7* (1): 38-56 (1977).

Nemeth, C., and Wachtler, J., Creating the perceptions of consistency and confidence: A necessary condition for minority influence. *Sociometry 37* (4): 529-40 (1974).

Nemeth, C., Endicott, J., and Wachtler, J., From the '50s to the '70s: Women in jury deliberations. *Sociometry 39* (4): 293-304 (1976).

Nemeth, C., Swedlund, M., and Kanki, B., Patterning of the minority's responses and their influence on the majority. *Eur. J. Soc. Psychol. 4:* 53-64 (1974).

Nemeth, C., Wachtler, J., and Endicott, J., Increasing the size of the minority: Some gains and some losses. *Eur. J. Soc. Psychol. 7* (1): 15-27 (1977).

Sherif, M., A study of some social factors in perception. *Arch. Psychol. 22,* No. 187 (1935).

Strodtbeck, F. L., and Hook, L. H., The social dimensions of a twelve man jury table. *Sociometry 24:* 397-415 (1961).

Strodtbeck, F. L., and Mann, R. D., Sex role differentiation in jury deliberations. *Sociometry 19:* 3-11 (1956).

Strodtbeck, F. L., James, R. M., and Hawkins, D., Social status in jury deliberations. *Amer. Sociol. Rev. 22:* 713-19 (1957).

Tribe, L., Trial by mathematics: Precision and ritual in the legal process. *Harvard Law Review 84:* 1391-92 (1971).

Zeisel, H., and Diamond, S. S., The jury selection in the Mitchell-Stans conspiracy trial. *American Bar Foundation Research Journal* (1): 151-74 (1976).

PART III
SELECTED AREAS IN THE
APPLICATION OF
DISCRETION

There are many areas in law in which the principle of discretion is applied, including its effects upon minority groups, upon corporate practices, and in the many issues and problems emerging in environmental concerns. All of these areas, and many others, are worthy of consideration and treatment within the focus of this book, but we have deliberately excluded them in favor of two issues of paramount importance, each of which is treated in depth.

The two concerns of Part III are the application of discretionary principles in the juvenile justice system and their application in the treatment of women citizens.

Barbara Flicker addresses the whole concept of discretion as applied to working with juvenile offenders, and she does so with a strong research background, extending over many years, in most of the important problems and issues in this area. She provides the reader with an in-depth consideration of present practices and the background and origin of the principles embodied in such practices, and a statement of a new point of view that looks toward changing what many experience in the administration of juvenile justice as current abuses.

Gary Glaser aggressively discusses the anomalies in the juvenile justice system by comparing testimony with judicial decisions from actual case records. The results are disturbing.

Aleta Wallach offers the reader a similar panoramic view of the uses and abuses of discretion in current laws and legal procedures dealing with women, whom she perceives as having constituted a class of legal second class citizens. She addresses herself to the history of the problems in this area and provides evidence that healthy change, in both the federal and state systems, is taking place, along with a wider understanding and appreciation of the role of women in American culture. Readers will be especially interested in the many problems that have had to be confronted because of long-outmoded views of the nature of women and of the full range of their capacities.

Responding to public criticism of the current juvenile justice with a careful examination of current practices throughout the country, Barbara Flicker documents its realities and problems as the former director of the IJA-ABA Juvenile Justice Standards Project.

She ascribes the system's seeming inability to cope with increasing juvenile contact with the law to permissible discretionary decisions deliberately incorporated into the law so the juvenile offender would be spared the destructive effects of the experiences of an adult criminal. Her major concern is how best to deal with juvenile offenders so that in the adjudication process they will not be irreparably harmed with consequent difficulty in adjusting to a free society.

Having completed an extensive study of the report by the Joint Commission on Juvenile Justice Standards of the American Bar Association, she applies its recommendations to contemporary discretionary procedures in actual cases. It is a rewarding effort, embodying practical suggestions for the immediate support of reconstruction of the current system without sacrificing its essential values.

1
Discretionary Law for Juveniles

Barbara Flicker

UNPREDICTABLE NATURE OF JUVENILE JUSTICE

Sample Cases

The most striking feature of the current juvenile justice system is the capricious and unpredictable relationship between the circumstances that occasion a juvenile's involvement with the system and the ultimate outcome of that involvement. Consider the cases of two 16-year-old high school students apprehended by the police on the same night in the same neighborhood. The girl was arrested for being on the street after midnight in violation of curfew regulations. The boy was picked up for an attempted burglary during the course of which he murdered an attendant. What dispositions of these cases should we expect?

The simple truth is that there is no way to know what to expect. After fact-finding and dispositional hearings, the boy might be released to his parents on condition that he receive psychiatric care or some other condition of probation, and the girl might be removed from her home and placed in a secure correctional facility. Or vice versa. Or practically any other disposition available in juvenile court. There are so many points at which decision-makers could exercise discretion—act officially according to the dictates of their own conscience and judgment—that it is impossible to predict the consequences of any unlawful act or conduct by a juvenile.

Jurisdictional Disparities Among States

The chancy nature of juvenile justice is evident even before the first local official— the police officer—makes his initial decision as to whether he should arrest or release the juvenile. Long before that, the state legislature has made a series of arbitrary decisions affecting juveniles in defining the jurisdiction of the juvenile court.[1]   The age, proscribed conduct, and range of penalties or treatment of the offenders who will be handled by the juvenile court vary so widely from state to state that the accident of geography can be the single most critical factor in determining the juvenile offender's fate.

Turning to our illustrative cases, jurisdictional disparities could be the difference between unrestricted freedom and severe deprivation of liberty for these youngsters.   In a state like New York, where the family court's jurisdiction over juvenile offenders ends with the sixteenth birthday, the girl's persistent late hours could not invoke any official intervention.[2]   She would be too old to be classified as a PINS, or Person in Need of Supervision; no charges could be brought in the criminal justice system, since she committed no criminal acts; and no curfew violation would apply, since New York has no curfew laws.   In California she would be within juvenile court jurisdiction until she reached age 18 as a 601 or status offender.[3]   In some states she also could be arrested for violation of curfew.[4]

The boy's felony murder would be grounds for indictment under the New York Penal Law for adults.[5]   Because of the seriousness of the crime, he would not be eligible for youthful offender treatment unless the prosecutor, in exercising his discretion, chose to file lesser charges. In California, he would be within the juvenile court's delinquency jurisdiction, but could be transferred to the adult criminal court for trial at the juvenile court judge's discretion after a fitness or transfer hearing on the issue of whether he would be "amenable to juvenile court care, treatment and training."[6]   Juveniles 16 years of age or older who are alleged to commit certain specified felonies can be found unfit for the juvenile court in California.

Until a few years ago, the girl's sex could have made her subject to the state's coercive intervention for conduct lawful for boys of the same age. In New York, PINS or status offense jurisdiction applied to girls between 16 and 18, although boys in that age group were free of such restraint, while in Oklahoma the same distinction was made for delinquency jurisdiction.   The New York State Court of Appeals and the federal court in Oklahoma declared both laws unconstitutional as discrimination against females in 1972.[7]   Ironically, the benign care and supervision deemed to be the purpose of the court's jurisdiction was not found so beneficial as to make it discriminatory against males to deny *them* that attention.

Having demonstrated some of the ways in which factors unrelated to the juvenile's conduct can determine the most preliminary question of whether a court is empowered to take jurisdiction, we have only begun to consider the imponderable elements that govern the disposition of juvenile misconduct. There seem to be boundless opportunities for the exercise of discretion in decisions vitally affecting the juvenile's life.

Multitude of Decision-Makers

As a juvenile proceeds sequentially through the justice system, there are over a dozen agencies and many more individuals who will make critical decisions concerning him or her: parents and other complainants, police, intake officers, prosecution and defense counsel, judges, social investigators, behavioral scientists, probation officers, child care agencies, youth correction authorities, parole boards, aftercare agencies, schools, neighbors and others in the community. At some point the juvenile may be diverted out of the system, which in itself is a major exercise of discretion, since a decision not to act can be as crucial as a choice of action. When we refer to discretionary decision-making in this context, we mean decisions in which an individual or agency makes a choice based on his or her own judgment, not one mandated by law or official guidelines. It is assumed that the official decision-makers are required to act reasonably and that abuses of discretion are grounds for reversal.

Nevertheless, discretionary decision-makers who are acting reasonably produce widely disparate results. Even the adult criminal justice system has fallen prey to the dictates of individualized justice, meting out sentences based on predictions concerning rehabilitation—the likelihood that a criminal can be reformed by the correctional system. Currently, legislators and criminologists are beginning to reverse the trend to indeterminate, individualized sentencing. California and Maine now require judges to impose fixed or determinate sentences.[8] The proposed revision of the federal criminal code presently before Congress would establish a sentencing commission to develop guidelines prescribing a range of sentences for each federal offense. As might be expected, the bill's most vociferous opponents are the judges who object to its restraint on their discretionary power.

In the adult system, discretionary power resides principally in the prosecutor, the judge, and the parole board. In the juvenile justice system, everyone gets a chance to decide. For example, in the adult criminal courts, the decision as to whether to bring formal charges against an alleged criminal is within the prosecutor's discretion. But in the juvenile court, parents, schools, neighbors, and other possible complainants, police officers, intake workers, child protective workers, child care agencies or treatment centers, as well as the juvenile prosecutor and the intake judge, have the power to decide whether a complaint will result in formal referral to the court.

Inherent Vagueness of Juvenile Court Goals

Most juvenile court acts recite the dual purpose of serving the best interests of the child and protecting the community. The patent difficulty of achieving these objectives through a judicial process is at the core of the uncertainty and confusion that pervade juvenile court decisions. How do you serve the interests of an adolescent who joins a street gang and commits a series of crimes with them? In theory, the court will arrange for an extensive investigation of the social, economic, familial, and psychological background of the juvenile, identify the factors that led to unlawful behavior, and devise a disposition that will meet the needs disclosed by the report. In practice, the courts lack the necessary resources, time, skill, and certainty as to programs that are capable of effectively dealing with antisocial behavior in adolescents. As for protection of the community, juveniles placed on probation go unsupervised because of unwieldy caseloads assigned to probation workers; juveniles assigned to community treatment programs receive little or no treatment; adjudicated delinquents the court might attempt to place in voluntary residential programs are rejected by the child care agencies as disruptive to their programming; and juveniles placed in public correctional or treatment facilities are confined for an indefinite term at the convenience of the correctional authority with little or no effective treatment or training.

Failures of the Current System

This grim assessment of the operation of the current juvenile justice system may suggest that the system is in serious trouble. Most observers would agree. However, they also agree that it can be salvaged. Wide-ranging proposals for reform of the juvenile justice system are being considered by the American Bar Association and the Office for Juvenile and Delinquency Prevention of the Law Enforcement Assistance Administration of the United States Department of Justice, as well as many other prominent organizations concerned about juvenile law. Before we consider some of those proposals, we will review the many facets of the exercise in discretion in juvenile justice, the effect it has on the children who may be subject to the court's jurisdiction, and the effect of discretionary law on the community the system is designed to serve.

THE DISCRETIONARY DECISION-MAKERS

The Complainant

The emphasis on the use of discretion in handling juveniles derived from the concept that the juvenile court and the officials functioning within its purview were acting as *parens patriae*—the state acting as parent—using their judgment and discretion as a substitute for the parent's control over the child. In reality, any adult is seen as entitled to some degree of authority over a child. Children are expected to obey the reasonable commands of teachers, neighbors, relatives, even shopkeepers. Unaccommodating children are described as fresh, unruly, incorrigible, beyond lawful control. In most states, that alone is ground for juvenile court jurisdiction over that child. Therefore, the first act of discretion on a local level is the decision by a complainant as to whether he or she will file a complaint against a juvenile.

A complaint is a report made to a juvenile court by the police, schools, social welfare agencies, parents, or other agencies and individuals. It sometimes is called a referral. Most complaints against juveniles for noncriminal misbehavior, like disobedience, ungovernability, incorrigibility, truancy, runaway, and so on, are filed by the juvenile's parents or school officials. Law enforcement officers, injured parties, or parents usually file delinquency complaints.

As an example, in one New York study,[9] 25 percent of PINS petitions were brought by school officials for truancy and 59 percent by parents for ungovernability. Of the ungovernability cases, 75 percent of the complainants were mothers, 16 percent fathers, and 9 percent parent-substitutes. The other 16 percent of the PINS complaints were filed by police, unrelated persons, and institutions.

It is difficult to isolate rational criteria for the decision to lodge a complaint, since the conduct alleged in PINS petitions for ungovernability include such ordinary misbehavior as late hours, undesirable companions, foul language, and general disobedience. The Report of the President's Commission on Law Enforcement and Administration of Justice in 1967 stated that "perhaps 90 percent of all young people have committed at least one act for which they could have been brought to juvenile court."

The arbitrary and patently unfair selection process by which certain juvenile offenses are reported and the overwhelming majority screened out without official intervention calls for safeguards, at least to limit the persons empowered to compel state action and to adopt definitions of acts constituting grounds for complaints that are objective and unbiased. In the New York study discussed above, 68 percent of the ungovernability complaints involved girls and 69 percent were for black or Hispanic youth.

Parental discretion can be the most insidious kind for a juvenile. The usual assumption is that parents and children have the same interests in protecting children's welfare. It is the parents who sign waivers, give consent, permit disclosures, and arrange for health and other care for their children. Yet it can be shown that frequently the presumed mutuality of interests between parents and children is a legal fiction. Cases of child abuse or neglect are merely dramatic manifestations of the breakdown in that relationship which courts and others should inquire into before permitting parents to act routinely on behalf of their children. In an issue still unsettled by the courts, the Supreme Court declined to decide whether a parent is authorized to commit a child to a mental institution under a state's *voluntary* commitment procedures without the child's informed consent.[10]   The same question of the validity of parent's "volunteering" their children's participation in treatment programs is brushed aside under traditional theories of juvenile justice on the ground that the juvenile is receiving a benefit by being placed in a treatment program, just as the parent is regarded as serving the child's best interests by initiating juvenile court action through the filing of a complaint of misconduct.

The Police

The decision of law enforcement officers about whether or not to take a juvenile into custody is considered by some authorities to be the most critical decision of the criminal justice system. The steamroller effect of official contact has been explained in many ways: damage to self-image, public labeling as deviant, being taken out of the mainstream, association with antisocial peer influences, adjustment to institutionalization, loss of dignity and privacy, exposure to official hypocrisy and corruption, adoption of new values, and so on. Whatever the explanation, it is a rare juvenile who emerges from the experience unchanged.

Therefore, the curbstone decision demanded of law enforcement officers as to whether to apprehend an individual juvenile should be based on something more tangible than instinct. Studies of the information used by the police in making custody or release decisions indicate that police consider more factors than expected.[11]   Although almost all of the officers studied did weigh the objective fact of the seriousness and nature of the offense, the most critical item was the attitude or demeanor of the juvenile. One report found that "the offender's visible attitudes toward the law, the police, and their own criminal behavior were the most important 'causal' factors relating to police decisions on whether to process a youth through the system." Another study stressed the importance of low socioeconomic status of the offender in influencing the police decision.

The second crucial decision that must be made by police officials is whether to refer the juvenile for formal court proceedings, release the individual, or divert him or her to a community program sponsored or approved by the police. Many modern local police units have developed neighborhood networks to provide diversified informal assistance to juveniles in trouble, and are active participants in experimental diversion programs.[12]

Police officials often acknowledge their own unease over exercising broad discretionary power without reliable guidelines to govern their handling of juvenile problems. Some police departments have been working with other community agencies to establish criteria for informal referrals, thus voluntarily placing restraints on their own discretion.

The Intake Officer

Juvenile court intake has a dual purpose: the screening of complaints to determine whether to file a petition for formal court processing or to adjust, refer, or
dismiss the complaint, and the informal nonjudicial handling of cases not referred to the court.

The screening out of cases involves a decision on the appropriateness or need
for judicial involvement. In most states, that decision is not exclusively within
the province of the intake officer. Complainants who insist upon a court hearing
and respondents who deny culpability and demand an opportunity to exonerate
themselves usually are deemed entitled to access to the courts. Furthermore,
even in cases in which the intake officer recommends the filing of a petition or
in which a complainant objects to dismissal or adjustment of the complaint, the
juvenile prosecutor may decide that the facts alleged in the complaint are not legally sufficient to constitute a triable case.

Aside from the exceptional cases noted above, the intake officer has broad discretionary powers for nonjudicial disposition of juvenile complaints. The manner in which that discretion is exercised has been the subject of many studies in
recent years.[13] The findings are similar to those in the police decision-making
study: that in the absence of mandatory criteria to guide the official, the decisions are largely impressionistic. The findings also disclose a wide range of variation among possible outcomes based on comparable sets of data, as in judicial
sentencing practices. For example, in a project sponsored by the Economic Development Council of New York City, the investigators found that the single
most reliable factor, the only real constant, was the identity of the intake
worker. Each individual worker's dispositions were consistent with that worker's
other decisions, demonstrating that he or she was functioning within a set of
self-imposed criteria.

The disparities in intake dispositions among New York City intake officers is
especially interesting because the Department of Probation has attempted at various times to remedy that problem. In December 1971 a Juvenile Intake Questionnaire[14] was distributed to officers in seven branch offices, eliciting answers
to inquiries concerning the criteria used for specific recommendations, such as
the decision that a juvenile be remanded or not, be referred to court or not, be
classified as delinquent or PINS, or be removed from home. The criteria and
items of information used by intake officers in making their recommendations
were analyzed, and hypotheses were drawn as to whether an officer had a rehabilitative, reintegrationist, or retribution approach to the intake function.

Conscientious efforts to prescribe criteria for the intake decision have been undertaken in many jurisdictions. However, to the extent that the criteria are informal and not strictly enforced either by supervisory review or a formal appeal

mechanism, they become part of a pro forma process of conforming dispositions actually based on individual perceptions and biases to the broad language of permissive guidelines. Decisions not exposed to the objective scrutiny of a third party tend to become increasingly subjective. And even objective factors, such as the availability of a suitable community agency for family services, can be an unfair basis for the intake decision as to whether to adjust a particular case informally or require formal court proceedings.

The Prosecutor and Defense Counsel

Prosecutorial discretion can arise in three ways: in the decisions to file a petition based on a particular charge, to withdraw or dismiss a petition after the action is commenced, and to accept or reject a plea by the respondent. The juvenile prosecutor does not possess all of these powers in all jurisdictions. Unlike the adult criminal justice system, where the prosecutor is the sole authority empowered to initiate a court proceeding, in juvenile court authority frequently is shared by or resides in the judge, complainant, police, or probation officer. Abuse or neglect petitions can be the province of the child protective service agency with its own prosecutor. In some jurisdictions, the prosecutor's office has become so reluctant to file a status offense case that it requires parents or other complainants to retain their own counsel to bring the action, tantamount to a civil proceeding. However, the trend is to provide powers more nearly equivalent to those of an adult prosecutor for the juvenile prosecutor. For more serious crimes, the tendency is to transfer the prosecutorial function to the district attorney from the county, city counsel, or corporation counsel usually assigned to juvenile cases.

As with most of the principal actors in juvenile law matters, the prosecutor is impeded in his or her ability to make decisions by the dichotomous nature of the role. Historically, the juvenile court was informal and nonadversarial. A juvenile proceeding was not designed to prosecute or to determine innocence or guilt, but to provide assistance to children in trouble. Therefore, as the need to have a prosecutor to present the petition brought an official law representative of the state into the proceedings, the object was to maintain a view of that function consonant with juvenile law concepts. To achieve that consistency, most states assigned juvenile cases to counsel responsible for civil rather than criminal matters. Where a special juvenile prosecutor's office was established, the prosecutor was expected to consider the best interests of the child as the paramount concern of the office. Even after protection of the community became an acceptable goal of the juvenile court, the prosecutor was charged with protecting both the child's and the community's interests. This confusion of roles, characteristic of probation workers, judges, and correction officers as well, was particularly difficult for prosecutors. They had to deal increasingly with single-minded opposition counsel, the respondent's attorney, who was dedicated to the traditional defense attorney's role of zealous representation of the client's interests. This role has been interpreted by juvenile defense counsel to mean extending every effort to get the charges dismissed, the client released, or the least restrictive disposition possible under the circumstances.

As a consequence, the professional duty of the juvenile's counsel has been clear and compatible with his or her training as an advocate, whereas the juvenile prosecutor's duty has been mired in confusion, euphemisms, and divided loyalties. After the landmark case of *In re Gault*[15] asserted the adversary nature of the fact-finding or adjudicatory proceeding (equivalent to the trial of a criminal case), the prosecutor's role at that stage became clearly and unequivocally that of a proponent of the state's or the petitioner's interests. Gradually, the prosecutor's role has become closer to the criminal justice counterpart. The result has been to establish a more coherent basis for discretionary decision-making by the juvenile prosecutor.[16]

On the other hand, it also has expanded the juvenile prosecutor's discretionary powers. Under the nonadversarial concept, the prosecutor did not participate in the dispositional stage of the proceeding, but relied upon the probation department to submit to the court the state's recommendation for the dispositional order. Today the prosecutor more commonly attends the dispositional hearing and argues for the state's preference. This places the prosecution squarely in opposition to the defense, unless the outcome has been negotiated and both sides agree to a stipulated dispositional alternative.

Another result of the increased recognition of the adversarial aspect of juvenile court proceedings is the effect the changed concept and the new role of both prosecution and defense counsel have had on the attitude and discretionary power of the judge, probation officer, and other officials involved in the juvenile court proceedings.

The Judge

Judges are the principal official decision-makers in any judicial system. Even in situations in which the judge is acting pursuant to the recommendation of another official, such as the prosecutor or the probation worker, it is the judge who is responsible for the ultimate decision.

In juvenile courts in most states, the judge will sit as presiding officer at preliminary hearings to determine whether an accused juvenile should be detained or released from detention, be removed from home and placed in temporary care, and remain within the jurisdiction of juvenile court, or be transferred to adult criminal court in particular cases. Other preadjudicatory decisions that the judge may be called upon to make pertain to such legal issues as (1) probable cause—whether there is probable cause to believe the juvenile committed the acts alleged; and (2) discovery motions—how much information the parties can be required to disclose to each other prior to the fact-finding hearing (also called the adjudication or trial). Other issues related to admissibility of evidence and the legal sufficiency of the complaint can be raised by formal motions and resolved by the court in preliminary hearings in some states. However, the rules governing that stage vary substantially from state to state, and frequently from court to court within a state or locality. The court may follow the rules governing civil procedures, criminal procedures, or juvenile procedures. There may be no written rules and, in some jurisdictions, no formal preliminary hearings. Preliminary hearings may also be recorded or not. The court's decision may be presented in writing or delivered orally. It may be reviewable by another juvenile court, by a superior court, or not at all.

The status of preadjudicatory proceedings is in flux. Currently, there is a trend toward more hearings, more disclosure, and more formality, especially where serious offenses are involved. There also is a trend toward requiring a probable cause hearing or a prompt detention hearing when a juvenile is in custody. Decisions concerning removal of children from their homes because of allegations of neglect or abuse by their parents also are being reexamined as to the information or proof necessary prior to adjudication.

The prevailing practice until recently, and in some jurisdictions the current practice, has been to regard intervention prior to trial as a benefit bestowed upon the juveniles and their families, a way of helping informally before the court has had an opportunity to make its final decision. Children removed temporarily from an allegedly undesirable environment were being protected from endangerment from others or from their own inability to resist misconduct. Further, since the court's procedures generally were designed to be informal, nonadversarial, and paternalistic, formal preliminary proceedings were unnecessary and inappropriate. The officials used their judgment to serve the best interests of the child. To those subscribing to that view of the court, demands for exclusionary rules, disclosure of data or social reports, proof of specified facts to sustain detention or temporary placement, and other preadjudicatory formalities needlessly obstructed the operation of a court distinguished by its reliance on discretionary decision-making by its officials.[17]

Before *In re Gault*, the same principles governed fact-finding hearings. Some states had adopted statutes requiring minimal due process at the trial, but most were informal in the extreme. They permitted hearsay testimony, unverified documentation, no defense counsel, no advance notice of charges, no transcript of the proceedings, no confrontation by accusers and opportunity for cross-examination of witnesses, no privilege against self-incrimination, and no right of appeal. Not all of these and other privileges were denied in all cases, since the judge was permitted to exercise his discretion as to the proper conduct of the hearing. States had begun to find abuses of discretion; courts and legislatures were beginning to adopt rules.

After *Gault* held juveniles entitled to certain procedural due process safeguards, significant changes took place in juvenile court.[18] Although the decision applied only to the adjudicatory hearing, and not the preliminary or dispositional stages, it brought more lawyers into the juvenile courts, reduced official discretion, opened the juvenile court process to greater scrutiny, and made the courts more accountable to the public. It also created even more confusion as to the purpose and functioning of the juvenile court system. What, before *Gault*, had been unquestionably a unique social court became an uncertain hybrid. Even when the officials could see that they were doing more harm than good, they blamed their failure on the lack of adequate resources. Doubt as to the propriety of their actions was rare before *Gault*. After *Gault* it became epidemic, affecting the public, court officials, and juveniles. If it was difficult to make decisions based solely on the best interests of the child, it was almost impossible when protection of the community, punishment, deterrence, and nonintervention were added considerations, not to mention the most confusing undefined term of all—the right to treatment.[19]

Although the court's discretion was radically curtailed at the adjudication stage through procedural requirements, it retained large areas of discretion as a result of vague substantive definitions characteristic of jurisdiction over juveniles.[20] Two obvious examples are the definitions of status offenders and emotional neglect. As discussed earlier, the definition of an ungovernable or incorrigible child could encompass the universe of childhood and adolescence. Similarly, emotional neglect is in the eye of the beholder, unaided by any nationally recognized technical definition. Therefore, almost any evidence could be relevant to introduce against juveniles or their parents to prove such charges, giving the judge broad discretionary power in these areas.

In the final stage of the juvenile court process, aside from appeals or collateral motions, the judge selects a disposition following adjudication. Once a juvenile has been brought into the juvenile justice system, the most important decision will be the outcome or disposition of the case. Here again the court has choices ranging from unconditional discharge to incarceration in a secure facility. In most states, the nature and severity of the offense do not limit the judge's discretion. Technically, the juvenile has not been found a felon, misdemeanant, murderer, rapist, or petty thief. He or she is a delinquent, and the dispositional choices specified by the legislature pertain to that finding. Under the "needs-plus," "conduct-plus," or "delinquency-plus" theory operating in some jurisdictions, the court must find that the juvenile committed the acts alleged in the petition *and* is in need of care, supervision, or confinement.[21] Therefore, the court would be empowered to discharge a juvenile found to have committed homicide on the ground that the parents will provide better care than the state in the form of supervision, training, psychiatric treatment, drug counseling, and so forth. Or, as in our other illustrative case, the judge can order a disobedient or ungovernable child to be confined for an indeterminate term in a state correctional institution on the ground that the parents are unable to control the child's behavior.

The judge is not always obliged to state the reasons for the dispositional choice, although the trend is to require a record of the dispositional order and for it to be reversible if it can be shown to be an abuse of judicial discretion. However, in the cases here described, it is reasonable to expect the judge's reasoning to be sustained in view of the special purpose of a juvenile court disposition.

That special purpose, so difficult to define, permeates juvenile law at every level. In denying a right to trial by jury in juvenile cases, the Supreme Court in *McKeiver v. Pennsylvania* cited "the juvenile court's assumed ability to function in a unique manner." It said:

> Concern about the inapplicability of exclusionary and other rules of evidence, about the juvenile court judge's possible awareness of the juvenile's prior record and of the contents of the social file; about repeated appearances of the same familiar witnesses in the persons of juvenile and probation officers and social workers— . . . chooses to ignore it seems to us, every aspect of fairness, of concern, of sympathy, and of paternal attention that the juvenile court system contemplates.[22]

That decision was rendered four years after *Gault*. Its preference for paternal attention and social files over exclusionary rules and impartial juries indicates the protected role of discretion in the ever unique juvenile court. That is why it is so difficult to overturn a court's disposition as inappropriate. Inappropriate for what purpose?

We are not suggesting that the juvenile court judge makes the dispositional decision in a vacuum. Usually he or she has received reports and recommendations from several sources. Traditionally, the judge is assisted at the dispositional stage by a probation officer, serving as court liaison official, who presents the probation department's investigative report, social profile, clinical and diagnostic studies, description of the juvenile's needs, and recommendation for a suitable disposition. Recent developments include an expanding role for defense counsel, frequently a public defender or other court-appointed legal services attorney, whose office may have prepared its own predispositional report and recommendation. Even more recently, the juvenile prosecutor has enlarged that office's participation in juvenile court proceedings to cover the dispositional stage, so that some prosecutors now represent the state's interest in advocating a particular disposition.

The judge makes the dispositional choice and issues the court's final order. However, the finality of the order may be more form than substance. Other decision-makers involved in executing the order will exercise discretion of their own. If the juvenile is unconditionally or conditionally discharged, the community's response will be significant. If he or she is placed on probation, that department's perception of its role and its ability to carry out its mandate will determine the extent of intervention and assistance. If the juvenile is referred to a child care agency for foster care placement, the factors of quality and duration of placement will be controlled by the agency. If the juvenile is placed with or committed to a private residential program or the state correctional authority, the type of treatment, supervision, and services to be provided, as well as the length of time spent in the programs, usually are decided by those agencies and not the court. These decision-makers also exercise significant discretionary powers over the life and liberty of juveniles involved in the justice system.

The Social Investigators and Behavioral Scientists

During the course of juvenile court proceedings, there are various points at which a judge or other official requests an investigative or diagnostic report about the juvenile or his or her family. The circumstances of the case usually are investigated by the police, although there are exceptions to the rule. In some jurisdictions, either the probation or the social services department conducts the entire investigation. Complaints of child abuse or neglect often are referred to a child protective agency for investigation and sometimes for direct service without referral to the court. Some states have experimented with youth service bureaus to handle certain types of juvenile misconduct, either noncriminal or minor criminal in nature. Dependency cases usually are handled by social investigators in the local or state social services department. Special matters within juvenile court jurisdiction, such as paternity and child support, interstate runaways, and retarded or handicapped children's programs, might be investigated by other agencies.

In general, the probation department has responsibility for coordinating and maintaining the file for all social, medical, and mental health reports pertaining to an individual juvenile. Therefore, the specialists or agencies actually reporting on the child or the child's family ordinarily have an ancillary role in juvenile court. Their findings become part of the social file and may be reinterpreted and integrated into a comprehensive report, with all the potential for distortion and error accompanying that process. Occasionally the social investigator, psychologist, psychiatrist, sociologist, or other specialist is asked to testify at a hearing, which provides the opportunity for direct evidence and cross-examination. Normally, their findings are part of a consolidated report, an amalgamation of hearsay, expert opinion, private impressions, fact, and fancy.

Even the best study of a juvenile can be irrelevant to the matter before the court. For example, it can introduce information that has no bearing on the case. At the inception of juvenile court, the view was widely held that the juvenile would benefit from extensive investigation, testing, and data collection because court officials would be aware of the juvenile's needs in formulating individualized dispositions. . Thus the motto was "more information is better information." With the proliferation of mechanized and computerized data collection, the increasing recognition of the dangers of retaining unverified statements, and the lack of time and personnel to screen and separate fact from fiction, the view today may be that the less such information, the better.[23]

Therefore, discretionary power to select salient fact, skills, deficiencies, and other qualities to measure and report concerning a juvenile in preparing a profile for the court can of itself produce a particular outcome. An emphasis on impulsive behavior may create a different impression (and lead to a different conclusion) from a report that stressed other features of the same juvenile's personality. In the same fashion, a description of the juvenile's family relationships, home environment, peer group patterns, school adjustment, neighborhood reputation, and other factors of socialization is easily presented to conform to an overall impression held by the investigator. In the absence of clear and explicit guidelines prescribing the data required by the court for a detention, placement, or treatment, the information disseminated in a juvenile's social file can unrecognizably distort or manipulate the objective image. The essence of the person can easily be lost in such fragmented data. The resultant subjective labeling, diagnostic or otherwise, can follow the juvenile for life.

The Probation Officer

The probation department generally performs three separate functions in the juvenile justice system: intake screening, social investigation, and community supervision. The intake and investigative roles were discussed earlier. Probation's supervisory activities are less easily appraised.

The probation officer embodies the juvenile justice ideal.[24] Empowered by the court to enforce its mandate, the officer usually is trained to function as a social worker in dealing with juveniles and their families. By being present in the community, probation workers are expected to maintain contact with their assigned juveniles in order to be aware of their needs and to be available to assist them. Through regularly scheduled meetings, they ensure the juvenile's meeting the conditions of his or her probation. Thus probation officers personify the benign authority and service concepts of the juvenile justice system.

Unfortunately, deficiencies in performance of this delicate dual role exemplify the true state of juvenile justice today. A chronic plea of probation departments across the nation is that they have too heavy a caseload. Their duty to provide adequate supervision, assistance, and services to juveniles on probation is buried under an unmanageable mass of reports and case files filled with unverified information. Their brief and infrequent meetings with the juveniles on their caseload provide an inadequate basis for sensitive and frequently significant evaluations of the juveniles' status. Family or school problems, drug use, or gang involvement may never come to the officer's attention. On the other hand, malicious gossip or anonymous complaints may provoke a flurry of official activity, including referrals back to the court or to another agency. Follow-up is rarely possible because of time pressures and bureaucratic obstacles.

The assumption that all adjudicated juveniles require treatment is cherished by the probation officer. Charles Shireman has suggested that the major unacknowledged function of probation is to provide the court with a dispositional choice that does not involve a placement, yet gives the appearance that something has been done. But Shireman rejects a "benign neglect" function and recommends the more positive intervention of "an offer of further help."[25]

Despite the limitations in their ability to familiarize themselves with individual juveniles and their families, probation officers continue to impose conditions of conduct on the juveniles in their charge, to refer them to programs that seem suitable to the officer, and to file official reports analyzing and assessing their adjustment to society regardless of the paucity of information available or the juveniles' actual needs or desires.

Youth Agencies: Child Care, Correctional, Parole, Aftercare

The judge's dispositional order sometimes directs that a juvenile be placed in a particular facility or program. More often it places the juvenile with an agency authorized to execute the dispositional order by selecting an appropriate nonresidential or residential program. The duration of the disposition usually is indeterminate.

Thus enormous discretionary power is delegated to public and nonpublic agencies for the ultimate response of the system to a juvenile found to be delinquent, neglected, abused, or dependent. Even if the court's dispositional order prescribes certain conditions, such as whether the correctional facility should be secure or nonsecure or the juvenile should receive specified treatment or services, the agency will be left with a wide area in which it can make significant choices.

Indeterminate dispositions and a broad range of available dispositions are the foundations of the kind of individualized justice on which the juvenile court is premised. The theory is that the correctional or child care agency should be provided with the flexibility to react appropriately to indications of rehabilitation or intransigence in a juvenile by having the power to change programs, transfer to other facilities, and reduce or extend the term of residence. In practice, that power has become primarily a disciplinary and management tool, enabling the agency to reward conformity and penalize individuality. Sometimes administrative convenience compels a contrary result, releasing those who are disruptive and detaining the quietly compliant inmates.

Although internal discipline is a legitimate concern of any institution, it bears little connection to the basis for the juvenile's assignment to a program. Adjustment to institutional authority does not presage adjustment to community life. Internal controls and the ability to make independent decisions are more important than obedience and submissiveness to a fixed routine. Moreover, the demands of institutional administration produce regimented conduct that is the antithesis of individualized treatment. With perennially inadequate resources, agencies are unable to provide the training, counseling, and personal attention that might help their charges to solve their problems. In addition, the physical and psychological environment of a facility remote from the juveniles' homes, as well as community living with other juveniles, equally stigmatized and ostracized by society, is unlikely to produce a beneficial climate for the normal growth and development essential to the health and well-being of youth.[26]

The two principal discretionary powers of the agencies authorized to implement dispositions, the nature and the duration of the disposition, present different problems for varying types of agencies. Child care agencies, for example, generally are given the responsibility of placing children in treatment programs and in foster homes. In both types of such dispositions, the problems are the quality of available placements, inadequate continuing supervision by the agency, and unnecessarily long placements in the program or foster home. In part the poor quality of available programming is the fault of limited funds, but it also results from defective planning and monitoring by the agency itself. The adoption and enforcement of guidelines for the operation of social, recreational, vocational, medical, and mental health programs should be the responsibility of the agency that places children in the programs.[27]

The same situation applies to foster care. Child care agencies often abdicate their duty to select, train, and supervise foster parents. After juveniles have been assigned to these programs and homes, agencies fail to use the power—sometimes a duty imposed by statute—of periodic reviews of the placement to determine whether it should be continued, modified, or terminated. The customary duty/power to involve juveniles' families in treatment programs, to encourage their ongoing relationship with their children, and to report to the court on the juveniles' progress or status frequently is performed in a perfunctory manner. Yet the effect of such reports and of the agencies' independent decisions to remand or release juveniles may be critical to their future.

State correctional authorities usually operate the secure juvenile facilities, as well as a variety of alternative residential programs.[28] In some states they also administer nonresidential programs for adjudicated juveniles. While child care agencies may be nonpublic, the correctional authority is public. However, the lines are becoming increasingly fuzzy as federal funds support a greater percentage of both public and nonpublic programs. In some jurisdictions, the voluntary or private (nonpublic) agencies receive as much as 95 percent of their funds from federal, state, and local reimbursement for services for juveniles, court-ordered or otherwise. With Title XII money from the Department of Health, Education and Welfare, and delinquency prevention and safe streets money from the Department of Justice, the state correctional authorities' funding patterns begin to resemble those of private agencies. Ironically, discretionary decision-making also has become similar. With the addition of less restrictive alternative programs, the public authority is as unwilling as private agencies to take a chance on the "hard-to-place acting out" older adolescent who may benefit from innovative handling. This usually means that alienated disadvantaged kids go to "training schools"—secure facilities—and less trouble-prone youngsters get the benefit of more relaxed settings, regardless of the seriousness of their respective offenses.

Some jurisdictions have established juvenile parole boards to make the decision of when to release juveniles from confinement. Such boards are not always independent of the correctional authority. Often they merely "rubber-stamp" the administrator's recommendation. And often their criteria are arbitrary and subjective, encouraging the same kind of manipulative and cynical behavior by juvenile inmates as seen in the adult system. Further, loose or nonexistent rules pertaining to written decisions and independent review of the parole decision permit unjust and discriminatory outcomes. Nevertheless, it can be argued that the addition of a separate forum to consider the question of a suitable release date provides the juvenile with an opportunity for a hearing as a safeguard against individual oppression. In some cases, dispersed rather than centralized discretion can be preferable.

The decision to release a juvenile from a correctional institution may be accompanied by a plan for aftercare or community services.[29] The plan sometimes is carried out by the local probation department and sometimes by a special aftercare division of the state correctional authority. Some child care agencies also arrange for continued supervision or service after the child returns to his or her parents, through their own social workers, the local department of social services, or referral to a special community-based program. In theory, such concern for the reentry problems of a juvenile who has been removed from family and friends is laudatory. Unfortunately, it often inhibits a return to normality. It can perpetuate the stigma of adjudication in the community and reinforce the youngster's self-image as a misfit or deviant. Also, the imposition of additional conditions to freedom and the continued presence of an authority that can continue to exercise discretionary judgment have a chilling effect on the juvenile's adustment to a free society.

The Community: Parents, Neighbors, Friends, Schools, Others

The way in which a community regards children and adolescents in its midst, especially those who have had contact with the justice system, is an important component of the juvenile justice system. The juvenile court and the legislatures have developed a vocabulary designed to immunize juveniles from the invidious labels of the adult criminal courts. The juvenile is not a criminal; he or she is a delinquent or a person in need of supervision. Juveniles are never defendants; they are respondents. They are not convicted, but adjudicated; not sentenced, but given a disposition; not imprisoned, but placed or committed. In addition, to preserve the secrecy of the proceedings and protect the juveniles' privacy, juvenile court hearings are closed, names are not published, and records are sealed.

Does it work? Not very well. The whole neighborhood and the school population know about every child's involvement with the courts, and even prospective employers, including the government and insurance agencies, manage to get the information. As for the pretty euphemisms, it is doubtful that a community fears its delinquent offenders less than its criminals. As for the juvenile *victims*—labeled abused, neglected, or dependent children—once they have been placed in an institution or in foster care, little difference can be found between them and the juvenile *offenders*.[30]

It seems that a key factor in the future path of a juvenile who has had court contact is the reaction of the community. The community must decide whether he or she is to be treated as a pariah, marked for life as potentially explosive, to be kept under surveillance and provided with perpetual preventive treatment services to ward off incipient criminality, or to be treated as an ordinary kid who has had some extraordinary experiences.

Everyone who comes into contact with an adjudicated juvenile has discretionary power. Parents decide on the rules governing the household and whether any special rules apply to the child. In addition, the school will decide whether it will permit the juvenile to rejoin the class or be reassigned, provide tutoring assistance, impose reasonable or harsh conditions for catching up academically, and, in general, whether it unobtrusively will help the juvenile regain lost ground or will single him or her out for watchful supervision. Neighbors' and friends' behavior will give the juvenile clues about whether he or she is accepted as is, rejected, or expected to change in some respects. Local law enforcement officers also have an obvious role in an adjudicated juvenile's future. Will he or she be part of the dragnet for every offense committed in the area? If the police do keep an eye on kids with records, will it be to help or prejudge, intrude or protect?

Finally, the role of employers must be considered. Many juveniles who return home choose not to go back to school. They may feel they have slipped off the track and be unwilling to get back on or be too experienced to be school children again. In either case, they need a job. Youth unemployment is so widespread that unskilled and undereducated youngsters have little chance even without a record. But it is doubtful that permanent psychic damage will result from being part of a national economic problem which probably will be resolved or ameliorated in due time. On the other hand, a juvenile rejected for a job because the employer knows of previous court contact confronts a different situation. The sense that he or she possesses a handicap, an ineradicable defect, can be the final push out of the mainstream. If the juvenile believes that there is no chance to succeed in acceptable activities, the next step may be to abandon any effort to engage in the acceptable. Then the task of creating a career criminal will have been completed, using the full discretionary powers of the community.

THE EFFECT OF DISCRETIONARY LAW ON JUVENILES AND ON SOCIETY

A rigid system of laws without recourse to the interjection of reasonable judgment in response to exceptional circumstances or other ground for appropriate modification would be inhumane. The law cannot be enforced by computers. Areas in which decisions must be tempered by values, experience, or special training beyond the strict rule of law are essential to a workable system of justice.[31]

Nevertheless, the single greatest problem in the juvenile justice system is the unrestrained exercise of official discretion. The dictionary definition of justice is merited reward or punishment. A minimal expectation on the part of society is a rational or reasonably predictable outcome in a given situation. But the current system, as a result of the multiple levels of discretionary decision-makers and the absence of known criteria for their decisions, is in a state of chaos.

The effect of this uncertainty on juveniles and the community is a lack of respect for and confidence in juvenile law. Juveniles persuaded by their friends that any smart kid can beat the system may try to do it. Premature cynics figure they will be able to find their Officer Krupke of "West Side Story" and persuade him that they should be exonerated of any responsibility for their actions because of the failings and depravity of their families and society as a whole: they're not bad, they're just misunderstood. This arrogant belief that the sharp and savvy youngster will be able to manipulate the prejudices and attitudes of court officials has a corollary—that the poor dull kid will be out of luck. Selective enforcement of the law impacts on those unable to protect themselves. Discrimination against juveniles unable to create the "right" impression produces detention facilities filled with minority, disabled, retarded, and other disadvantaged juveniles.

Discretionary justice also produces lawlessness in our law enforcement officers. For example, the police in certain communities in California have reacted indignantly to a legislative decision that juveniles apprehended under section 601 of the Welfare and Institutions Code, the status offenders, should not be held in secure facilities.[32]   As a protest against the statute, the police refuse to pick up runaways, truants, and absconders from nonsecure facilities on the ground that to do so would be futile, since the youngsters would only run away again. Therefore, instead of taking the lawful step of advocating a rational amendment to a law they find objectionable, they are unlawfully refusing to enforce a valid law. In their view, taking a status offender into custody is within their discretion. In a similar lawless response to an objectionable law, referred to in an earlier section, the prosecutors in a city in upstate New York have refused to file petitions by parents against PINS, the status offenders under New York law. The prosecutors argue that they are overburdened with delinquency petitions and that parents should obtain the assistance of private counsel to file the PINS petitions. This unorthodox exercise of prosecutorial discretion is of dubious legality.

Thus we see two different branches of the court's law enforcement arm, at opposite ends of the nation, reacting unlawfully to the vagaries of the noncriminal behavior jurisdiction of the juvenile court. Their lawlessness naturally is reflected in the behavior of local juveniles, who are running away from nonsecure placements in record numbers. It can be difficult to help people who don't want to be helped, especially if you can't lock them up to do it.

The combination of uncertainty, manipulability, bias, selective enforcement, disrespect for juvenile law, and the resultant lawlessness on the part of juveniles and officials, most of which derive from unfettered discretion permitted juvenile officials, has an ultimate undesirable effect—a sense of powerlessness in the community. Because of the lack of public accountability in the average citizen's inability to penetrate the elusive decision-making process in juvenile law, the community has reacted with a ferocious backlash. It demands mandatory incarceration for juvenile offenders, with fixed rather than indeterminate dispositions and special classifications for enhanced sentencing for violent offenders. In addition, the public also demands broad transfer criteria, urging removal of a vastly expanded class of juveniles from the jurisdiction of juvenile court to the more punitive ambience of adult criminal court. The rejection of traditional juvenile justice principles is based on two observations by the community: (1) the ineffectiveness of rehabilitative efforts and (2) the failure to protect the public from juvenile crime. Although those observations are valid, the proposed solutions will produce far greater dissatisfaction with the justice system. Abandonment of juvenile court and imposition of harsh punitive measures against juveniles are not the proper response to excessive discretionary power. In the following section, we consider more feasible recommendations for a reformed juvenile justice system.

RECOMMENDATIONS FOR A REFORMED JUVENILE JUSTICE SYSTEM

The need for reform of the juvenile justice system has become apparent to everyone concerned with its operation. What began as a noble social experiment is foundering in a mire of ambiguity, confusion, and ineffectuality. Yet there is little of value to emulate in the adult criminal courts, with their endless delays and plea bargaining, or in the civil courts pushing litigants to accept mutually disagreeable settlements because of six-year calendar backlogs. Despite its flaws, a court designed to handle the special problems of children and their families is worth preserving.

IJA-ABA Standards forJuvenile Justice

In recent years many commissions have studied the juvenile system and reported their findings. One group in particular, the Institute of Judicial Administration (IJA)-American Bar Association (ABA) Joint Commission on Juvenile Justice Standards, has produced a massive program to revise the entire system governing juveniles in their relationships with other social institutions. The 23 volumes comprising the proposed standards constitute a magnificent contribution to the literature, covering every aspect of juvenile law. Those recommendations are the basis for the proposals for reform to be tendered here.[33]

During its six-year study of the juvenile justice system, the Commission reached several major decisions: it adopted a justice, or due process, model for juvenile courts in preference to a rehabilitative or treatment model; it elected to maintain a separate juvenile court as a division of the court of original trial jurisdiction; it agreed to limit coercive intervention in the lives of juveniles and their families to situations of specific harm where intervention is likely to do more good than harm; and it stressed encouragement of recourse to voluntary services and dispositions based on the least restrictive alternative capable of achieving the purpose of the disposition.

A principal means of accomplishing these objectives was to promulgate standards that would reduce the discretionary powers of the decision-makers in the juvenile justice system. By articulating explicit criteria for the various rulings and actions that affect the juvenile's freedom, the standards aim for a coherent, predictable, and just outcome—one that both the juvenile and the community can anticipate as the consequence of a given set of facts. The relevant factors to consider in arriving at such decisions are spelled out in the standards. The underlying premise is that a community accustomed to a fair and even-handed system of justice will respect and adhere to its requirements—that official fairness and objectivity will reduce lawlessness.

Police Discretion

The initial step toward limiting discretionary powers was to adopt definitions of the court's jurisdiction that are clear, unambiguous, and consistent with fundamental values. Juveniles will not be apprehended nor will complaints be accepted by the court for conduct that does not warrant the court's attention. For example, the standards for *Police Handling of Juvenile Problems* distinguish among noncriminal misbehavior, minor criminal conduct, and serious juvenile crimes in selecting a course of action. The decision to confine juvenile court jurisdiction to cases of specific harm eliminated noncriminal misbehavior (unruliness, disobedience, running away, truancy, incorrigibility, and so forth) and victimless crimes (except drug use) as juvenile offenses in the standards on *Juvenile Delinquency and Sanctions* and *Noncriminal Misbehavior*. Therefore, police officers would be spared the decision of whether to take such children into custody in the absence of emergency or endangering circumstances. In the same way, removal of juveniles from their parents' care because of alleged child abuse or neglect is limited to carefully defined cases in the volume on *Abuse and Neglect*.

Discretion at Intake

Intake officers also are guided in their decisions by the definitions of the court's jurisdiction, as well as exact criteria for a choice between adjustment of complaints and referral to the court for formal proceedings. The officer's discretion is limited by standards such as those mandating release in the *Interim Status* volume. Referral to a youth services agency is required in all cases of first offense misdemeanors under the *Youth Services Agencies* standards, and the conditions permissible for a consent decree are set forth in the standards on *The Juvenile Probation Function*. Other standards in the probation volume prescribe the elements which must be found for a determination that a complaint is legally sufficient or that a disposition is in the best interests of a child. Further, the dispositional alternatives available at intake are restricted by the standards that bar the provision of long-term intake services and other nonjudicial dispositions, except unconditional dismissal or referral to a community agency.

Predisposition: Prosecutorial, Defense, and Judicial Discretion

Discretionary powers at the predispositional stages are prescribed by the standards in the volumes on *Counsel for Private Parties, Prosecution, Pretrial Court Procedures,* and *Adjudication.* With extensive discovery provisions requiring broad disclosure of evidence to be used at the fact-finding and dispositional hearings, preliminary procedures are accorded far greater importance under the proposed standards than in the current system, which stresses informality and secrecy. Furthermore, with the standards making the juveniles' right to counsel nonwaivable, it is necessary to protect juveniles from excessive power in their counsel. Therefore, limitations are imposed on plea bargaining, especially where the juvenile denies guilt. The judge is required to conduct a full inquiry into the juvenile's awareness of the consequences of any admission or confession before accepting a plea or admitting any statement against interest in testimony. As for the adjudicatory or fact-finding hearing itself, which traditionally is closed to the public unless the court in its discretion decides to open it, under the suggested standards the hearing may be public at the option of the respondent. Thus the judge's discretion to maintain secrecy would be shifted to the juveniles and their attorneys.

Dispositional Discretion

In a major shift in the dispositional stage, the standards on *Juvenile Delinquency and Sanctions* and *Dispositions* propose fixed terms, with maximum sanctions limited by the relative severity of the offense. The prevailing power of court officials to recommend or impose any available disposition in any proceeding, regardless of the nature or seriousness of the juvenile offense, and the power of the correctional authority or child care agency with which the juvenile is placed to decide on the duration of the placement would be eliminated. Although other objective factors could be considered in devising an appropriate disposition, such as age, prior record, and degree of culpability, under the principle of proportionality the duration and relative restrictiveness of the disposition would be governed by a classification of juvenile offenses based on the state's penal code. A class one juvenile offense, for example, would be an adult crime punishable by death or imprisonment for twenty years to life; a class two juvenile offense is akin to one punishable for adults by five to twenty years; and so on down to a class five offense, punishable for adults by six months or less, including a nominal sentence. Comparable juvenile dispositions would be for sanctions or placements suitable for juveniles, but would be limited by the principle of proportionality.

After the dispositional hearing, the standards on *Dispositional Procedures* require the judge to "state with particularity the precise terms of the disposition that is imposed." In the postdispositional stage, a disposition could not be changed by the correctional or placement agencies without petitioning of the court for a judicial proceeding for modification downward, based on subsequent circumstances rendering the disposition inequitable. The agency, the juvenile, or the juvenile's attorney or parents would be empowered to file for modification of the disposition. The only discretionary power to change the disposition retained by the agency in the standards on *Corrections Administration* would be for a prescribed percentage (5 percent) for "good time."

Parental Discretion

Parental powers are well protected by the standards. Parents are given a right to be represented by counsel at most stages of the juvenile justice process, both judicial and nonjudicial, including intake, dispositional, and appellate proceedings. They participate in diversion and plea negotiations and have an independent right to appeal final orders. However, in every instance in which parents are permitted to be present to assist their children, the court is required to consider possible conflicts of interest. If the parents are found to be hostile to their children, they are denied the right to appear unless their separate adverse interests are affected substantially by the matters in issue. Therefore, the presumption of mutuality of interests between parents and children is rebuttable under the standards.

Other Guides to Discretion

At every stage of the juvenile's contact with the juvenile justice system, the discretion of decision-makers is limited by well-defined standards. This extends from the decision about whether particular conduct constitutes a ground for official intervention, to the decision to return an adjudicated juvenile to the community after completion of a period of confinement. Decisions affecting juveniles' liberty in institutions unrelated to the courts also are constrained by guidelines, as in the standards for *Schools and Education* and *Youth Service Agencies.* Confused or unsettled areas of juvenile law, such as emancipation, family autonomy, right to health care without parental consent (for contraception, abortion, venereal disease, drug treatment), and youth employment are illuminated through standards in the *Rights of Minors* volume. Other relatively undeveloped but increasingly significant subjects for official decision-making are given coherence in standards proposed for *Appeals and Collateral Review* and *Transfer Between Courts.* Guidelines concerning the collection, retention, and dissemination of information by juvenile courts, police, and other juvenile agencies are expounded in intricate detail, especially with respect to social and psychological histories, in the volume on *Juvenile Records and Information Systems*. Finally, standards to eliminate some of the chaos in the administration and allocation of resources in the system are provided in *Court Organization and Administration*, *Architecture of Facilities*, *Planning for Juvenile Justice*, and *Monitoring*.

The Sample Cases Under the Standards

Under the proposed standards, our sample cases would have judiciously predictable outcomes. The girl who stayed out late at night would not have been within the jurisdiction of the juvenile courts, since she did not commit a crime. However, if the police officers who found her in the street reasonably determined her to be in "substantial and immediate danger" to her physical safety, they would be empowered to take her home or to another "appropriate residence," usually a relative's home. If she refused to be taken home, they could transport her to a temporary nonsecure residential facility for no more than six hours, while they tried to contact her parents. After six hours of limited custody, she could stay at the facility voluntarily or depart. No court action would follow.

The boy who committed the felony murder would be charged with a class one juvenile offense and be subject to the most severe juvenile court disposition. He also could be transferred to the adult criminal courts if a transfer hearing established that probable cause existed to believe he committed the class one offense and that he was not a proper person to be handled by the juvenile court. Explicit findings would have to be made to establish the inefficacy or inappropriateness of continuing juvenile court jurisdiction in the particular case.

Thus the new standards would allow discretionary power to be exercised: by the police in finding that a dangerous situation existed, the prosecutor in deciding whether to seek transfer, and the judge in determining whether the juvenile should be waived to adult court. But, in every instance, such discretion would be limited by clearly specified factors for the decision-makers to consider before reaching their conclusions and taking action.

CONCLUSION

The standards promulgated by the IJA-ABA Joint Commission are not the exclusive remedy for improvement of the juvenile justice system. Many problems basic to any system of justice remain. The long-range effects of incarcerating offenders, the societal benefits of any penal sanction, and the rational connection between any term of years and any particular offense, whether for purposes of deterrence, punishment, rehabilitation, protection of society, or "just desserts," are unsettled. The question of how we can fulfill our responsibility to raise children to be valued members of the community without unjustified coercive intervention is addressed throughout the standards, but never definitively answered.[34]

Through adherence to principles of fairness, reasonableness, and appropriateness in the adoption of standards to guide those who make decisions affecting juveniles in their relationships with social institutions, discretionary powers are given parameters. No one, whether judge or juror, attorney or petitioner, police or probation officer, social worker or psychiatrist, is totally free of bias. Decisions must bear the imprint of the training, experience, personality, and ethical values of the decision-maker. But a system of justice requires that the process by which discretion is exercised produce decisions that are perceived by those the system is designed to serve as a fair and even-handed response to the facts under consideration. A reformed juvenile justice system governed by standards limiting the exercise of discretionary powers can regain the respect of society and its children.

FOOTNOTES

1. Levin, M., and Sarri, R., Juvenile delinquency: A comparative analysis of legal codes in the United States. National Assessment of Juvenile Corrections (1974).
2. N.Y. Fam. Ct. Act §§711-18 (McKinney 1975).
3. Cal. Welf. 8 Inst'ns Code §601 (West 1972).
4. See Idaho Code §16-1803 (1a) (Supp. 1971); Ind. Ann. Stat. §9-3204 (10) (Supp. 1972); N.J. Rev. Stat. §2A:4-14 (2k) (Supp. 1973).
5. N.Y. Penal Law §125.25 (McKinney 1967).
6. Cal. Welf. & Inst'ns Code §707 (West 1972).
7. *In re Patricia A.*, 31 N.Y. 2d 3 (1972); *Lamb v. Brown*, 456 F. 2d 18 (10th Cir. 1972). See Besharov, D. J., *Juvenile Justice Advocacy*, 183. Practising Law Institute (1974).
8. See Wilson, J. Q., Changing criminal sentences. *Harpers 255:* 16 (November 1977).
9. Andrews, R. H., Jr. and Cohn, A. H., Ungovernability: The unjustifiable jurisdiction. *Yale Law Journal 7:* 1383 (1974).
10. *Bartley v. Kremens*, 423 U.S. 1028 (1976).
11. Sullivan, D., and Siegel, L., How police use information to make decisions. *Crime & Delinq. 18:* 253 (1972).
12. See Nejelski, P., Diversion: Unleashing the hound of heaven? In M. K. Rosenheim (ed.), *Pursuing Justice for the Child.* Chicago: University of Chicago Press (1976), p. 94.
13. Ferster, E. Z., and Courtless, T. F., The intake process in affluent county juvenile court. *Hastings L. J. 22:* 1127 (1971).
14. Office of Probation for the Court of New York City, Juvenile Intake Questionnaire. Research Center Report #1 (December 9, 1971). See Flicker, B., Summary report: Conference of New York City juvenile justice resources. IJA-LEAA (May 1974).
15. *In re Gault*, 387 U.S. 1 (1967).
16. See Fox, S., Prosecutors in the juvenile court: A statutory proposal. *Harv. J. Legis. 8:* 33 (1970).

17. Mack, J., The juvenile court. *Harvard Law Review 23:* 104 (1909). Platt, A. M., *The Child Savers: The Invention of Delinquency.* Chicago: University of Chicago Press (1969), pp. 137–75.
18. Dorsen, N., and Resneck, D., *In Re* Gault and the future of juvenile law. *Fam. L. Q. 1:* 34 (1967).
19. Bailey, W., and Pyfer, J., Jr., Deprivation of liberty and right to treatment. *Clearinghouse Rev. 7:* 519 (1974).
20. The California Welf. and Inst'ns Code §300 (West 1972), enumerating persons subject to juvenile court jurisdiction, does not attempt to define neglect or abuse, merely including juveniles whose home is unfit "by reason of neglect, cruelty, depravity or physical abuse of either of his parents. . . ."
21. See Besharov, *Juvenile Justice Advocacy,* p. 304, on motions to dismiss on the ground that there is no need for court intervention.
22. *McKeiver v. Pennsylvania,* 403 U.S. 528, 550 (1971).
23. Sussman, A., Psychological testing and juvenile justice: An invalid judicial function. *Crim. L. Bull. 10:* 117 (1974).
24. Schultz, J. L., The cycle of juvenile court history. *Crime & Delinq. 19:* 457 (1973).
25. Shireman, C. H., Perspectives on juvenile probation. In M. K. Rosenheim (ed.), *Pursuing Justice for the Child.* Chicago, University of Chicago Press, (1976), p. 138.
26. Goldstein, J., Freud, A., and Solnit, A. J., *Beyond the Best Interests of the Child.* New York: Macmillan Publishing Co. (1973). Rothman, D. J., *The Discovery of the Asylum.* Boston: Little, Brown and Co. (1971).
27. New York State Council of Voluntary Child Care Agencies, Reforming the child care system from within: The voluntary agencies' obligation–A beginning plan for action. Proceedings of Seminary/Retreat (November 5–6, 1975).
28. Luger, M., Tomorrow's training schools: Problems, progress, and challenges. *Crime & Delinq. 9:* 545 (1973). Vinter, R., Downs, G., and Hall, J., Juvenile corrections in the states: Residential programs and deinstitutionalization: A preliminary report. National Assessment of Juvenile Corrections (1975).
29. Ibid.
30. Council of Voluntary Child Care Agencies, Services to PINS and adolescents: The voluntary agencies' perspective (1973), p. 41.
31. Davis, K. C., *Discretionary Justice: A Preliminary Inquiry.* Baton Rouge: Louisiana State University Press (1969).
32. The much abused California Assembly Bill No. 3121, introduced in February 1976 and effective in January 1977, merely complied with the "deinstitutionalization" provisions of the Juvenile Justice and Delinquency Prevention Act of 1974, 18 U.S.C. 5031 *et. seq.* (modified by the 1977 amendments).
33. See Flicker, B., *Standards for Juvenile Justice: A Summary and Analysis,* Cambridge, Massachusetts: Ballinger Publishing Company (1977). This volume discusses the 23 volumes of standards approved by the IJA-ABA Joint Commission and published by Ballinger in 1976 and 1977 as tentative drafts, prior to anticipated adoption by the ABA House of Delegates in 1978.
34. Schur, E. M., *Radical Nonintervention: Rethinking the Delinquency Problem.* Englewood Cliffs, New Jersey: Prentice-Hall, Inc. (1973). Kaufman, I. R., Of Juvenile Justice and Injustice. *A.B.A.J. 62:* 730 (1976).

2
Discretion in Juvenile Justice

Gary Glaser

PARENS PATRIAE AND THE GAULT DECISION

> A recent study of juvenile court judges . . . revealed that half had not re-
> ceived undergraduate degrees; a fifth had received no college education at all; a
> fifth were not members of the bar.*

No single paragraph can awaken the uninitiated to the state of the juvenile justice system in the U.S. as the above statement can.

The creation of the family court system had the judge as its central focus: respected, wise, learned, probative, considerate, flexible, fatherly, and humane—a
figure who would benignly adjudicate disputes, always keeping in mind the high
purposes and goals of rehabilitating youngsters rather than punishing and chastis-
ing them. What then of the President's Commission report? What does it have
to do with our preconceptions about family courts? What does happen in family
courts?

The original purposes of the founders of the family court system were certainly laudable—to remove juvenile offenders from the proven failures and harshness of the adult system; to remove the stigma of appearances in court through
the use of informality with judges not robed and seated on a level equal to that
of the participants, with a small and informal courtroom, with confidentiality
through sealing of records, with juvenile offenses not treated as convictions, with
juvenile arrests not regarded as arrests but "taking into custody," and with new
facilities and institutions called schools, reformatories, or industrial homes.

To bring about change, a philosophy or doctrine is needed as a cornerstone.
The rock upon which the structure was to be built became known as *parens*

*Task Force Report Juvenile Delinquency and Youth Crime (President's Commission on
Law Enforcement and the Administration of Justice, 1967), pp. 7-9.

patriae. Simply explained, the state in its social welfare and parental role becomes parent, guardian, and benefactor to the wayward child.

To further the goals of rehabilitation and guidance, a concomitant legal development occurred. It included the reduction and stripping away of constitutional rights, of criminal procedures, of rules of evidence, and of formality. These later developments were justified because the young person was not to be punished, but to receive treatment. Furthermore, the goals of the new system were different from older, punitive goals; the wise, kindly father figure of the judge was to dispense benevolence rather than to do harm.

Two basic statutes developed to foster the concept of *parens patriae.* One was a body of juvenile delinquency statutes grounded in a charge related to penal law. The other statute is unique to the family court, having no counterpart in the adult world of the criminal court. This statute, in New York known as PINS (for Persons in Need of Supervision), has counterparts throughout the country, such as CINS (Children in Need of Supervision) and MINS (Minors in Need of Supervision), or some such variant designation. Such statutes provide jurisdiction and loss of freedom for truancy, ungovernability, disobedience, unruliness, and the like. The PINS statute is the true child of the *parens patriae* doctrine and gives the judiciary its greatest discretionary power; in it prevention is stressed.

To be an adult criminal offender, a person must commit an overt act with intent that results in the violation of a specific criminal statute. Not so, critics allege, with the PINS statute. Here the criteria are vague, and unacceptable; conduct is not explicitly set forth. The statute is subject to wide and unchecked interpretation. The wide use of judicial discretion that may involve personal and highly moralistic standards is a common outcome.

When a person speaks of discretion in the family court, it is in relation to failures in the law to define juvenile infraction. What do words like "ungovernable," "habitually disobedient," "beyond control," and "unruly" mean? Who is "in need of care and treatment"? And, on the other hand, who are the persons making these decisions? On what basis are these decisions being made and by what criteria?

The concept of *parens patriae* effected change. As a result the criminal justice system was divested of a large segment of its populace. Changes occurred with regard to detention pending trial. Youngsters in most states were no longer to be held with adults. Increased funding for social agencies occurred in some states.

But, at the same time, the sorry truth began to emerge as to the failings of the system. Ultimately the Supreme Court recognized these failings: that what we call a "hall of justice or courtroom" was an outer shell hiding the destruction and loss of freedom for thousands of youngsters without providing them benefits and rights comparable to those accorded to adults; that what were called "reformatories, schools," and the like were nothing more than juvenile penitentiaries, where social programs were minimal, if not nonexistent, and where brutality was the norm rather than the exception. Recognition came that the judges who manned these courts enjoyed greater discretion and latitude than judges dealing with adult cases, and greater abuses also resulted.

Thus the movement took a swing backward in time and concept. The youngster was indeed suffering a loss of freedom. Judges did act punitively. Institutions were corrupt. And so, due process—that mythical and sacred term embedded in our collective psyches, which had been removed by *parens patriae*— slowly and inexorably was ordered returned and expanded to the family court. Due process not only ensures an orderly and fair conviction, but in this author's view, protects the juvenile from his would-be benefactor, the judge.

A closer look is in order to examine the dangers that are posed by discretion and unlimited judicial leeway.

Most legal decisions one reads are appellate cases. The reader gleans the facts of the case, the legal issues involved, the reasoning behind the decision, and the specific holding. A study of the Gualt case will review these traditional breakdowns but will also center on the activities of the family court judge that gave rise to the appeal.

The keynote for modern juvenile justice is the case of *In Re Gault*, decided in 1967 by the Supreme Court. In *Gault* the *parens patriae* theory of juvenile justice was explicitly rejected. The actions of the particular judge in Arizona who committed Gault to a six-year term in an industrial school are illustrative of judicial abuse in family court. The case arose in Arizona, where Gault, a 15-year-old, had been placed in a state industrial school for six years for making a lewd phone call.

On Monday, June 8, 1964, at about 10 A.M., Gerald Francis Gault and a friend, Ronald Lewis, were taken into custody by the Sheriff of Gila County. Gerald was then still subject to a six months' probation order which had been entered on February 25, 1964, as a result of his having been in the company of another boy who had stolen a wallet from a lady's purse. The police action on June 8 was taken as the result of a verbal complaint by a neighbor of the boys, Mrs. Cook, about a telephone call made to her in which the caller or callers made lewd or indecent remarks. It will suffice for purposes of this opinion to say that the remarks or questions put to her were of the irritatingly offensive, adolescent, sex variety.

At the time Gerald was picked up, his mother and father were both at work. No notice that Gerald was being taken into custody was left at the home. No other steps were taken to advise them that their son had, in effect, been arrested. Gerald was taken to the Children's Detention Home. When his mother arrived home at about 6 o'clock, Gerald was not there. Gerald's older brother was sent to look for him at the trailer home of the Lewis family. He apparently learned then that Gerald was in custody. He so informed his mother. The two of them went to the Detention Home. The deputy probation officer, Flagg, who was also superintendent of the Detention Home, told Mrs. Gault "why Jerry was there" and said that a hearing would be held in Juvenile Court at 3 o'clock the following day, June 9.

Officer Flagg filed a petition with the court on the hearing day, June 9, 1964. It was not served on the Gaults. Indeed, none of them saw this petition until the habeas corpus hearing on August 17, 1964. The petition was entirely formal. It made no reference to any factual basis for the judicial action which it initiated. It recited only that "said minor is under the age of eighteen years, and is in need of the protection of this Honorable Court; (and that) said minor is a delinquent minor." It prayed for a hearing and an order regarding "the care and custody of said minor." Officer Flagg executed a formal affidavit in support of the petition.

On June 9, Gerald, his mother, his older brother, and Probation Officers Flagg and Henderson appeared before the Juvenile Judge in chambers. Gerald's father was not there. He was at work out of the city. Mrs. Cook, the complainant, was not there. No one was sworn at this hearing. No transcript or recording was made. No memorandum or record of the substance of the proceedings was prepared. Our information about the proceedings and the subsequent hearing on June 15, derives entirely from the testimony of the Juvenile Court Judge, Mr. and Mrs. Gault and Officer Flagg at the habeas corpus proceeding conducted two months later. From this, it appears that at the June 9 hearing Gerald was questioned by the judge about the telephone call. There was conflict as to what he said. His mother recalled that Gerald said he only dialed Mrs. Cook's number and handed the telephone to his friend, Ronald. Officer Flagg recalled that Gerald had admitted making the lewd remarks. Judge McGhee testified that Gerald "admitted making one of these (lewd) statements." At the conclusion of the hearing, the judge said he would "think about it." Gerald was taken back to the Detention Home. He was not sent to his own home with his parents. On June 11 or 12, after having been detained since June 8, Gerald was released and driven home. There is no explanation in the record as to why he was kept in the Detention Home or why he was released. At 5 P.M. on the day of Gerald's release, Mrs. Gault received a note signed by Officer Flagg. It was on plain paper, not letterhead. Its entire text was as follows:

Mrs. Gault: "Judge McGhee has set Monday June 15, 1964 at 11:00 A.M. as the date and time for further hearings on Gerald's delinquency."

At the appointed time on Monday, June 15, Gerald, his father and mother, Ronald Lewis and his father, and Officers Flagg and Henderson were present before Judge McGhee. Witnesses at the habeas corpus proceeding differed in their recollections of Gerald's testimony at the June 15 hearing. Mr. and Mrs. Gault recalled that Gerald again testified that he had only dialed the number and that the other boy had made the remarks. Officer Flagg agreed that at this hearing Gerald did not admit making the lewd remarks. But Judge McGhee recalled that "there was some admission again of some of the lewd statements. He—he didn't admit any of the more serious lewd statements." Again, the complainant, Mrs. Cook, was not present. Mrs. Gault asked that Mrs. Cook be present "so she could see which boy that done the talking, the dirty talking over the phone." The Juvenile Judge said "she didn't have to be present at that hearing." The judge did not speak to Mrs. Cook or communicate with her at any time. Probation Officer Flagg had talked to her once—over the telephone on June 9.

At this June 15 hearing a "referral report" made by the probation officers was filed with the court, although not disclosed to Gerald or his parents. This listed the charge as "Lewd Phone Calls." At the conclusion of the hearing, the judge committed Gerald as a juvenile delinquent to the State Industrial School "for the period of his minority (that is, until 21), unless sooner discharged by due process of law." An order to that effect was entered. It recites that "after a full hearing and due deliberation the Court finds that said minor is a delinquent child, and that said minor is of the age of 15 years."

No appeal is permitted by Arizona law in juvenile cases. On August 3, 1964, a petition for a writ of habeas corpus was filed with the Supreme Court of Arizona and referred by it to the Superior Court for hearing.

At the habeas corpus hearing on August 17, Judge McGhee was vigorously cross-examined as to the basis for his actions. He testified that he had taken into account the fact that Gerald was on probation. He was asked "under what section of . . . the code you found the boy delinquent?"

His answer is set forth in the margin.[1] In substance, he concluded that Gerald came within ARS 8-201, subsec. 6(a), which specifies that a "delinquent child" includes one "who has violated a law of the state or an ordinance or regulation of a political subdivision thereof." The law which Gerald was found to have violated is ARS 13-377.

[1] "Q. All right. Now, Judge, would you tell me under what section of the law or tell me under what section of—of the code you found the boy delinquent?

"A. Well, there is a—I think it amounts to disturbing the peace. I can't give you the section, but I can tell you the law, that when one person uses lewd language in the presence of another person, that it can amount to—and I consider that when a person makes it over the phone, that it is considered in the presence, I might be wrong, that is one section. The other section upon which I consider the boy delinquent is Section 8-201, Subsequent (d), habitually involved in immoral matters."

This section of the Arizona Criminal Code provides that a person who "in the presence or hearing of any woman or child . . . uses vulgar, abusive or obscene language, is guilty of a misdemeanor . . ." The penalty specified in the Criminal Code, which would apply to an adult, is $5 to $50, or imprisonment for not more than two months. The judge also testified that he acted under ARS 8-201, subsec. 6(d) which includes in the definition of a "delinquent child" one who, as the judge phrased it, is "habitually involved in immoral matters."

Asked about the basis for his conclusion that Gerald was "habitually involved in immoral matters," the judge testified, somewhat vaguely, that two years earlier, on June 2, 1962, a "referral" was made concerning Gerald, "where the boy had stolen a baseball glove from another boy and lied to the Police Department about it." The judge said there was "no hearing," and "no accusation" relating to this incident, "because of lack of material foundation." But it seems to have remained in his mind as a relevant factor. The judge also testified that Gerald had admitted making other nuisance phone calls in the past which, as the judge recalled the boy's testimony, were "silly calls, or funny calls, or something like that."

Note throughout the proceedings the wide discretion and arbitrary conduct in the proceedings involving detention, hearing, and placement. This situation was not limited to Arizona. Also to be stressed is that the case dealt with juvenile delinquents, leaving thousands of PINS still at the mercy of discretionary law.

The Supreme Court has granted delinquents the following specific rights:

1. Notice of the charges.
2. Right to counsel (free if indigent).
3. Right to confrontation and cross-examination.
4. Privilege against self-incrimination.

Furthermore the Court clearly admonished lower court judges not to treat their wards in a manner resembling a kangaroo court.

If Gerald had been over 18, he would not have been subject to Juvenile Court proceeding. For the particular offense immediately involved, the maximum punishment would have been a fine of $5 to $50, or imprisonment in jail for not more than two months. Instead, he was committed to custody for a maximum of six years. If he had been over 18 and had committed an offense to which such a sentence might apply, he would have been entitled to substantial rights under the Constitution of the United States as well as under Arizona's laws and constitution. The United States Constitution would guarantee him rights and protections with respect to arrest, search, and seizure, and pretrial interrogation. It would assure him of specific notice of charges and adequate time to decide his course of action and to prepare his defense. He would be entitled to clear advice that he could be represented by counsel, and, at least if a felony were involved, the State would be required to provide counsel if his parents were unable to afford it. If the court acted on the basis of his confession, careful procedures would be required to assure its voluntariness if the case went to trial, confrontation and opportunity for cross-examination would be guaranteed. So wide a gulf between the State's treatment of the adult and of the child requires a bridge sturdier than mere verbiage, and reasons more persuasive than cliche can provide. As Wheeler and Cottrell have put it, "The rhetoric of the juvenile court movement has developed without any necessarily close correspondence to the realities of court and institutional routines." . . .

In view of this, it would be extraordinary if our Constitution did not require the procedural regularity and the exercise of care implied in the phrase "due process." Under our Constitution, the condition of being a boy does not justify a kangaroo court. The traditional ideas of Juvenile Court procedure, indeed, contemplated that time would be available and care would be used to establish precisely what the juvenile did and why he did it—was it a prank of adolescence or a brutal act threatening serious consequences to himself or society unless corrected? Under traditional notions, one would assume that in a case like that of Gerald Gault, where the juvenile appears to have a home, a working mother and father, and an older brother, the Juvenile Judge would have made a careful inquiry and judgment as to the possibility that the boy could be disciplined and dealt with at home dispite his previous transgressions. Indeed, so far as appears in the record before us, except for some conversation with Gerald about his school work and his "wanting to go to . . . Grand Canyon with his father," the points to which the judge directed his attention were little different from those that would be involved in determining any charge of violation of a penal statute. The essential difference between Gerald's case and a normal criminal case is that safeguards available to adults were discarded in Gerald's case. The summary procedure as well as the long commitment was possible because Gerald was 15 years of age instead of over 18.

Thus due process protections were used to curtail judicial discretion and courtroom informality. Standards, rights, codification of rules, criminal procedure, attorneys, and stenographic records are all essentials and a prerequisite for a judicial system hoping to approach an ideal of fairness.

Cases such as *Gault* and others that followed have all too often incurred the anger of lower court judges. Where once their actions and opinions went unbridled and unchecked, greater accountability now exists. This curtailment of judicial power has not been met with understanding or enthusiasm.

In granting the juvenile in a delinquency case the fundamental rights of confrontation, non-self-incrimination, and cross-examination, the Court not only improved the nature of the fact-finding system, but also limited the role of the judge in family court. No longer could the judge ask the younster whether he wished to make a statement and then, in the guise of treatment, send him to a "rehabilitation" center. No longer would the youngster have to provide his own defense, ignorant of the law. No longer could the judge act as prosecutor, defense counsel, and ultimately decision-maker.

Given the facts of how the family court in Arizona handled *Gault*, the wonder is that, on appeal, such procedures were upheld by the highest state court in Arizona. If one reads the facts of this case to the average citizen today, and asks him to guess what year the case occurred, it is a fair assumption that the answer will be in terms of decades ago. It is frightening to contemplate that the decision, which is psychologically not very radical by today's standards, is only 11 years old.

THE EVERYDAY COURT

From theoretical matters and the decisions of the Supreme Court, we turn to the everyday workings of the family court.

As an illustration, I can recall working in the Family Court as a law guardian in New York City. As compared to working in the Criminal Court and representing adult defendants, judicial discretion based on moralistic conceptions is far more prevalent. Thus a pregnant teen-ager is adjudged a PINS. The judge asks the parent whether he or she wishes the child returned. The parent replies in the negative and the child is ordered detained. The child is on the road to "placement." meaning an institution or a foster home.

Another child is brought to court for running away. In the hallway of the court, the mother reveals to the law guardian that she carries a thick belt in her pocketbook for constant disciplinary use. She opens the pocketbook and proudly displays the weapon. The girl has large discolorations on her forearms where the belt was employed. Rather than find the girl a neglected child and legally justify the runaways, the judge comments that his father used the rod behind the woodshed on him, and therefore this discipline is justified. The youngster is then found guilty. It should be noted that our judge is not a caricature but is a basically humanistic person; his upbringing occurred near the turn of the century.

A seasoned and hardened law guardian is crying in the halls. She relates the following. A girl has been found to be a PINS for running away from home. Her defense: Her father would periodically inspect her to see if she was still a virgin. Defense denied.

Such examples can be duplicated in various forms and manner. What they reveal is a pattern of flexibility and discretion that is too great.

Any discussion of the psychology of discretion must include the role of the parent in the court.

When a youngster is brought to court on a juvenile delinquency or PINS petition, many states have a system whereby an intake part of court attempts to settle the dispute or see to it that it moves forward within the system. Particularly, in PINS cases should the parental decision be to keep the child pending a hearing, this decision is of overwhelming importance; for in a PINS case an initial decision not to take the child dooms the child to placement. Judges and probation officers are loath to order a recalcitrant parent to take a child home against his/her will. The same principle applies to delinquency cases. The detention of a child pending the hearing places this class of child in a far worse position than that of the child who is free pending trial. Most states do not provide for a bail system for juveniles, and even where such a system exists, the child again is at the mercy of the parent. The system is one of preventive detention, with the parent and intake judge as its chief components. The discretion of the intake judge lies in his desire and ability to pressure parents to prevent this system from being used as a dumping ground for children. Unfortunately, all too often, the mere initiation of a charge allows the parent psychologically to trigger the dumping process and use the court. Only a firm judge interested in due process can withstand this tactic.

Wide discretionary factors continue throughout the process. Once the hearing is over and the youngster is found to have committed PINS or juvenile delinquency violations, the next key decision must be made. Should the child be placed? Should the child be detained pending a placement? Should the child go home pending a placement? Should the child be sent for psychiatric or psychological workups? Should the child be placed in a foster home? A group home? An urban home? A drug program? A mental health facility? An after-school program? A different public school? The Army? An institution? An industrial home, training school, or other variant? With a different parent, a relative, or a guardian? Should he go home and be discharged? Should he go home with conditions on his conduct? Should he be supervised on probation?

Here, the family court process differs the most from the adult process, as here the family court judge has tremendous leeway in determining what to do with the child. In criminal court a sentence is affixed usually as a result of plea bargaining. In family court there is virtually no plea bargaining. The defendant in criminal court does his time in one of a few institutions selected by the corrections department rather than the judge. In family court, the judge can choose from a wide variety and range of programs. Again the parents' input is crucial. Should a parent plead for "another chance," the judge's decision may be made for him. Refusal to take a child home will trigger the all-important decision of what to do with the child.

The importance of the probation department should not be overlooked. In order for our judge to make his decision, probation will guide him. Probation, in theory, will provide an extensive work-up on the youngster and the family through interviews, school reports, other persons, past records, and psychiatric and psychological tests. For some youngsters it is a foregone conclusion that placement will occur. It is in marginal and difficult cases that discretion will play its greatest role.

The importance of well-qualified, humanistic, and intelligent judges is as crucial at this stage as it was in the fact-finding process.

Having discussed some aspects of the relationship of due process and discretion and some practical areas where discretion plays a large role, we turn to the psychology of appearing before family court judges.

Attorneys tend to catalogue judges. The resulting file is shared and constantly updated among practicing lawyers. Lawyers may ask each other questions and make comments to one another, such as: "What's he like on drugs?" "He's off the walls when it comes to guns." "He'll force a parent to take a kid home." "She'll never force a parent to take a kid home." "He doesn't know his law; maybe I can pull this one out." "He doesn't know his law; he won't know what the hell I'm talking about," And so on.

The day's work of a courtroom lawyer begins with a look at who the judge is. If the lawyer doesn't know the particular judge, he or she strikes up a conversation with a court officer whose attention and affection are essential in getting the case called. The court officer may key the lawyer in to who's sitting, the mood the judge is in today, and perhaps some of his philosophy and character traits. In addition, the novice will approach other attorneys, who are generally only too happy to swap shop talk as they await their turn. Within a very few minutes one can get a picture of what one will face.

In criminal court, the proceedings are open to the public, but this advantage is not available to the waiting attorney and his client. Once they are called into court, a few minutes tell a great deal. How is the stenographer acting, the court officer, the probation officer? What is the atmosphere—heavy, serious, jovial, friendly, loose, disrespectful, hostile? How does the judge look? How is he dressed—robes or street clothes? What sex, age, religion, race?

Based on our own preconceptions, these minute details will affect the handling and outcome of the case as much as and probably more than the application and knowledge of case law.

CONCLUSION

Conceptions of the judiciary in family court range from the old-fashioned image of protector and father figure to an image characterized by pervasive cynicism, corruption, and political maneuvering. The truth is that both caricatures are well represented.

Only increased curtailment of discretion can help foster the better of the two. Decisions such as *Kent v. U.S.* 383 U.S. 541 (1966) and *In Re Winship* 397 U.S. 358 (1970) have furthered this movement, while *McKeiver v. Pennsylvania* 403 U.S. 528 (1971), denying jury trials to juveniles, marked a set back.

Future case law and the selection process of judges will determine the role of discretion in the family courts.

Senior Judicial Attorney for the California Court of Appeal in Los Angeles, Aleta Wallach examines the role of discretionary law in securing fundamental human liberties to the citizens of the United States and in so doing demonstrates the new and significant institutional relationship that is emerging between state and federal courts as a consequence of the trend in some state courts toward independent activism in construing state constitutional counterparts of provisions of the Bill of Rights as guaranteeing citizens of their states more protection than the federal provisions. This trend toward state court activism is an important development for our constitutional jurisprudence and for our concept of federalism.

Moreover, in their effort to protect the freedoms of their citizens, state courts have not limited their activism to broadening the reach of state constitutional counterparts beyond the federal Constitution. State courts are also resorting to their common law as a source of protection for the basic rights of their citizens. While this permits judicial discretion to be exercised with unprecedented scope, such use of discretionary law in reality produces social legislation not traditionally the function or province of courts. Accordingly, state court activism is not only altering the institutional relationship of state and federal courts but is also rearranging the relationship of the judicial and legislative branches of state government.

While Ms. Wallach observes that these developments are evident in several substantive areas of judicial decision-making affecting liberty and property interests under the due process clause and classifications based upon race and national origin under the equal protection clause, she provides thematic unity by illustrating these aspects of discretionary law with court decisions in the law respecting women, a body grown misshapen through the ages by the withering antifeminist social values and class interests inherent in patriarchy and which presently is feeling the uncomfortable growing pains of our contemporary demand for justice and humanity. In this manner the author shows how our social consciousness respecting women has affected judicial decision-making in regard to the development of both substantive legal doctrines as well as institutional relationships in our state and federal courts. In drawing examples from judicial decisions in the law respecting women the author is also able to document how public opinion is creating an increasingly politicized judicial branch that threatens to vitiate the proper separation of powers.

3
Social Consciousness and Discretionary Law in the State and Federal Courts

Aleta Wallach

As a class of human beings women have not fared well under the democratic institutions constitutionally charged with promoting our well-being and protecting those individual rights and liberties fundamental to human dignity. It is through the medium of law that all three of our governmental branches undertake to discharge their constitutional duty to advance the public welfare and secure the blessings of liberty to all citizens. Insofar as women are concerned, however, law has been abused by those vested with the power and responsibility to make law as well as those authorized to apply it.

The long social struggle to dismantle the pervasive and complicated network of patriarchal law that decreed for female human beings a class status of deprivation, degradation, and general civil disability and to place in its stead a declaration of national commitment to equality has not been successfully waged in our representative bodies. Although the Equal Rights Amendment[1] had been reintroduced in every congressional session since its initial introduction in 1923, shortly after women attained suffrage with the adoption of the Nineteenth Amendment in 1920, it was not until March 22, 1972, that it was passed out of Congress and submitted to the state legislatures for ratification. Even more disturbing is the ineluctable reality that the Equal Rights Amendment is floundering in the state legislatures, where it has failed to achieve ratification by 38 states, and where several legislatures are currently seeking to rescind their previous ratification. Without congressional extension of the ratification period the proposed constitutional amendment certainly would have expired automatically in early 1979 for failure to achieve ratification by three quarters of the states. It was only through the most valiant, persistent, and organized efforts of committed women, whose tactics ranged from economic boycott of nonratified states to mass demonstration and lobbying in Washington, that the improbable ERA extension was attained in the eleventh hour as the 95th Congress, scurrying to conclude business and recess, with last minute haste extended the ratification period by three years and three months. Of course the validity of the extension itself has yet to withstand court challenges by ERA antagonists. Moreover, shortly after extension the 1978 November elections saw the electorates of two nonratified states defeat ERA measures: Nevadans rejected an advisory referendum that asked if they wanted their legislature to ratify the federal amendment and Floridians voted against an equal rights amendment to their state constitution. Clearly our social consciousness and will as thus expressed by our representative bodies, and by the people, continue women's dark heritage.

The primary restraint on the public will, however, is imposed by the judiciary. By its very nature, the United States Supreme Court is an antimajoritarian institution, whose trust it is to protect powerless minorities[2] and the expression of unpopular ideas from the tyranny of the majority. But only in recent years have we witnessed the emergence of the Supreme Court as a zealous and vigilant guardian of the fundamental federal law that protects us from the use of governmental powers in ways inconsistent with American conceptions of human liberty. As Justice Brennan has observed:

> Over the past two decades, decisions of the Supreme Court of the United States have returned to the fundamental promises wrought by the blood of those who fought our War between the States, promises which were thereafter embodied in our fourteenth amendment—that the citizens of all our states are also and no less citizens of our United States, that this birth right guarantees our federal constitutional liberties against encroachment by governmental action at any level of our federal system, and that each of us is entitled to due process of law and the equal protection of the laws from our state governments no less than from our national one.[3]

Because the Supreme Court's decisions under the Fourteenth Amendment have significantly affected state action, state courts, in addition to federal courts, have also become guardians of our liberties, affording their citizens the full protection of the federal Constitution.

State courts have followed the vigorous leadership of the Supreme Court, implementing its decisions enforcing the protections of the Fourteenth Amendment. The Court's expansive incorporation of the specific guarantees of the Bill of Rights into the Fourteenth Amendment enforced against encroachment by state action those rights previously ensured only against federal infringement.[4] The decisions enforcing the Fourteenth Amendment's guarantee against the deprivation of life, liberty, or property without due process of law have construed due process as ordinarily requiring that an individual be given an opportunity for a hearing before being deprived of any important liberty and property interest, and have fleshed out the essence of such liberty and property in light of conditions existing in contemporary society.[5]   And the Court's enforcement of the federal guarantee of equal protection of the laws has engendered decisions invalidating state legislative classifications that impermissibly impinge on the exercise of fundamental rights,[6] as well as decisions requiring exacting judicial scrutiny of classifications that disadvantage politically powerless groups whose members have historically been subjected to purposeful discrimination.   Thus classifications based upon race,[7] alienage,[8] and national origin[9] have been held to be inherently suspect.

This judicial activism, especially these new developments in the law of equal protection, held out to women a great hope in an otherwise not too auspicious and hospitable social milieu.   With the expectation of having our humanity vindicated, women turned to the Supreme Court for redress of two centuries of systematic oppression and exploitation by men.   Since it was through an elaborate system of patriarchal law that female disability was declared and enforced, it was particularly appropriate to look to the Court to sweep away the actual burdens of legislated inferiority and at the same time, by extending to women the democratic promise of liberty and dignity, to place in our constitutional gallery of normative national principles and policies a very important symbol.

Women, however, were left in the lurch.   The Supreme Court did not hold that legislative classifications based on gender are inherently suspect, even though the necessary analytical structure and legal precedent already existed.   Notwithstanding two decades of antecedent judicial activism, women arrived at the Court too late, amid a new current of judicial restraint.   Consequently women fared little better at the portals of the Supreme Court then than they did at the doors of the elective bodies.

Although the Supreme Court's decisions affecting women do not satisfy the need for the symbol of equality contained in a categorical statement of the principle, they have provided limited remedies in some cases by invalidating particular legislative enactments that disadvantage women.   The Court is clearly more sensitive to the aspect of gender classifications that infringes on tangible rights than to the aspect of these classifications that infringe on intangible rights—that denigrates status.   The Court's failure to bring a deep and broad vision to the nascent area of the law of women has resulted in judicial hopscotch: beginning in 1971 the Court has steered an unsteady course in ad hoc decisionmaking that is doctrinally disarrayed, analytically unsound, and bereft of a consistent and predictive rule of law.

An examination of the Court's exercise of discretion in this regard, in and of itself, is of interest. But equally compelling is the dramatic influence that this withdrawal has had in altering the relative roles of the Supreme Court and the state courts: a new and significant relationship between state courts and the Supreme Court is emerging as some states, in reaction to and in disagreement with the Court's retrenchment in recent opinions applying the federal Bill of Rights and the restraints of due process and equal protection clauses of the Fourteenth Amendment, increasingly rest their decisions on the authority of state constitutions and construe state constitutional counterparts of provisions of the Bill of Rights as guaranteeing citizens of their states even more protection than the federal provisions, even those identically worded. This burgeoning discretionary practice is an important development for both our constitutional jurisprudence and our concept of federalism.

Moreover, this trend in some state courts toward independent activism is affecting too the traditional institutional relationship of state courts to state legislatures. Judicial restraint is yielding to a broad exercise of discretion as state courts apply their power to its fullest limit in order to fashion law to meet the needs of a rapidly changing society.

Finally, in both the state and federal courts public opinion is a variable that shapes the exercise of judicial discretion. Consideration of judicial reaction to popular persuasion and social pressure will round out the view of different facets of judicial determination.

The illustration of these aspects of discretionary law also reveals the grave part the judiciary, as reflector, purveyor, and maintainer of social values, plays in the lives, liberty, and struggle for equality of American womanhood. It is hoped that the discussion which follows will illuminate the complex, ambivalent, and contradictory character of our social consciousness respecting women and the ways that it affects judicial decisionmaking in regard to the development of both legal doctrines and institutional relationships in our state and federal courts.

THE SUPREME COURT

The present attempt by the Supreme Court to reverse the direction of the law respecting women is complicated by certain indelible elements and durable interests fixed in the broader tradition of American jurisprudence and culture. These features, which concern the mechanism of law as superstructure as well as the very substance of patriarchal law itself, determine the nature and scope of today's decisions.

As a medium, discretionary law is not particularly suited to producing abrupt changes. Relying as it does on precedent and tradition, it is essentially a backward-looking rather than forward-looking institution. Since it functions to maintain the status quo, it is not, ordinarily, an instrument for social change. This function is usually reserved to the representative bodies. Yet it has also been recognized that the "genius of our Constitution resides not in any static meaning that it had in a world that is dead and gone, but in the adaptability of its great principles to cope with the problems of a developing America."[10]   Hence the decisions over the past two decades interpreting the Fourteenth Amendment have fulfilled the principle of *Boyd v. United States*, that ". . . constitutional provisions for the security of person and property should be liberally construed. . . . It is the duty of courts to be watchful for the constitutional rights of the citizen, and against any stealthy encroachments thereon."[11]   It is in the antagonism of the past and the future that the contemporary Court labors to meet tomorrow's challenge to its vision, and in a manner which does not today disrupt the long-term continuity and consistency essential to the Court's own authority and its survival as institutional mechanism.

The substance of patriarchal law is impressively neat; therein its form and content seem to merge into an identity and turn infinitely in upon itself. Just as law is the source of all power, males are the source of all law. Thus the men on the United States Supreme Court sit as the ultimate arbiters of a legal system whose vested interest has been relegating women to a class of nonpersons whose existences are relational to fathers, husbands, children. Males made law the archetypal institution that dictates and enforces antifeminist social values and class interests—the instrumentality to structure and control hierarchical relationships among all persons and classes of persons through the allocation of power, privileges, rights, duties, liabilities, and immunities. Inevitably, in the manipulation of these specific correlative legal relationships status itself became the basic subject matter of the law; men arrogated to themselves preeminent status while correspondingly according inferior chattel status to the class that composes over half of the United States population.

The form and substance of law thereby merged; the rule of law was indistinguishable from the rule of men because the premise was the systematic exclusion of women from the world. Apropos this subject I have elsewhere noted:

> In a game played by both women and men but for which men have made all the rules, it is unlikely that any woman would win. In law, women were never intended to "win" if "winning" means participating in the formulation (legislating) and application (judging) of a body of rules that controls conduct through the imposition of benefits and detriments upon persons and classes of persons. The intentional exclusion of women from participation in any aspect of law is evident in the fact that women were denied the right to vote, thus ensuring that men, the only voters, could electorally constitute themselves as the lawmakers—the legislators. . . . In addition men took it upon themselves to judicially declare, as a rule of law, that women could not be lawyers—the practitioners of law, and eventually the judges of law.[12]

The heart of the rule of law that required for women every imaginable civil disability was superbly expressed over 100 years ago in the concurring opinion of Justice Bradley in *Bradwell v. Illinois*, the Supreme Court case holding that women could constitutionally be denied a license to practice law:

Man is, or should be, woman's protector and defender. The natural and proper timidity and delicacy which belongs to the female sex evidently unfits it for many of the occupations of civil life. The constitution of the family organization, which is founded in the divine ordinance, as well as in the nature of things, indicates the domestic sphere as that which properly belongs to the domain and functions of womanhood. The harmony, not to say identity, of interests and views which belong, or should belong, to the family institution is repugnant to the idea of a woman adopting a distinct and independent career from that of her husband. . . . The paramount destiny and mission of woman are to fulfill the noble and benign offices of wife and mother. This is the law of the Creator. And the rules of civil society must be adapted to the general constitution of things, and cannot be based upon exceptional cases.[13]

It is striking that judges invoked the lofty natural and divine law, rather than civil law, as authority to create a rule of law that served their own privilege and freedom, that justified maintaining women in a position of servitude within the family in order to preserve male hegemony. By so confining women to the realm of home and family, men reserved to themselves as their exclusive domain all the worldly rest of civil life. In this respect it is truly the nulcear family (and all the restrictions on female choice and autonomy men perpetrate in its name) that has been the bane of women.

As a consequence, the cherished concept of neutral, doctrinal decisionmaking, so rooted in our idea of just laws, insofar as it concerns women has not been more than an illusive fancy. The applicable doctrines are, at this point, too contaminated with the arbitrary, oppressive self-interest of men to amount to more than a rule of males. Since it is this Anglo-American tradition that vests the men presently sitting on the Supreme Court with the power to make binding judgments, and it is the received doctrine of this tradition that they must now judge, they are the final arbiters of a finely tuned and ingrown organism of which they are a part.

The Supreme Court has refused expressly to characterize gender as a suspect legislative classification, even though it has declared suspect legislative classifications based upon race, alienage, and national origin. Such characterization has symbolic import in that it is a statement that there is something inherently wrong with gender-based classifications, that they violate deeply held American principles. It also means that, as a practical matter, the suspect classification is subjected to a strict scutiny standard of judicial review under which the burden is shifted to the state to show a compelling interest in validating the statute. Legislative classifications that are not suspect (traditionally those not based on race and not affecting a fundamental interest such as voting and privacy) are subjected to a more permissive standard of review requiring only "minimum rationality." These latter classifications have been upheld if there is a reasonable relationship between the statutory purpose and the challenged classification. But lately the Court has abandoned its previous two-tiered minimum rationality-strict scrutiny review framework in favor of a vaguer "intermediate" approach that, by avoiding a clear and principled statement of the rationale, permits unrestricted exercise of discretion. Often a guise for rigorous review, this intermediate posture also can justify a contrary position of noninterventionism.

Reed v. Reed[14] was the long-awaited first Supreme Court decision concerning discrimination against females. In that case the Court unanimously held that a statutory provision giving mandatory preference for appointment as estate administrator to a male applicant over a female applicant otherwise equally qualified and within the same entitlement class under the Idaho Probate Code violated the equal protection clause of the Fourteenth Amendment. Without formulating a rule of law, the Court unceremoniously announced that the statutory test was whether a difference in the gender of competing applicants for letters of administration bore a rational relationship to a state objective that was sought to be advanced by the statute. The state objective of administrative convenience appeared to meet this test, since the statute facilitated probate hearings by reducing hearings on the merits of the male and female applicants. Nevertheless, the Court stated that to give mandatory preferences to members of either sex over members of the other merely to avoid hearings on individual qualifications was arbitrary because it provided dissimilar treatment for males and females similarly situated. Had the Court openly proclaimed gender a suspect classification and invoked a strict scrutiny analysis, Idaho plainly would have failed to demonstrate a compelling interest in the statute on the basis of administrative convenience.

In thus using the reasonable relationship test instead of the more rigorous strict scrutiny standard, the Court signaled its willingness to invalidate irrational gender-based legislative classifications while simultaneously declining to establish gender as a suspect category. This *sub silentio* application of a higher standard of review has, as we will see, created a tangle of analytical inconsistencies and disagreements in the subsequent cases.

In *Frontiero v. Richardson*[15] eight of the nine members of the Court agreed that a federal statutory scheme allowing a serviceman to claim his wife as a dependent for quarters allowances and medical and dental benefits without regard to whether she was in fact dependent upon him for any part of her support but disallowing a servicewoman to claim her husband as a dependent unless he was in fact dependent upon her for over one-half of his support violated the due process clause of the Fifth Amendment. But this was a bare plurality decision because a majority could not agree on an opinion.

Frontiero is as significant for what it did not do as for what it did do. It did not say that the state interest in administrative convenience was not weighty enough to justify the differential treatment of servicemen and servicewomen, which alone would have been an important rejection of continued adherence to the rules of patriarchy articulated by Justice Bradley over a century ago.[16] For in view of that fact that "approximately 99 percent of all members of the uniformed services are male," and "since the husband in our society is generally the 'bread winner' in the family—and the wife typically the 'dependent' partner," Congress could have "rationally" concluded that it would be more economical to require married female members claiming husbands to prove actual dependency than to extend the presumption of dependency to them, and indeed the District Court had speculated that such differential treatment might conceivably lead to a "considerable saving of administrative expense and manpower."

Instead the Court acknowledged that *Reed v. Reed* had been a departure from "traditional" rational-basis analysis with respect to sex-based classifications, noting that:

> ... appellee argued that the mandatory preference for male applicants was in itself reasonable since "men [are] as a rule more conversant with business affairs than ... women." Indeed, appellee maintained that "it is a matter of common knowledge, that women still are not engaged in politics, the professions, business or industry to the extent that man are." And the Idaho Supreme Court, in upholding the constitutionality of this statute, suggested that the Idaho Legislature might reasonably have "concluded that in general men are better qualified to act as an administrator than are women."[17]

Perhaps recognizing that if the rational basis test were actually applied, all classifications disabling women would be constitutionally valid, owing to the self-fulfilling effect of past discrimination, Justice Brennan, writing for himself and Justices Douglas, White and Marshall, sought to formulate an appropriate analytical framework that could be the measure of future gender-based classifications. With insight and foresight he wrote:

> There can be no doubt that our Nation has had a long and unfortunate history of sex discrimination. Traditionally, such discrimination was rationalized by an attitude of "romantic paternalism" which, in practical effect, put women, not on a pedestal, but in a cage. . . .
> As a result of notions such as these [those expressed in *Bradwell v. Illinois*],

our statute books gradually became laden with gross, stereotyped distinctions between the sexes and, indeed, throughout much of the 19th century the position of women in our society was, in many respects, comparable to that of blacks under pre-Civil War slave codes. Neither slaves nor women could hold office, serve on juries, or bring suit in their own names, and married women traditionally were denied the legal capacity to hold or convey property or to serve as legal guardians of their own children. . . .

It is true, of course, that the position of women in America has improved markedly in recent decades. Nevertheless, it can hardly be doubted that, in part because of the high visibility of the sex characteristic, women still face pervasive, although at times more subtle, discrimination in our educational institutions, in the job market and, perhaps most conspicuously, in the political arena. . . .

Moreover, since sex, like race and national origin, is an immutable characteristic determined solely by the accident of birth, the imposition of special disabilities upon members of a particular sex because of their sex would seem to violate "the basic concept of our system that legal burdens should bear some relationship to individual responsibility. . . ." And what differentiates sex from such nonsuspect statuses as intelligence or physical disability, and aligns it with the recognized suspect criteria, is that the sex characteristic frequently bears no relation to ability to perform or contribute to society. As a result, statutory distinctions between the sexes often have the effect of invidiously relegating the entire class of females to inferior legal status without regard to the actual capabilities of its individual members.[18]

Accordingly Justice Brennan concluded that classifications based upon sex, like classifications based upon race, alienage, or national origin, are inherently suspect and must, therefore, be subjected to strict judicial scrutiny. Since the interest in efficacious administration of governmental programs was not compelling, it did not save the statute.

Because *Frontiero* is a plurality opinion, this doctrinal analysis is not authoritative. Three Justices who concurred in the judgment specifically disagreed with the view that all classifications based upon gender are inherently suspect and so must be subjected to close judicial scrutiny. Rather they would forego exercise of judicial discretion and impose self-restraint in deference to the legislative process:

The Equal Rights Amendment, which if adopted will resolve the substance of this precise question, has been approved by the Congress and submitted for ratification by the States. If this Amendment is duly adopted, it will represent the will of the people accomplished in the manner prescribed by the Constitution. By acting prematurely and unnecessarily . . . the Court has assumed a decisional responsibility at the very time when state legislatures, functioning within the traditional democratic process, are debating the proposed Amendment. . . . [T]his reaching out to pre-empt by judicial action a major political decision which is currently in process of resolution does not reflect appropriate respect for duly prescribed legislative processes.

There are times when this Court, under our system, cannot avoid a constitutional decision on issues which normally should be resolved by the elected representatives of the people. But democratic institutions are weakened, and confidence in the restraint of the Court is impaired, when we appear unnecessarily to decide sensitive issues of broad social and political importance at the very time they are under consideration within the prescribed constitutional processes.[19]

Particularly in view of the failure of the representative bodies to ratify the Equal Rights Amendment such restraint seems a bit extreme. A legislative classification that violates constitutional precepts is no less objectionable because legislatures engage to reconsider the underlying policy. These two opinions, however, illustrate well the divergent Court views regarding the antimarjoritarian function of the Court and the appropriate limits of discretion.

In *Kahn v. Shevin*[20] a gender-based classification discriminating against males revealed further divisions and doctrinal uncertainty in a Court already dissonant. Justice Douglas, previously joined with Justice Brennan in the plurality opinion in *Frontiero*, now writing for a majority of six, held that a Florida statute granting widows, but not widowers, an annual $500 property tax exemption did not violate the equal protection clause because the state's differing treatment of widows and widowers rested upon some ground of difference having a fair and substantial relation to the object of the legislation—not the state policy of furthering administrative convenience but of cushioning the financial impact of spousal loss upon the gender for whom that loss imposes a disproportionately heavy burden. *Kahn* thus established the principle that discrimination in favor of a certain class is permissible if it has the compensatory purpose of remedying past discrimination. The Court expressly acknowledged that compensatory discrimination was justified in this case because of women's continuing economic disadvantage: "whether from overt discrimination or from a male dominated culture, the job market is inhospitable to the woman seeking any but the lowest paid job."[21] While in *Reed* and *Frontiero* the effects of past discrimination could not be relied on as a justification for imposing additional disadvantages, *Kahn* permits those effects to be relied upon to justify favored treatment.

Although the opinion is doctrinally unclear, it appears that that Court tacitly viewed the gender-based classification as satisfying the minimum rationality standard of review. Justice Brennan, joined by Justice Marshall, however, dissented. He reaffirmed strict judicial scrutiny as the applicable standard of review, agreed that "in providing special benefits for a needy segment of society long the victim of purposeful discrimination and neglect, the statute serves the compelling state interest of achieving equality for such groups,"[22] but found that the statute nevertheless failed to satisfy the requirements of equal protection, since Florida had not borne its burden of proving that its compelling interest could not be achieved by a more precisely tailored statute. The statute was overinclusive, since the $500 property tax exemption was available to financially independent widows as well as to unemployed dependent widows, and the state did not explain why the inclusion of widows of substantial means was necessary to advance the state's interest in ameliorating the effects of past economic discrimination against women. Justice White separately dissented on the ground that the statute violated the equal protection clause because Florida did not sustain its burden of credibly explaining its tax exemption—presumably, if the state's purpose was to compensate for past discrimination against females, it would not have limited the exemption to women who are widows.

The four Justices who concurred in *Frontiero's* plurality opinion were now split three ways. Although they all seemed to agree that when the purpose and effect of a gender-based classification is ameliorative it neither stigmatizes nor denigrates males not also benefited by the legislation, that is all they seemed to agree upon.

Despite the presence in previous opinions of language suggesting the Court's understanding of the larger, institutional nature of discrimination against females, the Court's surprising unawareness of the ideology of patriarchy became disappointingly apparent in *Geduldig v. Aiello.*[23] A variety of social controls has been used to confine women to the domestic sphere and to deprive us of control of our bodies, thus making us prisoners of childbearing as well as child-rearing. Conspicuous examples are the prohibitions on contraception and abortion, absense of social alternatives to individual child care, and the imposition of pregnancy-related penalties on women employed outside the home in the public sphere, the only place that female labor is assigned monetary value. Although compulsory termination because of pregnancy is no longer permissible,[24] neither is paid maternity leave required, despite the fact that pregnancy and childbirth redound to the enormous collective benefit of all society, so much so, in fact, that is has mandated a system of legal detriments designed to ensure that women will reproduce, and will do so exclusively within the purview of the male-dominated nuclear family, by leaving us very little else to do and nowhere else to go.[25]

In *Geduldig v. Aiello* six members of the Court upheld the exclusion of coverage for disability that accompanies normal pregnancy and childbirth from the California disability insurance system which pays benefits to persons in private employment who are temporarily unable to work because of disability not covered by workers' compensation. The Court stated that the exclusion of normal pregnancy-related disabilities was valid because the legislative classification rationally promoted California's legitimate cost-saving interests, which provided an objective and noninvidious basis for the state's decision not to create a more comprehensive insurance program. Moreover, in a most extravagant and disturbing statement the Court declared there was no evidence that the selection of the risks incurred by the program worked to discriminate against any definable group or class:

> The dissenting opinion to the contrary, this case is . . . a far cry from cases like *Reed* v. *Reed* . . . and *Frontiero* v. *Richardson* . . . , involving discrimination based upon gender as such. The California insurance program does not exclude anyone from benefit eligibility because of gender but merely removes one physical condition—pregnancy—from the list of compensable disabilities. While it is true that only women can become pregnant, it does not follow that every legislative classification concerning pregnancy is a sex-based classification like those considered in *Reed* . . . and *Frontiero*. . . . Normal pregnancy is an objectively identifiable physical condition with unique characteristics. Absent a showing that distinctions involving pregnancy are mere pretexts designed to effect an invidious discrimination against the members of one sex or the other, lawmakers are constitutionally free to include or exclude pregnancy from the coverage of legislation such as this on any reasonable basis, just as with respect to any other physical condition.[26]

The decision in *Geduldig* was hostile to working women because it approved singling them out for less favorable treatment on the basis of a gender-linked disability peculiar to women. United again in dissent with Justices Douglas and Marshall, Justice Brennan observed that by so doing the state created a double standard for disability compensation in that a limitation is imposed upon the disabilities for which women workers may recover, while men receive full compensation for all disabilities suffered, including those that affect only or primarily their gender, such as prostatectomies, circumcision, hemophilia, and gout. In effect, one set of rules is applied to females and another to males. "Such dissimilar treatment of men and women, on the basis of physical characteristics inextricably linked to one sex, inevitably constitutes sex discrimination."[27]

Endeavoring to maintain a measure of analytical concordance, Justice Brennan reproached his brethren for decisional incoherence and the Court's "apparent retreat":

> . . . [B]y its decision today, the Court appears willing to abandon that higher standard of review without satisfactorily explaining what differentiates the

gender-based classification employed in this case from those found unconstitutional in *Reed* and *Frontiero*. The Court's decision threatens to return men and women to a time when "traditional" equal protection analysis sustained legislative classifications that treated differently members of a particular sex solely because of their sex. . . .[28]

The practical impact of *Geduldig* is acute because the economic effects caused by pregnancy-related disabilities are functionally indistinguishable from the effects caused by any other disability. Wages are lost because of a physical inability to work, and medical expenses are incurred for delivery of the child and for postpartum care. Especially in view of the fact that two-thirds of all women who work do so (at least) for economic necessity, the pregnancy exclusion policy confirmed by *Geduldig* can only discourage working women from reproduction, a consequence contrary to the objective of patriarchal law. It is obvious that the social attitude is nowhere near spreading the costs and minimizing the detriments that attach to this vital social function.[29]

In *Schlesinger v. Ballard*[30] the Court once again refused to find sex a suspect classification. In that case the Court held that a statutory scheme providing for men a shorter period of commissioned service before a mandatory discharge for want of promotion than that provided for women officers did not violate the due process clause of the Fifth Amendment, since the statutory classification was rational. Having decided that the classification could be saved by being reasonably related to the ameliorative purpose of the statute (which was to compensate female officers for lack of opportunity to compete with male officers in combat at sea), the Court found Congress could rationally conclude the longer tenure for women officers was "fair and equitable."

Writing for three of the four dissenting Justices, Justice Brennan again urged that legislative classifications based on gender be subjected to strict scrutiny. Under this standard the result in *Schlesinger* would be different because the state advanced no governmental interest fairly to be gleaned from the statutory scheme or its history which could justify the gender-based classification. Since female naval officers do not compete directly with male officers for promotion, the majority's reliance on the compensatory purpose of the statute (to aid female officers because they had not had the opportunity to compile seagoing records) was spurious. Besides the state did not show that the legislative design had this compensatory purpose. Rather the majority merely hypothesized that Congress *could* rationally conclude that a longer period of tenure for women officers comported with the goal of providing them with "fair and equitable career advancement programs." Hence even the minimum rationality standard was misapplied in *Schlesinger*, where the court again failed to provide a cogent methodology for analyzing a compensatory basis or an ameliorative purpose for a given legislative classification.

In *Weinberger v. Wiesenfeld*[31] and *Stanton v. Stanton*,[32] the cases following *Schlesinger*, the Court solidified its refusal to treat gender-based classifications as suspect. In *Stanton* the Court struck an ideologically significant blow at patriarchy but did not strengthen its own doctrinal approach. Under the minimum rationality test first articulated in *Reed*, the Court invalidated a Utah statute providing for female majority at age 18 while the age of majority for males was 21. Utah's basis for this difference was rational, if biased and self-perpetuating, given the premises and goals of patriarchy. It was alleged that females "mature" earlier and tend to marry earlier than do males, and that males needed extra time for education, and also child support to age 21 to facilitate education. Implicit in such a rule was the social purpose of channeling women into domesticity and preparing men to assume roles in public life. The overall pattern was aided by the historical and universal barriers prohibiting women from entrance into institutions of higher education.

Despite the "rationality" of the difference in age of majority for males and females, the Court invoked the rational relationship test and found the purpose of the statute, to lengthen the education of males, improper, the same result that would have been achieved with strict scrutiny. Increasingly "outdated" misconceptions concerning the role females in the home rather than in the "market place and world of ideas" were rejected as loose-fitting characterizations incapable of supporting state statutory schemes that were premised upon their accuracy. Utah's differential age of majority statute was invalidated, notwithstanding the statute's coincidence with and "rational" furtherance of the state's purpose of fostering "old notions" of role-typing and preparing males for their expected performance in the economic and political worlds.

In *Weinberger v. Wiesenfeld* the Court again reached a correct result but did not undertake a doctrinal analysis of the suspect classification question. Departing from his usual analytical consistency, Justice Brennan, expressing the views of seven members of the Court, held that the gender-based distinction mandated by provisions of the Social Security Act that granted survivors' benefits based on the earnings of a deceased husband and father to both his widow and to the couple's minor children in her care, but that granted benefits based on the earnings of a deceased wife and mother only to the minor children and not the widower, violated the right to equal protection secured by the Fifth Amendment's due process clause because it unjustifiably discriminated against female wage earners required to pay social security taxes by affording them less protection for their survivors than was provided for male wage earners. One of the impressive aspects of *Weinberger* was the Court's view that even though it was a widower who brought suit based upon denial to widowers of benefits equal to those allowed widows, nevertheless the class discriminated against was women and not men, because the gender-based distinction diminished the protection afforded working women and their families.

In this case the Court reaffirmed its prior discarding of a cornerstone of patriarchal structure.   In *Schlesinger* and *Frontiero* the challenged gender-based classifications were premised on overbroad generalizations that could not be tolerated under the Constitution.   The assumption was that female spouses of servicemen would normally be dependent upon their husbands while male spouses of servicewomen would not be dependent upon their wives. In *Weinberger* "[a] virtually identical 'archaic and overbroad' generalization . . . 'not . . . tolerated under the Constitution' underlies the distinction drawn by [the Social Security Act], namely, that male workers' earnings are vital to the support of their families, while the earnings of female wage earners do not significantly contribute to their families' support."[33]   The Court rejected the government's characterization of the classification as one designed to compensate women beneficiaries as a group "for the economic difficulties which still confront women who seek to support themselves and their families," and instead inquired into the actual purpose underlying the statutory scheme.

The Court stated that the statutory scheme itself and its legislative history revealed that the congressional purpose in providing benefits to widows with children was not to provide an income to women who were, because of economic discrimination, unable to provide for themselves. Rather, linked as it was directly to responsibility for minor children, the income was intended to permit women to elect not to work and to devote themselves to the care of children. Since this purpose was in no way premised upon any special disadvantages of women, it could not serve to justify a gender-based distinction that diminished the protection afforded to women who do work.

The conclusion that the Constitution forbids the gender-based distinction that results in the efforts of female workers required to pay social security taxes producing less protection for their families than is produced by the efforts of men, is a recognition of the equal value and importance of women's labor. But the court here again failed to establish a predictive model for review that can apply to all equal protection gender cases. Whereas in *Schlesinger* the Court accepted a hypothetical compensatory purpose in order to uphold the statute, in *Weinberger* it scrutinized the allegedly ameliorative statutory purpose and found it to be unrelated to the legislation in order to invalidate it.   In taking such a result-oriented approach with complete disregard of analytical conformity, the Court breaches its duty to articulate principled rules of decision and thus imprudently weakens its own authority. We see a Court divided and adrift.

The difficulty the Court has had in developing a coherent body of constitutional law respecting women was indirectly acknowledged in *Craig v. Boren*,[34] in which there were seven separate concurring and dissenting opinions. In that case the Court held that the gender-based differential under Oklahoma statutes prohibiting the sale of 3.2 percent beer to males under the age of 21 and to females under the age of 18 constituted a denial of equal protection to males 18–20 years of age because this disparity had not been shown to be substantially related to achievement of the asserted governmental objective of enhancing traffic safety; for the most relevant of the general statistical surveys offered to establish such relationship showed only that .18 percent of females and 2 percent of males in the 18-20 years of age group were arrested for driving while under the influence of liquor, and so did not warrant the conclusion that sex represents an accurate proxy for the regulation of drinking and driving.

Justice Powell, concurring in *Craig v. Boren*, stated that with respect to the equal protection standard, he agreed that *Reed v. Reed* was the most relevant precedent. Noting that *Reed* and subsequent cases involving gender-based classifications made it clear that the Court subjects such classification to a more critical examination than is normally applied when "fundamental" constitutional rights and "suspect classes" are not present, Justice Powell, almost apologetically, added as a footnote:

As is evident from our opinions, the Court has had difficulty in agreeing upon a standard of equal protection analysis that can be applied consistently to the wide variety of legislative classifications. There are valid reasons for dissatisfaction with the "two-tier" approach that has been prominent in the Court's decisions in the past decade. Although viewed by many as a result-oriented substitute for more critical analysis, that approach—with its narrowly limited "upper-tier"—now has substantial precedential support. As has been true of *Reed* and its progeny, our decision today will be viewed by some as a "middle-tier" approach. While I would not endorse that classification and would not welcome a further subdividing of equal protection analysis, candor compels the recognition that the relatively deferential "rational basis" standard of review normally applied takes on a sharper focus when we address a gender-based classification. So much is clear from our recent cases. . . .[35]

In *Califano v. Goldfarb*[36] a fragmented Supreme Court held that a provision of the Social Security Act that presumed dependency for a widow but required a widower to prove he had been receiving at least one-half of his support from his spouse violated equal protection under the due process clause of the Fifth Amendment. Although unable to agree on an opinion, five members concurred in this result, but even they could not agree on what class was discriminated against by this legislation. Justice Brennan, in a plurality opinion echoing *Weinberger*, expressed the view that the sex-based distinction was invalid since, as a result of it, the efforts of female workers who were required to pay social security taxes produced less protection for their spouses than was produced by the efforts of male workers, thus depriving women of the protection for their families which men receive. Such differentiation is forbidden by the Constitution, at least when supported by no more substantial justification than "archaic and overbroad" generalizations or "old notions" such as "assumptions as to dependency" that are more consistent with "the role-typing society has long imposed" than with contemporary reality.

Justice Stevens concurred in the judgment, but on the ground that the statute's sex-based discrepancy was violative of the rights of *male* spouses of female wage earners by denying them survivors' benefits absent proof of dependency. He was persuaded that this discrimination against a group of males was merely the accidental by-product of a traditional reflexive way of thinking about females (all widows as dependents) and not part of a purpose to compensate women for past wrongs. Justice Stevens acknowledged the antinomous precedents already created by the Court in *Kahn v. Shevin* and *Weinberger v. Wiesenfeld*. Since the gender-based distinction between surviving spouses in *Kahn* originated in 1885, it could not reasonably be supposed to have been motivated by a legislative decision to repudiate the nineteenth century presumption that females are inferior. Therefore, the Court erroneously upheld the Florida statute on the basis of a hypothetical justification for the discrimination that had nothing to do with the legislature's true motivation. Noting that the exclusion from eligibility benefits in *Weinberger* was apparently the accidental by-product of the same kind of legislative process that gave rise to *Kahn* and to *Califano*, Justice Stevens found *Weinberger*, not *Kahn*, controlling, since it was a later and unanimous holding, and rejected an attempt to use mere recitation of a benign, compensatory purpose as an automatic shield for a statute which was actually based on archaic and overbroad generalizations.

The concurrence of Justice Stevens exemplifies the confusion and inconsistency that have resulted from only a few years of ad hoc decisionmaking in the developing area of women's law. The desultory precedents have already split off into senseless distinctions and give contrary directions to the Justices at the forks in the doctrinal road, necessitating the creation of still further superfluous refinements. The problem the Court finds itself in today in gender discrimination cases is a result of both its failure expressly to declare sex a suspect classification, invoking the attendant strict scrutiny standard of review, and its subjective, random analysis of "ameliorative purpose" in legislative use of gender classification.

It is in women's struggle to attain self-determination in the intimate matters of personal life, sexual preference and family formation, control of our bodies and reproductive freedom, that the Court has been of critical importance. *Geduldig v. Aiello*, however, previewed the great difficulty the Court has with the subject of pregnancy. Regarding this most basic freedom, the Court has been most damaging and proved itself to be fickle and cowardly. When all is said and done, the Court does knuckle under the sway of public opinion and well-organized, well-financed special interests. The independence of the judiciary is sometimes a much exaggerated notion. But I do not think that in the entire history of the Supreme Court there has been a betrayal as startling and devastating as occurred in the second set of abortion cases.

In 1973 the Supreme Court proclaimed in *Roe v. Wade*[37] that the right of every woman to choose whether to bear a child is of fundamental importance and, therefore, protected by the Constitution against unwarranted governmental infringement. Yet only four years later, on June 20, 1977, the Court decided three cases adversely to women's newly won freedom. In *Beal v. Doe*[38] the Court, avoiding the constitutional question, held that Title XIX of the Social Security Act did not require a state to fund the cost of nontherapeutic abortions as a condition of participation in the Medicaid Program established by that Act. In *Maher v. Roe*[39] the Court held that the equal protection clause of the Fourteenth Amendment did not require a state participating in the Medicaid Program to pay the expenses incident to nontherapeutic abortions for indigent women simply because it has made a policy choice to pay expenses incident to childbirth. For purposes of the appropriate equal protection analysis inquiring whether the classification operated to the disadvantage of some suspect class or impinged upon a fundamental right explicitly or impliedly protected by the Constitution, thereby requiring strict judicial scrutiny, the Court stated that: indigent women desiring abortions did not constitute a suspect class, the exclusion of nontherapeutic abortions did not impinge upon the constitutional right of a woman to decide whether to terminate her pregnancy free from unduly burdensome interference, and the state, having an unquestionably strong and legitimate interest in encouraging normal childbirth, could rationally encourage it by subsidizing costs incident to childbirth while not subsidizing nontherapeutic abortions.

In the companion case, *Poelker v. Doe*,[40] the Court held that a city did not violate the equal protection clause in electing, as a policy decision, to provide publicly financed hospital services for childbirth without providing corresponding services for nontherapeutic abortions, since nothing in the Constitution forbade a state or a city, pursuant to democratic processes, from expressing a preference for normal childbirth.

What is disturbing about these decisions is that, in handing control of abortion back to the popular will ("democratic processes"), the Court has abnegated its responsibility, as our only antimajoritarian institution, to protect fundamental individual rights against despotism by the masses. No less distressing is the value system implicit in the Court's imperious assertion that childbirth may be socially encouraged by, in effect, prohibiting abortions to thousands of women. This announcement heralds a frightening reaffirmation of the patriarchal practice of directly and indirectly using power to manipulate women into subservience as a breeder population to be used as means to a social end rather than as ends in ourselves.

The Court's retrograde decision to endorse in these cases governmental policies constituting "coercion of women to bear children they do not wish to bear" provoked sensitive and passionate protests from three dissenting Justices. Justice Blackmun, joined by Justices Brennan and Marshall, rebuked the Court for allowing the states, and such municipalities as choose to do so, to accomplish indirectly what the Court in *Roe v. Wade* and *Doe v. Bolton*—"by a substantial majority and with some emphasis"—said they could not do directly:

> The Court concedes the existence of a constitutional right but denies the realization and enjoyment of that right on the ground that existence and realization are separate and distinct. For the individual woman concerned, indigent and financially helpless, as the Court's opinions in these three cases concede her to be, the result is punitive and tragic. Implicit in the Court's holdings is the condescension that she may go elsewhere for her abortion. I find that disingenuous and alarming, almost reminiscent of: "Let them eat cake."[41]

These decisions render the Court's prior decision a nullity for indigent women because the Court's construction can only result, as a practical matter, in forcing penniless pregnant women to have children they would not have borne if the state had not weighted the scales to make their choice to have abortions substantially more onerous. For a doctor who cannot afford to work for nothing, and a woman who cannot afford to pay a doctor, the state's refusal to fund an abortion is as effective an interdiction of it as would ever be necessary. Moreover, the infringement of the fundamental right of pregnant women to be free to decide whether to have an abortion was explained by the District Court:

> When Connecticut refuses to fund elective abortions while funding therapeutic abortions and prenatal and postnatal care, it weights the choice of the pregnant mother against choosing to exercise her constitutionally protected right to an elective abortion.... Her choice is affected not simply by the absence of payment for the abortion, but by the availability of public funds for childbirth if she chooses not to have the abortion. When the state thus infringes upon a fundamental interest, it must assert a compelling state interest.[42]

The magnitude of the danger adumbrated by the Court's retreat from *Roe v. Wade* was expressed in dissent by Justice Marshall:

> ...I fear that the Court's decisions will be an invitation to public officials, already under extraordinary pressure from well financed and carefully orches-

trated lobbying campaigns, to approve more such restrictions. The effect will be to relegate millions of people to lives of poverty and despair. When elected leaders cower before public pressure, this Court, more than ever, must not shirk its duty to enforce the Constitution for the benefit of the poor and powerless.[43]

Similarly concerned about the reckless, self-inflicted injury to the Court's institutional authority that is inevitably involved in its refusal to enforce its own prior rule of decision against the disobedience of the political branches of government, Justice Blackmun stated:

> The result the Court reaches is particularly distressing in *Poelker* v. *Doe*, where a presumed majority, in electing as mayor one whom the record shows campaigned on the issue of closing public hospitals to nontherapeutic abortions, punitively impresses upon a needy minority its own concepts of the socially desirable, the publicly acceptable, and the morally sound, with a touch of the devil-take-the-hindmost. This is not the kind of thing for which our Constitution stands. . . .
> Neither is it an acceptable answer, as the Court well knows, to say that the Congress and the States are free to authorize the use of funds for nontherapeutic abortions. Why should any politician incur the demonstrated wrath and noise of the abortion opponents when mere silence and nonactivity accomplish the results the opponents want?[44]

The noninterventionist policy of the Court was an intemperate act of deference to the political bodies that vitiates the proper separation of powers. Indeed the *per curiam* opinion in *Poelker* explicitly stated that

> [a]lthough the Mayor's personal position on abortion is irrelevant to our decision, we note that he is an elected official responsible to the people of St. Louis. His policy of denying city funds for abortions such as that desired by Doe is subject to public debate and approval or disapproval at the polls. We merely hold, for the reasons stated in *Maher*, that the Constitution does not forbid a State or a city, pursuant to democratic processes, from expressing a preference for normal childbirth as St. Louis has done.[45]

The salient inquiry is what makes the Court so willing to surrender to tyranny of the majority that very area of privacy invulnerable to the state's intrusion that it but four years earlier held surrounds the decision of a pregnant woman whether to carry her pregnancy to term. Why can the state now inhibit her fundamental right to make that choice free from state inference? And why is it that the

Court compromises its own integrity and perverts the doctrines of its own precedent for the sake of flight? For it is transparent that the Court, as Justice Marshall lamented,

> ...in its evident desire to avoid strict scrutiny—or indeed any meaningful scrutiny—of the challenged legislation, which would almost surely result in its invalidation, . . . pulls from thin air a distinction between laws that absolutely prevent exercise of the fundamental right to abortion and those that "merely" make its exercise difficult for some people. . . . [O]ur cases support no such distinction, . . . and I have argued . . . that the challenged regulations are little different from a total prohibition from the viewpoint of the poor. But the Court's legal legerdemain has produced the desired result: A fundamental right is no longer at stake and mere rationality becomes the appropriate mode of analysis. To no one's surprise, application of that test—combined with misreading of *Roe* v. *Wade* to generate a "strong" state interest in "potential life" during the first trimester of pregnancy, . . . —"leaves little doubt about the outcome; the challenged legislation is [as] always upheld." . . . And once again, "relevant factors [are] misapplied or ignored," . . . while the Court "forego[es] all judicial protection against discriminatory legislation bearing upon" a right "vital to the flourishing of a free society" and a class "unfairly burdened by invidious discrimination unrelated to the individual worth of [its] members." [46]

The answer illuminates an aspect of discretionary law that we customarily do not observe in process. The Court, which must be courageous "when elected leaders cower before public pressure" and "more than ever, must not shirk its duty to enforce the Constitution for the benefit of the poor and powerless," is, itself, sadly vulnerable to the same public pressures against which it stands guardian of individual liberties. Judicial change creeps along incrementally as wispy filaments of rules emerge, extend, wind, and eventually metamorphose into complex doctrinal webs. The progress is slow because it advances through case-by-case decisionmaking; any point along the doctrinal thread is usually firmly connected with its antecedent and consequent. Ordinarily the process itself is imperceptible; with the perspective of hindsight what was wrought becomes apparent. The stability and authority of such a system derive, at least in part, from society's confidence that it will yield fair and just decisions because the rules will not be changed without notice—giant steps will not be taken. The effectiveness of discretionary law resides in the social expectation that change will never be blatant, that the discovery of new rules will be gradual, and that they will not be announced *de jure* until they have become almost a *de facto* reality. With judicial restraint as its guiding procedural principle, discretionary law is not particularly suited to abrupt change.

In the past two decades, however, it has fallen to the judiciary to minister to our most serious social needs—in part owing to the abdication of our political bodies, caused by the reluctance of politicians to make unpopular choices,[47] and the nonresponsiveness of government bureaucracies in solving problems. We now turn to the courts to resolve our major socioeconomic issues. Consequently, it is with considerable activism that the judiciary undertakes to decide public issues when a great public need for decision of such an issue exists, and other branches of government cannot or will not tackle it.[48]   Although it is not the traditional role of the courts, we have come to accept, indeed, expect, such activism.

The Supreme Court fulfilled this high trust when it decided the landmark abortion cases in 1973.   In truth, when the Court decided *Roe v. Wade* and *Doe v. Bolton*,

...it properly embarked on a course of constitutional adjudication no less controversial than that begun by *Brown* v. *Board of Education.* . . . The abortion decisions are sound law and undoubtedly good policy. They have never been questioned by the Court and we are told that today's cases "signa[l] . . . no retreat from *Roe* or the cases applying it.". . . The logic of those cases inexorably requires invalidation of the present enactments.[49]

The Court's bouleversement—its refusal to enforce the constitutional right it declared fundamental four years earlier—portends ill for the institutional strength and leadership of the Supreme Court. The jump backward was too precipitous, startling, and unexpected. Not that the Court cannot, as it occasionally has done, subsequently decide that a prior rule of decision is incorrect; but in such a case it articulates the reasons therefor. However, to aver the probity of its rule of decision in an opinion that eviscerates the very rule it professes to still embrace, only enervates its own doctrinal verity and shakes to the core public faith and confidence in the authority of discretionary law. These abortion cases provide a rare insight into a gaping imperfection in the immune system of the Supreme Court and reveal that the Justices, though appointed for life tenure, do not have asbestos fingers. When the judiciary is so directly and immediately vulnerable to public pressure that it is impotent to follow its own established and just rule of decision, and in fact covertly contradicts it, institutional infirmity looms beyond the symptom. If the enduring values the Court finds for the society are not binding on the Court itself, all judicially ascertained values are threatened with transience and disobedience.[50]

To be sure, the authority of judge-made law depends upon voluntary compliance, since the Court lacks any mechanism of its own with which to compel enforcement of its judgments. But there are times when it must face public defiance, not by shrinking from its prior commitment to individual liberties, but rather by relying upon the military cooperation of a coordinate branch of government likewise obliged to uphold the Constitution of the United States, to enforce the law of the land, as happened after the Court decided *Brown v. Board of Education*. Only these toughest of moral decisions test the true strength of the United States Supreme Court and, ultimately, of our tripartite system of government.

As the institutional prominence of the Supreme Court recedes and its guiding beacon dims, attention is focusing on the state courts with hope that they will become the protective guardians of individual liberties. Responding to this social need, state courts are in the process of "discovering" state Constitutions by infusing them with a vitality that is revolutionizing American jurisprudence in a way never before imagined, although it seems perfectly natural that under our federal system state courts no less than federal courts ought to be the custodians of our liberties. And by resting their decisions in whole or in part on state law, state courts can not only afford greater protection of individual rights under state law than under federal law but also thereby immunize them against reversal by the United States Supreme Court, which is without jurisdiction to review such state court decisions.

THE STATE COURTS

More and more state courts are construing state constitutional counterparts of provisions of the Bill of Rights as guaranteeing citizens of their states even more protection than the federal provisions, even those identically phrased. Although it is unquestionably a highly significant development for our constitutional jurisprudence and for our concept of federalism, its cause is not completely clear. But it surely entails, to some extent, a stark change in the relationship of the state and federal courts. In this regard Justice Brennan has suggested:

> . . . [I] t was only natural that when during the 1960's our rights and liberties were in the process of becoming increasingly federalized, state courts saw no reason to consider what protections, if any, were secured by state constitutions. It is not easy to pinpoint why state courts are now beginning to emphasize the protections of their states' own bills of rights. It may not be wide of the mark, however, to suppose that these state courts discern, and disagree with, a trend in recent opinions of the United States Supreme Court to pull back from, or at least suspend for the time being, the enforcement of the *Boyd* principle with respect to application of the federal Bill of Rights and the restraints of the due process and equal protection clauses of the fourteenth amendment.[51]

The California Supreme Court has been in the vanguard among state courts that independently consider the merits of constitutional arguments and decline to follow opinions of the United States Supreme Court which they find unpersuasive, even where state and federal Constitutions are similarly or identically phrased.[52]   In 1971, the year that the United States Supreme Court decided *Reed v. Reed*,[53] its first decision under the new wave of attack on gender discrimination, the California Supreme Court, in the landmark case *Sail'er Inn, Inc. v. Kirby*,[54] held unconstitutional a California statutory provision prohibiting women from tending bar except when they are the licensees or are, singly or with their husbands, the sole shareholders of a corporation holding the license, notwithstanding a contrary 1948 decision of the United States Supreme Court, *Goesaert v. Cleary*,[55] holding that a Michigan statute forbidding any female to act as a bartender unless she was the wife or daughter of the male owner of a licensed liquor establishment did not offend the equal protection clause of the federal Constitution.   In order to accomplish this bold feat the California Supreme Court resourcefully invoked the equal protection clause of the Fourteenth Amendment to the United States Constitution *and* Article I, sections 11 and 21, of the California Constitution. Not only are these provisions substantially equivalent, but also the court stated that the California and federal tests for equal protection are essentially the same. Consequently, in interpreting the requirements of the state provision the California court not only found authority for its decision that did not exist under the federal equal protection clause because decisional law of the Supreme Court had already foreclosed that issue, but at the same time it also divergently construed the federal clause. Yet because *Sail'er Inn* was grounded on the state clause as well, the decision was based on an adequate state ground and thus insulated from Supreme Court review.

At the same time that the United States Supreme Court was unnecessarily eschewing established constitutional analysis and contorting the rational basis standard of review to strike down the gender-based classification in *Reed*, the California Supreme Court, with both independence and fidelity to existing principles of constitutional analysis, forthrightly announced in *Sail'er Inn* that ". . . [t] he instant case compels the application of the strict scrutiny standard of review, first, because the statute limits the fundamental right of one class of persons to pursue a lawful profession, and, second, because classifications based upon sex should be treated as suspect."[56]   Acknowledging that the United States Supreme Court "has not designated classifications based on sex 'suspect classifications' requiring close scrutiny and a compelling state justification for their constitutionality," although "an analysis of classifications which the Supreme Court has previously designated as suspect reveals why sex is properly placed among them," Justice Peters, with characteristic eloquence and perspicacity, wrote for a unanimous court:

> Sex, like race and lineage, is an immutable trait, a status into which the class members are locked by the accident of birth. What differentiates sex from

nonsuspect statuses, such as intelligence or physical disability, and aligns it with the recognized suspect classifications is that the characteristic frequently bears no relation to ability to perform or contribute to society. . . . The result is that the whole class is relegated to an inferior legal status without regard to the capabilities or characteristics of its individual members. . . . Where the relation between characteristic and evil to be prevented is so tenuous, courts must look closely at classifications based on that characteristic lest outdated social stereotypes result in invidious laws or practices.

Another characteristic which underlies all suspect classifications is the stigma of inferiority and second class citizenship associated with them. . . . Women, like Negroes, aliens, and the poor, have historically labored under severe legal and social disabilities. Like black citizens, they were, for many years, denied the right to vote and, until recently, the right to serve on juries in many states. They are excluded from or discriminated against in employment and educational opportunities. Married women in particular have been treated as inferior persons in numerous laws relating to property and independent business ownership and the right to make contracts.

Laws which disable women from full participation in the political, business and economic arenas are often characterized as "protective" and beneficial. Those same laws applied to racial or ethnic minorities would be readily recognized as invidious and impermissible. The pedestal upon which women have been placed has all too often, upon closer inspection, been revealed as a cage. We conclude that the sexual classifications are properly treated as suspect, particularly when those classifications are made with respect to a fundamental interest such as employment.[57]

Finally, considering whether the state had met its burden under the strict scrutiny review standard of establishing a compelling state interest to justify the classification, Justice Peters stated simply that the statutory classification was invidious and wholly arbitrary, and the state not only failed to establish a compelling interest served by it, but failed to establish any interest at all. The statute, therefore, was "unconstitutional under the equal protection clauses of the state and federal Constitutions."[58] A consistent, predictive, and principled rule of decision was thereby announced and explained. *Sail'er Inn, Inc. v. Kirby* is the seminal case in the "modern" law of women, and has had a profoundly shaping influence on its doctrinal development in many state courts and in the dissenting and plurality opinions of the Supreme Court cases discussed hereinabove.

In broadening the reach of state constitutional counterparts beyond the federal model to resist encroachment upon our fundamental rights, the California Supreme Court, and other state courts too, are fulfilling Justice Brennan's exhortation to vigilance:

... [S]tate courts cannot rest when they have afforded their citizens the full protections of the federal Constitution. State constitutions, too, are a font of individual liberties, their protections often extending beyond those required by the Supreme Court's interpretation of federal law. The legal revolution which has brought federal law to the fore must not be allowed to inhibit the independent protective force of state law—for without it, the full realization of our liberties cannot be guaranteed.[59]

While this new-found independent vigor in the state courts results in diverse meanings between words which are the same in both federal and state Constitutions, it is not inimical to federalism but rather strengthens it; the system of federalism envisaged by the United States Constitution not only tolerates but indeed requires such divergence where the result is greater protection of individual rights.[60]   How perfectly Mr. Justice Brennan expressed this view of federalism when he wrote:

Every believer in our concept of federalism, and I am a devout believer, must salute this development in our state courts. Unfortunately, federalism has taken on a new meaning of late. In its name, many ... door-closing decisions ... have been rendered. Under the banner of the vague, undefined notions of equity, comity and federalism the Court has condoned both isolated and systematic violations of civil liberties. Such decisions hardly bespeak a true concern for equity. Nor do they properly understand the nature of our federalism. Adopting the premise that state courts can be trusted to safeguard individual rights, the Supreme Court has gone on to limit the protective role of the federal judiciary. But in so doing, it has forgotten that one of the strengths of our federal system is that it provides a double source of protection for the rights of our citizens. Federalism is not served when the federal half of that protection is crippled.

   Yet, the very premise of the cases that foreclose federal remedies constitutes a clear call to state courts to step into the breach. With the federal locus of our double protections weakened, our liberties cannot survive if the states betray the trust the Court has put in them. And if that trust is, for the Court, strong enough to override the risk that some states may not live up to it, how much more strongly should we trust state courts whose manifest purpose is to expand constitutional protections. With federal scrutiny diminished, state courts must respond by increasing their own.

   ... Federalism need not be a mean-spirited doctrine that serves only to limit the scope of human liberty. Rather, it must necessarily be furthered significantly when state courts thrust themselves into a position of prominence in the struggle to protect the people of our nation from governmental intrusions on their freedoms.[61]

In their effort to protect the freedoms of their citizens, state courts have not limited their activism to broadening the reach of state constitutional counterparts beyond the federal Constitution. State courts are also resorting to their common law as a source of protection for the basic rights of their citizens. While this permits judicial discretion to be exercised with unprecedented scope, such use of discretionary law in reality produces social legislation not traditionally the function or province of courts. Accordingly, state court activism is not only altering the institutional relationship of state and federal courts but is also rearranging the relationship of the judicial and legislative branches of state government.

A very significant example of this judicial legislation is the recent far-reaching decision of the California Supreme Court in *Marvin v. Marvin*[62] which, in effect, materially revised California's family law to reflect an awareness of society's growing acceptance of nonmarital cohabitation as an alternative to formal marriage, by declaring that the laws of yesterday are inconsistent with the social reality of today. The court in *Marvin* narrowed the scope of the doctrine of illegality, which has been used to invalidate express property agreements between *de facto* spouses, and endorsed the application of several legal and equitable remedies to govern distribution of property acquired during a nonmarital relationship.

In *Marvin* the plaintiff had lived with the defendant for six years without marriage, during which time all property acquired was placed in the defendant's name. After termination of their relationship, the plaintiff filed a complaint alleging that under an oral agreement with the defendant she was entitled to half the property acquired and to support payments.[63] The trial court granted judgment on the pleadings for the defendant, and the Court of Appeal affirmed on the ground that applicable decisional law established the principle that no rights are acquired in meretricious relationships without an agreement between the parties. Where such an agreement is alleged, it is not *per se* invalid merely because the parties are living together, but a contract made in "contemplation" of the mertricious relationship is contrary to public policy and will not be enforced.

Before *Marvin* this doctrine of illegality had been invoked to render an agreement unenforceable as against public policy if the parties contemplated nonmarital sexual intercourse as any part of the consideration, although the California courts seldom refused to enforce a contract between unmarried cohabitants on that basis. In fact the courts developed a variety of exceptions to the doctrine in order to enforce agreements between unmarried cohabitants.[64] But this was done on a case-by-case basis. To the extent that public policy and legal doctrine disapproved nonmarital relationships, enforcement of property agreements pursuant thereto were not routinely sought in the courts. While *Marvin* does limit the discretionary nonenforcement of contracts to those that are separately and explicitly founded on sexual services, this is not a major departure from existing practice. Rather, the importance of the *Marvin* decision is that in rejecting the doctrine of illegality in favor of a principle that allows unmarried couples to order their economic affairs as they choose, it represents a statewide change in public policy in favor of the enforcement of agreements between cohabitants. By abandoning the meretricious and living-in-sin concepts of unlicensed cohabitation, *Marvin* provides a model code for protecting the basic civil rights of an increasing number of American citizens. (Some predict that the principles of *Marvin* will be adopted, legislatively or judicially, by every state within five years.)

Moreover, the court did not limit the enforcibility of these property rights to unmarried couples who make express agreements.[65]   The court also declared that courts may apportion property acquired during unmarried cohabitation even in the absence of an express agreement, holding that where the conduct of the parties demonstrates the requisite intent, it would be proper to find an implied-in-fact agreement, an implied agreement of partnership or joint venture, or a resulting trust. In addition to these remedies which implement the intent of the parties, the court also approved the use of constructive trusts, and recovery in quantum meruit for the reasonable value of household services rendered less the reasonable value of support received if one can show that services were furnished with the expectation of compensation.

It is clear that in giving courts this encompassing remedial power the California Supreme Court has, in effect, rewritten the Family Law Act (and, by implication, a good deal of other civil and criminal law as well), thereby responding with directness and courage to the change in social attitudes toward living-together relationships.[66]   *Marvin* attacks the central tenet of American family law because it withdraws support from antecedent statutory and decisional authority designed to reinforce the institution of marriage by disfavoring *de facto* spouses, especially unmarried women and their children. In its broadest and most pervasive sense the doctrine of illegality is the institution of "illegitimacy," with its myriad attendant forms of violation of the basic civil rights of women and children who are unattached to a male. Notwithstanding the court's disclaimer that "the structure of society itself largely depends upon the institution of marriage, and nothing we have said in this opinion should be taken to derogate from that institution,"[67] the reality is that women are being freed from the heavy oppression of the nuclear family, the glue that coheres patriarchal order.[68]

The implications of this ideological shift are of prodigious importance for the historical subjection of women. Within the nuclear family women have occupied the position of an inferior caste, but because the family supports and perpetuates patriarchal society, the legal mechanisms developed to protect it have inexorably refused to recognize alternative family arrangements. Undoubtedly the primary legal method of maintaining the nuclear family has been the institution of "illegitimacy," which makes unlawful that family unit consisting of an unmarried woman and her children. "Illegitimacy" has created a dual system of families based upon the presence or absence of marriage to a man, and has stigmatized with inferior status and deprivation of civil rights families in which traditional marriage does not exist.

The principle of "legitimacy," an insistence on the primacy of males, has been reinforced by awarding status to "moral" women who bear children within the patriarchal family while denying equal status to "immoral" women who bear children outside of the traditional family. Thus the institution of illegitimacy implements the principle of legitimacy by coercing women into marriage in which our identities are submerged and freedom limited. Insistence on the patriarchal family as the only valid family form and concomitant refusal even to recognize as a family the group composed of a woman and her children have discouraged women from exercising free choice in procreation, life-style, and personal association, and has thus violated a dear human right—the dignity of being recognized as a person[69] and citizen, which includes the right to be free to make independent personal choices.

Given, however, that domestic and worldly functions are equally essential to society, it is unlikely that the system of male power and preeminence and female dependency could have been consolidated without creating economic imparity in the value of male and female labor. Because the home has been decreed women's place, and our labor there without monetary worth, termination of familial relationships presents to us the spectre of financial crisis and hardship. In the absence of the contribution of funds and property, only legally married women had much chance for an equitable division of property acquired during the relationship. For all the women who have and who will provide our society with free domestic labor, the *Marvin* decision's explicit departure from judicial refusal to recognize an interest in property acquired during a relationship based upon the contribution of *services* is truly a triumph. Quoting a dissenting opinion in a 1943 case the court stated: "'Unless it can be argued that a woman's services as cook, housekeeper, and homemaker are valueless, it would seem logical that if, when she contributes money to the purchase of property, her interest will be protected, then when she contributes her services in the home, her interest in property accumulated should be protected.'"[70]

The *Marvin* decision has accentuated the ambivalence of our social attitude respecting women. On the one hand, the opinion reflects, indeed is inspired by, a desire to end an entrenched tradition of female abjection and servitude, as is required by our present level of societal enlightenment. Clearly a society must either abandon those practices that it comes to perceive as iniquitous or relinquish its claim of being a just society. At the same time, however, the *Marvin* decision has engendered considerable agitation among men "with a stake in it." Their supercilious attitude is illustrated by the following reactions:

I think it's ridiculous—there are girls who do it for a living, looking for guys to live with for a couple of years. I know a lot of these girls. They're getting paid while they're working, with a Mercedes and with tennis lessons. Why should they be paid something after it's over? And why should I pay someone to live with me? I can get a maid. You got the wrong guy, 'cause I'm hostile anyway; these women are high-class prostitutes. Who do they think is picking up all the dinner bills? By being tough I think they're alienating men. Every day there's a war constantly going on in this city, the M & W war, between men and women. It's disgusting that she can make money off his talent. It's one thing if the woman is involved in the guy's work. But other than that, you can't make a business off living together, can you? [71]

A prominent businessman has warned that "wealthy men are obvious targets for this type of suit. One unfortunate thing is that [the rights declared by *Marvin*] will probably enter the overall thinking of women involved with wealthy men." [72]

And a flamboyant Los Angeles attorney responded with petulance:

I'm considering making up a "One Night Stand" agreement, and if the woman doesn't agree to it, it automatically becomes a half-night stand. I'm very careful every time I let a girl stay overnight. Being successful and making a lot of money, I have to be careful for fear that some girl will get a portion of the money I've made that day. [73]

Preoccupation with the potential financial consequences of *Marvin* ignores the reality that women invest in their relationships even when they do not do housework. One female attorney has observed: "In some relationships . . . the unspoken agreement is that the man will provide a house, clothes and beauty parlor so that he might have the privilege and ego satisfaction of having a beautiful woman by his side. It boosts his status in the community and he can afford it. In essence, she's providing him with a service he needs." [74]

Anxiety has in fact been so strong that it has already provoked an effort in the California Legislature to limit the *Marvin* decision. Senate Bill 822 would create the legal presumption that property and earnings of an unmarried couple remain separate unless acquired jointly or under some sort of formal agreement, and hence would restrict the scope of judicial discretion to enforce under various common law doctrines implied agreements.

Women's struggle for liberty and autonomy is reconstructing the very basis of human relationships and, so too, the foundation of our social order. But the more than a little residual misogyny manifest in the various expressions of public will discussed herein has shown itself to be intense and powerful. The formidable difficulties inherent in this antagonism are being worked out in the judicial branch, where extraordinarily complex emotional conflicts present themselves for resolution. As the courts attempt to arbitrate the present antipathy between men and women and to accommodate their incompatible interests, it is evident that the most sensitive and primitive desires and needs of human beings have become their subject matter. Protecting us all from the use of power in ways inconsistent with American conceptions of human liberty has dramatically altered the grist of discretionary law in the state and federal courts. In the dialectic of this social revolution the concept of juridical function itself has been transformed, thereby generating a new arrangement of institutional relationships.

FOOTNOTES

1. Section 1 of the Equal Rights Amendment declares: "Equality of rights under the law shall not be denied or abridged by the United States or by any State on account of sex." [HRJ Res. No. 208, 92d Cong. 2d Sess. (1972)].
2. Despite the fact that women were granted suffrage more than a half century ago we still face fierce and pervasive discrimination in the political arena, as in other areas. "It is true, of course, that when viewed in the abstract, women do not constitute a small and powerless minority. Nevertheless, in part because of past discrimination, women are vastly underrepresented in this Nation's decisionmaking councils. There has never been a female President, nor a female member of this Court. Not a single woman presently sits in the United States Senate, and only 14 women hold seats in the House of Representatives. And, . . . this underrepresentation is present throughout all levels of our State and Federal Government." [*Frontiero v. Richardson*, 411 U.S. 677, 686, fn. 17 (1973)].
3. Brennan, W., Jr., State constitutions and the protection of individual rights. *Harvard Law Review 90:* 489, 490 (1977).
4. Between 1961 and 1969 the law underwent a revolution in a series of decisions binding the states to almost all of the restraints of the Bill of Rights. These decisions have had a profound impact on American life, requiring the close involvement of state courts in the application of federal law. *Mapp v. Ohio*, 367 U.S. 643 (1961) (exclusionary rule of the Fourth Amendment's prohibition of unreasonable searches and seizures); *Robinson v. California*, 370 U.S. 660 (1962) (Eighth Amendment's prohibition of cruel and unusual punishment); *Gideon v. Wainwright*, 372 U.S. 335 (1963) (Sixth Amendment's provision that in all prosecutions the accused shall have the assistance of counsel); *Malloy v. Hogan*, 378 U.S. 1 (1964) and *Miranda v. Arizona*, 384 U.S. 436 (1966) (Fifth Amendment's privilege against compulsory self-incrimination); *Pointer v. Texas*, 380 U.S. 400 (1965) (Sixth Amendment's right of an accused to be confronted by the witnesses against him); *Klopfer v. North Carolina*, 386 U.S. 213 (1967) (Sixth Amendment's right to a speedy and public trial); *Parker v. Gladden*, 385 U.S. 363 (1966) (Sixth Amendment's right to a trial by an impartial jury); *Washington v. Texas*, 388 U.S. 14 (1967) (Sixth Amendment's right to have compulsory process for obtaining witnesses); *Benton v. Maryland*, 395 U.S. 784 (1969) (Fifth Amendment's prohibition of double jeopardy). Some restraints against state action derive from the extension of the First Amendment: *School District v. Schempp*, 374 U.S. 203 (1963) (barring state required prayers in public schools); *New York Times v. Sullivan*, 376 U.S. 254 (1964) (limiting the availability of state libel laws to public officials and public figures); *NAACP v. Alabama*, 377 U.S. 288 (1964) (protecting the right of association).

5. These are the "property" interests recognized as mandating prior notice and the opportunity to be heard in order to guard against arbitrary deprivation: wages [*Snaidach v. Family Fin. Corp.*, 395 U.S. 337 (1969)] ; statutory entitlement to public support (welfare) [*Goldberg v. Kelly*, 397 U.S. 254 (1970)] ; driver's license [*Bell v. Burson*, 402 U.S. 535 (1971)] ; continued possession and use of goods purchased under conditional sales contracts [*Fuentes v. Shevin*, 407 U.S. 67 (1972)]. "Liberty" interests have been held to require that prison regulations and parole procedures provide some form of notice and hearing prior to solitary confinement [*Wolff v. McDonnell*, 418 U.S. 539 (1974)] or the revocation of parole [*Morrissey v. Brewer*, 408 U.S. 471 (1972)]. Together liberty and property interests are protected in the requirement that notice and an opportunity to be heard be given before revocation of tenured public employees' reasonable expectation of continued employment [*Perry v. Sindermann*, 408 U.S. 593 (1972)] and of school children's right to a public education [*Goss v. Lopez*, 419 U.S. 565 (1975)].

6. *Harper v. Virginia Bd. of Elections*, 383 U.S. 663 (1966) (right to vote); *Shapiro v. Thompson*, 394 U.S. 618 (1969) (right to travel interstate); *Eisenstadt v. Baird*, 405 U.S. 438 (1972) and *Griswold v. Connecticut*, 381 U.S. 479 (1965) (right to bear or beget child).

7. See, e.g., *Loving v. Virginia*, 388 U.S. 1 (1967).

8. *Sugarman v. Dougall*, 413 U.S. 634 (1973); *Graham v. Richardson*, 403 U.S. 365 (1971).

9. See, e.g., *Oyama v. California*, 332 U.S. 631 (1948).

10. Brennan, W., Jr., *supra*, State constitutions and the protection of individual rights. *Harvard Law Review 90:* 489, 495 (1977).

11. 116 U.S. 616, 635 (1886). Justice Brandeis called *Boyd v. United States* "a case that will be remembered so long as civil liberty lives in the United States" [*Olmstead v. United States*, 277 U.S. 438, 474 (1928) (dissenting opinion)]. It was, ironically, Justice Bradley who stated this principle—the author of the concurring opinion in *Bradwell v. Illinois* [83 U.S. (16 Wall.) 130 (1873)], the case in which the Supreme Court held that women could constitutionally be denied a license to practice law, a portion of which is quoted hereinafter. See text accompanying note 13 *infra*.

12. Wallach, A., A view from the law school. *Women and the Power to Change* (ed. F. Howe), pp. 81, 84 (1975).

13. 83 U.S. (16 Wall.) 130, 141–42 (1873) (Bradley, J., concurring).

14. 404 U.S. 71 (1971).

15. 411 U.S. 677 (1973). This case was decided under the due process clause of the Fifth Amendment, which has been interpreted to import safeguards equivalent to those under the equal protection clause of the Fourteenth Amendment.

16. See text accompanying note 13 *supra*.

17. 411 U.S. at 683 (1973) (footnotes omitted).

18. Id. at 684–87 (footnotes omitted).

19. Id. at 692 (Powell, J., concurring).

20. 416 U.S. 351 (1974).

21. Id. at 353.

22. Id. at 358–59 (Brennan, J., dissenting) (footnote omitted). "No one familiar with this country's history of pervasive sex discrimination can doubt the need for remedial measures to correct the resulting economic imbalances" Id.

23. 417 U.S. 484 (1974).

24. See, e.g., *Cleveland Bd. of Educ. v. LaFleur*, 414 U.S. 632 (1974).

25. The nuclear family has been promoted by the principle of legitimacy which insisted

that no child should be brought into the world without one man assuming the role of sociological father. Through the universal sanction of "illegitimacy," those family units consisting of women and their children are branded as unlawful. See generally Wallach, A., and Tenoso, P., A vindication of the rights of unmarried mothers and their children: An analysis of the institution of illegitimacy, equal protection and the Uniform Parentage Act. *University of Kansas Law Review 23:* 23 (1974). See also text following note 68 *infra.*

26. 417 U.S. at 496–97, fn. 20 (1974).

27. Id. at 501.

28. Id. at 503.

29. In 1976 the Court, again split six to three, held that exclusion of pregnancy-related disabilities from the employer's disability plan for employees did not constitute sex discrimination in violation of the 1964 Civil Rights Act [42 U.S.C. § § 2000e-2 (a) (1)]. *General Electric Co. v. Gilbert,* 429 U.S. 125 (1976).

   Justice Brennan, joined only by Justice Marshall, dissented, stating that the record as to the history of General Electric's practices showed that the pregnancy disability exclusion stemmed from a policy that purposefully downgraded women's role in the labor force, and that even if the classification was a facially neutral one, it had the effect of discriminating against members of a defined class, since it covered all risks except a commonplace one that was applicable to women but not to men.

   Justice Stevens, who since *Geduldig* had replaced Justice Douglas on the Supreme Court, separately dissented, stating that General Electric's rule placed the risk of absence caused by pregnancy in a class by itself, thus violating the statute as discrimination on the basis of sex, since it was the capacity to become pregnant which primarily differentiated the female from the male.

30. 419 U.S. 498 (1975).

31. 420 U.S. 636 (1975).

32. 421 U.S. 7 (1975).

33. 420 U.S. at 643 (footnote omitted).

34. 429 U.S. 190 (1976).

35. Id. at 210–11 (Powell, J., concurring).

36. 430 U.S. 199 (1977).

37. 410 U.S. 113 (1973). See also *Doe v. Bolton,* 410 U.S. 179 (1973).

38. 432 U.S. 438 (1977).

39. 432 U.S. 464 (1977).

40. 432 U.S. 519 (1977).

41. *Beal v. Doe, supra,* 432 U.S. at 462 (1977) (Blackmun, J., dissenting).

42. *Maher v. Roe, supra,* 432 U.S. at 482 (1977) (quoted by Brennan, J., dissenting).

43. *Beal v. Doe, supra,* 432 U.S. at 462 (1977) (Marshall, J., dissenting).

44. Id. at 463 (Blackmun, J., dissenting).

45. 432 U.S. at 521 (1977) (footnote omitted).

46. *Beal v. Doe, supra,* 438 U.S. at 457–58 (1977) (Marshall, J., dissenting).

47. About the relationship between the federal judiciary and Congress, Judge Shirley M. Hufstedler has written:

   Allocating scarce public resources and resolving conflicts between people asserting rights against the government or antithetical rights against each other is not a popular task because there are always losers. That's why some laws are deliberately phrased in such vague fashion. Legislators, understandably, prefer to delegate these hard choices to someone else—namely, judges—rather than absorb the wrath of the disappointed.

Federal judges are the congressionally favored catchers of these hot potatoes. They do not have to run for office and are therefore presumed to have asbestos fingers. Should Concorde landings prevail over enemies of noise pollution? Why not let the courts decide? The federal courts are already running ailing railroads, like the Penn Central, and they are supervising mental hospitals, prisons and school systems. Why shouldn't the city be adjudicated bankrupt and let the judiciary run that city, too? (S. Hufstedler, Americans simply expect too much of their courts and judges. *Los Angeles Times*, Pt. VI, p. 3, Sunday, October 16, 1977).

48.

We now expect courts to end racial tensions, sweep contaminants from the globe and bring about an armistice in the battle of the sexes. We expect courts to assure us of a right to be born and a right to die. We insist that courts protect our privacy, shield us from public wrong and private temptation, penalize us for our transgressions and restrain those who would transgress against us. (Id.).

49. *Beal v. Doe, supra*, 432 U.S. at 461–462 (1977) (Marshall, J., dissenting).
50. The increasing politicization of the judiciary is worrisome. Two other of several recent examples indicate an alarming immediacy in the impact that public pressure has upon the previously more insulated judicial function and decision-making. In May 1977, Judge Archie Simonson of Madison, Wisconsin, sentenced a boy convicted of second degree sexual assault to one year in a state home for boys, but told him he could stay at home if he kept out of trouble. The youth had attacked a young female in a stairwell at West Side High School; she was attired in blue jeans and a blouse over a turtle neck sweater. Before imposing sentence Simonson infelicitously implied that the rape victim had caused her rape by wearing sexually provocative clothing: "[Sex] is readily available. It is really wide open and we are supposed to take an impressionable person 15 or 16 years of age who can respond to something like that and punish that person severely because they [sic] react to it normally." Because biased and sexist prejudgments infect the impartiality and fairness of the judiciary, public outcry rose against Simonson, who was quickly removed from the bench in September 1977, in an unprecedented recall election. Without defending Simonson, it is apparent that the same mechanism could be engendered against any unpopular decision regardless of its merit and thus inhibit the exercise of discretion and harm the administration of justice.

A similar instance occurred in California after the Court of Appeal filed an opinion in July 1977, reversing a rape conviction because of an error in instructing the jury. In dictum, however, Justice Compton gratuitously offered the inflammatory and insolent view that it was not "unreasonable for a man" who picked up a woman hitchhiker "to believe that the female would consent to sexual relations. . . ." Such a woman "advises all who pass by that she is willing to enter the vehicle with anyone who stops and in so doing advertizes that she has less concern for the consequences than the average female." Angry public response blitzed television and newspapers, and a coalition of groups instantly picketed the Court of Appeal, protesting that the language of the decision was a perpetuation of the myth that rape is the fault of the victim. Instead of giving a warning to men that a female hitchhiker is not offering service, the judge warned women they should not hitchhike. Reacting to public pressure Justice Compton withdrew his attack, and on August 5, 1977, in an unparalleled retreat, modified his opinion by striking therefrom the offending remarks. *People v. Hunt*, 72 Cal. App. 3d 190 (1977).
51. Brennan, W., Jr., *supra*, State constitutions and the protection of individual rights. *Harvard Law Review 90:* 489, 495 (1977). See text accompanying note 11 *supra*.
52. The California Supreme Court has admitted a connection between recent decisions of the Supreme Court and the state court's reliance on the state's bill of rights. For exam-

ple, in holding that statements taken from suspects before first giving them *Miranda* warnings are inadmissible in California courts to impeach an accused who testifies in his or her own defense, the court stated: "[W]e . . . declare that [the decision to the contrary of the United States Supreme Court] is not persuasive authority in any state prosecution in California. . . . We pause . . . to reaffirm the independent nature of the California Constitution and our responsibility to separately define and protect the rights of California citizens despite conflicting decisions of the United States Supreme Court interpreting the federal Constitution." *People v. Disbrow*, 16 Cal. 3d. 101, 113–15 (1976) (footnote omitted). Similar positions have been taken by the Hawaii and Pennsylvania Supreme Courts. See *State v. Santiago*, 492 P.2d 657 (Ha. 1971); *Commonwealth v. Triplett*, 341 A.2d 62 (Pa. 1975).

In declining to follow the more restrictive interpretation of the privilege against self-incrimination defined by the United States Supreme Court in 1975 in *Michigan v. Mosley*, 423 U.S. 96, the California Supreme Court in *People v. Pettingill*, 21 Cal. 3d 231, 247–248 (1978), recently elaborated this view of its own constitutional power:

> Because of the importance of the legal issue we shall not attempt, as defendant urges us with some justification, to distinguish *Mosley* on its facts: for present purposes we shall concede that the "circumstances" relied on by the high court are essentially the same as those which we hold herein are inadequate to protect defendant's privilege against self-incrimination under the California Constitution. . . . We therefore proceed to the question of how this conflict between California and federal law is to be resolved.
>
> We need not be detained, in reaching that question, by the People's effort to reopen the entire issue of the authority of the courts of this state to construe provisions of the California Constitution to furnish greater protections to our citizens than do textually parallel provisions of the federal Constitution. We recently addressed that issue in various contexts and in considerable depth. . . .
>
> The construction of a provision of the California Constitution remains a matter of California law regardless of the narrower manner in which decisions of the United States Supreme Court may interpret provisions of the federal Constitution. Respect for our Constitution as "a document of independent force" . . . forbids us to abandon settled applications of its terms every time changes are announced in the interpretation of the federal charter. Indeed our Constitution expressly declares that "Rights guaranteed by this Constitution are not dependent on those guaranteed by the United States Constitution." (Cal. Const., art. I, § 24.)
>
> Finally, our right to decline to follow *Mosley* in construing state law was reaffirmed in Justice Brennan's dissenting opinion in that very case. . . . In language we have noted once before . . . he said: "In light of today's erosion of *Miranda* standards as a matter of federal constitutional law, it is appropriate to observe that no State is precluded by the decision from adhering to higher standards under state law. Each State has power to impose higher standards governing police practices under state law than is required by the Federal Constitution. . . . Understandably, state courts and legislatures are, as matters of state law, increasingly according protections once provided as federal rights but now increasingly depreciated by decisions of this Court. . . . I note that Michigan's Constitution has its own counterpart to the privilege against self-incrimination." So too, of course, does the California Constitution.
>
> The standard to be applied in resolving this issue is also now settled: "in the area of fundamental civil liberties—which includes not only freedom from unlawful search

and seizure but all protections of the California Declaration of Rights—we sit as a court of last resort, subject only to the qualification that our interpretations may not restrict the guarantees accorded the national citizenry under the federal charter. In such constitutional adjudication, our first referent is California law and the full panoply of rights Californians have come to expect as their due. Accordingly, decisions of the United States Supreme Court defining fundamental civil rights are persuasive authority to be afforded respectful consideration, but are to be followed by California courts only when they provide no less individual protection than is guaranteed by California law." . . . The question is not, as the People contend, whether the *Mosley* test "adequately protects" the rights of California citizens, but whether it provides *less* protection than has been guaranteed by the California Constitution since the *Fioritto* rule has been in effect. [*People v. Fioritto*, 68 Cal. 2d 714 (1968).]

And apparently some state courts seem even to be anticipating contrary rulings by the United States Supreme Court and are, therefore, resting decisions solely on state law grounds. Thus the California Supreme Court held, as a matter of state constitutional law, that bank depositors have a sufficient expectation of privacy in their bank records to invalidate the voluntary disclosure of such records by a bank to the police without the knowledge or consent of the depositor. Two years later the United States Supreme Court ruled that federal law was to the contrary. Compare *Burrows v. Superior Court*, 13 Cal.3d 238 (1974) with *United States v. Miller*, 425 U.S. 435 (1976).

Other state courts have similarly rejected United States Supreme Court decisions as unconvincing. The New Jersey Supreme Court has held that the validity of consent to a noncustodial search should be tested by a waiver standard requiring the state to demonstrate that the individual's consent was voluntary, an essential element of which is knowledge of the right to refuse consent [*State v. Johnson*, 346 A.2d 66 (N.J. 1975); cf. *Schneckloth v. Bustamonte*, 412 U.S. 218 (1973)]; the Hawaii and California Supreme Courts have held that searches incident to lawful arrest are to be tested by a standard of reasonableness rather than automatically validated as incident to such arrest [*State v. Kaluna*, 520 P.2d 51 (Ha. 1974) and *People v. Brisendine*, 13 Cal.3d 528 (1975); cf. *United States v. Robinson*, 414 U.S. 218 (1973)]; the Michigan Supreme Court has held that a suspect is entitled to the assistance of counsel at any pretrial lineup or photographic identification procedure [*People v. Jackson*, 217 N.W.2d 22 (Mich. 1974); cf. *United States v. Ash*, 413 U.S. 300 (1973)]; the South Dakota and Maine Supreme Courts have held that there is a right to trial by jury even for petty offenses [*Parham v. Municipal Court*, 199 N.W.2d 501 (S.D. 1972) and *State v. Sklar*, 317 A.2d 160 (Me. 1974); cf. *Baldwin v. New York*, 399 U.S. 66 (1970) and *Duncan v. Louisiana*, 391 U.S. 145 (1968)].

53. See text following note 14 *supra*.
54. 5 Cal.3d 1 (1971).
55. 335 U.S. 464 (1948).
56. 5 Cal.3d at 17.
57. Id. at 18–20 (footnotes omitted).
58. Id. at 22.
59. Brennan, W., Jr., *supra*, State constitutions and the protection of individual rights. *Harvard Law Review 90:* 489, 491 (1977).
60. "Why do we have two sets of Constitutions—federal and state—in this one nation?" Mr. Justice Mosk of the California Supreme Court asked recently. "Perhaps an answer can be found in this mythical quotation from Alice in Wonderland: 'Alice skwooched

up her forehead and ventured quietly, "If he writes the same thing, why does he do it twice?" "Because," said the White Rabbit, "he may write the same thing, but it reads differently.""""

61. Brennan, W., Jr., *supra*, State constitutions and the protection of individual rights. *Harvard Law Review 90:* 489, 502-3 (1977) (footnotes omitted).
62. 18 Cal.3d 660 (1976).
63. The plaintiff agreed to "give up her lucrative career as an entertainer [and] singer" in order to "devote her full time to defendant . . . as a companion, homemaker, housekeeper and cook." In return the defendant agreed to "provide for all of plaintiff's financial support and needs for the rest of her life." Id. at 666.
64. Two of the traditional devices used to avoid hardship upon the dissolution of a *de facto* marriage are the doctrines of common law marriage and putative spouses.
65. Significantly, nor does any language in the opinion limit the applicability of its principles to monogamous heterosexual relationships.
66. Indeed the dissent accused the court of as much: "By judicial overreach, the majority perform a nunc pro tunc marriage, dissolve it, and distribute its property on terms never contemplated by the parties, case law or the Legislature." *Marvin v. Marvin, supra*, 18 C.3d at 686 (1976) (Clark, J., dissenting).
67. Id. at 684.
68. For a discussion of family in relation to patriarchy see generally Wallach, A., and Tenoso, P., *supra*, A vindication of the rights of unmarried mothers and their children: An analysis of the institution of illegitimacy, equal protection and the Uniform Parentage Act. *University of Kansas Law Review 23:* 23 (1974). See also Wallach, A., Motherhood, Marshall, molecules: A passage through the heart of maternal darkness from God's creation to man's. *Black Law Journal 6:* 88-144 (1978).
69. "This right to be treated as a person is a fundamental right belonging to all human beings by virtue of their being human. It is natural, inalienable, and absolute right." Morris, H., Persons and punishment. *The Monist 52:* 475, 493 (1968).
70. *Marvin v. Marvin, supra*, 18 Cal.3d at 679, quoting *Vallera v. Vallera*, 21 Cal.2d 681, 686-87 (1943) (Curtis, J., dissenting).
71. Marks, M., Pal-imony: A brand new nightmare for L.A.'s swingers. *Los Angeles 22:* 10: 140, 143 (October 1977).
72. Id.
73. Id.
74. Id. at 144.

REFERENCES

Babcock, Barbara A., Freedman, Ann E., Norton, Eleanor H., and Ross, Susan C. *Sex Discrimination and the Law.* Boston: Little, Brown and Co. (1975).
Beal v. Doe, 432 United States Reports 438 (1977).
Boyd v. United States, 116 United States Reports 616 (1886).
Bradwell v. Illinois, 83 United States Reports (16 Wall.) 130 (1877).
Brennan, William, Jr., State constitutions and the protection of individual rights. *Harvard Law Review 90:* 489-504 (1977).
Califano v. Goldfarb, 430 United States Reports 199 (1977).
California Constitution, Article I, sections 11 and 21.
Cleveland Bd. of Educ. v. LaFleur, 414 United States Reports 632 (1974).

Craig v. Boren, 429 United States Reports 190 (1976).

Davidson, Kenneth M., Ginsberg, Ruth B., and Kay, Herma Hill. *Sex-Based Discrimination.* St. Paul: West Publishing Co. (1974).

Doe v. Bolton, 410 United States Reports 179 (1973).

Frontiero v. Richardson, 411 United States Reports 677 (1973).

Geduldig v. Aiello, 417 United States Report 484 (1974).

General Electric Co. v. Gilbert, 429 United States Reports 125 (1976).

Goesaert v. Cleary, 335 United States Reports 464 (1948).

Gunther, G., The Supreme Court, 1971 term—Foreword: In search of evolving doctrine on a changing Court: A model for a newer equal protection. *Harvard Law Review 86:* 1–48 (1972).

Hufstedler, S., Americans simply expect too much of their courts and judges. *Los Angeles Times*, Pt. VI, p. 3, Sunday, October 16, 1977.

Kahn v. Shevin, 416 United States Reports 351 (1974).

Maher v. Roe, 432 United States Reports 464 (1977).

Marks, M., Pal-imony: A brand new nightmare for L.A.'s swingers. *Los Angeles 22:*10: 140–47 (October 1977).

Marvin v. Marvin, 18 California Reports 3d 660 (1976).

Morris, H., Persons and punishment. *The Monist 52:* 475 (1968). Reprinted in Herbert Morris, *On Guilt and Innocence.* Berkeley and Los Angeles: University of California Press (1976), pp. 31–73.

People v. Hunt, 72 California Appellate Reports 3d 190 (1977).

Poelker v. Doe, 432 United States Reports 519 (1977).

Reed v. Reed, 404 United States Reports 71 (1971).

Roe v. Wade, 410 United States Reports 113 (1973).

Sail'er Inn, Inc. v. Kirby, 5 California Reports 3d 1 (1971).

Schlesinger v. Ballard, 419 United States Reports 498 (1975).

Stanton v. Stanton, 421 United States Reports 7 (1975).

United States Constitution, Fifth and Fourteenth Amendments.

Vallera v. Vallera, 21 California Reports 2d 681 (1943).

Wallach, A. A view from the law school. In Florence Howe (ed.), *Women and the Power to Change.* New York: McGraw-Hill Book Company (1975), pp. 81–125.

Wallach, A., Motherhood, Marshall, molecules: A passage through the heart of maternal darkness from God's creation to man's. *Black Law Journal 6:* 88–141 (1978).

Wallach, A., and Tenoso, P., A vindication of the rights of unmarried mothers and their children: An analysis of the institution of illegitimacy, equal protection and the Uniform Parentage Act. *University of Kansas Law Review 23:* 23–90 (1974).

Weinberger v. Wiesenfeld, 420 United States Reports 636 (1975).

Index